THIRD EDITION

Young Adult

LITERATURE

FROM ROMANCE TO REALISM

MICHAEL CART

Neal-Schuman

An imprint of the American Library Association

CHICAGO | 2016

© 2016 by the American Library Association

Extensive effort has gone into ensuring the reliability of the information in this book; however, the publisher makes no warranty, express or implied, with respect to the material contained herein.

ISBNs
978-0-8389-1462-5 (paper)
978-0-8389-1475-5 (PDF)
978-0-8389-1476-2 (ePub)
978-0-8389-1477-9 (Kindle)

Library of Congress Cataloging-in-Publication Data

Names: Cart, Michael, author.
Title: Young adult literature : from romance to realism / Michael Cart.
Description: Third edition. | Chicago : ALA Neal-Schuman, 2016. | Includes bibliographical references and index.
Identifiers: LCCN 2016014835 (print) | LCCN 2016014881 (ebook) | ISBN 9780838914625 (print : alk. paper) | ISBN 9780838914755 (pdf) | ISBN 9780838914762 (epub) | ISBN 9780838914779 (Kindle)
Subjects: LCSH: Young adult fiction, American—History and criticism. | Young adult literature—History and criticism. | Teenagers—Books and reading—United States. | Teenagers in literature.
Classification: LCC PS374.Y57 C37 2016 (print) | LCC PS374.Y57 (ebook) | DDC 813.009/92837—dc23
LC record available at http://lccn.loc.gov/2016014835

Book design by Kimberly Thornton in the Proxima Nova and Adelle typefaces.
Cover images: (top) © oneinchpunch/Shutterstock, Inc.; (bottom) © Marijus Auruskevicius/Shutterstock, Inc.

⊚ This paper meets the requirements of ANSI/NISO Z39.48–1992 (Permanence of Paper).

Printed in the United States of America

20 19 18 17 16   5 4 3 2 1

Young Adult
LITERATURE
FROM ROMANCE TO REALISM

ALA Neal-Schuman purchases fund advocacy, awareness, and accreditation programs for library professionals worldwide.

For Jack Ledwith
Still and always the best of friends

Contents

Preface | ix

PART ONE THAT WAS THEN

1 From Sue Barton to the Sixties 3

2 The Sixties and Seventies 23

3 The Eighties—Something Old, Something New 41

4 The Early Nineties 55

5 The Rest of the Nineties 63

PART TWO THIS IS NOW

6 A New Literature for a New Millennium? 81

7 Genre on the Agenda 97

8 Romancing the Retail 107

9 So, How Adult *Is* Young Adult? 131

10 Meanwhile, Back in the Real World 151

11 Reality Redux 163

12 Sex and Other Shibboleths 175

13 Lesbian, Gay, Bisexual, and Transgender Literature 187

14 Still the Controversies Continue 197

15 The Viz Biz 203

16 The New Nonfiction 223

17 Of Books and Bytes 233

References | 249

Appendix | 271

About the Author | 277

Index | 279

WELCOME TO THE THIRD EDITION OF *YOUNG ADULT LITERATURE: FROM Romance to Realism.* You'll find it has been completely revised, updated, and expanded to reflect the many dynamic changes and trends that have visited the field of young adult literature since the publication of the second edition in 2010.

Among the many trends you'll find addressed in this new edition are the following:

For starters, we are seeing a continuing increase in the sheer number of YA titles being published. Twenty-five years ago, when I first became involved with the field, we considered it a good year for YA if 250 titles appeared. Today the number is more like 7,000!

The explosion of titles being published is, in part, a reason that YA has become the tail that wags the dog of publishing, but in larger part it is the related fact that sales of the literature continue to escalate; for example: sales of books for young readers were up 22.4 percent in 2014, while adult sales took a nosedive, down 3.3 percent. Admittedly, sales of young readers' books were down about 3 percent in 2015, but continued to far outstrip the field, demonstrating that young adult literature is the most dynamic, lively area of contemporary publishing.

Speaking of sales, one of the most dramatic new trends in the field is the role of adults as buyers of YA books. Though estimates vary, it is safe to say that adults are now responsible for an astonishing 65 to 70 percent of all sales of young adult books. Why is this? The answer can be found in five little words: Rowling, Meyer, Collins, Roth, and Green—J. K. Rowling, Stephenie Meyer, Suzanne Collins, Veronica Roth, and John Green, that is. I think it is their tantalizing celebrity—thanks to their books *and* the movies that are being made from them—that is a major reason for this market phenomenon. It has driven sales of their books into the stratosphere and, accordingly, has landed the five on the *Forbes* 2015 list of the sixteen top-earning authors of the year. I should add another reason being offered for the new adult interest in YA is that a hallmark of the form is *story*. Unlike too many adult novels, YA books are simply enjoyable to read.

It's worth noting that the crossover readership we've been discussing has led to a growing sophistication of YA books in both subject and style, as evidenced by the increasing number of titles I see being published for grades 10 and up. The "up" now includes a special category of adults, those who are being called "The New Adult," that is, readers nineteen to twenty-five years of age. Publishers are increasingly targeting this category of crossover reader.

Another continuing trend that's related to crossover is the migration of adult authors to young adult literature. Publishers encourage this, of course, because it is presumed that these authors will bring their established readership to their forays into YA. As for the authors themselves, one reason for their interest in our genre is the opportunity to do something new and creatively different.

Unfortunately, there is not enough new to report about multicultural literature, which remains the most underpublished segment of YA. There are many reasons for this—there aren't enough editors of color for one thing—fully 90 percent of them self-identified as white on a recent *Publishers Weekly* survey. There aren't enough authors and illustrators of color either; sales of multicultural books remain modest; teens seem reluctant to read them (there are scarcely any multicultural titles on the various Teen Top Ten lists); and on and on. That said, we are finally seeing a modest rise in the number of multicultural books being published. According to the Cooperative Children's Book Center at the University of Wisconsin—Madison, which tracks diversity in books for young readers, the number of books with significant African-American content nearly doubled between 2013 and 2014 from 93 titles in 2013 to 179 in 2014. During the same period there was also a significant increase in Asian books, from 69 to 112. Unfortunately publishing for Native Americans (34 to 36) and Latinos (57 to 66) remained virtually flat. We obviously have a long way to go, but the modest increases hold out some hope for a more diverse field. K. T. Horning, Director of the CCBC, points to a new organization, We Need Diverse Books, as "really keeping diversity front and center." If you're not familiar with WNDB, check out its website at www.weneeddiversebooks.org.

Speaking of diversity: I'm happy to report that there has been a dramatic increase in the number of LGBTQI (Lesbian, Gay, Bisexual, Transgender, Queer/Questioning, Intersex) books; a new record of sixty-four titles with such content were published in 2015. This is twenty-four more than were published during the entire decade of the 1980s and only eleven less than were published in the 1990s. The field is broadening, too. The year 2015 saw the publication of two books with intersex characters; there were also three books about bisexuals, three about transgenders, and one each about gender fluid and genderqueer kids.

Finally, YA is returning to its roots. After a decade of obsessively focusing on speculative fiction, we are finally returning to a renascence of realistic fiction—thanks in large part to two authors, the teen whisperer John Green and Rainbow Rowell.

In addition to these general trends, here are some of the specific features you'll also find in this new edition:

1. New and expanded treatment of genre fiction, including dystopian literature and steampunk.
2. A new, detailed examination of the retail market for young adults, including such dramatic new trends and features as the appearance of the New Adult audience, the adult consumer, and the significant impact on the market of such best sellers as John Green, Suzanne Collins, Veronica Roth, and Rainbow Rowell.
3. Interviews with leaders in the field.
4. Updated and expanded coverage of lesbian, gay, bisexual, transgender, and intersex fiction.
5. New chapters focusing on teen demographics, multicultural literature, and teen literacy, including multiple literacies.
6. Coverage of the renascence of realistic fiction.
7. Coverage of new trends in graphic novels.
8. Revised treatment of the burgeoning audiobook field.

9. Discussion of the future of print.
10. Attention to the importance to the field of motion pictures being made from young adult novels.
11. Expanded attention given to narrative and creative nonfiction.

And much more. My hope is that the reading of this new edition may give you as much pleasure as the writing of it has given to me.

—*Michael Cart*

PART ONE

THAT WAS THEN

1

From Sue Barton to the Sixties

What's in a Name? And Other Uncertainties

THERE IS READY AND WELL-NIGH UNIVERSAL AGREEMENT AMONG EXPERTS that something called "young adult literature" is—like the Broadway musical, jazz, and the foot-long hot dog—an American gift to the world. But the happy concurrence ends when you then ask these experts to explain precisely what this *thing* called young adult literature is, because that act is about as easy as nailing Jell-O to a wall. Why? Because the term, like the gelatin, is inherently slippery and amorphous. Oh, the "literature" part is straightforward enough. Who can argue with the British literary critic John Rowe Townsend (1980, 26) who defines it as "all works of imagination which are transmitted primarily by means of the written word or spoken narrative—that is, in the main, novels, stories, and poetry." No, the amorphous part is the target audience for the literature: the young adults themselves. For it's anybody's guess who—or what—*they* are! Indeed, until World War II, the term *young adult*—like its ostensible synonym *teenager*—was scarcely used at all. For a while it was acknowledged that there were human beings who occupied an ill-defined developmental space somewhere between childhood and adulthood, the *idea*, the *concept*, the *notion* that this space comprised a separate and distinct part of the evolution from childhood to adulthood was still foreign in a society accustomed to seeing children become adults virtually overnight as a result of their entering the full-time workforce, often as early as age ten. Who, then, had the discursive leisure to grow up, to establish a culture of youth, to experience a *young* adulthood when there was so much adult work to be done? Indeed, as late as 1900 only 6.4 percent of American seventeen-year-olds postponed adult responsibilities long enough to earn high-school diplomas (Kett 1977); in fact, no more than 11.4 percent of the entire fourteen- to seventeen-year-old population was even enrolled in school, and those that were received—on average—only five years of education (Mondale and Patton 2001). Simply put, until 1900 we were a society with only two categories of citizens: children and adults.

This situation was about to change, however—and in only four years, at that. The agent of impending change was G. Stanley Hall, the first American to hold a doctorate in psychology and the first president of the American Psychological Association. It was in 1904 that he "invented" a whole new category of human being with the publication of his seminal work *Adolescence: Its Psychology and Its Relations to Physiology, Anthropology, Sociology, Sex, Crime, Religion and Education*. As the length of its title suggests, this was a massive, multidisciplinary, two-volume tome that Joseph F. Kett (1977, 26) has described as "a feverish, recondite, and at times incomprehensible book, the flawed achievement of eccentric genius."

It was flawed, because much of what Hall posited about this new stage of life that he called "adolescence" has been discredited, especially his notion of recapitulation (i.e., child development mirrors that of the "race"). Nevertheless, his theories were enormously influential in their time, particularly among educators and a growing population of youth workers. The latter embraced Hall's view of adolescence as a time of storm and stress (a phrase that invoked the German Sturm und Drang school and visions of Goethe's sorrowful young Werther), along with inner turmoil, awkwardness, and vulnerability, all phenomena that invited, even required, adult intervention and supervision in such controlled environments as schools and a growing number of youth organizations like the Boy Scouts and the YMCA. Neither Hall nor his disciples used the term *young adult*, of course, but their definitions of adolescence generally embraced our modern sense of young adults as somewhere between twelve and nineteen years of age. Indeed, Hall was prepared to extend his definition's reach as far as the early twenties, but educators generally stopped at nineteen and youth workers at sixteen. In addition to these two groups, Hall inspired two other sets of influential devotees: members of the vocational guidance movement (Hall believed in teaching

adolescents practical life and job skills) and the authors of "parents' manuals," which sought to guide the management of teenagers in middle-class
and upper-middle-class homes (Kett 1977, 221). Michael V. O'Shea, one of the
most prolific writers of these manuals, was also among the first to capitalize
on the potential economic importance of adolescents, so much so that Kett
(1977, 224) has dubbed him "the first entrepreneur of adolescence." As we will
see, there have been many others.

As a result of this new focus on the perceived needs of adolescents, the
percentage of young people in school gradually began to grow. By 1910, 15.4
percent were enrolled (Rollin 1999) and the old model of the six-year high
school was beginning to change, too, as over the next decade, more and more
junior high schools were created. "By 1920," Lucy Rollin (1999, 8) noted, "the
pattern of the four-year high school was well established," and by 1930 almost
half the adolescent population was enrolled there. This was the good news
for advocates of education, but the bad news was that slightly more than half
of America's adolescents were still not in school but in the workforce, where
they continued to be regarded as adults. But this, too, was about to change.
Indeed, it had already begun as the workplace was employing increasingly
sophisticated technology that required additional education, as—more
forcefully—had a spate of compulsory education laws.

It took the economic devastation of the 1930s, however, to effect truly seis-
mic change. As Grace Palladino (1996, 5) has written, "The Great Depression
finally pushed teenage youth out of the workplace and into the classroom."
Lucy Rollin (1999, 85) concurred: "The Thirties were a fulcrum for this shift."
The numbers alone, are telling: by 1939, 75 percent of fourteen- to seventeen-
year-olds were high-school students, and by 1940 nearly 51 percent of
seventeen-year-olds were earning diplomas (50.8 percent according to Kett
[1977]).

The Emergence of Youth Culture

This influx of students into high school was an important step in advancing
universal education, but what was even more important—in terms of the
later emergence of young adult literature—is that putting young people into
each other's company every day led to the emergence of a youth culture cen-
tered on high-school social life, especially in the newly popular sororities and
fraternities, which provided the context for a newish wrinkle in courtship rit-

uals: dances and dating. Quick to recognize this was the already entrenched *Scholastic* magazine, which had been founded in 1922 by M. R. "Robbie" Robinson, another of the early entrepreneurs of adolescence. In 1936, *Scholastic* introduced a new column to its pages. Titled "Boy Dates Girl," it was written by Gay Head (the pseudonym for Margaret L. Hauser), whose columns would provide the fodder for a number of later books, including *First Love; Hi There, High School!* and *Etiquette for Young Moderns*. As the last title suggests, the column focused more on manners than on advice to the lovelorn. Among the topics Hauser addressed, according to Grace Palladino (1996), were how to make proper introductions, which fork to use at a dinner party, and whether or not to wait for a boy to open a car door. Although boys took pride of place in the column's title, its intended readers were clearly girls, who were admonished not to correct their dates, because boys did not appreciate "brainy" girls. In the early days of youth culture, it was obvious that it was already a male-centered one. This was a reflection of the then-prevailing cultural attitudes, of course, as was Hall's almost single-minded focus on male adolescents in his own work. He had written so little about girls, in fact, that H. W. Gibson, an early disciple and social worker with the YMCA, dubbed adolescent psychology of the time "boyology" (Kett 1977, 224).

Although boys may have been the objects of lavish attention, the stereotypical image of the male adolescent that emerged in popular culture was an unflattering one: the socially awkward, blushing, stammering, accident-prone figure of fun typified by William Sylvanus Thaxter, the protagonist of Booth Tarkington's best-selling 1916 novel *Seventeen*, (the inspiration for Carl Ed's long-running comic strip *Harold Teen*, which first appeared in 1919. Twenty years later this image was still the rage, this time informing the spirit of radio's Henry Aldrich and the movies' Andy Hardy. (*The Aldrich Family* debuted on NBC in July 1939, while the first Andy Hardy movie, *A Family Affair*—starring Mickey Rooney—was released in 1937.) With the first appearance in 1941 of another soon-to-be youth icon, the comics' Archie Andrews (in *Pep Comics No. 22*, on December 22, 1941), it became clear that Hall's "adolescent" was fast morphing into a new kind of youth, the teenager. In fact, the first use in print of the term *teenager* occurred in the September 1941 issue of *Popular Science Monthly* (Hine 1999; see also Palladino 1996), and the term became commonplace in the decade that followed, though it wasn't until 1956 and Gale Storm's hit record *Teenage Prayer* that the term passed into currency in the world of popular music (the same year saw the debut of the singing group Frankie Lyman and the Teenagers).

The co-opting of the adolescent—now teenager—by popular culture did not mean that psychologists and other serious thinkers had abandoned the subject. Far from it. Two of the most significant works in the academic literature would appear less than a decade later: Robert James Havighurst's *Developmental Tasks and Education* and Erik Erikson's *Childhood and Society* both appeared in 1950, and both broke new ground in the field of psychology, especially as it pertains to stages of human development. Each writer defined specific stages of this development; Havighurst identified six stages and Erikson, eight. For both, two of these stages were "adolescence" and "young adulthood," which they identified—respectively—as thirteen through eighteen and nineteen through thirty (Havighurst), and twelve through eighteen and nineteen through forty (Erikson). In short order other significant work followed, most notably Jean Piaget's *The Growth of Logical Thinking from Childhood to Adolescence* (1958) on cognitive development, and Lawrence Kohlberg's on moral development (published intermittently throughout the 1970s).

All of this work—like that of Hall's—would have significant influence on therapists, youth workers, and especially educators, who found an equivalence between the tasks that Havighurst associated with each developmental stage and books for teens that dramatized the undertaking and accomplishing of these tasks. It's worth noting that the introduction of the term *young adulthood* into these various professional vocabularies may have been instrumental in the American Library Association's decision to form, in 1957, the Young Adult Services Division (YASD). This was a long overdue professional acknowledgment not only of a now au courant term, but also of the singular life needs of those we might as well now call young adults. Why "young adult" and not "adolescent," though? Well, there is no definitive answer. However, the term *young adult* was not altogether foreign to the library world. The youth services librarian Margaret Scoggin had first used it in the professional literature as early as 1944 (Jenkins 1999) and Kenneth R. Shaffer, then director of the School of Library Science at Simmons College, recalled in 1963 "our excitement of nearly a quarter of a century ago when we made the professional discovery of the adolescent—the 'young adult'— as a special kind of library client" (Shaffer 1963, 9). Also, one might presume that *adolescent* smacks a bit too much of the clinical, and some might even regard it as sounding faintly patronizing, though young adult might not be much better. As we will see, such uncertainty as to precisely what to call such youths has continued to invite much heated discussion and debate even to this day, though in 1991 YASD did finally decree, in concert with the National Center for Education Statistics, that young adults "are those individuals from twelve to eighteen years old" (Carter 1994).

A Literature for Young Adults

What impact did all of these developing attitudes and theories have on the writing and publishing of books targeted at such young people (however they might have been labeled and categorized at any given moment)? The short answer is "not much."

Because adolescents, teenagers, or young adults were—at least until the late 1930s—still widely regarded as children (even if the boys had mustaches and the girls, breasts!), there was no separate category of literature specifically targeted at them. However, as—over the course of the first four decades of the twentieth century—opinions began coalescing around the viability of recognizing a new category of human being with its own distinct life needs, books aimed at these "new" humans began to emerge. This happened very gradually, though, and may have had its roots in the long-ago publishing world of the immediate post-Civil War years when, as Nilsen and Donelson (2009, 42) have asserted, "Louisa May Alcott and Horatio Alger, Jr. were the first writers for young adults to gain national attention." The two authors' respective novels *Little Women* and *Ragged Dick* both appeared in 1868, and gave impetus to an era—already under way—of series fiction: dime adventure novels for boys and wholesome domestic stories like the Elsie Dinsmore books for girls. Then, as now, it was firmly believed there were girl books and boy books and never the twain would meet.[1] The always opinionated G. Stanley Hall had much to say about this, too. In a 1908 *Library Journal* article, he allowed: Boys loved adventure. Girls sentiment. Books dealing with domestic life and with young children in them, girls have almost entirely to themselves. Boys, on the other hand, excel in love of humor, rollicking fun, abandon, rough horse-play, and tales of wild escapade (Nilsen and Donelson 2009, 52).

Series books for both sexes hit their stride with the formation of the Stratemeyer Syndicate in 1900. Edward Stratemeyer, who had worked as a ghost writer for Alger, had the bright idea of hiring other ghosts to develop his own cascade of story ideas into novels. The result became what Carol Billman (1986) has called The Million Dollar Fiction Factory. Working pseudonymously, these otherwise-anonymous writers churned out hundreds of titles in endless series, most of them now forgotten, though a few—The Rover Boys, Tom Swift, the Bobbsey Twins, and Ruth Fielding—are still remembered with a twinge of pleasurable nostalgia.[2] Arguably the most successful of the Stratemeyer series—and the ones that come closest to our modern conception of young adult fiction—didn't appear until well after World War I. The Hardy Boys solved their first case (*The Tower Treasure*) in 1927, and Nancy Drew hers (*The Secret of the Old Clock*) in 1930.

Coincidentally 1930 is the year the ALA formed its Young People's Reading Roundtable, whose annual list of best books for "young readers" (think "young adults" here) contained a mixture of children's and adult books. The first list, for example, ran the gamut from Will James's *Lone Cowboy* (1929) to Edna Ferber's adult novel *Cimarron* (1930).

This situation endured until 1948 when librarians—realizing the new but still amorphous group of older "younger readers" no longer had any interest in children's books—changed the name and content of their list to Adult Books for Young People (Cart 1996).

Meanwhile, prescient publishers, taking notice of the emerging youth culture of the 1930s, began cautiously publishing—or at least remarketing— what they regarded as a new type of book. One of the first of these was Rose Wilder Lane's adult novel *Let the Hurricane Roar*. Published in 1933, this story of two teenage pioneers by the daughter of the Little House books' author offered intrinsic appeal to contemporary teens. Recognizing this, its publisher, Longmans Green, quickly began promoting it as the first in its promised new series Junior Books, a frankly patronizing phrase that lingered in publishing like a bad odor in the refrigerator for nearly a decade. Nevertheless, it may have set the stage for another book that would be published by Little, Brown in 1936.

This one caught the eye of the pioneering young adult librarian Margaret Alexander Edwards of the Enoch Pratt Free Library in Baltimore. Writing some years later in the *Saturday Review*, she reported Little, Brown's editorial bemusement when the publisher received a manuscript from the writer Helen Boylston. "While it was not a piece of literature, it was an entertaining story which did not fit into any category. It was too mature for children and too uncomplicated for adults. In the end Little, Brown took a chance and published the story under the title 'Sue Barton Student Nurse' *and the dawn of the modern teen-age story came up like thunder*" (Edwards 1954, 88, emphasis added).

The thunder was, presumably, the sound of fervent adolescent applause, as *Sue Barton* (for reasons that seem elusive to modern readers struggling through its turgid pages) quickly became one of the most popular books in the history of young adult literature. In 1947—eleven years after its publication—a survey of librarians in Illinois, Ohio, and New York chose it as "the most consistently popular book" among teenage readers, and it remained in print for years thereafter, along with its six sequels, which saw young Sue finish her training, serve in a variety of professional capacities (visiting nurse, superintendent of nurses, neighborhood nurse, staff nurse), and finally marry the young doctor she had met in book number one (Cart 1996, 41).

The popularity of the series may have derived in large part from its verisimilitude. Boylston was a professional nurse herself and there's truth in the details of her settings, but there are also stereotypes in her characters and clichés in the dramatic situations in which they find themselves embroiled. Told in an omniscient third-person voice, the books betray their author's often too-smug, patronizing attitude toward her material and her characters—not only Sue, but also, and especially, the "quaint" immigrants who are the chief patients at the big-city hospital where Sue receives her training.

Nevertheless, because of its careful accuracy regarding the quotidian details of the nurse's professional life, *Sue Barton* was the prototype of the career story, an enormously popular subgenre among the earliest young adult books.

Rivaling Sue for the affection of later nurse-story lovers was Helen Wells's own fledgling professional Cherry Ames, who debuted in 1943 (*Cherry Ames, Student Nurse*), and whose subsequent adventures filled twenty volumes. Wells also gave eager girl readers stories about plucky flight attendant Vicki Barr. Still another writer who re-created occupational worlds that she was personally familiar with was the remarkable Helen Hull Jacobs, whose many books about the world of championship tennis and military intelligence reflected her own life as the number-one world tennis player and a commander in the Office of Naval Intelligence during the World War II.

As for boys, they had been reading vocational stories since Horatio Alger offered his paeans to the rewards of hard work (and marrying the boss's daughter). More contemporary writers like Montgomery Atwater, Stephen W. Meader, and Henry Gregor Felsen offered fictions about such real-life jobs as avalanche patrolling, earth-moving, and automobile mechanics. In the years to come other less talented writers would report on virtually every other conceivable career—in often drearily didactic detail.

A decade before Boylston's initial publication another influential and wildly popular author for adolescents debuted: it was 1926 when Howard Pease published his first book, *The Tattooed Man*. A better writer than Boylston, Pease would soon rival her in popularity. In fact, a 1939 survey of 1,500 California students found that Pease—not Boylston—was their favorite author (Hutchinson 1973).

Like Boylston, Pease specialized in a literary subgenre: in his case, it was the boy's adventure story set—usually—at sea. And again, like Boylston, Pease knew his material from firsthand experience. For him, this was service in the United States Merchant Marine during World War I.

In 1938 still another important early writer, who also specialized in genre fiction based on personal experience, made his auspicious debut: John R. Tunis, the "inventor" of the modern sports story, published the first of his many novels, *The Iron Duke*. Tunis had played tennis and run track as a student at Harvard and, following service in World War I, had become a sportswriter for the *New York Post*. What set his work apart from that of earlier sportswriters was that he focused less on play-by-play accounts of the big game than on closely observed considerations of character, social issues, and challenges—not to his characters' hand-eye coordination but, instead, their personal integrity and maturation.

The First Young Adult Novel?

In retrospect any of these writers (though especially Pease, Boylston, and Tunis) could be reasonably identified as the first writer for young adults, but most observers (myself included) would opt to join the redoubtable Edwards (1954, 88) in declaring (on second thought in her case) that "it was in 1942 that the new field of writing for teen-agers became established."

The signal occasion was the publication of Maureen Daly's (1942) first, and for forty-four years *only* novel, *Seventeenth Summer*.

Amazingly, the author was only twenty-one when her history-making book appeared, though how old she was when she actually wrote the book is irrelevant. Ms. Daly herself claimed she was a teenager, but *The New York Times* reported that only fifty pages of the book had been written before the author turned twenty (Van Gelder 1942). Daly herself was quick to point out, though, that her novel was not published as a young adult book. "I would like, at this late date," she wrote in 1994, "to explain that 'Seventeenth Summer,' in my intention and at the time of publication, was considered a full adult novel and published and reviewed as such" (Berger 1994, 216).

John R. Tunis was similarly—and unpleasantly—surprised to learn from his publisher Alfred Harcourt that *The Iron Duke* was a book for young readers. He was still fuming thirty years later when he wrote, "That odious term juvenile is the product of a merchandising age" (Tunis 1977, 25).

The merchandising of and to "the juvenile" had begun in the late 1930s, coincident with the emergence of the new youth culture. The movement picked up steam in the 1940s as marketers realized these kids—whom they dubbed, variously, "teens," "teensters," and finally (in 1941) "teenagers"—were "an attractive new market in the making" (Palladino 1996, 52). That market wouldn't fully ripen until post-World War II prosperity put money into the kids' own pockets, money that had previously gone to support the entire family. The wild success of *Seventeenth Summer* was, however, an early indicator to publishers of an emerging market for a literature that spoke with immediacy and relevance to teenagers. In the case of Daly's novel these factors were not only due to her own youth and the autobiographical nature of her material ("What I've tried to do, you see," she told an interviewer, "is just write about the things that happened to me and that I knew about—that meant a lot to me." [Van Gelder 1942, 20]) but also to the fact that she chose to tell her story of sweet summer love in the first person voice of her protagonist, seventeen-year-old Angie Morrow. For its time, the book was also fairly bold and thus further reader-enticing because of its inclusion of scenes showing teenagers unapologetically smoking and drinking. And yet to modern readers Angie seems hopelessly naïve and much younger than her years. Her language now sounds quaintly old-fashioned and the pacing of her story is glacially slow, bogging down in far too many rhapsodic passages describing the flora and fauna of Fond du Lac, Wisconsin (the book's setting). If Angie's diction is now dated, so—more painfully—are her attitudes. Humiliated, for example, by the bad table manners of her new boyfriend, the otherwise desirable (and always very clean) Jack Duluth, Angie frets, "His family probably didn't even own a butter knife! No girl has to stand for that!" (Daly 1942, 147). Clearly Jack and his deprived family had never read Gay Head's column or her books!

Despite all this, *Seventeenth Summer* has remained tremendously popular; it's sold well over a million-and- a-half copies since its publication, and it's still in print in a smartly redesigned paperback edition.

Even more important than *Seventeenth Summer* to the cultivation of a readership for a newly relevant literature was the inaugural publication of the new girls' magazine *Seventeen* in September 1944. Teens were thrilled to be taken seriously at last. The first printing of 400,000 copies sold out in two days and the second—of 500,000—in the same short time. One reader wrote the editors to thank them for "looking upon us teenagers as future women and Americans, instead of swooning, giggling bobbysoxers." Another chorused, "For years I have been yearning for a magazine entirely dedicated to me" (Palladino 1996, 91–92).

Here was a niche to be exploited, and the editors of *Seventeen* were quick to recognize it, making theirs one of the first magazines to actually survey its readers—not to determine their editorial interests but, instead, their taste and interests in consumables. Oddly, such research was "unheard of at the time in fashion magazines." But *Seventeen* quickly changed that by hiring research company Benson and Benson to conduct the important market survey that it called "Life with Teena" (the name of the hypothetical everygirl it conjured up to report the survey's results breathlessly). "Teena has money of her own to spend," the editors enthused, "and what her allowance and pin money earnings won't buy, her parents can be counted on to supply. For our girl Teena won't take 'no' for an answer when she sees what she wants in 'Seventeen.'" The not-so subtle message to American business was "place your ads here." And the business wasn't confined to the manufacturers of sweater sets. "We're talking about eight million teenage girls who can afford to spend $170,000,000 a year on movies," the magazine trumpeted to motion picture producers (Palladino 1996, 103–106).

The year this happened was 1945. In Chicago, nineteen-year-old shoe clerk Eugene Gilbert was wondering why so few teenagers were buying shoes in his store. His conclusion: "Stores and manufacturers were losing a lot of money because they were largely blind to my contemporaries' tastes and habits. I started then to become a market researcher in a virtually unexplored field." Four years later, as head of the Youth Marketing Company in New York, Gilbert was sagely observing, "Our salient discovery within the last decade was that teenagers have become a separate and distinct group in our society" (Palladino 1996, 109–10).

It was a revelation and a revolution, such a liberating experience for teens that *The New York Times* published a Teen-Age Bill of Rights (Rollin 1999, 107–8). Here it is:

The right to let childhood be forgotten.

The right to a "say" about his own life.

The right to make mistakes, and find out about himself.

The right to have rules explained, not imposed.

The right to have fun and companions.

The right to question ideas.

The right to be at the Romantic Age.

The right to a fair chance and opportunity.

The right to struggle toward his own philosophy of life.

The right to professional help whenever necessary.

Oddly—if one is to judge by the gender of the pronoun employed throughout—these rights belonged exclusively to male teenagers! Odd, because—otherwise—the decade pretty much belonged to the girls, who certainly owned much of the media attention of the time. Not only did girls have *Seventeen*, they could also read another popular magazine devoted to them. *Calling All Girls* actually antedated *Seventeen;* it launched in late 1941. Meanwhile, manufacturers and the motion picture industry kowtowed to the girls, as did radio, which offered them such popular fare as *A Date with Judy, Meet Corliss Archer,* and *Your Hit Parade,* while newspaper comic strips served up daily doses of *Teena, Penny,* and *Bobby Sox.*

As for the fledgling young adult literature, imitation was definitely the sincerest form of flattery. For in the wake of *Seventeenth Summer's* success, romance fiction quickly captured the hearts—and balance sheets—of American publishers. One of the earliest of the faux Angie Morrows that followed was sixteen-year-old Julie Ferguson, the heroine of Betty Cavanna's 1946 *Going on Sixteen.* As its title suggests, the book is an almost homage to Daly. In fact, Cavanna's protagonist, Julie, actually mentions having "just last month read a newspaper account of a book written by a girl of seventeen" (Cavanna 1946, 89). This is offered in the context of Julie's own longing for a career in publishing—not as an author but as an illustrator. In this regard, Cavanna borrows not only from Daly, but also from career books like Boylston's. There are other similarities as well. Both books are about the interrelationship of dating and popularity; the book's dust jacket even claims that it offers "numerous useful tips on how to overcome shyness and how to become 'part of things.'"

Perhaps Cavanna's heroine read the book herself, because she finally does become "part of things" by finding true love (and dates) with a neighbor boy named Dick Webster, who habitually calls her Peanut and Small Fry. One supposes these are intended as endearments, but they sound merely condescending. Consider the following: "'Hey!' Dick scolded, suddenly masculine. 'We've got to get going.' Dick looked at her Dad in a way that said 'Women!' and grabbed her hand authoritatively. 'Come on.'" (Cavanna 1946, 220).

Girl readers were apparently quite ready to go along, too, because Cavanna, ultimately the author of more than seventy books, became one of the most popular authors for adolescents of forties and fifties. *Going on Sixteen* was the third most popular book in a 1959 survey of school and public libraries, close behind—yes—*Seventeenth Summer*.

Another romance author who rivaled Cavanna for popularity was Rosamund du Jardin (who was the only author to have two titles on that 1959 survey: *Double Date* and *Wait for Marcy*). Du Jardin's own first book, *Practically Seventeen* (do you detect a trend in these titles?) was published in 1949, and is yet another pale imitation of Daly.

Like *Seventeenth Summer, Practically Seventeen* is told in the first person, in the dumbfoundingly arch voice of Du Jardin's protagonist Tobey Heydon (which sounds too much like *hoyden* to be a coincidence). Like Daly's Angie, Du Jardin's Tobey has three sisters—two older and one younger. Like Angie's father, Tobey's is a traveling salesman. He is fond of saying that because he is "completely surrounded by females in his own home" he "would go crazy without a sense of humor and that he has had to develop his in self-defense." "But none of us mind," Tobey hastens to reassure the reader. "He is really sweet, as fathers go" (Du Jardin 1949, 4).

Like *Seventeenth Summer* (again), Du Jardin's book is a story of young love but much slighter in substance and lighter in tone. Tobey's big dilemma—and the theme that unifies the book's highly episodic plot—is whether her relationship with boyfriend Brose (short for Ambrose) will survive until he can lay hands on the class ring he has asked her to wear. Given the episodic structure of her first novel, it's no surprise to learn that Du Jardin had been a successful writer of magazine fiction, her short stories having appeared in such popular women's magazines as *Cosmopolitan, Redbook, Good Housekeeping,* and *McCall's.* Certainly her work is slicker, more innocent, and funnier than Daly's. For at-risk teens of the current day, there is something pleasantly nostalgic and comforting in reading about peers (even long-ago ones) whose biggest problems are pesky younger sisters, about who will take them to the big dance (the "Heart Hop" in this case), and about how to resolve a rivalry for a boy's affection with a visitor from the South named, appositely, Kentucky Jackson.

The book's dust-jacket blurb speaks, well, volumes—not only about *Practically Seventeen*, but also about the type of book that would prevail in publishing for young adults throughout the forties and fifties. Here's a sample paragraph:

> In recent years, permanent recognition and popularity have been accorded the junior novel . . . the story that records truthfully the modern girl's dream of life and romance and her ways of adjusting to her school and family experiences. *Practically Seventeen* is such a book—as full of life as the junior prom.

And about as relevant to today's readers, I would add, as *Rebecca of Sunnybrook Farm.*

And yet, were it and other such books relevant to and reflective of *their* contemporary readers' lives? Perhaps more than modern readers might realize. In 1951, J. B. Lippincott published a fascinating book called *Profile of Youth.* Edited by Maureen Daly (yes, *that* Maureen Daly), it collected profiles of twelve "representative" teenagers that had appeared in issues of *Ladies' Home Journal* throughout 1949 and 1950.

"We chose our young people from the North and South, the East and West," Daly writes, "From the hangouts and the libraries; from the popular and the aloof; the leaders and the followers. Some are planning professional careers; others are preparing themselves for marriage. Some just want a job—any job. We asked them about their lives—and let them tell their own stories. We asked them about their problems—and joined with them on the solutions" (1951, 9).

Although there are differences among the kids—especially in their circumstances (though none is homeless or impoverished)—the one thing they have overwhelmingly in common is, for twenty-first-century readers, an astonishing innocence. Almost none of them smokes or drinks; drugs are never mentioned; none of the students is gay or lesbian or a gang member. None is emotionally troubled or the victim of abuse. Instead, their biggest concern (the book calls it "A National Problem") is whether to go steady. They also "resent" parents who refuse to understand or recognize the importance of fads and customs in high school. (In her introduction, Daly [1951, 10] expresses hope that a parent reading this book "may listen with greater patience to a sixteen-year-old's plea for orange corduroy slacks or a red beanie when he realizes how vital 'fads' are to adolescent security.") Reading the profiles is eerily like reading the novels we have been discussing, especially when one comes to the editors' valedictory summing up of their findings ("American Youth—Full View"), where they affirm, "We have recorded, as told by youth itself, the things *they* find important—the good schools, the basketball rivalries, the college scholarships and Friday night dates" (Daly 1951, 256).

Perhaps life really was simpler back in the 1940s!

To the editors' credit, though, their book does differ from the YA literature of the 1940s by including one African American teen (called "Negro" here), though one wonders how representative she may be. Her name is Myrdice Thornton, and she is the daughter of an affluent mother (her father, the first African American member of the Chicago Park Police, was killed in the line of duty). Living in the North, she attends an integrated school in the Hyde Park neighborhood and seems to have experienced little racial prejudice or related problems, telling her profiler, "I never did feel different . . . I see no reason to act that way." Perhaps more indicative of reality was the reaction of the "Negro" boy who, when interviewed (though not profiled) expressed amazement that anyone would be interested in his opinion.

One other teen in the book, Hank Polsinelli, the son of Italian immigrants, is also "different." Alas, his parents are presented as the same kind of stereotyped and "quaint" eccentrics that Boylston featured in *Sue Barton*. Hank's mother, for example, is said to be "a real Italian mother; she believes it is her main business to cook, keep house and make a home for her husband and children and not ask too many questions." She does scold Hank when he misses mass, "but Hank takes reprimands lightly and his mother understands men. 'He is a good boy at home,' she says, 'I don't know what he does outside'" (Daly 1951,76).

That Hank and the several other working-class teens who are profiled seem much more mature than their privileged peers reminds us that adolescence, in its first several decades at least, was primarily an experience of middle- and upper-middle-class kids, who lived, for the most part, in all-white small towns. According to Kett (1977, 245), such "towns and small cities proved to be much more responsive to the institutions of adolescence than were rural and metropolitan areas, while a mixture of apathy and antipathy continued to mark the attitudes of lower class youth." Small wonder that urban settings and youth remained largely invisible in YA fiction until the social upheavals of the turbulent 1960s.

There are other disconnects between the idealized (fantasy?) world of early YA fiction and the real one. This is inadvertently reflected in the *Profile* book in a series of topical essays in which the editors and profilers step back from their individual subjects and do some actual research and investigative reporting, which leads to a somewhat less sunny picture of teenage life in the late forties. It's there we learn, for example, that "boys estimate that about half the eighteen- and nineteen-year-old boys have had sex experience" (Daly 1951, 153); that "in almost all cases the boys feel it is up to the girls 'to keep things under control.' She should know how and when to say 'stop,' for after all it's just *natural* for a fellow" (152), and that "pregnancy itself is still considered a social disgrace and a personal disaster" (153). Also, "society as a group has little sympathy for the unwed mother" (154), especially if she is economically deprived. "These girls may be placed in a charitable institution, to be trained in sewing or a trade while waiting out the birth of a child" (154). Sex, of course, remained absent from YA fiction until the late 1960s and it was equally absent from any serious discussion in the home. "Most teen-agers do *not* get sex information from their parents" (65). Nor did they get it from schools. "Oregon is the only one of the forty-eight states in which sex education is generally taught" (73). Nor, of course, did they get it from books—at least not the whole story. As one girl states, "I read all about 'that' in a book when I was eleven. But nobody ever told me I was going to get so emotional about it" (155). Too bad, for that's what a good work of realistic fiction, with fully realized characters whose lives invite empathy from the reader and with it emotional understanding can do—had there been any such books available. That there weren't may be evidence that adult authors (and publishers) did not yet trust YA readers with the truth of reality.

Another example of an invisible topic is the consideration—or lack thereof—of juvenile delinquency and the presence of gangs in teen life. Juvenile delinquency has been an issue in American life since the mid-nineteenth century; the 1930 White House Conference on Children and Youth formally defined it as "any such juvenile misconduct as might be dealt with under the law" (Kett 1977, 309). However, it wasn't until adolescents or teenagers had become a distinct—and distinctive—culture that popular attention turned, with a vengeance, toward the "problem." A significant catalyst was the universal hand-wringing over the spate of unsupervised—and possibly out of control—youths during World War II, a situation that was the product of fathers at war and mothers at work. Thus, "during the first six months of 1943 alone, twelve hundred magazine articles appeared on this subject (juvenile delinquency)" (Palladino 1996, 81). One of these, "Are These Our Children?" which appeared in the September 21, 1943, issue of *Look* magazine, inspired

RKO to produce a movie based on it. *Youth Runs Wild* was released in 1944 and ads promoting it featured such titillating headlines as "What Happens to These Unguarded Youngsters? The Truth about Modern Youth" (Barson and Heller 1998). The war ended in 1945, but the fascination with "dangerous" kids endured. In 1947, Irving Shulman published his adult novel *The Amboy Dukes*, about life in a Brooklyn gang. A host of original paperback novels, each more lurid than the last, followed in its wake. And then, suddenly, it was the 1950s, and not only were delinquents and gang members big news (and bigger box office), so were teenage rebels. The movie *The Wild One*, starring a leather jacket-clad, motorcycle-riding Marlon Brando, was released in 1954. It contained an unforgettably culture-defining moment in this priceless exchange between a horrified adult and Brando: HA: "What are you rebelling against?" MB, mumbling, "What have you got?"

Adults were further outraged (and teens, enthralled) the following year when not one but two cinematic classics of youthful disaffection were released: *Rebel without a Cause* starring the soon-to-be-iconic James Dean (who had died in an automobile crash only months before the movie was released) and *Blackboard Jungle,* a gritty film about an inner-city teacher's confrontation with his gang leader students. The most remembered aspect of the latter is the song that played over the movie's opening credits: it was, of course, Bill Haley and His Comets' "Rock Around the Clock." Forgive a personal note here: I was thirteen when this movie was released and I'll never forget sitting in the balcony of the old Logan Theater in my hometown (Logansport, Indiana) and hearing this song, the likes of which I had never heard before and the likes of which I couldn't wait to hear again! It was a transfixing and transforming experience that captured the imaginations and sensibilities of every teen in America, too, and presto, rock and roll was born and nothing was ever the same again.

Except young adult literature of the fifties, that is! Well, that's not quite true. One aspect of the new, harder-edged reality of teen life did find a place in that fiction: the car gang, a franchise that Henry Gregor Felsen seemed to own; he capitalized on it in such novels as *Hot Rod* (1953), *Street Rod* (1953), *Crash Club* (1958), and others.

The wave of prosperity that accompanied the end of World War II had turned America into a nation of car-crazy kids. *Profile of Youth* devoted an entire chapter, "Teen-Age Drivers Talk Back," to the topic, in fact. It began, rather breathlessly, "Sixteen, when a driver's license can be taken out in most states, is a far more important milestone in the life of the typical American male than twenty-one, when he reaches his majority and can vote, because 'cars are more fun than anything else in the world'" (Daly 1951, 46). Inevitably this phenomenon led to more adult hand-wringing ("I never close an eye any more until I know John or Mary is in at night!" [45]); a spate of popular songs about fatal car crashes involving teens; the magazine *Hot Rod*, which debuted in 1948; and a literary gold mine for Felsen.

The late forties and early fifties produced another wildly popular genre for boys. These books weren't about street rods but space rods! Science fiction found a welcoming home in young adult fiction with the publication of the already established adult author Robert A. Heinlein's first book for teens, *Rocket Ship Galileo*, in 1947. *Space Cadet* followed the next year and *Red Planet* the next. In short order Heinlein was joined in the science fiction lists by Andre Norton (pseudonym of Mary Alice Norton), whose first YA novel, *Star Man's Son, 2250 A.D.*, appeared in 1953—many, many others followed.

As in the forties, the books of the fifties continued to focus on romance for girls and other genre fiction for boys, who—in addition to car books and science fiction—were reading novels of adventure, sports, and animals.

For both sexes, there was a soupçon of more serious literature that focused principally on historical fiction and what the educator G. Robert Carlsen called stories of foreign culture. The latter had been a mainstay of juvenile fiction since the turn of the twentieth century, though most of the titles, written by well-intentioned white Americans, were of the "little-children-of-foreign-lands" type (most seemed to be twins). But there were exceptions. Elizabeth Foreman Lewis had written knowledgeably and insightfully about the lives of young people in China, having lived and taught there herself. Similarly, Anne Nolan Clark wrote widely about Latin America, but the best work in this category came from abroad in the years immediately following World War II, "an era," according to legendary editor and publisher Margaret McElderry (1994, 369), "in which American children's book editors actively sought out the best in writing and illustration from abroad." McElderry herself inaugurated this era when, in 1953, she published Margot Benary-Isbert's *The Ark*, the first German book to be published for American young readers following World War II. However, the strident imperative that books about other cultures could only be written by those from within that culture did not emerge until the 1980s and the advent of multiculturalism and political correctness.

For now, another advent—the arrival of a whole new decade and the dramatic changes it would visit on youth culture and the literature produced for it—is at hand. For a discussion of that we begin a new chapter!

Notes

1. Speaking of "twain," a singular work of fiction for boys—to match *Little Women* for girls—appeared in 1885: Mark Twain's *Huckleberry Finn*.

2. As "Victor Appleton," Howard R. Garis wrote many of the Tom Swift books, while under his own name he created the more enduring literary character of Uncle Wiggily. Interestingly, his wife, Lillian, was the pseudonymous Laura Lee Hope who penned the Bobbsey Twin books. Their two children also wrote for Stratemeyer, thus turning the Garis household into a mini-fiction factory of its own, though not, alas, a very happy one! See the ironically titled *House of Happy Endings* by Leslie Garis (2007).

2

The Sixties and Seventies

The Rise of Realism and the First Golden Age

"Teenagers today want to read about teenagers today."
—S.E. Hinton, *"Teen-Agers Are for Real,"* 1967

HINTON MAY HAVE BEEN WRITING IN 1967, BUT SHE WAS ECHOING A CON-
cern that had been expressed by American educators for at least two
decades. In 1946, for example, George W. Norvell wrote, "Our data shows
clearly that much literary material being used in our schools is too subtle,
too erudite." According to Nilsen and Donelson (2009, 59), he went on to
suggest, "Teachers should give priority to the reading interests of young
adults," concluding that "to increase reading skill, promote the reading
habit, and produce a generation of book-lovers, there is no factor so powerful as interest."

Although I can't imagine any of them had read or even heard of Norvell,
many of the early fifties teens featured in Daly's (1951) *Profile of Youth* echoed
his views, while acknowledging their personal dislike for reading. One senior
boy, for example, reported switching to journalism from English Literature
because "they were giving us English writers of the seventeenth century and
way back when" (41). A girl, it is reported, "doesn't like to read books and much
prefers articles with many pictures" (62). It took another girl six weeks to get
through the first hundred pages of *Pride and Prejudice* (163), and a horse-lov-
ing Wyoming boy asserted, "I read *A Tale of Two Cities* last month for English
class—didn't like it."

"Another young cowboy," the profiler writes, "looked up. 'Last month,' he
recalled morosely, 'last month we done *Macbeth*'" (215).

And so it goes. Would these teens have been more enthusiastic about reading if they had been permitted to self-select their books? Perhaps. The Dickens disliker did acknowledge reading about horses occasionally (though in farm and ranch magazines, not in books). And another boy demanded to know, "Why can't we read *Cheaper by the Dozen* in class instead of some old has-been?" (96).

The problem, of course, was that even if teachers had been inclined to use young adult books in the classroom instead of books by old has-beens, it's obvious from our survey of the field that few works of young adult litera-ture before 1960 would have qualified as literature. Indeed, many academ-ics would have asserted that putting the words "young adult" and "litera-ture" together produced nothing but an oxymoron. And yet enough serious work was being done that the first tentative attempts at critical analysis had already begun to appear by the mid-1950s. Richard S. Alm (1955, 315), for example, noted in 1955 that "the last twenty years has seen the coming of age of the novel of the adolescent," perhaps, he ventured, because writers, "noting the heightened attention given to adolescents and their problems by psychologists, educators, and librarians, have turned to the personal con-cerns of the teen-ager."

Perhaps, but the writers of the novel for the adolescent whom Alm sin-gled out for particular praise were all adult novelists like Maureen Daly, James Street, Dan Wickenden, William Maxwell, and Marjorie Kinnan Raw-lings. This was consistent, though, with the approach Dwight L. Burton had taken in an earlier essay, "The Novel for the Adolescent," that is often cited as being the first criticism of young adult literature. In it Burton (1951, 362) devoted the lion's share of his attention to an analysis of work by four adult authors whose novels either showed "a keen perception of the adolescent experience," or "have a peculiar appeal to certain elements of the adolescent reading public." (For the record, the four authors were Dan Wickenden, Ruth Moore, C. S. Forester, and Thomas Wolfe.)

The point we infer from both of these early pieces of criticism is that although there may—by the 1950s—have been a separate, identifiable body of books to be read by that separate, identifiable body of readers, that is, young adults, too many of its constituent titles were what Alm (1955, 315) himself had glumly described as "slick, patterned, rather inconsequential sto-ries written to capitalize on a rapidly expanding *market*" (emphasis added).

In 1956 a third early critic, Frank G. Jennings, was even blunter, grumbling, "The stuff of adolescent literature, for the most part, is mealy-mouthed, gutless, and pointless" (226). This may smack of overstatement for dramatic effect, but it is true, I think, that "much of the literature written for young adults from 1940 through 1966 goes largely and legitimately ignored today" (Nilsen and Donelson 1993, 574).

Books or Ladders?

Adolescence has always been viewed as a period of transition, of moving upward from one stage of development to another, and so it is not surprising that its literature, in the early years at least, should have been viewed as a ladder—or, more precisely, a rung on a ladder—between children's and adult literature. This idea of reading ladders may have been the inspiration of Dora V. Smith, who, in the 1930s at the University of Minnesota, taught the first college-level course in adolescent literature. At least one of her most celebrated students, G. Robert Carlsen (1984, 29), thinks so, recalling that "in her classes we constructed ladders placing titles on the rungs according to our judgment of quality . . . through reading guidance a teacher was to move readers from one level to a higher one."

Consistent with this concept is the corollary notion of stages of reading development (which echoes psychological stages of adolescent development!), that is, it is possible to identify certain specific types—or categories—of fiction that will appeal to young readers at specific ages or grade levels in school. In his influential 1980 work *Books and the Teen-Age Reader*, Carlsen identified three such stages: (1) Early Adolescence: ages eleven to fourteen, grades five to eight; (2) Middle Adolescence: fifteen to sixteen, grades nine and ten; and (3) Late Adolescence: seventeen to eighteen, grades eleven and twelve (Carlsen 1980). He then developed corollary categories of books that he believed offered unique appeal to students in each stage of development. For example, early adolescents would like animal, adventure, and mystery stories; middle adolescents would welcome war stories and historical novels; and late adolescents would dote on searches for personal values and books of social significance.

Carlsen linked these aspects of reading development to University of Chicago psychologist Robert J. Havighurst's influential theory of developmental tasks, which seemed to suggest that if teenagers were to successfully climb the ladder of personal development from childhood to adulthood, they must successfully complete seven distinct life tasks:

1. Achieve new and more mature relations with age-mates of both sexes.
2. Achieve masculine or feminine social roles.
3. Accept their physiques and use their bodies effectively.
4. Achieve emotional independence of parents and other adults.
5. Prepare for marriage and family life.
6. Prepare for economic careers.
7. Acquire a set of values and an ethical system as a guide to behavior; (i.e., develop an ideology that leads to socially responsible behavior).

"To accomplish [the tasks]," Havighurst claimed, "will lead to happiness and to success with later tasks, while failure leads to unhappiness in the individual, disapproval by society, and difficulty with later tasks" (Havighurst 1988, 61). Havighurst's ideas influenced work other than Carlsen's. Evidence of this may be inferred from the Alm article cited above, where the critic described what he perceived as the prevailing focus of young adult writers' attention: "In the main," he asserted, "these authors deal with an adolescent's relationships with others his own age, with his parents and other adults, and with such worries as deciding upon and preparing for a job, 'going steady,' marrying and facing the responsibilities of adulthood" (Alm 1955, 315). Though unacknowledged, this simply echoes Havighurst's list of developmental tasks.

Carlsen (1984, 29) was more candid, recalling of his own teaching methods, "I applied Robert Havighurst's concept of developmental tasks to adolescent books. It seemed to me that the most popular and successful titles, like Daly's *Seventeenth Summer*, were books in which characters were dealing with one or more of the developmental tasks. So we looked not only at the story content, but also at the conflicts and turmoils besetting the characters."

Personally I think this persistent attempt to transform literature into utilitarian ladders too often turned the early critics' attention from the work itself to the personal problems of the reader; that act, in turn, invited the transformation of a promising literature into the series of formula-driven, problem novels that would emerge in the sixties and seventies. I also think that frog-marching literature into ready-made category pens labeled for reading age suitability homogenizes readers, while also smacking of the didactic and dogmatic and threatening to turn literature from art to tool. Small wonder that young readers, beginning to feel manipulated, joined their voices in the chorus that greeted the looming new decade: "Never trust anybody over thirty."

The Times, They Were A'—Well, You Know . . .

This brings us to the 1960s, when the times and the literature would both be a-changin'! If one song—nasal balladeer Bob Dylan's 1964 release "The Times, They Are A' Changin'"—epitomized the social mood of this turbulent decade, one novel did the same for the nascent genre soon to be called "young adult literature." As had been the case in the 1940s with Maureen Daly and her *Seventeenth Summer*, this new sea change would arrive with the appearance of a single young writer—again, a teenaged girl—and the publication of her first novel. This time the book was *The Outsiders* by S. E. Hinton of Tulsa, Oklahoma.

And so it is that we have two young women and two books, each having far-reaching influence on young adult literature and each receiving enormous popular attention because of the novelty of their authors themselves being teenagers when their respective first novels were written. But there the similarities end and the differences begin. For starters, Hinton was writing about boys, not girls (one reason her publisher suggested she use her initials instead of her given name, Susan Elizabeth). And she wasn't writing about tree-shaded streets in small-town middle-America. Instead, she was writing about mean urban streets where teenagers didn't have time to agonize over first love and dates for the prom; they were too busy agonizing over whether they would survive the next skirmish in their ongoing war with a rival gang.

For it *was* warfare that Hinton (1967a) was writing about—class warfare as symbolized by the two gangs that appear in *The Outsiders*, the Greasers and the Socs. *Soc* was short for "Socials, the jet set, the Westside rich kids" who "wreck houses and throw beer blasts for kicks" (10–11). (The Soc, as both a term and a social type, had been around since the early fifties. One of the students in Daly's 1951 *Profile of Youth* is referred to as "a 'real sosh,' short for 'social.'" "That meant he was considered one of the right crowd, dated the right girls and went to the right dances") (109). As for the economically deprived "Greasers," they are "almost like hoods," and are given to their own antisocial behavior—they "steal things and drive old souped-up cars and hold up gas stations" (11).

Significantly, Hinton's story is told in the first-person voice of one of the Greasers: fourteen-year-old Ponyboy Curtis, who lives with his older brothers Sodapop and Darry, the latter of whom acts in loco parentis, because the Curtis boys' real parents have been killed in a car wreck before the story begins. As Ponyboy reports, "The three of us get to stay together only as long as we behave" (11). They try to avoid the more law-breaking Greaser activities outlined above, contenting themselves, instead, with wearing their "tuff" hair long, dressing in blue jeans and T-shirts, and lifting a fist in the inevitable rumble.

Hinton's was not the first novel to deal with gangs. Frank Bonham's story of Los Angeles, *Durango Street*, had been published in 1965, but there was something about *The Outsiders* that captured the imagination of its readers and spawned a new kind of literature, "books," as Richard Peck (1994, 154) put it, "about young people parents thought their children didn't know." Hinton knew them, though; she went to school with them every day in Tulsa. She knew from personal observation what their lives were like but, as a reader, she didn't find that kind of first-person reality being depicted in the pages of young adult literature.

"The world is changing," she wrote in an impassioned *New York Times Book Review* article, "yet the authors of books for teen-agers are still 15 years behind the times. In the fiction they write, romance is still the most popular theme, with a horse-and-the-girl-who-loved-it coming in a close second" (Hinton 1967b, 26). Hinton continues, "Nowhere is the drive-in social jungle mentioned . . . In short, where is the reality [?]" Hinton was not alone in wondering that.

In 1966, George Woods, then children's book editor of *The New York Times Book Review*, wrote, "One looks for modernity, boldness, for realism. The teenage novel, especially, should grapple with the delights and the dilemmas of today's teen-agers. Delicacy and restraint are necessarily called for, yet all too often this difficult problem is resolved through avoidance. A critic in touch with the world and aware of the needs of the young expects to see more handling of neglected subjects: narcotics, addiction, illegitimacy, alcoholism, pregnancy, discrimination, retardation. There are few, if any, definitive works in these areas" (169).

Not quite four months before Hinton's piece appeared, Nat Hentoff delivered a similarly scathing indictment of young adult literature in *The New York Times*. Writing of his own first YA novel, he asserted, "'Jazz Country' failed, as have most books directed at teen-agers . . . My point is that the reality of being young—the tensions, the sensual yearnings and sometime satisfactions, the resentment against the educational lock step that makes children fit the schools, the confusing recognition of their parents' hypocrisies and failures—all this is absent from most books for young readers" (Hentoff 1967, 3).

A year later Newbery Medal–winning author Maia Wojciechowska (1968, 13) joined the chorus, criticizing authors of books for the young, who keep going back to their own turn-of-the-century childhoods, or write tepid little stories of high-school proms, broken and amended friendships, phony-sounding conflicts between parents and children, and boring accounts of what they consider "problems." The gulf between the real child of today and his fictional counterpart must be bridged.

Hinton's great success came from managing to bridge that gap and, by giving fictional counterparts to the real teenagers she knew, introducing to young adult fiction new kinds of "real" characters—whether they were the alienated, socioeconomically disadvantaged Greasers or the equally alienated but socioeconomically advantaged Socials.

Her novel was innovative, too, in its introduction of thematic relevance. Hinton (1967b) had been quite right when she pointed out in her *New York Times* piece, that "violence, too, is part of teenagers' lives." Before her, though, authors had tended to ignore this basic reality of adolescent life. But Hinton used it as a tool to define the daily lives of her characters, both as individuals and as gang members, and this use was groundbreaking and consistent with the demands of the realistic novel.

As we have seen, Hinton rejected the literature that had been written for her generation, calling it "the inane junk lining the teen-age shelf of the library." And her rejection of the established literature for young adults is also consistent with the universal rejection of the status quo that was such a hallmark of the iconoclastic sixties, a decade that belonged to the young.

Because of her own youth, Hinton came to symbolize that rejection as well as its replacement by a new kind of literature. Richard Peck (1993, 19), writing of authors like himself whose work would follow Hinton's, said she "may be the mother of us all."

The Young Adult Library Services Association confirmed that assessment in 1988 with the presentation, to Hinton, of the first Margaret A. Edwards Award, which recognizes lifetime achievement in writing young adult books.

Hinton's significant place in the evolution of young adult literature is secure, yet reading her first novel today one is struck by what an odd hybrid it is: part realistic fiction and part romantic fantasy that, at its self-indulgent worst, exemplifies what critic Terrence Rafferty (1994, 93) has called "morbid adolescent romanticism." Her Greasers are such romantically idealized figures, in fact, that it is small wonder that Ponyboy is, himself, enchanted by other romantic figures—the Southern cavaliers of Margaret Mitchell's *Gone with the Wind*. There is some verisimilitude in this, however. The sociologist Frederic Thrasher had earlier, in his 1929 study of 1,313 Chicago gangs, pointed out that gang members placed a high value on physical prowess, peer loyalty, and even chivalry (Kett 1977).

Another element of romanticism is Hinton's sometimes sentimental treatment of her theme of lost innocence that may, in turn, invite some revisionist comparisons with Barrie's *Peter Pan* and his band of lost boys.

This loss of innocence was also the theme of J. D. Salinger's *The Catcher in the Rye* (1951), a more distinguished work of fiction that, though published for adults, is also a more viable model for the modern young adult novel than Hinton's. *Catcher's* most powerful contribution is the idiosyncratic, first-person voice of its narrator, Holden Caulfield. But the book is also quintessentially adolescent in its tone, attitude, and choice of narrative incidents, many of which are ritually rite-of-passage, including the obligatory (and obligatorily embarrassing) encounter with a prostitute. The latter introduction of sexuality may explain why none of the early critics of YA—Alm, Burton, Jennings, Carlsen—included *Catcher* in their analyses (*Catcher* did make it into Carlsen's 1971 revision).

Wry, cynical, funny, and intensely self-conscious, Holden's voice is one of the more original in American fiction, and the story he tells is a marvel of sustained style and tone. Even more than *Seventeenth Summer*, *Catcher* helped to establish a tradition of first-person narrative voice for young adult fiction.

Holden's tone and manner are clearly echoed in the work of Paul Zindel, whose own first novel *The Pigman* was published in 1968, a scant year after Hinton's. Zindel's debt to Salinger is the more obvious, as his characters, like Salinger's, hail from the urban East—New York City, to be precise. Another YA pioneer, John Donovan, whose first novel, *I'll Get There. It Better Be Worth the Trip*, published in 1969, also employed the New York setting and, like Zindel, echoed Holden's unmistakable voice and attitude.

Because Zindel was an accomplished playwright and a demonstrated master of dialogue (he won the Pulitzer Prize for drama in 1971), it's not surprising that he chose to tell his story in not one but two first-person voices: those of teenage friends John and Lorraine, whose brash, colloquial tone invites further comparison with Holden's. There are other similarities: John, like Holden, is both "extremely handsome" and a prodigiously gifted liar. He hates school, too, and has a horror of being a "phony in the crowd" (Zindel 1968, 71).

Holden's favorite word is "madman," and after having some kind of indeterminate breakdown, he tells his story "about this madman stuff" from a sanitarium where he has been sent "to take it easy" (Salinger 1951, 1). There are numerous references to mental illness in *The Pigman*, too. Lorraine tells readers "how really disturbed" two of her classmates are. and believes herself to be paranoid. For his part, John announces he is a lunatic. Neither of the two is really insane, of course, only terminally smart-alecky.

Zindel's biographer Jack Forman (1994, 933) summarized critical opinion: "'The Pigman' was a groundbreaking event because—along with S. E. Hinton's 'The Outsiders'—it transformed what had been called the teen 'junior novel' from a predictable, stereotyped story about high-school sports and dances to one about complex teenage protagonists dealing with real concerns."

Complex? Real? Perhaps—but John and Lorraine seem more types of disaffected modern youth than real characters (and, frankly, their narrative voices are so similar as to be sometimes indistinguishable). Compared with their parents, however, they are positively Chekovian in their complexities. Zindel seems to have taken George Wood's thoughts about adult hypocrisy to heart, for John and Lorraine's respective parents are one-dimensional cartoon versions of prevailing adult stereotypes. John thinks, "I would rather be dead than to turn into the kind of grown-up people I knew" (Zindel 1968, 178).

Given their respective romanticism and dramatic hyperbole, it's a bit surprising that Hinton and Zindel have traditionally been accorded the lion's share of the credit for ushering in a new age of modern, realistic young adult fiction. Especially when a third writer, whose first young adult novel was also published in 1967, served up an authentically realistic work of fiction in terms of theme, character, setting, style, and resolution. I refer to Robert Lipsyte, whose gritty, often hard-edged novel *The Contender* offers a richly realized theme—becoming an individual and transforming the self—that speaks to the quintessential adolescent experience. His protagonist, Alfred Brooks, is an African American teenager living with his aunt in a tiny Harlem apartment. For Alfred, the future offers nothing but dead ends—until he discovers Donatelli's Gym and learns that although he may not have the killer instinct necessary to become a successful boxer, he does have the necessary strength of character to become a contender in the larger arena of life.

Lipsyte, like Zindel, was already an established writer before turning to young adult fiction. At the age of twenty-seven, he was one of two internationally syndicated sports columnists for *The New York Times*. His experience as a journalist, trained to search for the telling detail and for reporting the unflinching, though often unpleasant truth, guaranteed a book that is a marvel of verisimilitude in the details of its setting: the boxing world and its gritty backdrop of New York streets. The characters, even the minor ones, are real people, not conventional types. They have believable motivations and authentic reactions to each other and to the situations in which they find themselves. With four decades of hindsight, it now seems that it is *The Contender*, rather than *The Outsiders* or *The Pigman*, that is a model for the kind of novel that Woods, Hentoff, and Hinton herself had called for in the articles cited earlier in this chapter. This revisionist critical opinion was reflected when a long-overdue Margaret A. Edwards Award was bestowed on Lipsyte in 2001.

Regardless of who was first responsible, it is inarguable that, in the late sixties, YA literature was in a hectic period of transition from being a literature that had traditionally offered a head-in-the-sand approach to one that offered a more clear-eyed and unflinching look at the often unpleasant realities of American adolescent life.

It would be an uphill battle, though, for not only are young adults inherently romantic, they are also inherently reality-denying. Richard Peck (1994, 159), as usual, put it well:

> In depicting reality our books are often on a collision course with our readers' most deeply felt beliefs: that they cannot die or be infected with sexually transmitted diseases, or get pregnant unless they want to, or become addicted to anything. Our books regularly challenge their conviction that the rules don't apply to them. There are limits to the amount of reality the novel form can encompass. Young adults test the boundaries.

Lipsyte—and Hinton and Zindel and Donovan, and even Bonham and Hentoff—were among the first to test these boundaries and, in the process, to set aside certain shibboleths that had contributed to the rosy unreality of previous YA novels. The taboos that had hobbled the literature in terms of subject and style had flourished in the complicity of silence that authors had maintained in the forties and fifties. But in the late sixties and early seventies, a new and bolder generation of authors began to break the silence with the power and candor of their voices. "Authors [now] wrote the way people really talked—often ungrammatically, sometimes profanely" (Nilsen and Donelson 1988, 275).

Zindel had written the way two people really talked; in 1973 Alice Childress would go him ten better and write in twelve different voices while also addressing the hard-edged issue of heroin abuse in her novel *A Hero Ain't Nothin' But a Sandwich*. Hinton would also write about drug abuse (*That Was Then This Is Now* [1971]). As for other taboo-breaking topics, Zindel would write about abortion (*My Darling, My Hamburger* [1969]); Norma Klein would write about a happily unwed mother (*Mom, the Wolfman and Me* [1972]); John Donovan would break one of the strictest taboos of all when he introduced the subject of homosexuality (*I'll Get There. It Better Be Worth the Trip* [1969]); and in the era of the Vietnam War, Nat Hentoff explored the ethics of the military draft and the hotly topical issue of avoiding it (*I'm Really Dragged but Nothing Gets Me Down* [1968]).

Robert Cormier and the Seventies

In retrospect, the period from 1967 to 1975 is remarkable for the boldness with which writers began to break new ground, both in terms of subject and style. The single most important innovation of the seventies, however, came at the very end of this period with the 1974 publication of Robert Cormier's first young adult novel, *The Chocolate War*. In it, this working journalist and already established author of adult fiction single-handedly turned the genre in a dramatic new direction by having the courage to write a novel of unprecedented thematic weight and substance for young adults, one that dared to disturb the comfortable universe of both adolescents and the adults who continued to protect their tender sensibilities. It did this by boldly acknowledging that not all endings of novels and real lives are happy ones. In this story of Jerry Renault, a teenage boy who resolutely refuses to sell chocolates in his school's annual fund-raiser and thereby challenges the accepted order of things, which has dire consequences, Cormier took his young adult readers into the very heart of darkness for the first time, turned the lights on, and showed them what the landscape there looked like. Alas, it looked alarmingly like the real one we all inhabit and read about in our morning papers and see depicted daily on the evening news. In that novel and in the fourteen that would be published before Cormier's death in 2000, he continued to disturb the too-comfortable universe by challenging complacency, by reminding us that, as he himself later said, "adolescence is such a lacerating time that most of us carry the baggage of our adolescence with us all our lives" (Sutton 1982, 33).

Dark forces are at work in the world Cormier limned not only in *The Chocolate War* but also in such other indispensable novels as *I Am the Cheese* (1977), *After the First Death* (1979), *Fade* (1988), *The Bumblebee Flies Anyway* (1983), *We All Fall Down* (1991), and so many more. Cormier's is a deterministic view that sees evil—sometimes institutionalized—in a world where conventional morality may not prevail, and where there are powerful, faceless forces that will destroy us if we disturb them. Such a revolutionary view opened enormous areas of thematic possibility for writers who would come after him. In turn, this amazing author was always quick to acknowledge his own debt to a writer who came before him: Grahame Greene, whom he called "the writer-mentor of my mature years" (Cart 2000b), and whom he was fond of quoting: "The creative writer perceives his world once and for all time in childhood and adolescence and his whole career is an effort to illustrate his private world in terms of the public world we all share" (Cormier 1998, 22). Students of young adult literature will know how brilliantly he succeeded.

Had the seventies produced no other writer than Robert Cormier, they would be remembered as the first golden age of young adult literature. Wonderfully, however, this decade also saw the first work of at least half a dozen others who would become grandmasters of the field by receiving the Margaret A. Edwards Award (Cormier himself received the honor in 1991). These others include Judy Blume, whose novel *Are You There God? It's Me Margaret* appeared in 1970; M. E. Kerr, whose first YA novel *Dinky Hocker Shoots Smack* was published in 1972; Richard Peck, who debuted the same year with *Don't Look and It Won't Hurt*, Lois Duncan, whose *I Know What You Did Last Summer* came along in 1973;[1] Walter Dean Myers with *Fast Sam, Cool Clyde and Stuff* in 1975; and Lois Lowry's *A Summer to Die* in 1977. What an extraordinary roster—what an extraordinary decade!

The emergence of a serious body of literature expressly written and published for young adults was also acknowledged—however belatedly—when the Young Adult Library Services Association (YALSA) in 1973, finally began considering YA titles for inclusion on its annual Best Books for Young Adults List (the list had been called by that name since 1966 but had included only adult titles). Three young adult novels were selected for the historic 1973 list, which also contained thirty-one adult titles. The three were Alice Childress's *A Hero Ain't Nothin' but a Sandwich*, Rosa Guy's *The Friends* and Robert Newton Peck's *A Day No Pigs Would Die.*

The Problem with the Problem Novel

Unfortunately, success and innovation often breed not only more success and innovation, but also pale imitation as new techniques are turned into recycled formula, making subject (think "problem") and theme the tail that wags the dog of the novel. Such was the case in the later seventies with the appearance and swift ascendancy of what has come to be called the *problem novel.*

The Canadian critic Sheila Egoff (1980, 196) has described its characteristic deficiencies as well as any other observer: "It was very strongly subject-oriented with the interest primarily residing in the topic rather than the telling. The topics—all adult oriented—sound like chapter titles from a textbook on social pathology: divorce, drugs, disappearing parents, desertion and death." Or, I'd add, think of it this way and you'll understand the problem with the problem novel: it is to young adult literature what soap opera is to legitimate drama.

Just why the new novel of realism so often degenerated into the single-issue problem novel may be an unanswerable question. But it surely has something to do with the rapid pace of change overtaking the lives of young people in the late sixties and early seventies and the perhaps belated recognition by writers and publishers that the novel, if it is to have any hope of offering not only relevance but also revelation to its readers, must keep pace with the ever-changing and ever-more sophisticated ingredients of their daily, real-world lives.

Looking back at the seventies, Egoff (1980, 194) pointed out that "adolescents had been steadily assuming more and more of the attributes, perquisites, and problems of their elders. Like adults, teenagers now had money, cars, jobs, and also drugs, liquor, sex, and the assorted difficulties arising therefrom." The powerful newness of these difficulties and the intoxicatingly sudden freedom to write about them caused some writers to forget the totality of the realistic novel's mission: that it must portray not only real-life circumstances—call them problems, if you must—but also the real people living in real settings. Hence, this thought from critic (and later *Horn Book* editor) Roger Sutton (1982, 33): "Instead of a character being the focus of the novel, a condition (or social concern) became the subject of examination" Or, as Sheila Egoff (1980, 67) argued, "The realistic novel grows out of the personal vision of the writer," while the problem novel "stems from the writer's social conscience."

The writer who, by this measure, apparently boasted the most highly developed social conscience of the sixties and seventies was Jeanette Eyerly, who might be called the queen of the problem novel. One remembers her many, many books not by the richness of their settings or the complexities of the characters but, instead, by the problems her interchangeable kids were forced to deal with. Thus, *Drop Out* (1963) is not about people but about the perils and consequences of dropping out of school; *A Girl Like Me* (1966) is about the wages of teenage pregnancy; abortion is all we remember of *Bonnie Jo, Go Home* (1972); similarly, the only memorable aspect of *The World of Ellen March* (1964) is the divorce of the title character's parents; and this ongoing inventory of woe includes suicide (*The Girl Inside* [1968]), drugs (*Escape from Nowhere* [1969]), runaways (*See Dave Run* [1978]), and—well, you get the idea.

It's ironic, however, that while such books were receiving scorn and disapproval from adult reviewers, they were enjoying enormous success with young adult readers. "Teens," Sutton (1982, 33) wryly observed, "don't even read these books so much as they gobble them like peanuts, picking them up by the handful, one right after the other."

Deny though they might the relevance of the problems to their own lives, teens seemed to dote on reading about how they plagued other people's lives. In retrospect, it seems that the problem novel offered readers the same sort of appeal that horror fiction would a decade later: the frisson of reading about darkness from the comfort of a clean, well-lit room.

If the problem novel received an often well-deserved drubbing from reviewers, the early novels of realism did not escape unscathed, either. As early as November 1969, Diane Gersoni Stavn (1969, 139) noted that "an unusual number of juvenile novels aimed at an audience of young teens and attempting realism" had been published in 1968 and 1969, but "these stories [were] often written according to the language, structure, and content specifications of children's books."

The next broadside came in 1976 with Jane Abramson's "Still Playing It Safe: Restricted Realism in Teen Novels" in which the author argued that "the restrictions on teen fiction result in books that succeed only in mirroring a slick surface realism that too often acts as a cover up . . . Books that set out to tackle painful subjects turn into weak testimonies to life's essential goodness" (38). There is nothing wrong with testimonies, of course, unless they compromise aesthetic inevitability by forcing an unrealistically happy ending on an otherwise realistically downbeat story: suppose, for example, it turns out that the woman Oedipus slept with wasn't his mother after all, and at the play's end a gifted eye surgeon is found whose uncanny abilities enable him to restore the self-blinded king's eyesight. *Rex redux!*

This kind of manipulation transforms realism into romance and demonstrates the kind of "cockeyed optimism" and "false notes of uplift" that Abramson objected to in teen novels (38). I think she was quite correct in this aspect of her criticism. On the other hand, it should be remembered that the kind of realistic novel that was being written in the late sixties and early seventies was still firmly rooted in the traditions of nineteenth-century American realism and its essentially optimistic view that goodness would prevail and that man had the power of free will to make it so. It was not until Cormier's *Chocolate War* arrived in 1974 that there was the first hint of determinism and the notion that evil might conceivably carry the day. But it could also be argued that Cormier was operating not in the tradition of realism at all but in that of naturalism, which views human beings as hapless victims of social and natural forces.

Be that as it may, I suspect most readers will be happy simply to acknowledge that whatever these novels were, they were at least different from those of the forties and fifties, and the best of them were good enough for some to call the seventies a golden age of young adult literature.

Others, those who use the phrase "problem novel" as a pejorative, will be less sanguine. Though technically the problem novel and the realistic novel are synonymous ("What's a novel without a problem?" Marilyn Kriney, the former publisher of HarperCollins Children's Books, asked cogently), there are, practically speaking, differences that we have already discussed (Cart 1996, 71). As the seventies drew to a close, those differences loomed large, indeed. For if—despite its occasional lapses—the novel of realism was gradually evolving into something richer and more rewarding, the problem novel was evolving into something ridiculous. As competition for readers' attention became ever brisker, the problems being addressed had to become ever more sensational until the problem novel reached an arguable nadir in two books whose publication bracketed the decade. The first was *Go Ask Alice* by Anonymous (1971) and the second was Scott Bunn's *Just Hold On* (1982).

Though presented as the "authentic" diary of a "real" fifteen-year-old girl who ultimately dies of a drug overdose, *Go Ask Alice* was actually a work of fiction coauthored by two adults: Beatrice Sparks and Linda Glovach. Nevertheless, as late as 2015, the amazon.com review was calling this "a true life diary." Over the years the question of the book's authenticity has become something of a *cause célèbre* and the issue is even discussed at the urban legends website Snopes.com.

Perhaps because its treatment of the dangers of drug use is so sensational, lurid, and over the top, *Go Ask Alice* has been hugely successful, never going out of print and selling millions of copies to credulous teenagers. Most modern readers find it unintentionally hilarious in its melodramatic overstatements and, though originally aimed at high-school-age students, it is now principally middle-school students who read *Alice.*

Scott Bunn's *Just Hold On*, a more serious portrayal of the tragic consequences of being a teen, proved less enduringly successful, though not for lack of its own sensational content. *Time* magazine[2] helpfully summarized its plot: "Heroine Charlotte Maag, 16, is raped by her father, an Albany pediatrician. She befriends fellow loner Stephen Hendron, who is hiding the shame and rejection of his own physician-father's alcoholism. By mid-story Charlotte is on the sauce, Stephen is involved in a homosexual affair with a football star named Rolf, and both tumble into bed with another couple after a bourbon and pot party. At novel's end Stephen is near catatonia and Charlotte is institutionalized" (Reed 1982, 66).

This kind of wretched excess suggested that the genre was not only overripe but also overdue for satire. The irrepressible Daniel M. Pinkwater took the cue and responded with his own *Young Adult Novel* (1982), a hilarious take-off on the problem novel. A nice coincidence is that Pinkwater's novel was published the same year as Bunn's, sounding the death knell for the subgenre it represented. Unfortunately, by this time the shrill sensationalism of the subgenre had exhausted readers and accordingly, they rejected not only the problem novel but also the novel of realism and maybe even reality itself. And small wonder, for although it may be true that, in popular culture, "The Seventies are often considered a joke decade, defined by shag carpet, pet rocks, streaking, polyester leisure suits, and the thump-thump of Beethoven to a disco beat" (Rollin 1999, 241), it is also true that this was the decade of the Kent State shootings; the forced resignation of Vice President Spiro Agnew; Watergate; the resignation, in disgrace, of President Richard Nixon; the ignominious end of the Vietnam War; the economic hard times of the Carter administration; the Iran hostage crisis; anxiety over the environment (the first Earth Day was held in 1970); the kidnapping of Patty Hearst, and the violent deaths of her captors. Times were hard; the daily business of life was unsettling, and so it's no small wonder that young readers began turning for relief to a resurgence of the sweetly unrealistic romance novel. Welcome, reader, to the 1980s.

Notes

1. Much of the analysis of early YA literature came from professors of education, that is, teachers who were teaching prospective teachers. Critical

writing from teachers of library science came later, as—still later—did work from university English and comparative literature departments. Duncan had actually begun publishing in the 1960s, but her early work was, for the most part, forgettable formula romance.

2. It's worth noting that the mass media only takes note of YA literature when it's at its most outrageous!

The Eighties—Something Old, Something New

The Rise of the Paperback Series, Multicultural Literature, and Political Correctness

IF THE LAWS OF PHYSICS APPLIED TO YOUNG ADULT LITERATURE, FOR EVERY action (read "innovation"), there would be an equal and opposite reaction. One doubts that it was physics—more probably a combination of publishing economics and weariness with hard-edged realism—but it is a fact that the decade-long emergence of such realism with its relatively unsparing and unrelenting focus on life's darker aspects was followed by just such a reaction. That this should have manifested itself as an early eighties renascence of forties- and fifties-style romance fiction may, at first, seem surprising until one remembers the conservatively nostalgic climate of a country that had also swept a forties movie star and former host of the fifties TV series *Death Valley Days* into the White House.

Critic Margo Jefferson finds effect in this cause. Writing in 1982, when the romance revival was still in its early innings, she concluded that these emotionally recidivist titles were "grown-up nostalgia repackaged for the young, very like those remakes of 1950s and 1960s songs by people in their 30s and 40s pretending to be ten or twenty years younger" (Jefferson 1982, 613).

As early as 1974, the journalist Edwin Miller was warning readers of *Seventeen* magazine about just such a grown-up nostalgia that seemed to be skewing Hollywood's portrayal of teens in the seventies. "Young people have become more troublesome in recent years," he wrote. "Even nice kids. If (however) you have a teen-ager pinned down in the past like a butterfly under glass, you've got the upper hand" (Rollin 1999, 262). This sounds a bit paranoid but it's true that Hollywood was busily harvesting the past for display both on America's large and small screens. *American Graffiti*, George Lucas's sentimental salute to the early sixties, was a box office sensation in 1973, and *Happy Days*, a nostalgic nod to the simpler—and arguably happier—times of the 1950s, was the number-one rated television show of the 1976–1977 season.

When it was their turn, publishers cranked the clock back even farther, to the 1940s, with their fictional treatment of the innocent romantic lives of young people who Barson and Heller (1989), in their amusing book *Teenage Confidential*, call "Kleen Teens."

If the adolescent lives portrayed in the eighties' romances were an almost eerie replication of those already unreal lives found in the pages of the forties and fifties versions, their packaging at least was different this time around. Although there had been a certain sameness to the content of the earlier titles, they were, at least, published as individual, stand-alone hardcovers by writers whose names—Janet Lambert, Betty Cavanna, Rosamund Du Jardin, Anne Emery—quickly became household words. The new romances, however, had little individual identity; they were slick, mass-market paperback series appearing at the rate of one new title per month under such saccharine rubrics as Wildfire, Caprice, Sweet Dreams, First Love, Wishing Star, and so on and on. If they were branded, it was with the name of their series, not that of their authors.

This decision to revive romance was not made in a vacuum, however; marketing decisions seldom are. Editor Pamela Pollack (1981, 25) explained, "Mass market paperback publishers gave teens what they 'want' as determined by market research, rather than what they 'need' based on their problems as reflected by social statistics."

In fact, what teens wanted in the eighties was what their parents had already been demanding—and getting—for a decade or more: genre romances and formulaic bodice-ripper-of-the-month gothic paperbacks. The latter—the adult gothics—had hit the paperback racks at least two decades earlier, led by the 1960 publication of Victoria Holt's *Mistress of Mellyn*.

However, it was not until the seventies, according to Kristin Ramsdell, that the (adult) romance boom really began, and although historical romances were especially popular at first, "light, innocent, Category (usually contemporary) Romances were popular, as well" (Ramsdell 1987, 8). It was this latter type that began trickling down into YA publishing at about the time that President Reagan's trickle-down theories of economics hit the marketplace.

Both offered what many readers have always, not unreasonably, wanted: escape from life's cares and woes. The author Jane Yolen told *Seventeen* magazine that "the trend is a teenager's way of saying 'enough.' Teenagers have seen their adolescence taken away by graphic television shows and movies and books. The return to romance is a way to return to the mystery and beauty of love, even if only on a superficial level" (Kellogg 1983, 158).

Well, maybe. But it's worth noting that Yolen is, most famously, an author of fantasy, and the lives portrayed in these romances had more of the never-never to them than reality. Here's how Pollack (1981, 28) described them: "The heroines—shy, inexperienced, small-town girls—live in happy homes and tend to have names that end in 'ie.' Their primary interest in life is boys; having a steady ensures a place in the high-school hierarchy. They are not interested in college or career and are not involved in the women's movement. Their mothers are their role models. Their fathers are shadowy but benign breadwinners. There are no grandparents—in fact, there are few elderly, black, or handicapped people to be found."[1]

The predictably hand-wringing adult reaction to this was not long in coming. As early as 1981, when the romance boom was only two years old, a coalition of organizations led by the Council on Interracial Books for Children issued a report charging, among other things, that these books "teach girls that their primary value is their attractiveness to boys; devalue relationships and encourage competition between girls, discount the possibility of nonromantic friendships between boys and girls; depict middle-class, white, small-town families as the norm, and portray adults in stereotypical sex roles" (Ramsdell 1983, 177).

Apparently, however, stereotypes sell, for the many new romance series were wildly successful from their very inception. Scholastic's Wildfire, which debuted in 1979, sold 1.8 million copies of sixteen titles in one year. Dell's Young Love followed in February 1981; Bantam's Sweet Dreams, in September 1981; Simon and Schuster's First Love, in February 1982; and in 1985 the first YA novel ever to reach *The New York Times* paperback best-seller list, the Sweet Valley High super edition *Perfect Summer*. Created by Francine Pascal, the Sweet Valley empire soon spawned countless spin-offs, and by the end of the eighties there were thirty-four million Sweet Valley High books in print (Huntwork 1990).

Speaking, still, of sales: another significant difference between the new romance and that of the forties was that, for the first time, teens themselves were the targeted consumers. Affluent though the eighties may have been in consumer terms, they were a period of economic hardship for schools and libraries. With this traditional market for YA in eclipse, publishers began looking for a new one. As Ramsdell (1987, 19) points out, Scholastic's launch of its Wildfire series "changed the way materials were marketed to young adults . . . Previously publishers had concentrated on reaching young adults indirectly through the schools and libraries; now they tried selling to them directly with spectacular results."

By the early 1980s American teens were spending a staggering $45 billion per year on nonessential consumables, and new marketing companies like Teen Research Unlimited, of Northbrook, Illinois, had been founded to poll them and otherwise study their tastes and habits. It was another example of history's repeating itself. It was in the 1940s, remember, that teens were first identified as potential consumers and, to study them, pioneer marketing maven Eugene Gilbert founded his Youth Marketing Company.

By 1986, 93 percent of high-school students in one national survey had worked for pay. "You want to talk revolution?" *Forbes* magazine cynically asked. "Not to this generation of adolescents. They have seen the future—and they want to buy it, not change it" (Rollin 1999, 282).

And where were they buying it? In the new American consumer paradise, the shopping mall. The first enclosed shopping mall in America opened in 1957 in Edina, Minnesota, and in the succeeding two decades the mall had become such a fixture of American life and a home away from home for America's teenagers that Richard Peck had become its unofficial laureate with his 1979 novel *Secrets of the Shopping Mall*.

The omnipresence of the malls quickly led to the evolution of the chain bookstore. Announcing Pacer Books, a new line of YA paperbacks from Putnam, then editor-in-chief Beverly Horowitz explained that Pacer titles would be found in display racks in these new fixtures of the omnipresent malls, "hangout places where kids go on a boring Saturday. You will find Pacer positioned right between the fast-food haven and the record store. There is a teen-aged consumer force out there, and the only way to reach them is to go where *their* action is" (Baldwin 1984, 15).

George Nicholson, then editor-in-chief of Dell/Delacorte Books and a pioneer in paperback publishing for young readers with Dell's Yearling Books, agreed, explaining that chain bookstores in malls "demystified the traditional bookstore concept for kids. Now they can buy anything they want. They have the power to come in, pay their money, and out they go, without being harassed. No one questions them" (Baldwin 1984, 18).

The stupendous success of paperback romance series soon inspired other genre incursions into the marketplace, most notably horror. Christopher Pike is generally credited with creating the bloodcurdling stampede with the 1985 publication of his novel *Slumber Party*. However, R. L. Stine quickly followed with his first foray into horror (writing as Jovial Bob Stine, he had previously been known as an author of joke books); his *Blind Date* was published in 1987. Both men became phenomenally popular, though Stine took the lead with the 1990 introduction of his Fear Street series and the 1992 debut of the Goosebumps books. By 1994 there were twenty-one Goosebumps titles and each had sold in excess of 1 million copies in paperback (Cart 1996).

As were the romance series, horror fiction was formula-driven, produced according to multipage specification sheets that virtually guaranteed predictable plots and cardboard characters. Settings were as blandly white, middle-class, and suburban as those of romance novels, and equally devoid of sex (though gouts of blood were always welcome.)

New Voices and Multicultural Stirrings

Despite the glut of paperback series, the eighties also saw the debut of a number of literarily and culturally important new voices, including the likes of Francesca Lia Block, Bruce Brooks, Brock Cole, Chris Crutcher, Ron Koertge, Gary Paulsen, Cynthia Voigt, and Virginia Euwer Wolff. (Block, Crutcher, Paulsen, and Voigt would go on to receive the Margaret A. Edwards Award for their contributions to the field).

Meanwhile, already established voices continued to be heard. Major work was published by such stalwarts as Sue Ellen Bridgers (*Permanent Connections* [1987]); S. E. Hinton (*Tex* [1980] and *Taming the Star Runner* [1988]); Robert Cormier (*The Bumblebee Flies Anyway* [1983], *Beyond the Chocolate War* [1985], and *Fade* [1988]); M. E. Kerr (*Little Little* [1981], *Me, Me, Me, Me, Me: Not a Novel* [1983], and *Night Kites,* [1986]); Robert Lipsyte (*Summer Rules* [1981] and *The Summer Boy* [1982]); and Richard Peck (*Remembering the Good Times* [1985] and *Princess Ashley* [1987]).

As the legendary editor Charlotte Zolotow—who worked with Block, Kerr, Lipsyte, Zindel, and others—noted, "The more original you are in publishing, the harder it is to be commercially successful but good writing survives trends," adding that young adult novels in the eighties were "becoming more honest and realistic, authors writing out of heart, feeling, and genuine motivation" (Baldwin 1984, 17).

Another legendary editor, Jean Karl, who had founded the children's book department at Athenaeum, agreed: "Young adults are moving into new areas of their lives," she said, "where they need to find books which will provide them with literary experiences that will broaden their view of the world" (Baldwin 1984, 20).

Clearly, this view needed broadening because the world of the 1980s that young (and old) adults inhabited was changing dramatically. One of the most significant of these changes had begun quietly enough back in 1965 when the United States Congress passed amendments to the Immigration and Nationality Act that not only placed a ceiling on immigration from European countries for the first time, but set it lower than the newly established limits for those from other parts of the world. The result was a major change in patterns of immigration. The numbers of immigrants from Europe began dropping precipitously, while those from Asia and the West Indies increased dramatically. In 1940, 70 percent of immigrants had still come from Europe. By 1992, only 15 percent came from there, whereas 37 percent were coming from Asia and 44 percent from Latin America and the Caribbean (*Time,* "Numbers Game" 1993). Moreover, not only did the pattern change, so also did the scope, for the 1980s began seeing the greatest wave of immigration to the United States since the nineteenth century (8.9 million people entered the United States legally between 1980 and 1990 and roughly 3 million more, illegally) (Mydans 1993). Significantly, most of the new immigrants hailed from such countries as Mexico, the Philippines, Haiti, South Korea, China, the Dominican Republic, India, Vietnam, and Jamaica—all of which had previously been represented only modestly.

Just as it had taken a decade for adult romances to trickle down into the YA field, so it would take nearly a decade and a half—from 1965 to 1980—for publishers to begin to take cognizance of these new facts of demographic life, and to start offering a new body of literature called "multicultural" that would give faces to these new American peoples.

And not a moment too soon.

According to "Kids Need Libraries" (Matthews et. al. 1990, 202), a position paper developed by the youth-serving divisions of the American Library Association and adopted by the Second White House Conference on Libraries and Information, "Kids need preparation to live in a multicultural world and to respect the rights and dignity of all people."

A search for those rights had brought yet another huge immigrant swell to our shores: political refugees who came to America from countries like Iran, El Salvador, and Cuba seeking not only economic opportunity but also sanctuary.

The arrival of both groups of new peoples created enormous problems of acculturation not only for them but also for established residents, as each group tried to cope with innumerable daily crossings of the borders of strange languages and baffling customs and mores. In this potentially explosive, newly multicultural environment, books had never been more important, for—as Hazel Rochman (1993, 9) wisely put it: "The best books break down borders."

The editor and publisher Margaret K. McElderry (1994, 379), who had been the first to publish a children's book from Germany following World War II, had this to say: "What is of immense importance now, as I see it, is to find writers among the new wave of immigrants, authors who can portray creatively what it is like to adjust to life in the United States, what their own experiences have been, written in either fictionalized form or as expository nonfiction."

Such writers had already appeared in the world of adult publishing: authors like Gish Jen, Bharatee Mukerjee, Gus Lee, Maxine Hong Kingston, Amy Tan, Sandra Cisneros, Nicholosa Mohr, Gary Soto, David Wong Louie, Betty Bao Lord, Ghita Mehta, Frank Chin, and still others. Who would match their eloquence in the world of young adult literature?

Before we can answer that question, we need to pause for a belated word or two of definition. *Multiculturalism* is an expansive word, containing in its definition and in its resonant connotations as many concepts—and sometimes hotly expressed opinions—as a suitcase full of unmatched socks.

I have been using the word *multiculturalism* to refer simply to aspects of the cultural and social lives and experiences of the newly immigrant populations who began arriving here in the seventies and the eighties. For others, however, the issues surrounding the word were more complex—and controversial.

Sarah Bullard explained: "Educators disagree, first, over which groups should be included in multicultural plans—racial and ethnic groups, certainly, but what about regional, social class, gender, disability, religious, language and sexual orientation grouping?" (Smith 1993, 341).

Similarly, Masha Kabakow Rudman (2006, 111) has written, "Multiculturalism can be defined simply as the inclusion of, appreciation of, and respect for all cultures; but a more complex formulation includes a challenge to the power structure that subordinates people on the basis of race, ethnicity, class, gender, sexual orientation, ability, age, and religion." This more expansive definition conjures up the image of a very—almost unmanageably—large tent, and so, when addressing this issue in the context of the decade of the eighties, I agree with Karen Patricia Smith, who argued in a 1993 article about the concept of multiculturalism and literature that "it is . . . necessary, for the sake of coherence, to narrow the scope of one's discussion." For her purposes—and for mine, at least in this chapter—"the term will be used to refer to people of color, that is, individuals who identify with African-American, Hispanic, American Indian, Eskimo or Aleut, and Asian or Pacific Islander heritage" (Smith 1993, 341–42).

Race was an important consideration, because—until the end of the sixties—it was nearly absent from the world of books for young readers. It was in 1965 that educator-writer Nancy Larrick published a hugely influential— and, again, controversial—article in the *Saturday Review* Titled "The All-White World of Children's Books," the article excoriated American publishers for failing to give faces to the growing populations of children of color. Surveying the 5,206 books for young readers published between 1962 and 1964, she found that only 6.7 percent contained any reference in text or illustration to African Americans, and 60 percent of that 6.7 percent were set either outside the United States or in the period before World War II. And even when African Americans did appear, they were too often presented as caricatures and stereotypes in books that, as Henrietta Smith (1995, 5) has observed, "were replete with the exaggerated use of dialect and illustrations that showed the Negro child with heavy lips, bulging eyes, night-black skin and wooly hair."

But it was still the sixties, and the times, they were actually a-changin'. In the wake of Larrick's seminal article, of the burgeoning Civil Rights movement, and of such long overdue legislation as the Voting Rights Act of 1965, the world of African Americans as depicted in literature began changing dramatically. Within five years a black literary renaissance was under way, marked by the emergence of such celebrated illustrators as Jerry Pinkney, Ashley Bryan, John Steptoe, Tom Feelings, and such distinguished writers as Rosa Guy, Alice Childress, Walter Dean Myers, Julius Lester, Mildred Taylor, and Virginia Hamilton, who—in 1975—became the first African American writer to win the prestigious Newbery Medal for *M. C. Higgins the Great*.

Two years later, Taylor became the second for *Roll of Thunder, Hear My Cry*. To further encourage this creative flowering, the American Library Association, working through its Social Responsibilities Roundtable, established the annual Coretta Scott King Awards in 1969 to recognize outstanding works written and illustrated by African American authors and artists.

It was in the mid-seventies that Chinese Americans also found an early literary champion of their own in Laurence Yep, who began writing about their cultural experience in his second book, *Dragonwings* (Harper, 1975). Yep's own experience of growing up as an outsider between cultures had actually found expression—though metaphorically—in his first book, a fantasy titled *Sweetwater* (1973). Yep continued to write powerfully about this experience throughout the seventies and eighties in such other novels as *Child of the Owl* (1977), *Sea Glass* (1979), *The Serpent's Children* (1984), and *Mountain Light* (1985).

Though Japanese Americans also found their faces and stories represented in the early work of Jeanne Wakatsuki Houston, Lensey Namioka, and Yoshiko Uchida, it would not be until the nineties that the true diversity of other Asian peoples found expression in young adult literature. In the preface to his important anthology *American Dragons* (1993), a collection of creative short works by twenty-five contemporary Asian American writers, Yep stressed the diversity of Asian cultures in America. "Asian Americans," he noted, "come not only from China and Japan but from the many countries around the Pacific rim, including the Philippines, Korea, India and even Tibet. Recently there have been new waves of immigrants, especially from Southeast Asia, countries such as Vietnam, Thailand, Cambodia, and Laos" (Yep 1993, xi–xii).

This is an important point, because the umbrella term *Asian American* tends to treat individuals from dramatically different countries and cultures as a single, homogeneous whole, and nothing could be further from the truth. The same problem has plagued literature about Native Americans and, especially, literature about Latinos and Latinas, who come from a world so diverse (twenty-one different nations comprise Latin America alone) that no one can even agree on a uniform term to embrace it. Although I will typically use *Latino* or *Latina*, others prefer *Hispanic* as being a broader term that emphasizes the common denominator of the Spanish language, even though there is no one universal form of the language in this hemisphere and the more politically conscious regard *Hispanic* as being too Eurocentric (and too often a language of oppression, to boot).

These disagreements aside, there is universal agreement that no viable body of literature for and about Latinos existed until the 1970s and 1980s, and even then the growing size of the populations that remained, in large part, invisible far outpaced the amount of work available. There were a number of interrelated reasons for this, beginning with the very language of Latino literature. "Most of what we write," Roberto Rodriguez and Patrisia Gonzalez (1994, B7) declared, "is considered noise, foreign chatter at best. We are often unable to find a medium for our rich and textured prose—the amalgam of Spanish, English, Indian and *calo* (street talk). Many publishers not only find our writing unacceptable; they can't read it."

Why they can't read it brings us to a second reason: there were—and, perhaps, still are—too few Latinos working in children's book publishing, resulting in a lack of knowledge of how to acquire, evaluate, and publish for this market. And a reason for that is there was no significant tradition of creating an indigenous literature for young readers in most Latin American countries, the few available books there being imported from Spain. And much of that was drearily didactic and moralistic. As a result, most of the Latino and Latina writers for young people who began appearing in the seventies and eighties were already established authors for adults, writers like Rudolfo Anaya, Gary Soto, Nicholosa Mohr, Sandra Cisneros, and others. It was not until the nineties and the creation of literary prizes like the Pura Belpre and Americas awards for excellence in Latino literature that a new generation of writers began focusing exclusively on writing for young readers. Further encouragement came both from mainstream publishers' creation of Spanish-language imprints (e.g., Rayo from HarperCollins; Mirasol from Farrar, Straus and Giroux; and Libros Viajeros from Harcourt), and also from the emergence of small independent publishers like Arte Publico, Cinco Puntos, Lee and Low, and Children's Book Press.

Even then, books for and about young people from other cultures remained a hard sell. Donald Barr (1986, 50), writing in *The New York Times Book Review*, noted, "American adolescents, for the most part, have little interest in their own traditions and almost none in anyone else's." Six years later, Margaret McElderry (1994, 379) agreed, noting in her 1994 May Hill Arbuthnot lecture, "The number of such books has drastically diminished in the last fifteen or twenty years. In part this has happened," she continued, "because our young readers some while ago seemed to lose interest in other countries, other peoples, other ways, tending instead to concentrate on themselves and their peers and their life-styles."

Political Correctness

Speaking of other cultures . . . the term *political correctness* implies the idea that attention must be paid to ensuring that language or actions do not offend or disadvantage individuals or groups, and as such can be applied to a wide range of such groups or topics. Our attention here will be given to literature in the context of multicultural awareness that arose in the later eighties as the sheer number of foreign-born demanded that attention be paid. But that raised the vexing question "By whom?" An increasing number of critics were beginning to question the authenticity of literature created by those writing from outside a cultural experience. Writing in *Library Trends*, Karen Patricia Smith (1993, 345) noted, "For years, minority populaces have been written about and 'described' by essentially white authors who are outside the cultures about whom they are writing or illustrating . . . the question posed and often debated is whether or not material written by so-called 'outsiders' is actually valid material."

As I pointed out in chapter 1, this issue was being debated as early as the 1950s and may be one that can never be satisfactorily resolved, for at its core it asks an unanswerable question: Can a writer's imagination be powerful enough to create a viable work of fiction about a culture he or she has observed only from the outside?

Richard Peck (1993, 21–22), for one, believes it can:

> Now in the nineties, we're being told to march to the beat of multiculturalism. This baffles novelists who thought we'd been celebrating the cultural mix of this country well before the textbooks touched on it. . . . Unless—unless a book is to be judged by the race or ethnicity of its author. In which case we are standing at the edge of an abyss. Fortunately a novel need not brand the race of its characters as a film must. A novel can begin at the next epidermal level down, to explore what we all have in common.

Jane Yolen (1994, 705) added a similarly cautionary thought in 1994:

> What we are seeing now in children's books is an increasing push toward what I can only call the "Balkanization" of literature. We are drawing rigid borders across the world of story, demanding that people tell only their own stories. Not only does this deny

the ability of gifted storytellers to re-invigorate the literature with cross-cultural fertilization, but it would mean that no stories at all could be told about some peoples or cultures until such time as a powerful voice from within that culture emerges.

Both Peck's and Yolen's observations bring us to the brink of another abyss: that aspect of multiculturalism that, in the later 1980s, came to be called "political correctness," or what I have dubbed "multiculturalism without a sense of humor." It is related to a certain stridency that accompanied efforts to maintain the cultural identity and separate integrity of the newly immigrant populations. The traditional image of America as a melting pot seemed to be in the process of being replaced by a new metaphor, America as stir-fry, the ingredients of which, of course, remain distinct.

Hazel Rochman, (1993, 17) who herself came to this country from South Africa, has been fearless in her indictment of this movement.

> *Multiculturalism* is a trendy word, trumpeted by the politically correct with a stridency that has provoked a sneering backlash. There are P.C. watchdogs eager to strip from the library shelves anything that presents a group as less than perfect. The ethnic "character" must always be strong, dignified, courageous, loving, sensitive, wise. Then there are those who watch for authenticity: how dare a white write about blacks? What's a gentile doing writing about a Jewish old lady and her African-American neighbors? The chilling effect of this is a kind of censorship and a reinforcement of apartheid.

Of course, this works both ways. One of the Latino books most often challenged by Anglo censors is Rudolfo Anaya's *Bless Me, Ultima* (1972) which—according to the watchdogs—celebrates witchcraft in its story of a New Mexican boy's magical encounter with a *curandera* (healer) and her owl spirit. Rodriguez and Gonzalez (1994, B7) explain: "The objections to Anaya's book indicate that those who would ban it do not understand Latino culture or its indigenous roots: the practice of healing is part of our indigenous memory."

Native American culture has been particularly subject to misrepresentation and, accordingly, has engendered some of the hottest debates, including challenges to the authenticity of the treatment of Native Americans in Laura Ingalls Wilder's Little House books, in the work of Jamake Highwater (three of whose novels were selected as ALA Best Books for Young Adults), and in individual titles by Lynn Reid Banks, Ann Rinaldi, Gerald McDermott, and others.

In 1970, futurist Alvin Toffler (1970, 4) coined the now-familiar phrase "future shock," which he defined as "the shattering stress and disorientation that we induce in individuals by subjecting them to too much change in too short a time." Future shock had certainly played a part in the first great wave of immigration that occurred in the late nineteenth century, but to a lesser degree, certainly, than in the one that followed in the 1980s—principally because the former was more gradual, spread out over a period of some four decades (roughly 1880 to 1920). However, the second great wave about which we've been writing in this chapter came crashing down on our shores in the space of only a single decade, bringing with it future shock in spades! Too few people deal well with such rapid change; it induces in them not only disorientation but also fear—principally fear of the unknown—which is why good books that provide information about not only the culture, but also about the individual human conditions of the lives of new immigrants, are so important.

Even by the dawn of the new decade of the nineties, the issues continued to be so complex and so various as to baffle minds and perplex hearts. But I believe—as I wrote in the first edition of this book—that it remains literature, whether imported from other lands in other languages, imported in translation, written in English in this country by immigrants who describe the invention of new selves here or recall the realities of former lives in the lands of their national origins—that will prove to be the place of illumination, the neutral center where all of us can go to find out about each other and, come to think of it, ourselves. "We" need to read books about "them," and "they" need to read about "us," and in the process perhaps we will find that we are all simply "we."

Note

1. This changed dramatically later in the decade when, for the first time, African American teens were represented in a romance series of their own. Called *18 Pine Street*, it had been "created" by Walter Dean Myers, according to Bantam Doubleday Dell.

4

The Early Nineties

A Near-Death Experience

AS THE NEW DECADE OF THE NINETIES DAWNED, CONNIE C. EPSTEIN, FORMER editor-in-chief of Morrow Junior Books, reflected on the condition of young adult publishing. Noting reports of "weakening sales for what had come to be called 'problem stories,'" she reported that "some editors, marketing directors, and subsidiary rights directors, discouraged by this downturn, have been wondering whether the young adult novel was ready for burial, and certainly most would agree that the genre is in turmoil" (Epstein 1990, 237).

Four years later, in 1994, the critic Alleen Pace Nilsen (1994, 30) agreed that assessing "the health of the genre" had become tantamount to "gathering at the bedside of an ailing loved one," though she qualified her diagnosis by explaining she was referring specifically to "the realistic problem novel" rather than "the entire body of modern young adult literature."

But what else, one is tempted to ask, was there? Well, there was horror, of course, the market for which continued to thrive in the early nineties. "Adolescents now constitute a booming niche market for the peddling of published gore and violence," Paul Gray (1993, 54) explained in *Time* magazine, noting that Christopher Pike had 8 million copies of his books in print in 1993 and that R. L. Stine boasted 7.6 million copies of his books. Shortly thereafter, the entertainment journalist Ken Tucker, in a reference too good not to mention, dubbed Pike and Stine the "Beavis and Butthead of horror." "It's easy to understand why young adult horror is so popular," he continued. "It's a combination of youth's eternal desire to shock its elders and a budding interest in all things odd and uncomfortable" (Tucker 1993, 27).

That interest was reflected not only in books, but also in the spate of increasingly violent slasher movies that had been dominating the box office since the eighties, starting with Sean Cunningham's *Friday the Thirteenth* and Wes Craven's *Nightmare on Elm Street.* The interest in the "odd and uncomfortable" was also finding expression in the popularity of the daytime confessional reality shows that had started with Phil Donahue in 1970; come of age with Oprah Winfrey, whose show debuted in 1986; and had then taken a swan dive into the sensational in the early nineties with increasingly over-the-top programs hosted by the likes of Jerry Springer, Sally Jesse Raphael, Geraldo Rivera, Ricki Lake, Maury Povich, and others. As a result, Penn State sociologist Vicki Apt said, "Television emphasizes the deviant; if you really are normal, no one cares" (Roan 1994, E1).

Nilsen felt that this was another reason for the decline in realistic YA fiction. "The daily media glut of stories about the personal foibles and tragedies in which young people get involved . . . leaves little unexplored territory for authors to mine," she said (Nilsen 1994, 32).

Although it was small comfort, this phenomenon was not confined to literature for young adults. Adam Hochschild (1994, 11), founder of *Mother Jones* magazine, offered a similar observation about adult fiction in the 1990s. "One reason people write fewer traditional realist novels these days," he said, "is that modern readers are jaded. Film, radio, first-person journalism, prying biographers and, above all, TV have saturated us with reality."

Small wonder, then, that readers continued to search for escape in the borderline fantasy pages of series romance, which, accordingly, continued to sell every bit as briskly as horror, with Sweet Valley setting a particularly blistering pace. According to the series' publisher, Bantam Doubleday Dell, there were more than eighty-one million copies of Sweet Valley titles in print in 1994 with more to come, for, as the publisher trumpeted, "Sweet Valley continues to offer teens all the racy romance, drama, and adventures they're looking for in a series" (1994, 90).

The popularity of such genre series is perhaps the most durable phenomenon in the ongoing history of publishing for young readers. Such series were, as we have seen, staples of the twenties and thirties, thanks in large part to the Stratemeyer Syndicate. Today's writing factories, which are still turning out similar titles on the creative assembly line as fast as kids can read them, are no longer called syndicates, however, but packagers. Their typical function is to develop an idea for a series, sell it to a mainstream publisher, and then assemble the talent—including author, editor, and illustrator—necessary to produce a finished product for delivery to (and manufacture and distribution by) the publisher. One of the leading packagers of the eighties was Daniel Weiss Associates, which produced ten series a month in "a market-driven style and standard" according to Elise Howard, who was then the company's vice-president (Cart 1996, 148). Packagers would become even more important and influential, as we will see, in the late nineties and early aughts with the explosion of what came to be called "chick lit."

For the moment, it bears repeating here that teens themselves were purchasing these original paperback genre series—unlike hardcover novels of realism, which adult librarians and teachers usually bought—usually at mall-based chain bookstores. And fewer and fewer hardcovers were being published and purchased. Thanks to a combination of taxpayer revolts (spearheaded by California's notorious Proposition 13), diminishing federal funding, and the American economy's recessionary malaise, the institutional market continued its precipitous decline throughout the eighties and into the early nineties. If anything, the school library market was even punier than that of the public library, as educators were increasingly spending their dwindling resources on new technology instead of books. By 1993, the industry magazine *Publishers Weekly* noted that the market had dropped from 80–90 percent institutional to only 50–60 percent (Dunleavy 1993). As a result, Nilsen observed, major publishing houses "have moved from the past practice of bringing out about 80% fiction and 20% nonfiction to doing 80% nonfiction and 20% fiction"—the point being that while cash-strapped institutions were now avoiding "nonessential" fiction, they did continue to buy nonfiction to support curricular needs. The publisher Beverly Horowitz confirmed this, citing growing pressure to increase profit margins by eliminating whatever books or kinds of books that didn't turn a profit that was "both quick and high" (Eaglen 1990, 54).

Middle-school Literature

Something else equally significant was happening to young adult books: the typical age of their protagonists was decreasing from sixteen or seventeen to as young as twelve to fourteen. This radical change was due to several interrelated factors. First was the rise of the middle-school movement. From 1966 to 1981 the number of these new schools, which typically served grades six to eight, increased from 499 to 6,003. Unlike the old junior highs, which might have been described as high schools with training wheels, these new schools were specifically designed to meet the unique developmental needs of eleven- to fourteen-year-olds, young people who were no longer children but not quite young adults, either. As Lucy Rollin (1999, 252) notes, "The term 'middle school' emphasized a separate identity, a school and a group of students who were not 'junior' to anything but in transition." As had happened in the thirties with the emergence of the first generation of teenagers, this new group offered a de facto challenge to publishers to create a new kind of literature expressly for them, one that publishers continued to call young adult but now targeted at this new, younger age range. Simultaneously, the amount of traditional YA literature continued to dwindle as fewer and fewer books appeared for high-school-aged readers. As a result, though it might have appeared to the casual observer that the age of YA protagonists was simply decreasing, what was actually happening was that a new kind of literature—middle-school literature—was being born (while the traditional form was dying). This shift dovetailed nicely with the sales strategies of the chain bookstores, many of which were morphing into superbookstores. The Barnes and Noble chain led this evolution, opening 105 such superstores between 1989 and 1992. Though much larger than the earlier chain stores, none of these new behemoths contained separate young adult sections; instead, everything labeled YA was simply—and summarily—shoved into the children's department. This practice further encouraged the "youthening" of protagonists because at the same time the stores avoided stocking any titles containing controversial subjects or themes. As George Nicholson noted in 1990, the chains would not buy a novel "with anything difficult in it" (Cart 1996, 150). No wonder that another legendary editor, Richard Jackson, flatly declared in 1994, "Young adult (now) stops at fourteen" (Cart 1996, 150).

Unfortunately, this new middle-school YA literature did have at least one thing in common with the traditional form: it didn't sell well in hardcover. In fact, in 1993 hardcover sales to both the institutional and retail markets were down for the first time, though paperback sales continued to soar. As a result, publishers—though they still produced small hardcover editions of 1,000 copies or less for the institutional market (Eaglen 1990)—were typically acquiring for hardcover release only titles that promised steep sales when they would be published a year later in their paperback editions, editions that were sold directly to teens through the chain bookstores.

Recognizing the dwindling market for hardcovers, why didn't publishers begin issuing quality fiction for those largely ignored older teens in original trade paperback formats? After all, adult publishers were finding success with this more cost-effective strategy. One reason was that the children's book-review media tended not to cover paperbacks (hence the continued small hardcover releases), and many libraries remained reluctant to stock such a relatively ephemeral format; another reason was the claim that the chains would not stock such paperbacks; and still another was authors' alleged preference for the cachet of hardback publication, along with the more practical reason that publishers paid larger advances for hardcovers than for paperbacks. To its credit, the publisher Harcourt, Brace did experiment with issuing selected titles in simultaneous hard- and soft-cover editions in a uniform trim size but, unfortunately, with little or no success.

Farewell, YA?

Thanks to all these many factors, the number of YA titles continued to decline, though it is difficult to ascertain by how much with any degree of precision. Publishers and the reference media have historically (and a bit unceremoniously) lumped statistics for children's and YA books together into one generic children's books category. Nevertheless, Audrey Eaglen (1990, 54) noted in her *School Library Journal* column that "even the biggest publishers seldom do more than a dozen or so YAs a year."

What did editors have to say about this? A panel of five leaders in the field shared their views with participants in a 1994 YALSA conference in Miami Beach. The five were Marc Aronson of Henry Holt; David Gale, of Simon and Schuster; Richard Jackson, of Orchard Books; Robert Warren, of HarperCollins; and Linda Zuckerman, of Harcourt, Brace. With five strong-minded, independent individuals on the platform, consensus on some issues was predictably elusive; however, there did seem to be agreement that young adult publishing—though still alive—was, indeed, ailing. Aronson delicately called it "a time of transition." Zuckerman was probably the least sanguine of the five, saying frankly, "I think young adult literature is dying." She explained that there was only a limited amount of time and risk that publishers were willing to take with developing new authors. As a result, she predicted, the YA field would continue to diminish, becoming increasingly focused on series and on the work of a handful of established name authors.

There was consensus that publishers were, indeed, increasingly targeting the twelve- to fourteen-year-old reader. In fact, of the five, Gale was the only one who still actively searched for books for older readers, though he acknowledged he had to exercise caution in accepting manuscripts with too much sex or violence, because they might be rejected by an increasingly conservative school library market. He also agreed that books for older readers were "nonexistent" in bookstores, echoing Nilsen's comment that fiction didn't sell particularly well in the prevailing market and, accordingly, fewer novels were being published.

Several of the editors also acknowledged that a major factor in their decision to publish a book in hardcover was its demonstrated potential for paperback reprint sales. "Do paperback sales drive the market?" Warren asked rhetorically. "Yes."

Warren then turned the discussion from a focus on the field of YA to the individual writer when he reminded his audience that "we're not publishing a genre; we're publishing an author. And," he concluded, "a good book will always, always be published" (Cart 1996, 163).

This salutary affirmation aside, an overall air of the valedictory pervaded a conference that found little to celebrate in the present but much to laud in the past. Indeed, the principal business of the conference attendees was the selection of the one hundred best YA books published between 1967 and 1992.

This 1994 list, "Here We Go Again . . . 25 Years of Best Books," included a number of titles that, in terms of their topical and thematic content, were historically important. *Go Ask Alice* and *A Hero Ain't Nothin' but a Sandwich* were, for example, classic treatments of drug abuse, whereas Richard Peck's *Are You in the House Alone?* (1976) was the first YA novel to deal with rape. Like Zindel's earlier *The Pigman*, Lois Duncan's *Killing Mr. Griffin* (1978) continued to explore the important issue of adolescent acceptance of responsibility, a theme also treated in her earlier classic *I Know What You Did Last Summer* (1973). Felice Holman, in her *Slake's Limbo* (1974) introduced an element of allegory into the prevailing mode of YA realism and in her story of young Artemis Slake's 121-day odyssey in New York's subways also gave readers a classic story of survival. Finally, Barbara Wersba's *Run Softly, Go Fast* (1970) explored another timeless theme: the uneasy relationship of fathers and sons, a topic that also informed such other novels of the seventies as Robert Newton Peck's *A Day No Pigs Would Die* (1973) and Richard Peck's *Father Figure* (1978).[1]

Despite its golden past, young adult literature was, by 1994, clearly at risk of extinction. Ironically so were young adults themselves, whose lives were becoming increasingly endangered by societal and personal problems that ranged from poverty to homelessness, from fractured families to violence (in 1991 one fifteen- to nineteen-year-old was murdered every three-and-a-half hours!), from increased drug use to sexual harassment and rape and—perhaps as a result of all this—an exponential increase (200 percent in the preceding four decades) in teenage suicide (Waters 1994, 49).

Sadly, this coincided with a continuing decline in the purchasing power of school and public libraries, and a critical shortage of trained young adult librarians who might have helped endangered young adults weather their stormy lives. According to a 1988 survey conducted by the National Center for Education Statistics, only 11 percent of America's libraries had young adult specialists on staff. A later survey, conducted in 1992 by the Young Adult Library Services Association, confirmed this, reporting a continued "dearth of qualified staff" and the prevailing feeling, among librarians, that YA funding was the first area to be cut during times of fiscal crisis and that "the loss of library funding" had become "a national epidemic" (Latrobe 1994, 238).

How, I asked in the first edition of this book, can we solve problems of such magnitude? How can we even comprehend them? Well, if knowledge is power, I continued, there was no shortage of powerful nonfiction being published to describe the shape and scope of the problems. More important, a trend in early nineties nonfiction was the inclusion, through interviews, of the authentic voices of the young people themselves, especially those whose lives were at risk or who lived at the narrower margins of society. Such books included Susan Kuklin's *Speaking Out: Teenagers Take on Race, Sex, and Identity* (1993), Judith Berck's *No Place to Be. Voices of Homeless Children* (1992), and Susan Goodwillie's *Voices from the Future: Our Children Tell Us about Violence in America* (1993). Such books gave not only voices but also faces to too often invisible young people. But, good as those books were, we needed more.

"We need more than information," I argued in "Of Risk and Revelation," my keynote speech at the 1994 preconference, "we need *wisdom*. And for that we must turn to fiction—to young adult fiction, which is written for and about YAs and the unique problems that plague and perplex them. Why fiction?

Because of its unique capacity to educate not only the mind but the heart and spirit as well. The late Italo Calvino put it this way in his *Six Memos for the Next Millennium:* 'My confidence in the future of literature consists in the knowledge that there are things only literature can give us by means specific to it'" (Calvino 1988, 1).

"Really good fiction," the novelist and critic John Gardner once wrote, "has a staying power that comes from its ability to jar, to turn on, to move the whole intellectual and emotional history of the reader" (Yardley 1994, 3). If young adult literature is to have a future, it must be more than a formula-driven fiction that begins and ends with a problem. It must be as real as headlines, but it must be more than the simple retailing of fact. It must also be enriched by the best means literature can offer: an expansive, fully realized setting; a memorably artful narrative voice; complex and fully realized characters; and unsparing honesty and candor in its use of language and treatment of material. Young adult literature, in short, must take creative (and marketing) risks to present hard-edged issues of relevance so that it may offer its readers not only reality but also revelation and, ultimately, that desired wisdom.

This is the spirit in which I wrote the first edition of this book, and it remains one of the guiding principles by which I evaluate the success or failure of the literature that followed in the second half of the 1990s. For more about that we turn, now, to the next chapter and a consideration of the balance of that formative decade.

Note

1. The complete list can be found in Betty Carter, ed. *Best Books for Young Adults,* 2nd ed. Chicago: ALA, 2000.

5

The Rest of the Nineties

Revival and Renaissance

IN RETROSPECT, THE 1994 MIAMI BEACH CONFERENCE TURNED OUT TO BE A dramatic turning point for young adult literature, marking not the death of the genre as had been predicted but, instead, its rebirth and the beginning of a remarkable period of renaissance that has continued to the time of this writing in 2016.

The first stirrings of this revival had actually taken place in US schools in the late eighties and very early nineties in the form of the nascent whole-language movement, a method of teaching reading that employed trade books instead of classic basal readers (Dick and Jane, anyone?). Although at first this phenomenon primarily impacted the children's book market, it would have a more long-range and salutary impact on young adult literature by bringing contemporary books into the classroom. As Lori Benton, then with The Book Shop in Boise, Idaho, told *Publishers Weekly*. There's "a huge demand for us to give in-service workshops. Teachers want help finding what literature is available and appropriate" (Ohanian 1991, 127).

Another phenomenon of equal if not greater importance arrived in 1992 when, following a fifteen-year period of decline, America's teen (twelve to nineteen) population spiked significantly, growing 16.6 percent from 1990 to 2000 when it totaled 32 million. That rate of increase was widely expected to outstrip that of the general population before peaking in 2010 (in fact, it continued to increase—see chapter 10).

In the meantime, January 1994 had seen the publication in *School Library Journal* of Chris Lynch's important article, "Today's YA Writers: Pulling No Punches." Himself an emerging writer of hard-hitting literary fiction for young adults, Lynch underscored the importance to the field of allowing authors the luxury of "taking the gloves off" when writing for young adults. "My plea is authenticity," he wrote, adding "the teen experience is unlike any other and it deserves its own literature" (Lynch 1994, 94, 37–38).

An early intimation that this process might already be under way was a new column on young adult literature that had debuted in the venerable *Horn Book* magazine in its September/October 1993 issue: "The Sand in the Oyster," by writer, critic, and editor Patty Campbell. In her first column Campbell (1993, 568) promised "to do some heavy breathing, since (the) subject will be controversial: books and issues in young-adult literature, focusing not only on sex and censorship but also on debatable matters of literary style and other social and intellectual concerns." Lynch's article and Campbell's new column would be only the first in a series of similar writings to help spur the revival of young adult literature. In June 1994, for example, I began my own monthly column, "Carte Blanche," in *Booklist* magazine. And 1995 saw Marc Aronson's memorably titled "The Young Adult Novel Is Dead and Other Fairly Stupid Tales" in *School Library Journal* and my own "Of Risk and Revelation: The Current State of Young Adult Literature" in *Journal of Youth Services.*

In retrospect, it's clear that 1996 marked another significant turning point in young adult literature's coming of age as literature. In a radical departure from its previous focus on scholarship and research in children's literature, the Children's Literature Association devoted the entire contents of the spring issue of its quarterly journal to "Critical Theory and Young Adult Literature." That fall the annual workshop of the National Council of Teachers of English's Assembly on Literature for Adolescents (ALAN) had as its theme "Exploding the Canon," which offered true believers another opportunity to trumpet the news that young adult literature was now literature that deserved a place in a literary canon long overdue for reexamination and reassessment; surely, conferees argued, YA books deserved a place in America's classrooms where they could be taught and appreciated in the company of long-established—but increasingly dusty—classics.

This argument found more discursive expression that same year in two book-length publications: Sarah K. Hertz and Don Gallo's *From Hinton to*

Hamlet: Building Bridges between Young Adult Literature and the Classics (1996) and the first edition of this book (1996). Scarcely a year later another important book appeared, John Noell Moore's *Interpreting Young Adult Literature: Literary Theory in the Secondary Classroom* (1997).

How Adult Is Young Adult?

In summer 1996, YALSA presented still another significant program. Titled "How Adult Is Young Adult?" and held at the American Library Association's Annual Conference and Exhibition in New York, it attracted a standing-room-only audience and excited considerable discussion and debate. Campbell (1997, 366), in fact, devoted one of her "Oyster" columns to its content, noting, "We have lost the upper half of YA—those fourteen- to nineteen-year-olds who were the original readership for the genre."

How to recover and even expand that audience was, in fact, the central purpose of the program's co-conveners (literary agent George Nicholson and myself). To that end, a number of influential speakers addressed the importance of redefining and expanding the audience for young adult literature. As moderator, my role was to provide context; accordingly, I noted, "The borders of the land of young adult have always been ill-defined and subject to negotiation and many titles that have found their way onto YALSA's annual Best Books for Young Adults list have slipped across from the land of children's literature as well as from the world of books published for adults."[1]

The editor Marc Aronson picked up on this theme, noting that the most successful titles in his own EDGE imprint at Henry Holt were those that crossed markets. "They reach YA and Asian American adult [readers], YA and Latino adult, YA and Jewish adult, YA and African American adult." In fact, he suggested, "We have frozen our terms around a late sixties reality that no longer exists and we may be doing ourselves harm by calling books that deal with older teenage life or deal with coming of age in a sophisticated way, 'YA.'" His point here, of course, was that YA had become synonymous with middle-school literature and therefore the term was an implicit turnoff for older readers, as was Barnes and Noble's policy of shelving YA titles in its children's departments. In that respect, there was good news from another of the speakers, Carla Parker, senior buyer for the Barnes and Noble chain, who reported—to loud applause—that Barnes and Noble would reconfigure older stores and create separate, stand-alone YA areas in all of its new stores, so that by 1997, all of the YA sections would be "outside of not in their children's departments."

What to call these new departments—and the more sophisticated literature they might stock—excited considerable discussion. For example, another speaker, the writer Francesca Lia Block, suggested the term "X-Over" to describe its multigenerational, crossover appeal, the same appeal that her category-defying Weetzie Bat novels had excited among both teens and readers in their twenties.

Whatever it might be called, it was surely true, as Anna Lawrence-Pietroni (1996, 34) had written in that landmark issue of the *Children's Literature Association Quarterly,* "Young adult fiction defies easy categorization, and by its nature proposes a more liberating view of genre as process rather than as circumspection and definition." Block seemed to echo this view at the YALSA program:

> Society is beginning to understand that childhood and adulthood are not really as separate as people think they are . . . Childhood is filled with darkness, the need for love, the search for acceptance. Why can't we create a category which all the barriers will cross? This is the intention in bookstores and libraries: books that appeal to young and old, gay and straight, open-minded and representative of different racial backgrounds. Maybe we can begin here to use literature as a way to connect rather than to divide.

The issue, however, was not so much what such a new and free-ranging category of literature might be called or could offer in the way of connections, but instead how it might be created, published, marketed, and sold. In 1992, the editor and publisher Stephen Roxburgh, then still at Farrar, Straus and Giroux, had written, "Publishing, in order to work, has to fit into boxes. One has to be clear on whether the publishing strategy for a title is adult or YA. A book's primary support, in terms of advertising and the review media must be defined" (Lodge 1992, 38).

Because of the undefined composition of her multigenerational readership, Block acknowledged that most readers found her books by word of mouth. Speaking to the same issue in her address, Parker suggested, "We need to see more book reviewing and advertising done on MTV and in the magazines that teens actually look at: *Seventeen, Sassy* and *Spin*. I don't think YA is dead, I think it's changed and we must change with it."

Some strategies for change that were suggested during the program included the cross-promotion of titles by listing them in both children's and adult catalogs as Houghton Mifflin had done with David Macaulay's *The Way Things Work* (1988). The literary agent George Nicholson, another speaker, offered the model of Robert Cormier's novel *Fade* with which he had been involved when he was publisher of books for young readers at Dell/Delacorte. This most ambitious of Cormier's books was published, he explained, in both adult and young adult editions and was listed in both catalogs. Another possibility broached was the publication of adult paperback editions of more sophisticated YA titles as had been done with *Fade*, Walter Dean Myers's *Fallen Angels* (1988), and A. M. Homes's *Jack* (1989).

By program's end the panel had carved out an ambitious agenda that publisher Andre Schiffrin seemed to be describing in another context (the venturesome creation of his nonprofit company The New Press): "We would need," he wrote in *American Bookseller*, "to show that audiences deemed unreachable" (think sixteen- to twenty-five-year-olds here) "by many publishers will respond to materials and formats designed to reach them. The search for new audiences is, of course, as essential to the future of the bookstore as it is to that of publishers. We hope to be increasingly successful at finding new ways to reach those readers with meaningful, affordable books" (Schiffrin 1995, 17).

Hope keeps dreams alive, but much of what the panelists were calling for seemed, at the time, to be just such a dream—and an impossible one at that, given the rapidly changing world of publishing. The traditional model of the private, often family-owned, small company had morphed, through relentless mergers and acquisitions, into a new model: the multinational, publicly held infotainment conglomerate. According to a 1997 issue of the *Nation*, eight such behemoths (Hearst, News Corporation, Pearson, Viacom, Advance Publications, Bertelsmann, Time Warner, and Holtzbrinck) owned virtually every publisher in America. Many of these were headed by a new kind of executive "brought in, often from finance or banking, with a commitment to their new owners (international media conglomerates) to increase profits, which now are gauged against those of other conglomerate holdings" (which were often television and motion picture companies) (Schiffrin 1995, 17).

This constant pressure to perform resulted in the increased commodification of books as publishers focused on the next hot new property to be

exploited. Morgan Entrekin, of Grove/Atlantic, one of the few surviving inde-
pendents, said, "Nowadays there is a burning impatience to find the next big
hit, to pigeonhole authors and books in easy categories. The large corpora-
tions that control American publishing care more about product than prose"
(Getlin 1997, E5).

The massive size of these operations further encouraged maintaining the
status quo, rather than embarking on the sort of experimentations that the
YALSA panel had called for. Imagine asking a giant ocean liner to turn on a
dime, and you have a good idea of the condition of American publishing in
the late nineties. And as publishing grew, so did the noninstitutional market.
By 1997, Barnes and Noble operated more than 1,000 stores (454 superstores
and 559 smaller mall outlets), and retail outlets controlled 85 percent of the
market (Campbell 1997).

And yet progress did continue to be made. For example, another important advance took place in 1995, when the National Book Foundation rees-
tablished a long-moribund category among its prestigious National Book
Award: a prize for the most distinguished book of the year for young readers.
The first award, presented in 1996, went to the young adult novel *Parrot in
the Oven* by the California writer Victor Martinez. In the succeeding six years
the award would go four times to a young adult book (the remaining two
were awarded to children's titles). Two years later, recognizing the increasing
artistic sophistication of young adult literature, *The Los Angeles Times* added
the category of "Young Adult Novel" to its roster of annual book awards. The
founding judges—Patty Campbell, Selma Lanes, and myself—selected Joan
Bauer's wonderfully funny and heartfelt *Rules of the Road* as the first recipient of this major new award.

Inarguably, however, the most important of the new YA literary prizes
would be YALSA's Michael L. Printz Award, which was created in 1999 and
presented for the first time in 2000. I have more to say about the creation of
this new award for a new millennium and its far-reaching significance later
in this chapter.

A Renaissance of Youth Culture

It was clear, by the mid-1990s, that there was "a renaissance of youth culture in this country" (Bernstein 1996, 25). This was, once again, a largely
market-driven phenomenon, rooted in the extraordinary growth of this seg-

ment of the population, which would grow by 4.5 million between 1990 and 2000 (a 17 percent increase). Record numbers of students were enrolled in US schools in 1996 and 1997, with "the bulk of the increase at the high school level," according to the US Department of Education. "From the fall of 1997 through 2007, the nation's schools can expect a 13 percent increase in grades nine through twelve" (American Library Association Washington Office Newsline 1977, 73).

That this record number of young people commanded record amounts of disposable income was catnip to the American marketplace. According to *The New York Times*, "In 1995 people between 13 and 19 spent $68.8 billion on personal items, up from $49.8 billion in 1985. 'The teen market has got tremendous buying power and is growing by leaps and bounds,' said Page Thompson, the head of United States Media at the ad agency DDB Needham. 'If you take a look down the line, four or five years from now, it's going to be huge. Long term, it's a bonanza'" (Pogrebin 1996, C8).

Seldom in our history had so much attention been lavished on teens, who now seemed virtually omnipresent, not only in America's malls and gallerias but also in every medium of popular culture: magazines, movies, television, and more.

Among magazines, *Teen People* debuted to much fanfare in 1998, and quickly became second only to the venerable *Seventeen* magazine in its popularity (*Teen* and *YM* rounded out the "big four" magazines for this demographic). *Cosmo Girl* followed in 1999, and *Elle Girl* and *Teen Vogue* in 2001 and 2003, respectively. Oddly there have been no general interest magazines for boys with the possible exception of *MH-18*, which debuted in 2000 but folded in less than a year. There have, however, been a number of special interest magazines including *Thrasher*, *Transworld Skateboarding*, and *Game Pro*.

If no single director dominated teen-oriented motion pictures in the nineties as John Hughes had in the eighties, movies nevertheless continued to capture the teen zeitgeist, none more cleverly than two 1995 releases: Amy Heckerling's *Clueless* and Kevin Smith's *Mall Rats*. The former, according to *Time* magazine, "is about conspicuous consumption: wanting, having and wearing in style," while the latter telegraphs its message when a character walks into the mall that is the film's setting and exclaims, "I love the smell of commerce in the morning" (Corliss 1995, 77–8).

Television began its increasingly single-minded focus on teens in 1989 with the series *Saved by the Bell* (which was followed in 1993 by *Saved by the Bell: The New Class*). The trash classic *Beverly Hills 90210* followed in 1990. MTV then launched its hugely popular and influential series *The Real World* in 1992 (it would still be on the air in 2016, having become the network's longest-running series). *My So-Called Life* and *Party of Five* debuted in 1994, and *Sabrina the Teenage Witch* and *Clueless* followed in 1996. Meanwhile, in 1995, the teen-oriented WB television network launched, and within five years had become home to such blockbuster teen-centric TV series as *Buffy the Vampire Slayer, Dawson's Creek, Felicity, Charmed, Roswell, Popular,* and *Angel.*

"In network TV, WB defines hot because (1) its audience is young, (2) it's the only network to make solid ratings gains this past season, and (3) its audience is young," TV critic Rick Kushman (1999, G1) noted sardonically. The most critically acclaimed of all of the youth-oriented series, *Freaks and Geeks,* came along at the very end of the decade in 1999, a year when eighteen of the thirty-six new shows starred people in their teens or early twenties (Kushman 1999).

According to *Time,* "The economics alone don't explain the high school vogue, nor why the shows include a couple of the fall's better premieres. 'Adolescence is a great period of time to write about,' says Jason Katims, creator of the acclaimed *Relativity.* 'It's where so much of you is formed and the themes that will follow you your whole adult life are born'" (Poniewozik 1999, 77–78).

Publishers already knew this, of course, and were publishing not only books for adolescents but also a new genre of books for adult readers about adolescents. One of the first of these was Grace Palladino's lively and informative *Teenagers: An American History* (1996). Another important title—and one that would be widely imitated—was journalist Patricia Hersch's moving and unsparing *A Tribe Apart: A Journey into the Heart of American Adolescence* (1998); in doing her research, Hersch, the mother of four adolescent boys, spent three years in the company of eight other teenagers in Reston, Virginia.[2] William Finnegan's *Cold New World* was a sobering look at adolescent alienation and impoverishment (1998), and Peter Zollo's *Wise Up to Teens: Insights into Marketing and Advertising to Teenagers* (1999), examined the lives and consuming interests of more privileged teens, as did Don Tapscott's *Growing Up Digital* (1998), which profiled the emergence of the "net" generation.

No longer limited to the traditional twelve-eighteen demographic, this new culture embraced young adults as old as thirty, giving shape and form to the previously amorphous *Weetzie Bat* readership and acknowledging the growing commercial and cultural influence of the MTV demographic. Booksellers were starting to call this group the alternative audience and a number of venturesome small presses—Last Gasp, Serpent's Tail, City Lights, Manic D Press, and so on—were starting to publish quirky, offbeat titles for it. Significantly, this phenomenon was not limited to major urban centers. "In the suburbs kids are absolutely starving for, and fanatical about, anything that is weird, funky, extreme," publisher Katherine Gates told *Publishers Weekly*. "Also don't forget that books are the current required accessories of hipdom, the way CDs used to be" (Bernstein 1996, 26). As a result, such hip outlets as Tower Records and Virgin Atlantic began to carry books for these wired and with-it young readers, right alongside their staple music products.

The Advent of the Edgy

All of the elements I've been discussing breathed new life into the nearly moribund YA genre, sparking a rapid and energetic recovery from its near-death experience. With a newly expanded reader demographic and a new retail marketplace in which to reach them, publishers began issuing a newly hard-edged and gritty fiction of realism that targeted a crossover readership. Quickly dubbed *bleak books*, this new subgenre excited considerable discussion and even more considerable controversy.

The movies had anticipated this turn to darkness in 1995 and 1996 with such landmark *noir* films as Larry Clark's horrifying *Kids* (with a screenplay by teenager Harmony Korine), and—from Britain—Danny Boyle's *Trainspotting* (based on the sensationally popular novel of the same title by Irvine Welsh).

As *The New York Times* critic Jon Pareles (1995, sec. 2, 1) correctly noted, "*Kids* is, for now, the most extreme of a long line of films in which teens are amoral, irrational, hormone-crazed and oblivious to consequences."

Bellwether book titles in this new genre began appearing in 1997, and included Brock Cole's *The Facts Speak for Themselves* (Front Street), Norma Fox Mazer's *When She Was Good* (Levine/Scholastic), Robert Cormier's *Tenderness* (Delacorte Press), Han Nolan's *Dancing on the Edge* (Harcourt Brace), and Adam Rapp's *The Buffalo Tree* (Front Street). Not only was the content of these books newly sophisticated (subjects ranged from pedophilia to insanity to murder to rape to juvenile incarceration to serial slaying); so also was the physical design of the books themselves. *Publishers Weekly* took notice of this in an article titled "Hipper, Brighter, and Bolder" (Stevenson 1997), which acknowledged the importance of the new retail market, (which also included the online retailers Amazon.com and Barnes and Noble.com, both of which would create new, separate teen sections at their websites in 1998).

In the same spirit, the editor and publisher Arthur Levine told me in an interview, "It's first of all important to pay careful attention to the dust jacket art in order to excite all of your potential audiences" (Cart 1997b, 553).

While all of this dynamic activity was happening, libraries remained a staple—though slightly diminished—market for these books and the institutional world was actually the first to acknowledge the changes that were sweeping the YA world. In fact, one of the very first strands of discussion on the newly created electronic book discussion forum YALSA-BK was "Bleak Books." Soon thereafter, *Booklist* magazine's Children's Books Editor Ilene Cooper wrote a thoughtful article, "Facts of Life" about Cole's *The Facts Speak for Themselves* (1997) and followed this with "Publishing on the Edge," coauthored with the YA Books Editor Stephanie Zvirin. At the 1998 ALA conference, *Booklist* sponsored an important panel discussion, "On the Edge: Personal Perspectives on Writing for Today's Young Adults." The speakers included authors Brock Cole, Annette Curtis Klause, Norma Fox Mazer, Han Nolan, and editor Richard Jackson, publisher Virginia Walter's controversial bleak book *Making up Megaboy* (1997), the story of a suburban white California teen who inexplicably murders a Korean shopkeeper.

The eloquent Jackson (1998, 1985) put the entire controversy in perspective: "When reviewers today worry about bleak stories, they are worrying, on behalf of the audience, about the readiness of young readers to face life's darkest corners. But in America there are kids *living* in those dark corners, and they need our attention as much as the feisty, pert, athletic, and popular youth so reassuring to adults. Even children in the sun will enter the darkness. They *all* need our tenderness. And we need our tenderness as art inspires us to feel it."

This should have been the last word on this controversy, but there would be many more to come as the mainstream media belatedly discovered this debate and a yearlong spate of increasingly sensational stories about this new trend in publishing began appearing. The media hubbub seems to have started with an article that appeared in *The New York Times Sunday Magazine* on August 2, 1998. Written by Sara Mosle and titled "The Outlook's Bleak," the article was a hand-wringing account of the eruption of edgy young adult novels that were offering unsparingly dark looks at the lives of contemporary teens. By reading bleak books, Mosle argued, teens were growing old before their time, "shouldering burdens far beyond their years."

And so they were but not because they were reading young adult books. Rather, it was because they themselves were a generation at risk. The first edition of this book was chockablock with statistics demonstrating that reality. This time around it may suffice simply to quote Thomas A. Jacobs (1997, 39), who—in his book *What Are My Rights? 95 Questions and Answers about Teens and the Law*—wrote, "In the Forties the top discipline problems in school were talking, chewing gum, making noise, running in the halls, getting out of turn in line, and not putting trash in the wastebaskets. In the Nineties, the top problem [was] alcohol and drug abuse, followed by pregnancy, suicide, rape, assault, arson, murder, vandalism, and gang fights."

Nevertheless, the *Times* piece proved to be only the tip of the iceberg as a titanic number of similar articles began appearing in such outlets as *Time, US News and World Report,* the *Wall Street Journal,* and *Brill's Content,* all of them tut-tutting at the spurt in bleak books. The titles of the articles betrayed the sensational slant of their content: "Reads Like Teen Spirit," "Frank Tales Tempt Teens," "Luring Today's Teen Back to Books," and "Sex, Serial Killers, and Suicide." Use of words like "tempt" and "luring" suggested, to over-credulous adults, that publishing had become a dirty old man approaching a group of innocent teens and wheezing, "Hey, kids, wanna see some—heh, heh, heh—*books?*"

Such oversimplification did both publishers and the new young adult literature a disservice. In retrospect it seems more than likely that the mainstream media were not responding to any perceived changes in or problems with young adult literature, but instead were simply riding the crest of the wave of interest in young adults themselves and in some of the darker aspects of their real lives, including an inarguable increase in teenage drug use (Bass 1997; Wren 1997) and a wave of gun-related school violence that crested (but did not end) with the Columbine shootings in 1999.

The result, unsurprisingly, was a rise in the adult demonization of youth. "According to a new poll," the late columnist Molly Ivins (1997, A19) wrote in 1997, "we don't like our own children. The public policy research group Agenda found that only 37 percent of adults polled believe that today's youngsters will eventually make this country a better place. It seems we consider our teenagers, whom we have long disliked, to be 'rude,' 'wild,' and 'irresponsible.'"

The reporter Lynn Smith (1997, E3), writing in *The Los Angeles Times,* made a cogent point in this connection: "Some youth advocates said such perceptions may be misinformed, largely because many adults shape their opinions from sensational news coverage and studies that focus on problems, rather than actual contact with young people."

As for those young people themselves, a New York teen named Julia Rosen (1998, 347) may have spoken for her entire generation when she wrote, in *VOYA* magazine, "Reading 'bleak books' helps us to realize what kinds of problems actual teens have. They broaden our outlook and help us become less apathetic about the world's problems. Until we live in a world where no problems exist, where adults always behave responsibly, and where there are always happy endings, adults must learn to accept that some of the books we read will describe the harsh realities of life."

The journalist David Spitz (1999, 49) noted what else such reading could do: "Teen books," he wrote in *Time*, "may not be able to compete with the visuals of 'The Matrix' but they do provide for a few hours what teens may need most: time to think. And there's nothing bleak about that."

A Profusion of Prizes

Even though the cutting edge of the new YA literature was inarguably sharper than before, its art was even more acute. *The Facts Speak for Themselves* was a finalist for the National Book Award, while *Dancing on the Edge* (1997) was the winner of the award that same year. Also, *Tenderness* (1997) and *When She Was Good* (1997) were both selected as ALA Best Books for Young Adults (1998), as were *Blood and Chocolate* and *Making up Megaboy* (1997).

The editorial latitude being given authors for new candor, vigorous truth-telling, the use of ambiguity, and sharing the sad truth that not all endings are happy ones may have resulted in occasional eruptions of bleakness, but it was also clearly elevating young adult literature to new heights of artistry.

Hence, as noted earlier, the profusion of new awards that began appearing to acknowledge this salutary aesthetic reality. Surely, true believers in the viability of young adult literature felt, the time was now right for the creation of another award, one that would serve the same purpose for young adult literature that the Newbery Medal did for children's literature, that is, to recognize the most distinguished contribution to American literature published in the United States during the preceding year for its intended readership. A noble purpose, but one not easily realized. The creation of awards can be a fraught process, I discovered when I became president of the Young Adult Library Services Association in 1997 and found myself taxed with effecting a decision that an earlier YALSA Board had made in 1995: to accept, in concept, the proposal of author Amelia Elizabeth Walden to fund the creation of an annual book award for young adults. Walden, the author of some forty-three YA novels published between 1946 and 1977, had, in 1971, established a testamentary trust in the amount of $25,000 for that purpose, I learned. And in 1991 the trust had been raised to $50,000.00.

Such munificence seemed the answer to a YA believer's prayer until its specific petitions were examined to reveal that in her offer Walden had stipulated that the award committee be required to choose a book relevant to teens, preferably fiction; give equal consideration to literary merit and popularity; and choose a book that reflects a positive approach to life. Alas, the latter two criteria were inherently contentious. As long as there has been a young adult literature, there has been a raging debate over the relative importance, in evaluating it, of merit and popularity. Worse, at a time when YA was finally able to eschew forced happy endings and acknowledge, with candor, the often bleak realities of contemporary teen life, the requirement that the winning book "reflects a positive approach to life" seemed, at best, limiting and at worst, self-defeating.

Dirk P. Mattson (1997) reported the ensuing brouhaha, at painful length in his article "Beware of Donors Bearing Book Prizes?" and I needn't elaborate further on it here except to say that, in retrospect, the incident brought new urgency to the discussion of what might constitute a meaningful award. Ultimately, after much debate, the YALSA Board chose not to take action on Walden's offer, tacitly consigning it to the department of benign neglect. A decade or so later, the Assembly on Literature for Adolescents (ALAN) of the National Council of Teachers of English revived it, and in 2008 announced its creation of the Amelia Elizabeth Walden Award. To be presented annually to the author of a young adult book selected by an ALAN committee, the $5,000 prize would recognize a book "demonstrating a positive approach to life, widespread teen appeal, and literary merit." *Plus ça change . . .* [3]

The Printz of Prizes

Many of us were still determined to seize the day, however. With the enthusiastic support of YALSA's deputy executive director, Linda Waddle, and the YALSA Executive Committee (consisting of Pam Spencer Holley, Deborah D. Taylor, and Joel Shoemaker), I appointed—in the spring of 1998—a nine-member task force (with myself as chair) to investigate "the feasibility of an annual award for the best young adult book *based solely on literary merit,* to establish criteria for selection with necessary policies and procedures, and to explore the mechanisms for effectuating the award."

I felt it was imperative that the other eight members reflect the diversity of audience and opinion that is the world of young adult literature and YALSA. To that end I appointed two young adult book editors, Marc Aronson (Henry Holt) and David Gale (Simon and Schuster); a professional reviewer and critic, Hazel Rochman of *Booklist* magazine; a reading specialist, Dr. Gwendolyn Davis; two public librarians, Kirsten Edwards and Ed Sullivan; and two school librarians, Frances Bradburn and Mary Purucker. Geographically, the task force members represented the West (California and Washington), the Midwest (Illinois), the South (North Carolina), and the East (New York).

Although the Task Force members also came from different segments of the young adult world, the members quickly arrived at a happy commonality of opinion on many major issues that might have been contentious. For example, they found themselves in unanimous agreement that an award for best young adult book was not only feasible but also long overdue. They also agreed that *Booklist* should sponsor it, and they concurred on a number of necessary definitions: "best" meant books of exemplary literary merit but not of immense popularity; "young adult" meant persons aged twelve through eighteen; and "young adult book" meant a book published expressly for that readership. Thus, books published for adults—even though they might find a young adult audience—would not be eligible. The reasoning? This was to be an award for the best young adult book, not the best book for young adults. This distinction set the proposed award apart from YALSA's Best Books for Young Adults list, which does include titles published for adults and also includes popularity as a factor to be considered in selecting books for the list.

The second part of the mission—to establish criteria with necessary policies and procedures—was a bit more problematic, though again many points were quickly, and unanimously, agreed on. Here are the most important: The winning book must have been published in the United States during the year preceding its selection; however, it may have been published in another country first. Eligibility is not confined to novels; anthologies are eligible, as are poetry and other works of nonfiction. Works of joint authorship are eligible, too. In addition to a winning title, as many as four honor books can be named. And if no title is deemed sufficiently worthy in a given year, no award will be given.

Following six months of intensive work, the Task Force presented its recommendations to the YALSA Board at the 1999 Midwinter Conference. They were unanimously adopted and—just like that—the Michael L. Printz Award became a reality.[4]

From the beginning, it was the belief of the task force that an award recognizing literary merit was essential not only as acknowledgment that some of the most risk-taking, artful, and creatively stimulating work in publishing was happening in the field of young adult literature, but also as evidence of its belief that teenagers need books that are created for them, books that are relevant to their interests, and, indeed, to their life needs. It was, finally, our belief that the Michael L. Printz Award would stimulate the further publication of such books, books that have the enduring power to change the lives of their readers—and perhaps the world they inhabit—for the better. This, as we will see in the next chapter, proved to be the case, guaranteeing that the Michael L. Printz Award would be one not only for a new millennium but also for all times and for all seasons.

Notes

1. Direct quotations in the following section come from unpublished MS copies of the participants' speeches.

2. Hersch was one of the more memorable keynote speakers at the YALSA President's Program at the 1998 ALA conference in Washington, DC.

3. The first Walden Award was presented at the 2009 ALAN conference to Steve Kluger for his antic novel *My Most Excellent Year: A Novel of Love, Mary Poppins, and Fenway Park.* (New York: Dial, 2008).

4. Of course, it wasn't quite that simple. Those who are interested in a more detailed account of the prize's creation are referred to "Creating the Michael L. Printz Award," *Journal of Youth Services in Libraries* 12 (Summer 1999): 30–33.

PART TWO

THIS IS NOW

6

A New Literature for a New Millennium?

Revival and Renaissance

HISTORY WAS MADE ON JANUARY 17, 2000, WHEN—AT THE ALA MIDWINTER conference in San Antonio, Texas—the first-ever winner of the Michael L. Printz Award was announced, along with three honor titles. Together these four books exemplified the newly literary, innovative, and diverse nature of young adult literature, which the award had been created to recognize.

Consider:

Ever since 1989 when Francesca Lia Block, in her first novel *Weetzie Bat* introduced magic realism and the verbal conventions of Imagist poetry into YA, the field had become increasingly open to experiments in style, structure, and narrative form. Walter Dean Meyer's *Monster*—the winner of the first Printz—is an excellent example of this. Originally conceived by the author as a screenplay, the resulting novel about Steve Harmon, an African American teenager on trial for his life, is told in two different but interrelated dramatic forms: the first is a screenplay, written by the boy himself, who observes of his surreal experience, "I feel like I have walked into the middle of a movie;" the second is his journal (printed on grey paper and set in a handwritten font) in which he is able to record the more visceral reality of his interior life and emotional responses (of the prison he writes, "The best time to cry is at night when the lights are out and someone is being beaten up and screaming for help").

Reflecting the increasingly visual context of contemporary teens' Internet-ridden lives, the book also includes a number of black-and-white, often digitally manipulated, photographs that—the work of Meyers's gifted artist son, Christopher—further ratchet up the reader's interest and engagement.

Though notable for its innovations, *Monster* is also very much of its time, rooted in adult America's abiding fear and distrust of teenagers, especially those of color. The title of the book, in fact, is a reference to the prosecuting attorney's reference to Steve as being a monster.

Two of the three Printz honor books, Ellen Wittlinger's *Hard Love* (1999) and Laurie Halse Anderson's *Speak* (1999), are also notable for having innovative formats and structures. The former, the ill-starred love story of a straight boy and a lesbian, features the inclusion of pages from teen 'zines (those self-designed, self-written, self-published magazines that captivated teen energies and imaginations in the late nineties), along with such other textual anomalies as handwritten letters, poems, and pages from journals.

The latter is also notable for its nontraditional structure. Eschewing chapters, Anderson divides her debut novel into four sections that reflect a school year's traditional grading periods. The story is then presented in a series of short scenes told in the first person voice of protagonist Melinda, who brings a sense of imperative action to her almost cinematic account of being outcast by using the present tense and introducing scenes with headings ("Hard Labor," "Death by Algebra," "Lunch Doom," etc.) that may recall title cards from silent films.

Though more traditional in its structure, David Almond's *Skellig* (1999), the third honor title, is a departure in two other senses. First published in England, it evidences that young adult literature—born though it might have been in the United States—has increasingly become a global phenomenon. Additionally, the novel is a metaphysical exercise in ambiguity, raising—but never resolving—the central question of the identity of the eponymous Skellig, while also tacitly acknowledging British mystic William Blake's aesthetic and intellectual influence on its author. A staple of literary fiction, ambiguity had been largely absent from young adult literature but it is an essential constituent of both *Skellig* and *Monster* (the question of Steve's guilt is left to the reader to adjudicate) and its use is another herald of the coming-of-age of young adult literature. It should be added in this context that *Hard Love* represents the maturation of fiction addressing gay and lesbian issues and experiences. Its protagonist, John, falls in love with an out lesbian named Marisol, but the reality remains that—though the two appealing teens are kindred spirits—Marisol is not emotionally equipped to reciprocate John's tender feelings and, at the book's bittersweet end, the two part.

The decade-and-a-half that has passed since the publication of these four landmark titles has, it seems in retrospect, only reinforced the validity of what I wrote about them in my "Carte Blanche" column for March 15, 2000: "Clearly, each of these books is extraordinary in its own individual way, but each has in common with the others innovation, creative courage, unimpeachable style, and, in sum, literary excellence" (Cart 2000a, 1370).

These words also serve to describe the Printz winners and honor titles in the years that have followed. Many of them also exemplify innovation and new trends that have characterized the literature's continuing aesthetic evolution and, all in all, confirm one of the most exciting trends of the new decade: the emergence of the literary novel for young adults.

Defining Literary Merit

For the reviewer, critic, and serious reader, one of the most interesting opportunities for discussion of this new literature is the matter of exactly what constitutes literary excellence. The Printz Award Task Force acknowledged this challenge when it wrote the policies and procedures that guide the selection process. Accordingly, it's worth quoting the Criteria section in full:

> "What is quality?" the Task Force wrote, "We know what it is *not*. While we hope the award will have a wide audience among readers 12 to 18, *popularity* is not the criterion for this award. Nor is message. In accordance with the Library Bill of Rights, controversy is not something to avoid. In fact, we want a book that readers will talk about.
>
> Having established what the award is not, it is much harder to formulate what it is. As every reader knows, a great book can redefine what we mean by quality. Criteria change with time. Therefore, flexibility and an avoidance of the too-rigid are essential components of these criteria. [Thus] the following criteria are only suggested guidelines and should in no way be considered as absolutes. They will always be open to change and adaptation. Depending on the book, one or more of these criteria will apply: Story, Setting, Theme, Voice, Accuracy" (remember

that nonfiction is eligible), "Illustration" (as are graphic works), "Style, Characters, Design (including format, organization, etc.). For each book the questions and answers will be different, the weight of the various criteria will be different." (www.ala.org/yalsa/printz-award)

Given this latitude for uncertainty and interpretation, the Printz Committees that have served in the years since 2000 have done a heroic job of finding and honoring titles that will stand yet another taxing test of excellence: the test of time. Having chaired the 2006 Printz committee, I can testify that the process of selecting the single best YA book of the year is no easy task. It is, indeed, a process, for many, many worthy books are nominated both from within the committee and also from the field. Discussion and sometimes heated debate follow (book lovers are passionate people!), and it is unlikely that the first choice of every single member of every single committee will be the title to receive the top award (or even to be named an honor title). Nor has every choice been a universally popular one with the reading public. And yet, as the following list of winners evidences, these books are not only timely in speaking with relevance to the lives of their contemporary adolescent readers, but they are also timeless in the universality of their art and in their ability to expand the meaning of the word excellence. Consider the Printz winners:

2000 *Monster* by Walter Dean Myers
2001 *Kit's Wilderness* by David Almond
2002 *A Step from Heaven* by An Na
2003 *Postcards from No Man's Land* by Aidan Chambers
2004 *The Last Part First* by Angela Johnson
2005 *How I Live Now* by Meg Rosoff
2006 *Looking for Alaska* by John Green
2007 *American Born Chinese* by Gene Luen Yang
2008 *The White Darkness* by Geraldine McCaughrean
2009 *Jellicoe Road* by Melina Marchetta
2010 *Going Bovine* by Libba Bray
2011 *Ship Breaker* by Paolo Bacigalupi
2012 *Where Things Come Back* by John Corey Whaley
2013 *In Darkness* by Nick Lake
2014 *Midwinterblood* by Marcus Sedgwick

2015   *I'll Give You the Sun* by Jandy Nelson
2016   *Bone Gap* by Laura Ruby

No matter how diverse and disparate they may be, what all of these winning titles have in common is richness of character, an attribute that, more than any other, separates literary from popular fiction, in which character often takes a back seat to plot. This is not to say these Printz Award books are thinly or awkwardly plotted or do not have compelling, reader-involving stories to tell. They do, all of them. But in these books story is typically in service to character. And although the actions of the characters may often contain an element of ambiguity, they are never arbitrary or dictated by the needs of a formula or a plot device. It is because they feature such fully formed, beautifully realized, multidimensional characters that these books will endure, just as the human spirit will.

This focus on character should not obscure the fact that many of the Printz titles have been notable for their unusual style and structure. I've already mentioned *Monster, Hard Love,* and *Speak,* but more recently there are Gene Luen Yang's graphic novel *American Born Chinese,* John Corey Whaley's *Where Things Come Back* with its multiple themes and viewpoints, and Marcus Sedgwick's novels in the form of linked short stories—*Midwinterblood* and *The Ghosts of Heaven.*

In addition to this stirring and life-affirming commonality, all of these books are also distinguished by their diversity, which is emblematic of the wonderful welter of innovations that are redefining the meaning of young adult literature. Note, for example, that more than 40 percent (seven of the seventeen) were first published in a country other than the United States (*Kit's Wilderness, Postcards from No Man's Land, How I Live Now, The White Darkness, In Darkness,* and *Midwinterblood* were first published in England, and *Jellicoe Road* in Australia). *American Born Chinese* is the first graphic novel to win the Printz, which augurs well for the continued aesthetic growth of a form that was once dismissed, sniffily, as "just comics." That two winners, *Looking for Alaska* and *A Step from Heaven,* are first novels also evidences the field's attraction of powerful new voices (as does the recent establishment of YALSA's William C. Morris YA Debut Award).

In the case of several of these books, the Task Force proved almost prescient when it noted, "Controversy is not something to avoid. In fact, we want a book that readers will talk about." Three of the Printz winners were particularly notable for exciting controversy and discussion: *Postcards from*

No Man's Land, How I Live Now, and *Looking for Alaska.* All invited visceral reactions from some readers (and reviewers) for their inclusion of sexual content. In the case of *Postcards,* it was the homosexuality of several characters and the ambiguous sexuality of the protagonist; with *How I Live Now* it was the inclusion of a sexual relationship between two young cousins that was regarded by many as incestuous; and with *Alaska* the grumbles revolved around a scene involving oral sex (and others involving teenage drinking and smoking—lots of smoking!).

Equally—if not more—controversial has been the regular appearance, in discussion, of another *C* word that was invoked—and invited—by the Task Force: complexity. Many observers have charged that the complexity of plots and characterizations in such winning titles as *Midwinterblood, Jellicoe Road, The White Darkness, Postcards from No Man's Land,* and *Kit's Wilderness* made them uninviting or inaccessible to teen readers. "In particular," Sarah Cornish and Patrick Jones (2002, 353) wrote, "the buzz about several 2001 winners was that while they might be great literature, they would be a hard sell to many young adults."

The title that has most often excited this objection is not, however, a Printz winner, but a Printz honor title: M. T. Anderson's epic novel *Octavian Nothing: Traitor to the Nation* (2006). Published in two volumes (each of which received an honor), this ambitious historical novel of the American Revolution as seen through the eyes of a sixteen-year-old slave has been much criticized (another *C* word), not only for the complexity of its plot, structure, and theme, but also for the elaborate eighteenth-century voice Anderson created for his first-person protagonist. Some (myself included) find such criticism particularly egregious in its wholesale discounting of the abilities of its intended audience. Anderson himself has addressed this issue: "I think people don't always give teens credit for how well they read," he told an interviewer in 2008, "I think kids are excited by language, and they've not always been given credit for that" (Sellers 2008a).

In addition to the two volumes of *Octavian Nothing,* the Printz committees have named an additional sixty-one honor titles, many of which are also notably sophisticated in their use of language, in their structure, and in their thematic content. Among these are Janne Teller's *Nothing* (2011), Margo Lanagan's *Tender Morsels* (2009), Sonya Hartnett's *Surrender,* and Markus Zusak's *The Book Thief* (both 2007), Jennifer Donnelley's *A Northern Light* (2004), and Chris Lynch's *Freewill* (2002). Still other of the honor titles evidence emerging trends that we will discuss later, including the appearance of literary nonfiction (e.g., Jack Gantos's compelling memoir *Hole in My Life* [2002] and Elizabeth Partridge's ambitious biography of John Lennon *All I Want Is Truth* [2005]). Also in evidence is the renaissance of the short story (*Black Juice* by Margo Lanagan, 2006) and poetry for young adults (*Your Own Sylvia* [2008] by Stephanie Hemphill; *A Wreath for Emmet Till* [2006] by Marilyn Nelson; *Keesha's House* [2004] by Helen Frost; *Heart to Heart*, a poetry anthology edited by Jan Greenberg [2002]; and *True Believer* by Virginia Euwer Wolff [2002]).[1]

But Will They Read It?

Despite the Printz Award's success in recognizing and encouraging literary excellence while also serving as a bellwether for exciting new trends in YA literature, the prize has not been without its critics. It was dealt something of an implicit rebuff at the 2005 YALSA Best of the Best conference, in fact. The 127 conferees were charged with selecting the best of the best YA books published in the decade between 1994 and 2003. Not only were three of the five Printz winners from that period (*Kit's Wilderness*, *Postcards from No Man's Land*, and *A Step from Heaven*) excluded, so were ten of the eighteen honor titles.[2]

Printz winners have fared little better in another de facto best of the best ranking: YALSA's annual Best Books for Young Adults/Best Fiction for Young Adults (BBYA/BFYA)[3] top ten list. Long part of the process of selecting the BBYA list, the BBYA committee also chooses the top ten. Once the master list has been selected, each member votes for his or her personal top ten books. The ballots are then tabulated and the books receiving the most votes constitute the top ten for that year. Through 2016, less than half (seven of the sixteen) of the Printz winners have made this list. Though it is supposed to represent a balance of literary quality and reader popularity, it seems that the scales have definitely been tilted in the direction of popularity—or participating librarians' notion of what will be popular with teens (though, to be fair, teen input is solicited throughout the BBYA/BFYA selection process). The long-standing dialectic between popularity and literary merit will probably never be resolved and such debate can be a healthy and intellectually stimulating process. Nevertheless, when one is talking about selecting best books, popularity alone is no measure of merit. If it were, the Printz would automatically be awarded to Suzanne Collins (Hunger Games series) each year and there would be no need for discussion. Nor is it enough simply to toss an aesthetically noteworthy title into a new book bin and expect it to sell itself. After all, one reason adult gatekeepers—librarians and teachers—are involved with young adult literature is to bring their maturity of judgment and their greater experience of reading to the process of putting teens and excellent books together. Sometimes this means fast talking and strenuous selling, but surely a successful sale is worth the labor, no matter how herculean.

If literary fiction is often regarded as being more popular with adults than with teens, the same is routinely said of two of its constituent forms—the short story and poetry, both of which experienced a period of rapid revival and growth in the wake of the YA renaissance. This presumed unpopularity is puzzling, for, after all, the defining aspect of the short story—its shortness—would seem to be an irresistible lure for attention-span-challenged teens. Poetry, too, is often an exercise in brevity, and teens seem to love the emotionally cathartic experience of writing it. But the received wisdom is that teens resist every effort to persuade them to read either short stories or poetry. Is the received wisdom wrong? Let's examine each form in turn and try to find out.

The Short Story Revival

The short story as an American literary form dates back to the early 1800s and the work of Washington Irving, Nathaniel Hawthorne, and Edgar Allan Poe. Later in the same century, it flourished in the hands of such as Stephen Crane, Jack London, Frank R. Stockton, Bret Harte, O. Henry, and—in the early twentieth century—Sherwood Anderson. The form hit its stride in the thirties and forties in the work of F. Scott Fitzgerald and Ernest Hemingway and, in the fifties, of J. D. Salinger, John O'Hara, John Cheever, and the whole coterie of *New Yorker* writers who redefined the form. But then, in the sixties and seventies, the market for the short story began to decline as general-interest magazines, which had always been its home, went into eclipse. But the story is a durable form and it rebounded in the eighties in the minimalist work of Raymond Carver, Richard Ford, Tobias Wolff, and others. This was also the decade in which MFA programs in creative writing began appearing in America's universities and fastened on the short story as the instructional form of choice. "The majority of people who enroll in these programs want to be novelists," Charles McGrath (McGrath, 2004b, B1) wryly wrote in *The New York Times*, "but novels don't lend themselves very readily to the workshop format, and so would-be novelists these days spend at least part of their apprenticeship working on stories."

This equation of the form with the academic suggests a major reason why short stories have been such a hard sell: they have traditionally been used for instructional purposes in America's high-school classrooms. Worse, like most other required reading, they have too often been dusty works from the adult literary canon that offer little of relevance to the lives or interests of contemporary teens. Happily, this situation began to change in the mid-to-late eighties when—encouraged by the renaissance of the form in adult publishing—pioneering young adult anthologists like Donald Gallo and Hazel Rochman started assembling thematically related collections of short stories, many of them written specifically for the collection by established young adult authors.

Gallo, who must be regarded as the godfather of the contemporary YA short story collection, published his first, *Sixteen*, in 1985. This was followed by *Visions* in 1988 and *Connections* in 1990. Rochman's first, *Somehow Tenderness Survives*, a collection of stories about South Africa, appeared in 1988, and was followed in 1993 by *Who Do You Think You Are? Stories of Friends and Enemies* (coedited with Darlene Z. McCampbell).

Rochman has written about the necessary characteristics of such anthologies. "It's helpful," she noted in a 1998 "YA Talk" piece for *Booklist*, "for teen readers, especially reluctant ones, to have a theme that grabs them, a cover that looks like them, and some connection to lead them from one story to the next" (Rochman 1998, 1234).

This new kind of anthology—the theme-driven collection of original work commissioned expressly for the book—became enormously popular. In 1997 half-a-dozen such were included on YALSA's Best Books and Quick Picks lists. In the meantime, well-known YA novelists had begun assembling anthologies, too, among them Harry Mazer, Anne Mazer, Lois Duncan, Marilyn Singer, Judy Blume, James Howe, and others. Such name authors excited new interest among young adult readers already familiar with and well-disposed to their work.

Of perhaps greater interest in literary terms, however, was the quick emergence of single-author collections. Among the first of these were Gary Soto's *Baseball in April* (1990) and Chris Crutcher's *Athletic Shorts* (1991). Others by a veritable who's who of writers have followed, including David Almond, Francesca Lia Block, Bruce Coville, Diana Wynne Jones, Kelly Link, Chris Lynch,

Beverly Naidoo, Graham Salisbury, Tim Wynne-Jones, and many others. In terms of sheer literary excellence, such collections hit a new peak with the publication of Australian author Margo Lanagan's *Black Juice*, a brilliantly imaginative collection of speculative stories that was selected as a 2006 Printz honor title. (Though a single author collection, it is also an example of another newish kind of anthology in which it is genre, not theme, which provides the basis for commonality: e.g., Kelly Link's *Pretty Monster* [2008], Deborah Noyes's *Gothic* [2004], Carrie Ryan's *Foretold* [2012], Holly Black and Justine Larbalestier's *Zombies vs. Unicorns* [2010], and my own *How Beautiful the Ordinary* [2009].) In fact, though the popularity of short stories has gone into a temporary period of eclipse, collections of genre stories—especially science fiction and fantasy—continue to be published and read. The popularity of the short story (and the decreasing attention span of teens) is also responsible for a new literary form that began to emerge in the 1990s: the novel as a collection of linked stories. Among the first of these were three heart-stoppingly good books: Bruce Brooks's *What Hearts* (1992), Chris Lynch's *Whitechurch* (1999), and E. R. Franks's *Life Is Funny* (2000). Other notable works in this form that have followed include Kathi Appelt's *Kissing Tennessee* (2000), Walter Dean Myers's *145th Street* (2000), Richard Peck's *A Long Way from Chicago* 1998) and *A Year Down Yonder* (2000), Ellen Wittlinger's *What's in a Name?* (2000), and most recently, Margo Rabb's critically acclaimed *Cures for Heartbreak* (2007) and Marc Aronson and Charles R. Smith Jr.'s *One Death, Nine Stories* (2014), which differs from the others because the stories are not by one author but, rather by nine different authors writing about the same characters, incident, and theme.

By far the most artful and sophisticated novel in stories is surely British author Marcus Sedgwick's 2014 Printz Award–winning *Midwinterblood*. This collection of seven stories, presented in reverse chronological order is, as Daniel Kraus has written in his *Booklist* review, part love story, part mystery, part horror. "This is as much about the twisting hand of fate as it is about the mutability of folktales" (Kraus 2012, 52). A more recent Sedgwick novel in stories is *The Ghosts of Heaven*, a Printz honor title; its four constituents can, Sedgwick says, be read in any order but most readers (this one, certainly) will prefer to read them in the order presented, that is, chronologically. Like Lanagan, Sedgwick elevates the short story form to the loftiest reaches of literary art.

A Poetry Renaissance

"The dirty secret of poetry is that it is loved by some,
loathed by many, and bought by almost no one."
—*William Logan, New York Times (June 15, 2014)*

Logan aside, the evergreen appeal of Mother Goose evidences that small children love rhythm and rhyme. However, their taste for poetry does seem to decrease as an inverse function of their age, so by the time they have finished elementary school, most kids are no longer engaged by verse. Once again, this diminishing interest is pretty clearly a function of adolescents' association of the form with the classroom and the dreaded phrase "required reading." "No wonder kids don't like it," Logan writes, "it becomes another way to bully them into feeling compassion or tolerance, part of a curriculum that makes them good citizens but bad readers of poetry" (2014).

Holly Koelling (2007) discusses this lack of popularity (and audience!) in her analysis of the Best Books for Young Adults lists from 2000–2006. There she notes that only three works of poetry (0.5 percent of the total) appear on these seven annual lists. This is hardly an anomaly. In looking at the six Best of the Best Books lists that YALSA has assembled periodically since 1974, one finds only 6 works of poetry represented out of 530 titles (0.01 percent)! Four of the titles are anthologies—Stephen Dunning's *Reflections on a Gift of Watermelon Pickle* (1967); R. R. Knudson and May Swenson's *American Sports Poems* (1988); Paul B. Janeczko's *The Place My Words Are Looking For: What Poets Say about and through Their Poems* (1990); and Lori Carlson's *Cool Salsa: Bilingual Poems on Growing Up Latino in the United States* (1994), and two—Mel Glenn's *Class Dismissed: High School Poems* (1982) and Cynthia Rylant's *Something Permanent* (1994)—are single author works.

As is the case with short story anthologies, theme is of overarching importance. The poet and anthologist Paul Janeczko has said, "If poetry is to do more than furnish answers on a multiple-choice test, we must relate poetry to the real world, finding poems that are connected with something that happened at school, in the community, or in the world" (Cart 2001, 1390).

Another successful anthologist, Ruth Gordon, agreed that "a theme that will appeal" makes a successful collection, but noted that a fundamental cause of poetry's lack of popularity is that "so many people are afraid of it because of the form and its perceived formality; they have been read to incorrectly and they are not taught how to read poetry for themselves" (Cart 1997a, 1570).

Poetry began to undergo something of a sea change in the mid-nineties when American culture started taking new cognizance of the form. In 1996, the Academy of American Poets, with the support of a number of other organizations including the American Library Association, succeeded in having April designated as National Poetry Month. A decade earlier, in 1986, the Librarian of Congress had appointed Robert Penn Warren as America's first official Poet Laureate, further raising the public profile of the literary form. Public television and the Internet also made poetry vastly more accessible, as did the surge in popularity of coffeehouses which—shades of the beat poetry movement of the 1950s—began sponsoring open mic poetry nights and poetry slams, events that young adult librarians discovered and that became, almost overnight, staple fixtures of their programming for teens.

Ironically, the same teens who have traditionally been reluctant readers of poetry have, nevertheless, always loved writing it. "Poetry is a perfect medium for adolescence: it lends itself to the fierce dramas and false clarities of these years," author and teacher Katie Roiphe (2009, 14) writes in *The New York Times Book Review*.

The Internet has begun providing teens exciting new opportunities for writing and hearing poetry. A number of sites like former Poet Laureate Robert Pinsky's www.favoritepoem.org/ present opportunities for hearing both poets and ordinary Americans reading work, while sites like www.teenink .com offer them abundant opportunities for publishing their work online. Book publishers, too, have issued collections of teen-written work. Betsy Franco's *You Hear Me? Poems and Writing by Teenage Boys* was selected as a 2001 Best Book for Young Adults. Other collections include Lee Francis's *When the Rain Sings: Poems by Young Native Americans* (1999) and Lydia Omolola Okutoro's *Quiet Storm: Voices of Young Black Poets* (2008).

Franco (the mother of celebrated actor James Franco) is one of a new generation of poetry anthologists—others are Naomi Shihab Nye, Liz Rosenberg, and Lori Carlsen—who have brought enhanced popularity to poetry for teen readers. Nye and Carlsen have also enriched multicultural literature by editing anthologies of poetry from the Middle East (Nye) and from Latin America (Carlsen). Jan Greenberg, known for her many books about art and artists, received a Printz honor for her innovative anthology *Heart to Heart: New Poems Inspired by Twentieth Century Art* (2001).

Another measure of the new popularity of poetry may be found in the annual Top Ten Best Books for Young Adults. Since this list was established in 1997, a total of 11 works of poetry—out of 200 total titles—have been included (a fairly robust 5 percent of the total, pretty good for "a major art with a minor audience") (Logan 2014).

Arguably the most visible manifestation of poetry's new popularity, however, is the profusion of novels in verse (book-length works of narrative poetry). *Booklist* magazine reviewed seventy-seven of them between 2009 and 2015. Though hardly a new form in world literature (Homer, anyone?), the modern verse novel began to excite interest about the same time as poetry in general did. In the young adult world two of the first were Mel Glenn's *My Friend's Got This Problem, Mr. Candler* (1991) and Virginia Euwer Wolff's *Make Lemonade* (1994). Interestingly, unlike reviewers and readers, Wolff does not herself consider *Make Lemonade* or its two sequels (*True Believer* [2001] and *This Full House* [2009]) as being novels in verse. "Reviewers have called my books 'novels in verse,'" she told *Publishers Weekly*, but "I consider them as written in prose but I do use stanzas. Stanza means 'room' in Latin, and I wanted there to be 'room'—breathing opportunities to receive thoughts and have time to come out of them before starting again at the left margin. I thought of young mothers reading my books, and I wanted to give them lots of white space, so they could read entire chapters at a time and feel a sense of accomplishment" (Comerford 2009).

The accessibility of verse novels—pages set with short lines surrounded by white space—has made them popular for use with reluctant readers as well as those who have English as a second language. "Many who work with English-language learners and others who struggle with reading seek novels that promote fluency and a sense of competence in readers. Verse novels can accomplish that," says poet and teacher Terry Farish (2013, 11).

The narrative nature of verse novels' content is a further inducement to teen readers; because almost all of them are written in free verse, no one needs fear the rigors of form or perceived formality.

Though free verse sometimes invites self-indulgent writing that has more to it of prose than poetry, it can—when properly executed—prove to be not only reader-friendly but also exceedingly artful. Another example is the California poet Sonya Sones's first book, *Stop Pretending: What Happened When My Big Sister Went Crazy* (1999). Telling the story of the emotional breakdown and subsequent institutionalization of the narrator's older sister, these first person poems from the point of view of a thirteen-year-old girl have a cumulative emotional power that is quietly devastating, which makes the first evidence of the older girl's recovery dizzyingly cathartic: "I blink/ and there you suddenly are/ inhabiting your eyes again . . . and I'm feeling all lit up/ like a jar filled/ with a thousand fireflies."

Sones's subsequent work—*One of Those Hideous Books Where the Mother Dies* (2004), *What My Mother Doesn't Know* (2001), and *What My Girlfriend Doesn't Know* (2007)—similarly demonstrated the capacity of poetry to record the personal. Through the use of figurative language, rhythm, verbal economy, emotional insight, and honesty they translate it into the universal. Small wonder that Sones has become one of the most popular practitioners of the verse novel form.

Another notable practitioner is the versatile Ron Koertge. The author of such celebrated prose novels as *The Arizona Kid* (1988), *Stoner and Spaz* (2001), and *Margaux with an X* (2004). Koertge is also an award-winning adult poet, who has demonstrated these skills in his YA novels in verse, *Shakespeare Bats Cleanup* (2003) and *The Brimstone Journals* (2001), an ALA Best Book for Young Adults. The latter, told in the different voices of fifteen members of the graduating class of Branston High School, fluidly demonstrates poetry's wonderful capacity for presenting multiple points of view. Other notable titles that do this are Nikki Grimes's *Bronx Masquerade* (2002) and David Levithan's *The Realm of Possibilities* (2004).

A few writers—Helen Frost and Marilyn Nelson among them—have written verse novels employing either traditional or newly created poetic forms. Nelson, for example, wrote her Printz honor award-winning *A Wreath for Emmet Till* in the exquisitely difficult form of a heroic crown of sonnets. Frost, another Printz honor winner for *Keesha's House*, which is written in the form of sonnets and sestinas, specializes in creating forms that match the thematic or narrative material of her novels in verse. In *The Braid*, for example, she invented, as she notes in an afterword, "a formal structure for this book, derived in part from my admiration for Celtic knots" (Frost 2006, 91).

Other talented authors of verse novels include Ann Burg (*All the Broken Pieces* [2009]) Martine Leavitt (*My Book of Life by Angel* [2012]), Kristin Elizabeth Clark (*Freakboy* [2013]), and Padma Venkatraman (*A Time to Dance* [2014]).

All in all, the book-length work of verse has proven to be marvelously versatile, lending itself to a variety of forms and genres, including, recently, biography and memoir. Stephanie Hemphill's *Your Own Sylvia: A Verse Portrait of Sylvia Plath* (2007) received a Printz honor; another more recent—and equally superb—memoir in verse is Cuban-American author Margarita

Engle's 2015 *Enchanted Air* (2015). The same may be said of Jacqueline Woodson's Newbery Medal–winning *Brown Girl Dreaming* (2014), Marilyn Nelson's *How I Discovered Poetry* (2014), and Cordelia Jensen's *Skyscraping* (2015). Other genres include mystery (especially the work of Mel Glenn), fantasy (Lisa Ann Sandell's novel of the Lady of Shalott, *Song of the Sparrow* [2007]), historical fiction (Jen Bryant's two novels about the Scopes trial, *Trial* and *Ringside, 1925* [2004 and 2008]), and even problem novels (examples are Ellen Hopkins's wildly popular *Crank* [2004], *Glass* [2007], *Burned* [2006], *Identical* [2008] , and so forth).

A question remains: why write novels in verse instead of prose? Farish (2013, 33) asked this question of poet Margarita Engle (*Silver People* [2014] and *Hurricane Dancers* [2011]). Speaking of her book *The Surrender Tree: Poems of Cuba's Struggle for Freedom* (2008), Engle said, "Poetry and music play such an essential role in Cuban culture that it was natural to include them." Poet Caroline Starr Rose (33) explains that she wrote her novel *May B* (2014) in verse because "I love the immediacy verse gives, not only to the character but to the setting." In sum, Farish says, "I learned multiple reasons for using the verse form: To reflect a culture's music and literary heritage; to offer reprises of the rhythm of a language; to create a fast pace of lines that mirrors the character's own ride; to bring the cinematic camera intimately close" (33).

Trends are transient and, doubtless, the novel in verse will pass in, out, and out of favor with writers and readers for years to come, but one thing seems certain: poetry itself will remain one of literature's most durable—and universal—forms, a lesson that was brought home when—in June 2015—Juan Felipe Herrera became not only the first Mexican American United States Poet Laureate but also the first to have written for young readers as well as adults. Indeed, Herrera recommends that those unfamiliar with his work start their acquaintance with his young adult collection *Laughing Out Loud, I Fly* (1998). "I did a lot of experimental work in that," he told *The Washington Post*. "I was inspired by Picasso. I had a great time. It's a 3,000-color kite" (Charles 2015).

One, his readers will discover, that soars.

Notes

1. A complete list of Printz winners and honor titles is available online at www.ala.org/yalsa.

2. Those interested in reading more about this preconference might take a look at my Carte Blanche column of September 15, 2005.

3. BBYA (Best Books for Young Adults) was changed to BFYA (Best Fiction for Young Adults) in 2010.

Genre on the Agenda

More of the Millennial

GENRE FICTION IS, BY CONVENTIONAL DEFINITION, POPULAR, PLOT-DRIVEN category fiction. In this chapter we examine five genres: Speculative Fiction, Historical Fiction, Romance, Horror, and Mystery/Suspense.

Speculative Fiction

Much of contemporary imaginative fiction has become an interesting mélange, an exercise in bending and blending, in shape-shifting and morphing. Thus, many observers regard science fiction as having now merged with fantasy to form something called "speculative fiction." Of the two genres, it is fantasy that has arguably—in the wake of the Harry Potter phenomenon (see chapter 8 for details)—maintained the stronger sense of separate identity.

Nevertheless, science fiction, this youngest of the genres (it's often regarded as a twentieth-century phenomenon, though its early antecedents are actually the mid-to-late nineteenth-century work of Jules Verne and H. G. Wells), remains sufficiently sui generis to be represented by three winners of the prestigious Margaret A. Edwards Award: Anne McCaffrey, Ursula K. LeGuin, and Orson Scott Card. Even here, though, there is some room for ambiguity. McCaffrey's most celebrated work—her Pern novels—are often regarded as fantasy, because they feature dragons (the late McCaffrey strongly disagreed, pointing out her dragons were genetically engineered); LeGuin's books also operate on the cusp between traditional science fiction and fantasy, and Card—though more clearly a science fiction practitioner—has never been published for young adults, though he is widely read by them. All this said, science fiction—after a decade of being eclipsed by fantasy—has, in the mid-2010s, begun a cautious comeback in the work of such writers as Neal Shusterman, Paolo Bacigalupi, Cory Doctorow, Philip Reeve, Suzanne Collins (see chapter 8). and others.

Of all the genres, however, it is classic fantasy that seems to have produced the most serious works of literature, perhaps because it is the oldest category. In fact, a case could be made that it originated as early as the eighth century with *Beowulf* (the writer Harlan Ellison dates it even earlier, to the *Epic of Gilgamesh!*). As a form, it also incorporates timeless folklore and fairy tales, though the most memorable codifications of such stories date only to the early nineteenth century, and what we regard as modern fantasy fiction didn't appear until 1865 with *Alice in Wonderland.* And like *Alice,* much of classic fantasy is regarded as children's literature. In fact, very little successful work of the imagination has been published specifically for young adults, perhaps because the field—with its narrow focus on realistic fiction—has been regarded as inhospitable. This is not to say that fantasy hasn't been published, but established gatekeepers, have generally failed to recognize it, and its fans have long been critical of the annual Best Books for Young Adults lists, which, in the past, conspicuously lacked such genre titles.

But times change and fantasy has, for the past decade, been in the ascendant. Writing in 2007, Holly Koelling (2007, 64) observed, "Fantasy accounts for almost fifteen percent of the 577 books on BBYA lists since 2000, the same share as nonfiction and exceeded only by general fiction." Writing a year earlier, the critic and former publisher Anita Silvey (2006, 47) drew a similar conclusion: "Instead of craving realistic stories about people like themselves, today's teens are crazy about characters (and scenarios) that have little in common with their everyday lives. Today's adolescents are flocking to fantasy, suspense, and mystery." Ten years later, they continue to do so, for consider that fully 22 percent of the fifty-eight titles on the 2015 Best Fiction for Young Adults list were fantasy, while 6 percent were science fiction.

Was this all due to the success of Harry Potter? Not entirely, I think. One of fantasy's most attractive features has been its implicit invitation to escape this careworn world for a visit to a more appealing one, if only in one's imagination. Some need this escape more than others. As the fantasist Tamora Pierce (1993, 51) has eloquently stated, "Fantasy is also important to a group that I deeply hope is small: those whose lives are so grim that they cling to everything that takes them completely away for *any* length of time." In the wake of the 9/11 tragedy, the wars in Afghanistan and Iraq, worldwide economic distress, international terrorism, and the specter of global warming, this invitation to escape has surely become increasingly attractive—and the group accepting it, ever larger. "Fantasy," Pierce rightly noted, "creates hope and optimism in readers. It is the pure stuff of wonder."

The two writers in the overall field of speculative fiction whose work offers—in my estimation—the richest infusion of the imaginative into assessments of what can only be called the human condition are the British writers David Almond and Philip Pullman. Almond's first book to appear in the United States, *Skellig*, was a Printz honor book, while his second—*Kit's Wilderness*—won the Printz outright (In England, *Skellig* won the Carnegie Medal, and *Kit's Wilderness* was shortlisted for the same prize). These two haunting books, as well as those that have followed—*Heaven Eyes* (2002), *Secret Heart* (2002), *The Fire Eaters, The True Tale of the Monster Billy Dean as Telt by Hisself,* and *The Tight-Rope Walkers* (2015) among them—are nearly impossible to classify but abound in wonders and challenges to their readers' imaginations. As a character in his novel *Secret Heart* aptly puts it, "The most important things are the most mysterious." The character might well be speaking for Almond himself and, as a result, his books are filled with magical realism and exquisite examinations of light and dark, good and evil, finding magic, metaphor and larger meaning in their North of England settings that provide the quotidian foundation for so many of his books. One of Almond's latest novels, *The Tight-Rope Walkers,* is more firmly rooted in reality than others but is nevertheless equally powerful in its examination of good and evil.

Like Almond, Pullman is also interested in the large issues that generally find expression in high fantasy. In his most ambitious work, the His Dark Materials trilogy, this is clearly the same dialectic between good and evil that inspired Milton's *Paradise Lost*. Though Pullman writes prose, not poetry, his language—like Almond's—is often soaring and even majestic, resulting in a style that matches the richness and complexity of his thematic material. The final volume of the trilogy, *The Amber Spyglass,* received the 2001 Whitbread Prize for best children's book of the year in England and was then also named The Whitbread Book of the Year, the first time a children's book has ever won this prestigious prize. This speaks not only to the intrinsic excellence of the book, but also to coming-of-age books for young readers as literature. And, it should be noted, though published as a children's book, *Amber Spyglass* is very clearly a young adult novel. Just as each succeeding volume of the Harry Potter series became more sophisticated, so did each volume in Pullman's trilogy.

Unlike the Harry Potter books, which stimulated numerous challenges from religious conservatives, Pullman's have excited somewhat less controversy in the United States. This is ironic, as Pullman's are by far the more subversive books. Though he is hardly "the most dangerous author in Britain" as one conservative columnist dubbed him, he does have serious reservations about organized religion and one of his characters calls Christianity "a very powerful and convincing mistake" (Miller 2005/2006, 52).

Nevertheless, Pullman is a passionate believer in the moral authority—or perhaps capacity would be a better word—of fiction, remarking in a lecture, "We can learn what's good and what's bad, what's generous and unselfish, what's cruel and mean from fiction." Or, as he has also noted, "'Thou shalt not' might reach the head, but it takes 'Once upon a time' to reach the heart" (Miller 2005/2006, 54). His stories—and Almond's too—bear eloquent witness to the truth of that.

Historical Fiction

Like fantasy, historical fiction has a long and distinguished, uh, history, beginning with Sir Walter Scott's 1814 novel *Waverly*. But like fantasy it, too, was not a terribly significant presence in young adult literature until recently. The belief among publishers and adult gatekeepers alike was that young readers were too interested in their contemporary selves to embrace stories of the long ago and far away. "'Children only want to read about people like themselves,' teachers assure me," the distinguished, multiple-award-winning novelist Katherine Paterson (1999, 1430) has lamented. A decade later, the historical novelist Ann Rinaldi (2009) agreed. "When I wrote my first historical novel 21 years ago [1988], all the publishers said much the same thing. 'We can't give children history. No bookstore will carry it, no child will read it.'"

This belief seems to have become even more firmly entrenched when applied to notoriously solipsistic young adults who, it was believed, would read only realistic fiction with contemporary settings. "In my experience," the librarian Jen Hubert wrote at her popular website Reading Rants, "most teens won't even look at hist. fic. unless they have to read it for a school assignment" (www.readingrants.org).

This began to change as YA literature became more expansive starting in the mid-1990s. And, indeed, by the end of that decade historical fiction—which we might define as fiction that is set at least fifty years in the past or that requires its author to conduct research—had become a significantly popular category of young adult literature. In 2000, when I assembled my annual list of the best young adult books of the year, I was startled to see that fully twenty-one of the sixty-one works of fiction on my list fell into the historical fiction category, while twenty-seven subsequently appeared on my 2001 list.

A major catalyst for the rise of historical fiction in the 1990s was Scholastic's introduction, in 1996, of its soon-to-be hugely popular Dear America series. These fictional girls' diaries, set in various significant periods of American history, rapidly became enormously popular. Within two years, there were 3.5 million copies of the first twelve in print. Ultimately there were forty-two titles in the series, which concluded in 2004.

A companion series for boys, My Name Is America, soon followed as, in turn, did two others for girls: The Royal Diaries, and—for younger readers—My America. All three of these companion series also concluded in 2004.

The immediacy of the diary form may well have been part of the series' appeal, but so was its innovative format: Scholastic's Jean Feiwel told *Publishers Weekly*, "Our intention was to create a book that was a replica of an actual diary" (Lodge 1998, 31). This meant publication in hardcover (a novelty for series fiction at the time) and in a trim size that was slightly smaller than the standard. The price, a low $9.95, was also unusual and, as it turned out, unusually attractive to booksellers. So once again the retail market became instrumental in developing a new YA trend.

The hardcover format itself lent a certain patina of respectability to this new exercise in series fiction but so, too, did the extraordinary roster of distinguished authors whom Scholastic commissioned to write for the series: people like Joseph Bruchac, Karen Hesse, Carolyn Meyer, Jim Murphy, Walter Dean Myers, Ann Rinaldi, and still more. (Interestingly, though, to maintain the polite fiction that the books were actual diaries, the authors' names—no matter how celebrated—did not appear on the books' covers.)

Like the other genres we have explored, historical fiction also lends itself to genre bending and blending. Indeed, "blending with other genres is the most conspicuous trend in historical fiction," the reader's adviser Joyce Saricks (2008, 33) has written. There are, for example, historical romances, historical mysteries, historical adventures, and even historical fantasies (see Robin LaFevers's His Fair Assassins trilogy [2012–2014]). Sometimes the blending includes more than two genres: consider Libba Bray's *The Diviners* (2012) and *Lair of Dreams* (2015). Set in the Roaring Twenties, they combine a historical setting with fantasy, horror, and romance. Saricks has also noted one more interesting trend: "Books that combine historical elements with contemporary story lines have become enormously popular" (2008). Two excellent YA examples of this are Aidan Chambers's *Postcards from No Man's Land* (2002) and the late Mal Peet's *Tamar* (2007), both of which find meaning for contemporary lives by revisiting World War II. (The routine injection of lengthy flashbacks as in these two novels is another fairly recent innovation in YA fiction.)

All of these disparate elements have conspired to turn historical fiction from required to pleasure reading. As the hip Hubert noted, when presenting teens with her own list of Historical Fiction for Hipsters: Stories from the Past That Won't Make You Snore, "Sure, you may not know much about history, but learning it from these juicy fictional accounts is way more fun than memorizing any old, dry textbook."

The growing popularity of historical fiction has expanded the genre's portfolio well beyond series fiction. Like the entire field of YA, historical fiction has, since the Millennium, become home to significant works of literature. Indeed, I would argue that four of the best young adult novels of the past quarter-century are historical novels: Aidan Chambers's *Postcards from No Man's Land* (2002), Mildred Taylor's *The Land* (2007), Markus Zusak's *The Book Thief* (2006), and M. T. Anderson's two-volume *The Astonishing Life of Octavian Nothing* (2006). All brilliantly conceived and written, these four titles are further enriched by the very largeness and complexity of their themes, which include war, slavery and the Holocaust. Each invites us to reexamine our understanding of the human condition and to expand our moral sensibility. One can hardly ask for or expect more from literature.

Literature is inherently dynamic and never more so than when it is young adult literature. Trends come and go, and so it is no surprise that—here in 2016—the boom in young adult historical fiction may well have peaked, though I would not go so far as Ann Rinaldi (2009), who earlier lamented, "Now, all of a sudden, the whole ball game seems to be over. We're back where we began. Things have come full circle. Historical novels for teens seem to be chopped liver again."

I daresay such authors as Jennifer Donnelly, Walter Dean Myers, Ruta Sepetys, and Elizabeth Wein might disagree!

But time, as always, will tell.[1]

Romance

We have already discussed the genesis of young adult romance in the 1940s and its later renascence in the 1980s and 1990s. But the form itself is much older; indeed, it dates to the eighteenth century and the very beginning of the novel form in such books as Samuel Richardson's *Pamela, or Virtue Rewarded* (1740), and the novels of Jane Austen and the Bronte sisters. Perhaps as a result, the historical romance for both adult and young adult readers has remained a staple of the genre. We will see another, the trendy paranormal romance, in the next chapter. In the meantime, romance remains arguably the most popular of all the genres. Despite its subgenres—and there are many—all romances have two things in common according to the Romance Writers of America: a central love story and an emotionally satisfying and optimistic ending. ("The loves . . . are rewarded with emotional justice and unconditional love.") (RWA nd).

Romance itself will reward further consideration but for that we must wait until the next chapter. In the meantime, let us induce a shudder as we turn to another presently popular genre; yes, it's...

Horror

Like romance, horror—the 2015 trend du jour—has its roots in the eighteenth century, specifically in Horace Walpole's 1764 novel *The Castle of Otranto*, which is the progenitor of contemporary gothic fiction. Mary Shelley's 1818 classic *Frankenstein: Or the Modern Prometheus* followed to introduce the monster subgenre, and the vampire novel traces its beginnings to Bram Stoker's *Dracula*, published in 1897. The werewolf subgenre is a more modern phenomenon. Though there were a handful of forgettable nineteenth century werewolf stories, it wasn't until the 1933 publication of novelist Guy Endore's

The Werewolf of Paris that the subgenre gained any literary traction, and at that it wasn't until the 1941 movie *The Wolf Man,* starring Lon Chaney Jr., that werewolves became the flavor of the month for horror connoisseurs

As all of this suggests, horror is a fiction of monsters but not merely monsters. "It's any work where," Kelly Jensen (2013, 41) writes, "the emotions of fear, dread, and/or disgust" (think splatterpunk with its blood and gore) "drive the narrative." When written for young adult readers, the genre typically finds its expression not in stand-alone titles but in series, instead, some—like the horror fictions of R. L. Stein and Christopher Pike—disposable; others—those by Amelia Atwater-Rhodes and Clive Barker spring to mind—may have slightly more substance. Too, a few memorable individual titles have appeared: think M. T. Anderson's first novel *Thirsty* (1998), and some of the later work of Neil Gaiman, notably *Coraline* (2008) and his Newbery Medal–winning *The Grave-yard Book* (2008), (though Gaiman told *Booklist's* Ray Olsen, "Do I think of myself as a horror writer? No, I don't except that I love horror") (Olsen 2002, 1949).

One who does consider himself a horror writer is the redoubtable R. L. Stein who, in 2014, returned to the field with six new Fear Street novels notable for being grittier and more adult than were the originals written in the 1990s. "For me it's thinking of new scares, plot twists and cliff-hanger chapter endings I haven't done before, moving into the modern world," Stein told the CNN correspondent Ashley Strickland (2013a), adding of Fear Street redux, "It will be a roller coaster ride of fearful suspense."

Stein is an old hand at this, having written more than 300 novels in his long career. An emerging talent, though, is Daniel Kraus. His fiendish imagination was on display in his novel, *Rotters* (2011), which focused on grave-robbing, while his second, *Scowler* (2013), featured the most horrific father in contemporary fiction, a monster of a man who escapes from prison and returns home to terrorize his family and murder his son. Kraus's *pièce de résistance,* however, is his ambitious two-volume novel *The Death and Life of Zebulon Finch* (2015–2016), the story of a boy who is murdered at the age of seventeen and then comes back to life, continuing to live this death in life (or vice-versa) for the next century or so, becoming increasingly desiccated as the years pass. This work transcends genre fiction and attains the status of authentic, not to be missed literature.

Although not always easy to classify, some of the novels of the late William Sleator may also be regarded as horror. His 2004 novel *The Boy Who Couldn't Die,* for example, helped usher in a mini-trend of zombie books, though the undead as subject had its much earlier origins in Haitian and West African religion and folklore, as the literary genre had its pre-Sleator beginnings in adult fiction in the 1920s work of horrormeister H. P. Lovecraft, later becoming part of a larger public consciousness with the release of the 1968 George A. Romano film *The Night of the Living Dead*. It then became a staple of contemporary young adult genre fiction with the 2008 publication of Daniel Waters's *Generation Dead*. Though interest in zombie fiction has waned somewhat since the late aughts, novelist Jonathan Maberry (*Rot and Ruin, Dust and Decay, Flesh and Bone, Fire and Ash*) remains a lively exponent of the undead, helping keep the flame alive with his blog, "It's Scary out There" (www.horror.org/yahorror).

Mystery and Suspense

Speaking of scary . . .

For many years, it seems to me, mystery/suspense was the genre that offered the fewest titles published specifically for YAs—and those that were all seemed to be written by either Lois Duncan or Joan Lowery Nixon. But like every other aspect of the YA field this, too, has changed. One evidence of the new significance of YA mystery/suspense was the 1989 establishment of a young adult category among the annual Mystery Writers of America Edgar Awards.

Perhaps as a consequence, a host of new writers have begun experimenting with this form—writers like Carol Plum-Ucci, whose *The Body of Christopher Creed* received a Printz Honor Award in 2001; Nancy Werlin, whose work often evokes that of Robert Cormier; and—more recently—Kevin Brooks, a British writer whose publisher, The Chicken House, specializes in mystery and speculative fiction and whose books are distributed in the United States by Scholastic. Other notable names include Caroline Cooney, Joyce Armstrong, Willo Davis Roberts, Chap Reaver, Gail Giles, Alex Flinn, Graham McNamee, Charles Benoit, and more.

As is the case with other genres, there is no shortage of popular mystery series, although most are for middle-school readers, among them Wendelin Van Draanen's Sammy Keyes series; Alex Horowitz's hugely popular Alex Rider novels; Julia Golding's Cat Royal series of historical mysteries; Dorothy and Thomas Hoobler's Samurai mysteries set in eighteenth century Japan; and, most recently—for older readers—Barry Lyga's ambitious (and terrific)

I Hunt Killers trilogy; and Elizabeth George's The Edge of Nowhere series. However, none of these, it is safe to predict, will ever match the enduring popularity—or influence—of that indefatigable girl sleuth Nancy Drew, whose name was once again in the news when Supreme Court justice Sonia Sotomayor acknowledged her early passion for the series, a passion that had previously been acknowledged by Justice Ruth Bader Ginsburg and retired jurist Sandra Day O'Connor. Such other movers and shakers as Hilary Clinton, Laura Bush, Oprah Winfrey, and Washington Post columnist Kathleen Parker have also publicly pledged their own undying allegiance to Nancy.

Finally, the crossover phenomenon has also visited this genre. Among the established adult authors who have begun writing mysteries for young readers are Peter Abrahams, John Feinstein, Michael Winerip, Harlan Coben and, most notably, Carl Hiaasen and James Patterson. And in the old-is-new-again department, British writer Charlie Higson has begun writing a series of thrillers about Ian Fleming's James Bond as a teenager. Such pastiches have become a mini-trend in the mid-twenty teens. The young Sherlock Holmes, for example, is being featured in novels by Andrew Lane, while Jackaby by William Ritter is a clever Holmes pastiche. Others are mystery/horror mash-ups; for example, Victor Frankenstein is the protagonist of Kenneth Oppel's Such Wicked Intent (2012) and This Dark Endeavor (2011), and Suzanne Weyn has extrapolated from Mary Shelley's classic to give us Dr. Frankenstein's Daughters (2013). Similarly, Robert Lewis Stevenson's characters Dr. Jekyll and Mr. Hyde have inspired a quartet of tales: Beth Fantesky's Jekyll Loves Hyde (2010), Daniel Levine's Hyde (2014), James Reese's The Strange Case of Doctor Jekyll and Mademoiselle Odile (2012), and Daniel and Dina Nayeri's Another Jekyll, Another Hyde (2012). Meanwhile, L. Frank Baum's Wizard of Oz has inspired Danielle Paige's Dorothy Must Die (2014) and H. G. Wells's The Island of Dr. Moreau has given us Megan Shepherd's Her Dark Curiosity (2013).

Clearly, in literature as in life, imitation is the sincerest form of flattery.

Note

1. Ironically, five months after Rinaldi's dire evaluation her next historical novel, Leigh Ann's Civil War (Boston: Harcourt, 2009), was published.

Romancing the Retail

Of Series, Superstores, Harry Potter, and Suchial

NOT EVERY TWENTY-FIRST-CENTURY TREND IN YOUNG ADULT LITERATURE has evidenced the field's artistic evolution. Some have demonstrated its ever-expanding commercial possibilities instead. Principal among these trends is the inexorable rise of what came to be called chick lit: those often (though not always) humorous novels aimed at female readers in pursuit of romance and/or designer labels. Arguably the first of these epidemic novels was Helen Fielding's adult title *The Diary of Bridget Jones,* published in England in 1996. Wildly popular, the book quickly inspired a host of similar titles and thus a major trend—"perhaps the only new one of the past 25 years," according to Laura Miller (2004, 27)—was born. The phenomenon arrived in the United States with the 2000 publication here of British comedian Louise Rennison's young adult novel *Angus, Thongs and Full-Frontal Snogging.* To the surprise of many this became a 2001 Printz honor title, turning the usual controversy on its head as—for once—a book was criticized as being too popular to receive Printz recognition! Be that as it may, *Angus* was so successful that at last count ten more addled adventures of its protagonist Georgia Nicholson have followed, clearly demonstrating that the operative word in any discussion of chick lit is *popular,* followed closely by *commercial.*

For many readers, the first indication that a new genre was in the offing was the unheralded appearance of book display tables at their neighborhood Barnes and Noble bookstore bearing signs saying, simply, "Chick Lit." This suggested several things: first, that the principal market for this new kind of genre fiction was the retail, not the traditional institutional, and second, that the major chain bookstores were playing an increasingly active role in the process of book publishing for young readers and were able to create and develop trends. One of the earliest indicators of this had been an article that appeared in the August 12, 1997 *New York Times.* In it the reporter Doreen Carvajal noted, "Publishing executives in search of oracles have begun turning to the dominant chains like Barnes and Noble and Borders for guidance about a broad range of issues—from dust jacket colors and punchy titles to authors' precise sales histories and forecasts of customer demand—that could determine a manuscript's destiny." To affirm this, Carvajal (1997, C5) quoted Ira Silverberg, then Grove Press's editor in chief: "Barnes & Noble and Borders have an increasing presence, so we really must spend more time with them to get our books across to a wider audience."

Silverberg was an adult publisher, of course, but a similar influence was also being felt on the juvenile side of publishing houses. Children's book reviewer Barbara Elleman noted in a 1998 *School Library Journal* article:

> Juvenile trade marketing staffs have begun close contact with bookstore chains, as their adult counterparts have done for some time. Barnes & Noble has 35 central buyers who make the (purchasing) decisions for all the stores across the country. In the children's field, there are only one or two buyers. Their selections are usually based on an author's reputation, the number of awards he or she has won, the 'spin' the sales and marketing people have put on the book, and how much money the publishers are willing to put into marketing it in the bookstore. (Elleman 1998, 44)

Whether these buyers have ever actually exercised veto power over the publication of any particular book(s) is moot, but I know from personal experience that their opinions are taken very seriously. When, in the late nineties, I served as a consultant to Houghton Mifflin on the development of their prospective new YA series, The Best American Nonrequired Reading (the term *young adult literature* was considered to be too noncommercial!), I was flown to New York for a meeting with Joe Monti, then children's book buyer for Barnes and Noble, to solicit his views on the viability of the series and whether it should be published as a YA or an adult title. Later, in the mid-aughts when I was developing *Rush Hour*, my YA literary journal, its publisher Delacorte also sought advice and feedback from Barnes and Noble regarding marketing, jacket art, and price points.

The growing influence of the chains affirmed another equally significant trend: the increasing purchasing power of the young adults themselves. "Attracting teens' business has become a Holy Grail for marketers," the reporter Dave Carpenter (2000, D1) wrote in a November 2000 article for the Associated Press, adding that American teens were projected to spend "a staggering" $155 billion that year.

The following year *The Los Angeles Times* reported that literature for young adults (which it defined—à la YALSA—as twelve- to eighteen-year-olds) had become a $1.5 billion industry (DiMassa 2001). That same year *USA Today* reported that teens aged fourteen to seventeen had bought 35.6 million books in 2001, an increase of about 6 million over the previous year.

Two years later *The Washington Post* reported, "Teenagers are the demographic that almost everyone in the book industry—librarians, publishers, booksellers—wants. As the number of teenagers in the population has risen (the 2000 census had shown 5.5 million more ten- to nineteen-year-olds than in 1990), so has teen buying power for all kinds of items, including books" (Bacon 2002, B1). Since then, with a current population of 42,715,537 ten- to nineteen-year-olds, the 2010 census has shown growth of a more modest 1,820,453, but that is still a 5 percent growth with increased buying power. Indeed, the market has continued its relentless expansion in the years since. By 2012, for example, sales totaled $3.3 billion dollars, more than twice the 2001 total (Milliot 2014, 15). Though dollar totals for 2014 remain elusive, the total number of YA books sold increased by a healthy 22.4 percent (even as adult sales were down 3.3 percent) (Stampler 2014).

When I interviewed David Gale, vice president and editorial director of Simon and Schuster Books for Young Readers, on May 28, 2015, he confirmed that "YA over the past few years has been sustaining the industry." Yet that may be changing, for he then interjected a cautionary note, saying, "We're over-publishing; there are just too many YA books; we're not seeing the overall growth (in the market) we used to see" (Gale, personal communication, May 28, 2015).

One understands his point about over-publishing: when I first became involved with the young adult world in the late 1980s, approximately 250 to

500 YA books were published in a good year; today (2016) it's closer to 7,000!

Another downside to this volume is that it's difficult to give books the editorial attention they require and, accordingly, it's not hard to find examples of sloppy publishing; also, because the business is currently trend-driven, the literature runs the risk of becoming homogenized, lacking innovation and originality. All that said, wonderful books are still being published; it's just harder to find them among the welter. Be that as it may, it's clear that, for the time being at least, YA continues to be the tail that wags the dog of the publishing business.

Another trend that continues to inform the market is a focus on hardcover publishing in a field where paperbacks in the 1980s and 1990s had reigned supreme. This began to change with the Millennium. The editor-publishers Brenda Bowen (Simon and Schuster) and Elise Howard (Avon) both told *Publishers Weekly* in 1999 that they were finding a new receptivity to hardcovers on the part of the chains (Maughan 1999, 93); a year later Andrew Smith, then Vice President of Marketing for Random House, agreed, saying, "We're selling more hardcovers to teens than we have in the past. The format and price point don't seem to be a problem for them" (Maughan 2000, 28).[1] Apparently not, for five years later, the Association of American Publishers reported that children's and young adult hardcover sales in 2005 were up an amazing 59.6 percent over the previous year (2006).

YA Imprints Arrive

Although it was publishers' children's divisions that had previously released young adult books, it is small wonder—considering its robust market—that as early as 1999 publishers were starting to launch separate young adult imprints, many of them specializing in reader-friendly (i.e., commercial) fiction. Some twenty-seven of these imprints would emerge between 1999 and 2016, all designed to "capitalize on a unique moment in publishing: the teen wave" (Corbett 2014, 23).

Jacquelyn Mitchard, author and editor-in-chief of Merit Press agrees, saying, "YA is where the big emotion is right now" (i.e., 2014). "YA is where the stories are right now. Readers go to where the stories are" (23).

The new imprints, in order of their founding, are:

1999: Avon (later Harper) TEMPEST and Simon and Schuster PULSE

2002: Scholastic PUSH, TOR Starscape, Penguin SPEAK, Penguin FIREBIRD

2004: Penguin RAZORBILL, Houghton Mifflin GRAPHIA

2005: Abrams AMULET

2006: Llewellyn FLUX

2007: Aladdin MIX (aimed at tween readers), Harlequin Kimani TRU

2009: Sourcebook

2010: Carolrhoda Lab, Sourcebooks Fire

2012: F&W/Merit Press, Soho Teen, Seven Stories Press/Triangle Square Editions

2013: Amazon Skyscape, Ig Publishing/Lizzie Skurnick Books, Zondervan Blink, Algonquin Young Readers

2014: Capstone Switch, Swoon

2015: Abdo Epic, Rock the Boat/One World

2016: Flatiron Books (Macmillan)

In addition to the twenty-seven YA imprints, two important adult imprints—Pocket Books' MTV Books (1995) and Simon and Schuster's Spotlight Entertainment (2004)—were aimed directly at a newly emerging crossover audience, that is, eighteen to twenty-five-year-olds. Though MTV Books were notably edgy and clearly aimed at the older end of the MTV demographic, many of the titles it published could easily have been released as YA and—in one notable case—should have been. I refer to Stephen Chbosky's *Perks of Being a Wallflower*, an extraordinary epistolary novel with a haunting sensibility, an unforgettable protagonist, and an exquisite narrative voice. Published in 1999, it became an instant YA classic and—had it been published as YA—surely would have been a very strong contender for the Michael L. Printz Award.

Not every commercial effort to reach teens has been successful, however. One of the most notable failures was the Teen People Book Club, launched in March 2000 by the magazine of the same name, in cooperation with the Book of the Month Club. Sadly, this promising effort, which initially brought in four to five times more new members than expected (Maughan and Milliot 2001, 12), lasted only a year before it fell victim not so much to disappointing sales as to the fraught merger of its owner Time Warner with AOL. In the meantime, the categories of books offered by the club and deemed to be especially attractive to teens remain instructive. Here, for those interested in the equation between teens and popular reading, they are:

> Amazing books about real teens and real issues
> Great novels that will make you laugh or make you cry or make
> your heart pound with fear
> Star-studded books on today's hottest celebrities
> Useful guides with advice that's truly relevant to your life
> And all the new, new, NEW stuff you just won't hear about any-
> where else

It's also worth noting that—in a further effort to establish credibility with YAs—titles for the Club's catalog were selected with the advice and counsel of a panel of teenagers recruited from across the country and called "The Review Crew."

The Book Club may not have survived, but the habit of consulting teens has; for example, Merit Books in 2014 maintained a teen focus group it called Merit 66. The young people received a shipment of prepublication copies of forthcoming books every three months "in exchange for posting their reactions on Twitter, Instagram, and YouTube" (Corbett 2014).

Mean Girls Materialize

Ironically or not, the emergence of teens as uberconsumers influenced the emergence of a new chick lit subgenre that was quickly dubbed both "mean girl" books and "privileged chick lit." A *New York Times* article about this new subgenre with its relentless focus on designer labels and other consumables was amusingly titled "Poor Little Rich Girls Throbbing to Shop!" (Bellafante 2003). The chief exemplar of this new subgenre was Cecily von Ziegesar's Gossip Girl series, which detailed the designer label-ridden lives of the fabulously wealthy girls Blair Waldorf and Serena van der Woodsen, both of whom attend the exclusive (and fictitious) Constance Billard School on Manhattan's Upper East Side. Though loosely based on the author's own teenage experience of being a student at the tony Nightingale-Bamford School ("if she wasn't precisely Paris Hilton, Von Ziegesar was an unusually astute observer among her glittering set"), (Nussbaum 2005) these are books in which—*The*

New York Times dryly noted—"No cliché of Upper East Side privilege goes unnoticed" (Bellafonte 2003, F1).

The genesis of the series was an outline proposal that von Ziegesar wrote when she was working as an editor at the book packager 17th Street Productions (later part of Alloy Entertainment). One of the first such proposals to be shopped around by e-mail, the project was quickly snapped up by Little, Brown editor Cynthia Eagen and the rest is literary history—of a sort. Within two years, the incipient series had sold 1.3 million copies and spawned a companion spin-off series, The A List, which was set on the other coast—in Hollywood. The only difference between the two cultures under examination was that the kids in the A-List titles didn't attend a private school; instead they were students at Beverly Hills High, a milieu that irresistibly recalls the once-popular TV series Beverly Hills 90210 and underscores the growing symbiosis between commercial fiction and its electronic counterpart, television and motion pictures.

There would ultimately be a dozen Gossip Girl titles[2] that, through 2011, had sold six million copies and spawned at least two other spin-off series from von Ziegesar: The It Girls and The Carlyles. The latter, which debuted in 2008 with a two-hundred-thousand-copy first printing, (Lodge 2008) featured triplet sisters who, newcomers to Manhattan, happened to move into the penthouse that Blair Waldorf's family had previously occupied (precisely why von Ziegesar names her characters for hotels is one of the more tantalizing imponderables about these series; perhaps it's for the same reason that Antonio Pagliarulo's The Celebutantes, another series starring wealthy triplets, named its protagonists after fashionable Manhattan streets: Madison, Lexington, and Park!)[3]

Gossip Girl publisher Little, Brown found the Holy Grail of synergy in 2007 when the books inspired a highly touted television series on the CW network. Interestingly enough, it was an earlier television series, Sex and the City, which has often been cited as the source of inspiration for the whole burgeoning mean girl movement. "I give you Sex and the City as told by Carrie Bradshaw's kid sister," the Manchester Guardian observed when the Gossip Girl books debuted in Britain in 2003 (Cooke 2003).

Sex—casual and otherwise—was certainly a fixture in many of these books, but it was couture that might have been their most deliciously meretricious aspect. The New York Times education columnist Michael Winerip (himself an author of fiction for middle-school readers) wrote an interesting piece about this in July 2008. Headlined "In Novels for Girls, Fashion Trumps Romance," it quotes an academic study of Gossip Girl and two of the series it spawned—Clique and the A List—that found 1,553 brand-name references in the books' collective 1,431 pages—slightly more than one "commercial" per page (though none of them were actually paid placements, Winerip decided after some reportorial digging) (Winerip 2008).

It's hard, thus, to disagree with cultural observer Naomi Wolf (2006), who concluded that in these books "success and failure are entirely signaled by material possessions—specifically by brands. Sex and shopping take their place on a barren stage, as though, even for teenagers, these are the only dramas left."

Given this commercial patina, it's no surprise that many of these series—though published by all the major houses including Little, Brown, Simon and Schuster, HarperCollins, Delacorte Press, and others—were created by book packagers, the most successful being Alloy Entertainment, which produces some forty books a year and is responsible not only for Gossip Girl and The A-List, but also The Clique, the Au Pairs, Pretty Little Liars, Privilege, Luxe, and the more benign Sisterhood of the Traveling Pants. According to Elise Howard, then Associate Publisher of HarperCollins Books for Young Readers, "They (Alloy executives) have a no-holds-barred approach to giving readers exactly what they want to find" (Mead 2009). Significantly, Alloy Entertainment is a division of the larger Alloy Media + Marketing, one of the largest and most successful marketers and merchandisers to the youth market.

The goal in this still-burgeoning field is to create an instantly recognizable brand or franchise (a word that is increasingly heard) that can be spun off into a variety of economic opportunities—books, television series, movies, products—and then promoted through interactive websites, contests, and, increasingly, social networks.

Typically published as trade paperbacks (though some—Luxe, Traveling Pants, etc.—may also appear in hardcover editions), the books are targeted at the retail market, their covers replete with references to *The New York Times* Best Seller List and to contests ("Win Shopping Spree. Details Inside"). Their sophisticated cover art, usually featuring photographs of drop-dead gorgeous girls (and boys), is designed to appeal to a broad age range. "Though 'Gossip Girl' was originally published as a YA novel," its editor Cynthia Eagen told *Publishers Weekly,* "we thought the book would have crossover appeal and we specifically designed the cover to have an older, cosmopolitan look. Pretty soon we discovered that women and gay men in their 20s and 30s were buying a ton of these books. Our first Gossip Girl 'Win a Trip to New

York' contest winner was actually a 32-year-old woman" (Alderdice 2004, 26).

Genre fiction of all sorts has always had considerable crossover potential, though it has traditionally been manifested as teens reading adult titles. The discovery of YA books by adult readers is a new—and fascinating—development that we will examine in greater detail a bit later. In the meantime, it should be noted that just as the lines of demarcation dividing adult and young adult readers has increasingly blurred since the late 1990s, so have the lines separating genres. Nowhere is this more evident than in the field of romance fiction, where genre bending and blending have become commonplace.[4] In addition to the chick lit, Brit lit, mean girl, and privileged chick lit we've been discussing, there are historical romances (Libba Bray's Gemma Doyle trilogy and the Luxe novels of Anna Godbersen), mystery/suspense romances (virtually anything by Joan Lowery Nixon), gay and lesbian romances (*Annie on My Mind, Boy Meets Boy*) and the myriad marriages of science fiction, paranormal, fantasy, and horror with romance (think Melissa Marr and Stephenie Meyer).

Contemporary romance (which includes chick lit) continues to lead the other subgenres in terms of reader popularity, and it's here that we find many of the most popular contemporary authors for YAs—writers like Anne Brashares, Kate Brian, Meg Cabot, Zoey Dean, Melissa De La Cruz, Megan McCafferty, Lurlene McDaniel (all hail the uncrowned Queen of the Weepies!), and the more mainstream writers who tend to combine romance and realistic fiction—writers like Sarah Dessen, Maureen Johnson, Lauren Myracle, Catherine Gilbert Murdock, and others.

Though these authors remain popular, adult chick lit itself went into a period of decline circa 2012; an editor at Kensington Books told a *BuzzFeed* reporter, "We've pretty much stopped publishing chick lit" (North 2012).

As a result, a number of formerly adult authors have migrated to young adult; they include such stellar talents as collaborators Nicola Kraus and Emma McLaughlin, "Sex and the City's" Candace Bushnell, Jessica Brody, Donna Cooner, and others.

What Harry Wrought

No matter how successful the many-splendored subgenres of romance fiction have been in the twenty-first century, they are all eclipsed by the jaw-dropping success of the fantasy field in the wake of one of the most extraordinary phenomena in the history of publishing: the international success of the Harry Potter series. From the 1997 British publication of volume one, *Harry Potter and the Philosopher's Stone* (re-titled *Harry Potter and the Sorcerer's Stone*, the American edition was published in 1998) to the seventh and final volume, *Harry Potter and the Deathly Hallows*, published in 2007, the series broke record after record while dramatically—some might say seismically—changing the world of publishing for young readers.

Although no one could have predicted the ultimate enormity of the phenomenon when the first book was published, the seeds of that success were already sown. It didn't hurt, for example, that the book arrived with an irresistible back story: its previously unpublished author, J. K. Rowling, was an attractive, divorced, unemployed single mother who was on the dole and living in an unheated Edinburgh flat while she was writing the book. To keep warm, she reportedly wheeled her baby daughter into cafes and coffeeshops where she wrote the book in longhand (the now legendary story varies in its details, of course: according to *Time* magazine she would "sometimes jot down Harry Potter ideas on napkins" (Gray 1999, 71). That its British publisher then paid £100,000 for this first novel added a fairy tale glow to the story, which was further burnished when Scholastic ponied up $100,000 for the US rights, an unprecedented sum for an American children's book. Sales more than met expectations as the book became a best seller in both the United Kingdom and the United States, where it appeared on *The New York Times* Best Seller List within three months of its publication. A mere year-and-a-half later, the top three hardcover slots were held by Potter titles and a fourth was on its way with a first printing of 3.8 million copies, the largest ever for any book.[5]

Harry had appeared on the cover of *Time* (September 20, 1999), Warner Brothers had acquired film rights (the first film was released in 2001), and Harry Potter was now more than a series of enchanting books; it was a full-fledged publishing phenomenon, including Harry Potter theme parks! Ultimately, of course, there would be seven novels that, together, have sold more than 375 million copies to date and have been translated into 65 languages. By 2004, *The New York Times* had received enough complaints from adult publishers about the Potter books taking so many slots on its Best Seller List that it responded by inaugurating a new—and separate—children's best-seller list! (*The Times* would change the list again in the fall of 2015, separating hardcover middle grade and young adult titles from paperback and e-book best sellers) (Gilmore 2015b).

This was only one of the significant changes that the Potter books visited on the worlds of publishing and bookselling. Their international success also encouraged the more widespread publication in the United States (and in the United Kingdom) of books first published in other countries as international cooperation was served when Bloomsbury (the books' British publisher) and Scholastic quickly agreed that each new Potter book should be released simultaneously in the United Kingdom and the United States (typically the American release would have followed the British publication by a year or so). Each new Potter release subsequently became an event—no, make that an EVENT! The books were embargoed until their official publication date: no advance reading or review copies were released prior to publication, and bookstores put them on sale at precisely one minute after midnight on the official publication date, staying open until the wee hours to accommodate the hordes of over-stimulated children (most of them dressed as Potter characters) and their bleary-eyed parents (some also in costume), all waiting in serpentine lines to purchase their anxiously anticipated copies. Because no advance review copies were available, I waited in one such line myself to purchase a copy of *Harry Potter and the Order of the Phoenix*, as I had been hired by *The Los Angeles Times* to review it. Because the paper wanted to run the review as close to the publication date as possible, I was given only a day-and-a-half to read the 870-page behemoth and write the review. Reader, I did it . . . barely.

The normally book-shy mass media ate all this up and hyped Harry relentlessly. Each new printing or sales record was greeted with rapturous headlines and when the motion picture versions of the books began appearing, the hoopla approached hysteria. In the meantime, the Internet came alive with fan sites and fan fiction; there were fan gatherings (à la Star Trek conventions), promotional tours, rock bands, and more—so much more that Melissa Anelli, webmistress of the Leaky Cauldron, the premiere Potter fan site, wrote a fascinating account of it all in *Harry: A History* (2008), a book of interest not only to Potter fans but also to future literary historians and cultural anthropologists alike.

The books themselves soon became almost lost in the larger phenomenon that was Pottermania. And that's a pity, because they remain extraordinary works of fantasy, and J. K. Rowling is a brilliant writer, a fact that is not compromised by her now being wealthier than Queen Elizabeth. My personal feelings about the Potter titles have not changed since I gave a starred review in *Booklist* to the very first one in 1998, calling it "brilliantly imagined, beautifully written, and utterly captivating."

These seventeen years later I would use the same words to describe the books that followed. Rowling proved herself to be a gifted storyteller with a remarkable ability to create a detailed alternative world that coexists with ours. Yet, having read all seven volumes, I believe it is the characters and their interrelationships that will remain with me longest, in part because Rowling permitted them to grow up with their readers over the course of the series (Harry is a year older in each new volume). Thus, though the first several titles were clearly aimed at middle-school readers (I recommended the first for fifth to eighth graders and the literary historian Leonard Marcus [2008] regarded the early titles for eight- to twelve-year-old tweens), each volume thereafter became increasingly sophisticated and, frankly, darker. The final three—*Order of the Phoenix, Half-Blood Prince,* and *Deathly Hallows*—are clearly young adult novels. Thus, the changes that Harry Potter visited on publishing impacted not only children's books but YA ones, as well. At this writing, nine years have passed since the publication of volume seven and another decade or two must flow under the bridge of history before one can, with any validity, assess the series' lasting place in world literature (or describe them as "classic").

That said, it is already indisputably clear that they will command a very large place in all future histories of publishing, for their impact there is already abundantly evident. The international success of the series helped turn young adult literature into an increasingly global phenomenon and also sparked a new interest in fantasy as a genre not only for children but also—and perhaps more importantly—for young adults. It is hard to argue with Holly Koelling's (2007, 64) flat declaration, "Plain and simple, fantasy is a predominant trend in current teen literature," an assessment as true today (2016) as it was in 2007. Not only did Harry's success stimulate an amazing outpouring of new fantasy titles (that virtually every one of these must now be part of an ongoing series and many hundreds of pages long à la Harry may be less salutary trends), it also spurred readers to discover other long-established fantasists whose work had not previously received its due—writers like Diana Wynne Jones, Eva Ibbotson, Margaret Mahy, and others.

Meanwhile, the multigenerational appeal of the Potter books spurred a rush to publish crossover titles and also began attracting record numbers of established adult authors to the newly profitable field of books for young readers. The books also sparked an interest in family reading, and demonstrated that, given something they actually wanted to read, boys would embrace books as enthusiastically as girls. The increasing length of the individual volumes (three of the last four exceeded 700 pages!) also proved that, contrary to traditional wisdom, contemporary young readers would welcome books more than 200 pages in length, and as a result YA novels have now routinely become many hundreds of pages longer—whether they need to be or not. When my YA novel *My Father's Scar* was issued in 1996, its publisher, Simon and Schuster, dictated that it could be no longer than 200 pages, the industry standard for that era. Today, most YAs are at least 350 pages in length and often longer—much longer!

One of the less benign aspects of the Potter books was their introduction into the children's field of what is called "event publishing," which had long been a fixture of the world of adult publishing. Indeed, the runaway financial success of the Rowling series seems to have accelerated a trend that had already begun: the transformation of children's publishing into its adult counterpart, with its relentless focus on the next big, high concept "thing," and its corollary shrinking of the backlist and its neglect—benign or otherwise—of more modest-selling midlist titles.

Fangs for the Memories

No surprise that publishing became relentlessly—some might say obsessively—focused on finding the next Harry Potter. It found it in an unlikely place: Stephenie Meyer's fevered Twilight series, the four-volume saga of teenage Bella's love for the exotically beautiful vegetarian vampire Edward Cullen, a boy who has been seventeen since 1918! (I'm not making this up).

The first volume of the series, *Twilight,* was published in 2005, the same year as *Harry Potter and the Half-Blood Prince.* It, too, came with an interesting—and highly marketable—back story. Its previously unpublished author, Stephenie Meyer, was an attractive, 31-year-old Phoenix housewife who reportedly found the inspiration for her series in a dream so vivid that, on waking, she felt compelled to write it down. Three months later it had become a 498-page novel. Over the next three years it would sell 1.5 million copies. In the meantime, three more volumes quickly followed, each one more successful—and longer—than the previous ones. *New Moon,* which introduced Edward's rival Jacob—a werewolf no less—appeared in 2006 and weighed in at 564 pages; *Eclipse* (640 pages) followed in 2007; and *Breaking Dawn* (768 pages) came along in 2008, selling 1.3 million copies in its first twenty-four hours of publication, a record for its publisher Little, Brown/Hachette.

To the unbridled delight of the media, some of the same promotional hoopla that had surrounded the publication of the various Harry Potter titles quickly began to gather around the Twilight titles. "Yes," *The Washington Post* observed, "the creation of Stephenie Meyer's 'Twilight Saga' series, and its subsequent arc toward fame, recall J. K. Rowling's 'Harry Potter' success story to no small extent" (Yao 2008). "Stephanie Meyer: A New J. K. Rowling?" *Time* trumpeted (April 24, 2008); "Harry Potter and the Rival Teen Franchise" the *Wall Street Journal* chorused (July 9, 2009), while *Entertainment Weekly* hailed "the second coming of J. K. Rowling" (Valby 2008).

The similarities between the two as publishing phenomena were startling: once again, each new title was embargoed until one minute after midnight on the official publication date. when it would go on sale to hordes of costume-wearing fans (many of whom called themselves either Twilighters or Twihards); no advance review copies were released; there were a plethora of Internet sites (including one for adult fans called Twilight Moms), fan fiction,[6] Twilight-themed rock bands, and more. As a result, Meyer—with twenty-two million sales—became *USA Today's* best-selling author of 2008. The next year she was named to *Forbes* magazine's Celebrity 100 List of the world's most powerful celebrities.

There were—and are—differences between the two series, however. Unlike Rowling, Meyer launched hers with an implicit fan base, that is, romance readers. According to the Romance Writers of America, 71 percent of the 58.1 million American romance readers opened their first adult romance novel when they were sixteen (Engberg 2004) The runaway success of Meyer's series is surely at least in part responsible for making the genre the biggest fiction category in 2007 (Hesse 2009) As for the vampire romance subgenre: thanks to Anne Rice it, too, was already a hugely popular genre with an established crossover readership. Ironically its hallmark is often steamy sex, though the hallmark of the first three Twilight volumes was sexual abstinence. This changed dramatically with volume four, however, when Bella and Edward finally married. Sonya Bolle wryly wrote in her *Los Angeles Times* article "Why 'Twilight' Isn't for Everybody," "The fourth book answers the burning question about what vampires do with all their free time, since they don't sleep. It turns out that married vampires have a lot of sex" (Bolle 2008).

There's no gainsaying the sex appeal of the books and the part it has played in their popularity with pubescent teens, a popularity reinforced by the November 2008 release of the first *Twilight* film, which grossed more than $382 million worldwide (Schuker 2009). The second film was released exactly a year later in November 2009 to similar heavy breathing. As for Harry, sex was always a secondary consideration, though as the boy wizard and his friends grew into adolescence, romantic attraction certainly became a subtext, which then became a major marketing point for the sixth Potter film. "As the new Harry Potter movie opens next week," the *Wall Street Journal* reported, "the bespectacled wizard faces a new challenge: how to compete for the attention of a young audience that has been growing up—and is starting to prefer the angsty teen romances and cooler, edgier characters of the 'Twilight' books and movies" (2009).

Perhaps. But there is one area where there is no competition between the rival franchises and that is literary quality. There Rowling is clearly the superior—and more serious—writer. Meyer, though a natural storyteller with a thorough understanding of her readers' interests, is no stylist, and her four-volume saga shows little promise of ever becoming part of any literary canon. This is as much the genre's fault as it is hers, however. It's hard to take books that focus on "sculpted, incandescent chests," "scintillating arms," and "glistening pale lavender lids" very seriously (quotes from *Twilight*, 260), although Annette Curtis Klause did quite a memorable job with the vampire romance in her first YA novel *Silver Kiss* (1990) and later served the werewolf romance well, too, with *Blood and Chocolate*.

Critics may not have taken paranormal romance, a spin-off from *Twilight*, seriously but fans and booksellers surely did. This subgenre, which coupled romance and speculative fiction, became enormously popular, so much so that behemoth bookseller Barnes and Noble separated it out from other YA titles and formed a stand-alone section devoted to these outré romances about girls who fall in love with vampires, werewolves, demons, fallen angels, and so on.

Next in Line

If Harry Potter and Twilight visited revolutionary changes on YA, a third series may have put those trendsetters into the shade. I refer to Suzanne Collins's The Hunger Games trilogy.

Unlike Rowling and Meyer, Collins was already an established author in the series form, having previously written the five-volume Underland Chronicles, which became a *New York Times* best seller and was sold in twenty-one foreign territories. Yet that fledgling series didn't have a patch on The Hunger Games trilogy, which became an international best seller and was sold into fifty-six territories and translated into fifty-one languages.

Its plot is well-known: set in the fictional country of Panem, it posits the notion that each of its twelve districts must choose two young people to represent it in the so-called Hunger Games, an annual competition in which the chosen must fight to the death, the sole survivor being the winner. The competition is broadcast to rapt audiences à la real world television reality shows. Representing District 12 are the two competitors Katniss Everdeen and Peeta Mellark, the baker's son. Peeta, it turns out, is in love with Katniss, who gradually begins to return his affection, though this is complicated by the fact that she retains tender feelings for her erstwhile hunting partner Gale Hawthorne (who, despite his ambiguous first name, is a boy—definitely a boy!). The three volumes in the series—*The Hunger Games, Catching Fire,* and *Mockingjay*—follow the fortunes of the love triangle and, increasingly, the rebellion against Panem's repressive government.

Well-written, fast-paced, and boasting both an irresistible premise and memorable characters, the trilogy became enormously successful, selling more than sixty-five million copies, each volume becoming a *New York Times* best seller (the three have spent a combined 260 consecutive weeks on *The Times* list) [Scholastic News Room, nd].

By 2012 (*The Hunger Games* was published in 2008), the trilogy had become the all-time bestselling book series, surpassing even the success of the Harry Potter series (Gaudios 2012). (Harry got a bit of his own back when, in a 2012 NPR reader poll of the best young adult books of all time, he edged out *The Hunger Games* for the top spot [Fantozzi. 2012]).

Inevitably the books were turned into equally successful films; *The Hunger Games,* the first in a quartet of movies based on the trilogy, became the third biggest grossing weekend film in Hollywood history (#1 for a spring release) (Barnes 2012).

Though not quite as successful, another important publishing phenomenon is the recent Divergent trilogy by Veronica Roth. Like Harry Potter and Twilight, this one comes with a backstory. Roth, a first novelist, wrote *Divergent,* the first volume in her trilogy (*Divergent, Insurgent,* and *Allegiant*), when she was still a senior at Northwestern University, and sold it in a major preemptive bid. Set in a dystopian future Chicago, the novel posits a society in which everyone is born into one of five factions (Abnegation,

Candor, Amity, Erudite, and Dauntless). At age sixteen, everyone must choose whether to stay in the faction into which they were born or to opt for a different one. Our protagonist Tris Prior, born into Abnegation, chooses to switch to Dauntless, with predictably dire results. Divergent has often been compared to The Hunger Games (dystopian setting, repressive regime, plucky heroine, etc.) but—though thoroughly successful commercially (more than ten million copies were sold as of January 1, 2014, while the first printing of volume 3, Allegiant, boasted a press run of two million copies), it pales by comparison, as do the inevitable movie versions. Yet "this is the next series— the next to follow in that line of Stephenie Meyers's 'Twilight' and Suzanne Collins's 'Hunger Games,'" says Brian Monahan (Borelli 2013), a book buyer for the all-powerful Barnes and Noble chain. "It is the next YA phenomenon."

Phenomenon though it may have been, Divergent is more notable for what it—in tandem with The Hunger Games—helped usher in: the next important trend in young adult literature, the dystopian novel.

Dystopian Fiction

Some trace the dystopian novel back to the eighteenth century and Jonathan Swift's Gulliver's Travels. Others argue for the nineteenth century and Samuel Butler's Erehwon. Be that as it may, the genre is surely best-known for two twentieth century examples: Brave New World by Aldous Huxley and George Orwell's 1984. In the ranks of young adult literature, the arguable progenitor is Lois Lowry's 1993 novel The Giver.

Dystopias are usually set in future, often post-apocalyptic societies marked by nightmarish repression, ruin, corruption, squalor, darkness, or devolution to a woeful, preindustrial agrarian society. Some are not set on this world at all, the best example of this being Patrick Ness's superlative Chaos Walking trilogy. Regardless of setting, however, the best contemporary example remains Suzanne Collins's Panem.

Other notable examples of the dystopian include:

M. T. Anderson, Feed (2002)
Scott Westerfeld, Uglies (2005)
Catherine Fisher, Incarceron (2007)
Patrick Ness, Chaos Walking (2008)
Michael Grant, Gone (2008)

Cory Doctorow, *Little Brother* (2008)
Saci Lloyd, *The Carbon Diaries* (2009)
James Dashner, *The Maze Runner* (2009)
James Patterson, *Witch and Wizard* (2009)
Ally Condie, *Matched* (2010)
Carrie Ryan, *The Forest of Hands and Teeth* (2010)
Marie Lu, *Legend* (2011)
Lauren Oliver, *Delirium* (2012)
Jeff Hirsch, *The Darkest Path* (2013)
Rachel Caine, *Ink and Bone* (2015)

There are as many reasons as examples for the genre's post-Hunger Games proliferation. One, surely, is publishers' hope of recapturing the sheer popularity—and financial success—of Collins's magnum opus. But others are rooted in the *zeitgeist*. "Adults write books for teenagers," author Moira Young (2011) explains, "So anxious adults—worried about the planet, the degradation of civil society and the bitter inheritance we're leaving for the young—write dystopian books."

Others point to the existential fallout from 9/11: Here is editor Karen Grove: "After 9/11, it seemed people started thinking about the destruction of the world" (Springen 2010, 21). And Laura Godwin, vice-president and publisher of Henry Holt Books for young readers: "They really are kind of cautionary tales. These books are all believable metaphors that arise from the social milieu or situation of the time. They're taken to their logical extreme" (22).

But this begs the question: why are these books so popular with teens? Some argue it's because they reflect the uncertainties and anxieties of their lives and times. "Dystopian novels," Debra Donston-Miller (2014) writes, "are merely all speaking to these anxieties of young people today." Others would argue that they address teens' psyches: "They (dystopian novels) speak to the young adult inside us all, the part whose identity is yet unformed, full of rage and fear and longing. No wonder teens love stories about dystopias: they feel like they're in one" (Penny 2014). "It's about what's happening, right this minute, in the stormy psyche of the adolescent reader," Laura Miller (2010) adds.

Still others point to a more quotidian cause: these books reflect the ghastly horrors of high school! "The success of *Uglies*," its author Scott Westerfeld writes, "is partly thanks to high school being a dystopia" (Miller 2010). Dana Stevens chimes in: "The word dystopia comes from a Greek root that roughly translates as 'bad place' and what place could be worse than high school?" (Stevens 2014).

So, yes, teens want dystopian novels. But do they *need* them? Janie Slater says yes and offers four reasons why. Dystopia:

1. Provides a healthy outlet for exploring socially unacceptable topics within our own spheres and communities.
2. Helps us see new, different perspectives than we're capable of from our own limited experience.
3. Helps us sort out and express feelings and emotions, providing cathartic release and relief.
4. Inspires us with often courageous, defiant (in a healthy way), quirky and unique protagonists who overcome barriers and limitations (Slater 2011).

These reasons suggest the difference between adult dystopias and teenage ones. Moira Young (2011) offers a more abiding difference: "These are dark, sometimes bleak stories, but that doesn't mean they are hopeless. Those of us who write for young people are reluctant to leave our readers without hope. It wouldn't be right. We always leave a candle burning in the darkness." Always? So long as the genre is flourishing, yes. But has it run its course? Lois Lowry thinks so: "I think that trend is ending," she said in August 2014. "We'll go on to the next trend and we all wish we knew what it was so we could go out and write it. Dystopian fiction is passe now" (Riley 2014).

And who am I to argue with the godmother of the genre?

Steampunk

Less dark than the dystopian—though sometimes gloomy—is the latest sub-genre of speculative fiction: steampunk. Though its origins are hard to trace, some observers claim it began as an offshoot of cyberpunk science fiction. Be that as it may, steampunk is usually set in Victorian England—though sometimes it is in a dystopian future. This mashup of science and historical-fiction is further distinguished by its inclusion of real or imagined steam-powered machinery. Arguably the most popular writer of steampunk is the prolific Cassandra Clare, but other authors and books worth consideration are

Scott Westerfeld's Leviathan quartet (2009–2012), William Alexander's *Goblin Secrets* (2012), which is a National Book Award–winner, and Kelly Link and Gavin J. Grant's *Steampunk! An Anthology of Fantastically Rich and Strange Stories* (2011).

The Return of Realism

Clearly the market is changing. Not only is the demise of the dystopian imminent, but paranormal romance is already yesterday's news, according to editor/publisher David Gale. The multivolume series also seems to be fading. Gale says that he is now looking for stories with "a two-book arc or maybe a trilogy but nothing longer than that" (David Gale, personal communication, May 28, 2015). This comes at a time when Gale sees a new trend: a return to the form that founded young adult literature: the novel of contemporary realism.

Gale is hardly the only one to see this trend. The publisher Macmillan has recently sought to capitalize on it by inaugurating a new imprint, the ReaLI-TyReads program, "which is designed to shine a light on Macmillan's realistic literary fiction." Most of these spotlighted books are backlist titles (e.g., Laurie Halse Anderson's *Speak,* Marcus Sedgwick's *She Is Not Invisible,* etc.), but others such as the short story collection *I See Reality* are new releases

The renascence of realistic fiction is driven by a single author, the so-called "teen whisperer" (Talbot 2014) and latter-day young adult Pied Piper, John Green.

The phenomenal Green hit the ground running with the 2005 publication of his first novel *Looking for Alaska,* which won that most prestigious of YA prizes, the Michael L. Printz Award, in 2006. And he has never looked back, cementing his place as contemporary YA's premiere creator with his subsequent novels *An Abundance of Katherines* (2006), a Printz honor title; *Paper Towns* (2008), *Will Grayson, Will Grayson* (with David Levithan) (2010), and the remarkable *The Fault in Our Stars* (2012), which was the best-selling book in America in 2014 in both print and Kindle editions.

Its story is reprised—along with my critical reaction—in my January 2012 starred *Booklist* review:

> At 16, Hazel Grace Lancaster, a three-year stage IV-cancer survivor, is clinically depressed. To help her deal with this, her doctor

sends her to a weekly support group where she meets Augustus Waters, a fellow cancer survivor, and the two fall in love. Both kids are preternaturally intelligent and Hazel is fascinated with a novel about cancer called "An Imperial Affliction." Most particularly she longs to know what happened to its characters after an ambiguous ending. To find out, the enterprising Augustus makes it possible for them to travel to Amsterdam, where "Imperial's" author, an expatriate American, lives. What happens when they meet him must be left to readers to discover. Suffice to say, it is significant. Writing about kids with cancer is an invitation to sentimentality and pathos—or worse, in unskilled hands, bathos. Happily, Green is able to transcend such pitfalls in his best and most ambitious novel to date. Beautifully conceived and executed, this story artfully examines the largest possible considerations—life, love and death—with sensitivity, intelligence, honesty, and integrity. In the process, Green shows his readers what it is like to live with cancer, sometimes no more than a breath or a heartbeat away from death. But it is life that Green spiritedly celebrates here, even while acknowledging its pain. In its every aspect, this novel is a triumph. (Cart 2012a)

• • •

Legions of its fans rushed to the epically popular film into which the book was made. This translated into equally epic box office receipts (grosses of more than $125 million as of February 2016), but the film was also a *succès d'estime*—of sorts. In his *New York Times* review, critic A. O. Scott wrote, "The movie, like the book before it, is an expertly built machine for the mass production of tears. Directed by Josh Boone with scrupulous respect for John Green's best-selling young adult novel, the film sets out to make you weep—not just sniffle or choke up a little, but sob until your nose runs and your face turns blotchy. It succeeds" (Scott 2014).

More than a successful novelist, Green has become a force of nature, named to *Times's* list of 100 most influential people and to *Forbes* magazine's Celebrity 100 list. His status as a celebrity has been cemented by the videos that—as the Vlogbrothers—he and his brother Hank began posting in 2006 to YouTube. This led to Green's creation of the Nerdfighters, a loose confederation of fans who now number in the millions.

"Nerdfighters weren't against anything," Margaret Talbot explains in the *New Yorker*, "they were simply proud to immerse themselves in interests that others might find geeky and arcane. Through an annual charity event, the Project for Awesome, nerdfighters have raised hundreds of thousands of dollars for one another's favorite causes" (Talbot, 61). In 2013, an appearance by the Green brothers sold out Carnegie Hall ("The sold-out show put on full view Mr. Green's uncanny knack for channeling the voice of marginalized but smart, self-identifying nerds") (Kaufman 2013).

In the meantime, Vlogbrothers, "which has more than two million subscribers, has become the anchor of an online empire that now includes the Crash Course videos, short educational lectures with animation accompaniments" (Talbot 2014, 64).

All this hyperactivity has impacted the way teens read Green's books. According to Talbot: "In a different era, 'The Fault in Our Stars' could have been that kind of cultish book. For many young people today, however, reading is not an act of private communication with an author whom they imagine vaguely, if at all, but a prelude to a social experience—following the author on Twitter (Green has 1.4 million followers), meeting other readers, collaborating with them on projects, writing fan fiction. In our connected age, even books have become interactive phenomena" (68).

Green's many-splendored successes have had their downside. Author and publisher David Levithan says that Green does not always get his professional due. "People think of him as a great marketer, when in fact he is a great writer" (Kaufman 2013).

Whether as marketer or as writer, Green remains remarkably influential in the field of young adult literature and his work, as I mentioned earlier, has sparked the form's return to realism. Indeed, the *Wall Street Journal* has praised Green for "ushering in a new golden era for contemporary, realistic, literary teen fiction, following more than a decade of dominance by books about young wizards, sparkly vampires, and dystopia" (Badavi 2014).

"Everybody benefits from his popularity," Joy Peskin, vice-president and editorial director at Farrar Straus and Giroux, says. "He's brought countless readers into stores, and a rising tide lifts all ships" (Corbett 2014, 28).

However, Sue Corbett suggests that a non-Green novel, Rainbow Rowell's *Eleanor and Park,* also helped spark the return to realism: "St. Martin's" (the book's publisher) "has gone back to print 28 times for a total of nearly 500,000 copies since *Eleanor and Park's* March 2013 release. Combine that with the astronomical success of John Green's *The Fault in Our Stars*—more than 7 million copies in print—and you have a one-two punch that has gotten the entire publishing world's attention" (26).

"I'm sure there are editors all over town saying, 'I'm comping' (comparing) this to *Eleanor and Park* or to *The Fault in Our Stars,*'" says Peskin. "Right now taking on a contemporary book is not seen as an indulgence. There's a recognition that there are opportunities to break these books out" (28). "Especially if the books have crossover appeal," adds Beverly Horowitz, who edited Delacorte's big spring 2014 YA title *We Were Liars* by E. Lockhart (28).

Crossover? To explore *that* phenomenon, we turn to chapter nine. But first a quick nod to the importance to contemporary YA of film adaptations, the most successful recently being that of, yes, *The Fault in Our Stars.*

What is significant is the healthy symbiosis going on here, that is, book fans promise successful movies, while successful movies promise book fans. "After all the idea behind movie adaptations, besides franchise-building, is to give readers a new opportunity to walk through their favorite world. It's a chance to fall in love with the characters all over again when readers can see the books come to life. It's like a little reward for loving the books" (Strickland 2013b).

Ellie Berger, president of trade publishing at Scholastic, adds: "When a great book finds a new life on the big screen, it drives people who have never discovered them from movies to the books" (Robehmed 2015). Berger (2015) explains that publishers can see more than a 10 percent lift in book sales around the time a movie version is released. "Once the movie comes and goes, we are still able to sell strongly as we do now with the Hunger Games."

In addition to inspiring readers to return to their favorite books, I would argue, films inspire new fans for YA who are looking for pleasure in reading as well as in viewing.

The economic impact of this is staggering. Largely because of the sales of their books for motion picture development, four of the sixteen writers on the *Forbes* 2015 list of top-earning authors were YA writers: John Green, Veronica Roth, Suzanne Collins, and J. K. Rowling.

If there is a downside to this, it is that it reinforces the blockbuster mentality that is endemic to the field. "It's all tied into movies," David Gale says (personal correspondence, May 28, 2015). The International Movie Data Base agrees: "Adapting movies from Young Adult books has become an unstoppable juggernaut" (www.imdb.com/poll/imoLBOnpld4/). The scope of the movement is reflected in a recent *Los Angeles Times* article describing twenty-five young adult novels turned into films. MTV went *The Times* twenty-five better with its survey ranking fifty Young Adult film adaptations from "worst to first."

What's fascinating about this is the fact that history is, in a way, repeating itself. In the late eighties and early nineties, a manuscript wasn't accepted unless it showed potential for lavish paperback sales. Today the same manuscript won't be accepted unless it shows a potential for development as a movie. *Plus* ça *change* . . .

Now as to those crossovers . . .

Notes

1. My own personal affirmation of this came when, in the fall of 2000, I was browsing in the YA section of the Barnes and Noble store in my then hometown of Chico, CA, and—to my astonishment—came across several hardcover copies of my then newly published book *Tomorrowland*.

2. A thirteenth, *Gossip Girl Psycho Killer*, brought Blair and Serena back for an encore appearance as serial killers!

3. It should be noted, at least in passing, that starting with volume nine, the Gossip Girl books—and the later spin-off series—were all ghost-written, though they continued to bear von Ziegesar's name as "author."

4. Such "blended" books are usually called "mashups."

5. By the time the seventh title was published in 2007, the first printing had grown to 12 million copies and the book sold an unbelievable 8.3 million copies in the first twenty-four hours of publication—that's 50,000 copies per minute!

6. Fascinatingly, E. L. James's steamy adult novel *50 Shades of Grey* began as *Twilight* fan fiction!

9

So, How Adult *Is* Young Adult?

The Crossover Conundrum

THOUGH *CROSSOVER BOOKS* IS A RELATIVELY NEW TERM, AT LEAST ONE aspect of the phenomenon it contemplates—the notion that young people will read books published for adults—is scarcely a new one. Three hundred years ago, for example, children were avidly reading *Robinson Crusoe* and *Gulliver's Travels*—so many, in fact, that over the years these classics have come to be regarded as children's books. More recently, so many teens have read and embraced *Seventeenth Summer, The Catcher in the Rye, A Separate Peace, To Kill a Mockingbird,* and *Lord of the Flies* that it is now commonplace to say that if these books were published today, they'd be released as YA. But until recently publishers seemed oddly unwilling to capitalize on this.

Only twenty-seven years ago, for example, Betty Carter (1988, 60), who had chaired the 1986 Best Books for Young Adults Committee, wrote a fascinating article for *School Library Journal* in which she wryly noted that *The New York Times*, in its review of Marianne Gingher's newly published short story collection *Teen Angel*, stated, "It is perhaps even more damaging to the author's reputation as a writer for grown ups that the American Library Association named Ms. Gingher's novel *Bobby Rex's Greatest Hit* one of its Best Books for Young Adults for 1986."

That situation was about to change. In fact, it already had in another category of publishing: picture books for children.

Picture Book Crossovers

"Say 'crossover book' to most people in the industry," Sally Lodge (1992, 38) wrote in 1992, "and they immediately focus on the picture book that appeals to adults as well as kids." This new interest in a form that previously had been targeted at kids in the kindergarten through grade three group had begun in the late 1980s with the publication of Jon Scieszka and Lane Smith's *The True Story of the Three Little Pigs* (Viking 1989). The instant success of this wackily irreverent, ironic, sophisticated, and offbeat retelling of a classic story quickly attracted the attention of other innovative authors and artists such as William Joyce, J. Otto Sebold, Maira Kalman, and Istvan Banyai. When Scieszka and Smith's second collaboration, *The Stinky Cheese Man* (Viking 1992), received both a Caldecott honor medal and a spot on the Best Books for Young Adults list in 1993, the success of this new crossover form was cemented. I experienced the new crossover phenomenon at first hand when, in the early nineties, I served as a consultant for a children's bookstore in Beverly Hills, California, and each afternoon began noticing a clutch of teenagers entering the store, heading to the picture book section, and spending the rest of the afternoon there admiring and exclaiming over the books they were finding. Clearly something was afoot.

When I subsequently spoke with Viking's president and publisher Regina Hayes about this, she acknowledged the sophistication of these picture books but argued, "There's very little that escapes kids. They're growing up in a highly visual age and because they are subject to influences that are so much broader than they used to be—sophisticated graphics, TV, comics, magazines, and so forth—they grow up with a sense of parody that wasn't part of kids' consciousness before." Hayes also saluted the earlier, seminal influence of the late James Marshall (creator of The Stupids, George and Martha, The Cutups, Miss Nelson, and so on). "When I first saw Jim's books, I said 'This is something really new.' I began to realize," she continued, "in part because my own kids responded so strongly to his books and never seemed to outgrow them that his humor appealed on many different levels" (Cart 1995b, 695).

Another artist who shook up the storytelling strategies and design conventions of the picture book while expanding its audience to older readers was David Macaulay, whose groundbreaking *Black and White* received the Caldecott Medal in 1989 and inspired the late Eliza Dresang's pioneering critical work *Radical Change: Books for Youth in a Digital Age* (Wilson 1999).

Macaulay, of course, is notable not only for his interest in the architecture of the picture book. but also that of cathedrals, castles, pyramids, mosques, and even the human body, all subjects of his continuing series of nonfiction picture books that examine, in extraordinarily detailed drawings, how things are built and the way they work. In book after book, Macaulay (1991, 419) showed, as he stated in his Caldecott acceptance speech, "that it is essential to see, not merely to look, that words and pictures can support each other; that it isn't necessary to think in a straight line to make sense; and, finally, that risk can be rewarded."

Still other risk-taking artists have followed, all of them creating unconventional picture books that challenge expectations and excite the attention of older readers. Chief among them is Peter Sis, the Czech-American artist, whose sometimes autobiographical books like *The Wall* (2007), *Tibet: Inside the Red Box* (1998), and *The Three Golden Keys* (1994) are marvels of creative energy, thematic subtlety, and visual imagination. Both his picture book biography of Charles Darwin, *The Tree of Life*, and his autobiographical book *The Wall* were selected as Best Books for Young Adults.

The Marketing and Maturing of the Crossover

With the ice of a multigenerational market broken, publishers reversed direction and began cautiously experimenting with promoting YA books to adults, helped along by the word-of-mouth discovery by twenty- and thirty-something-aged readers of Francesca Lia Block's five Weetzie Bat books. These were collected and published in an omnibus volume in 1998 with the title *Dangerous Angels*.

"We're giving it an adult trade trim with an adult look and a quote from 'Spin' magazine," its publisher Joanna Cotler explained, adding, "We're also giving it a reading group brochure like our adult books"[1] (Rosen 1997, 29). To further its cross-market appeal, the book was listed in both Harper's adult and children's catalogs.

Robert Cormier was another author whose work had always demonstrated potential crossover appeal, never more so than with his most ambitious novel *Fade*, which Delacorte published as a YA title in 1988 and then released as a mass-market adult paperback the next year. Two years after that, the book was reissued as a YA trade paperback. Similarly, Scholastic first issued

Walter Dean Myers's Vietnam War novel *Fallen Angels* as a YA hardcover and then as a mass market adult paperback. The same thing would happen with A. M. Homes's novel *Jack* and Philip Pullman's *Golden Compass.*

Pullman's extremely sophisticated metaphysical fantasy would probably have excited adult interest without any particular help from its American publisher, Knopf. But Knopf's parent company, Random House, pulled out all the promotional stops, giving the 1996 book a $250,000[2] marketing budget and offering a classic case study of how a children's book could cut across the lines implicitly dividing the myriad imprints that comprise a major publishing house. Thus, Del Ray, Random's adult fantasy/science fiction imprint, quickly acquired paperback rights to *Compass* and its two projected sequels, while Random House Audio Books acquired its own rights, making *Compass* the first so-called children's book that Random House had ever put on tape. Carl Lennertz, then Director of Marketing for the Knopf Group, ordered a thousand advance reading copies and sent them to independent booksellers and wholesalers with a note saying (rather patronizingly, it now seems), "Dear Bookseller: Be a kid again" (Alderdice 1996, 24). Subsequently 7,000 copies of a more lavish advance reader's copy were distributed to librarians, reviewers, and booksellers. Both the Book of the Month Club and the Children's Book of the Month Club then chose *Compass* as an Alternate Selection.

In the years since, the crossover book has become such an engrained publishing phenomenon that it is hard to believe that, as relatively recently as 1992, Sally Lodge was writing, "[adults] seem to shun the idea of reading a novel published as a young adult book. One of the key barriers appears to be adults' lack of interest in reading about a young protagonist" (Lodge 1992, 38). Or that *Bobby Rex's Greatest Hit* could ever have been called "one of the relatively rare books that transcends age as a criterion for potential readership" (Carter 1988, 60).

If Block, Cormier, Pullman, and—later—Rowling and Collins demonstrated that adults would, indeed, read about young protagonists in books published (at least initially) for young readers, then three other books clearly evidenced the coming of age of the crossover phenomenon and the increased blurring of the line that divided adult from young adult books (and vice versa): the first of these was British writer Mark Haddon's *The Curious Incident of the Dog in the Nighttime* (2003), the second was Canadian author Yann Martel's *Life of Pi* (2001), and the third was American author Curtis Sittenfeld's *Prep* (2004).

Perhaps because Haddon was already an established writer for children in England, *Curious Incident,* a haunting story of a teenage boy with Asperger's Syndrome, was published there in simultaneous children's and adult editions. When it was subsequently released in the United States, however, it appeared only as an adult title, although it immediately became hugely popular with young adult readers. A similar thing happened with Martel's exquisitely inventive *Life of Pi,* which was also published in the United States as an adult title. In this case, however, Harcourt, its publisher, recognized the title's crossover appeal and subsequently issued a YA paperback edition.

Why American publishers cannot simply replicate the sensible British model of simultaneous publication has been much discussed and debated in the years since. Meg Rosoff, an American-born author living in London whose Printz Award–winning *How I Live Now* was published there in both YA and adult editions, has said "there's less of a stigma against young adult literature" in Britain (Rabb 2008, 23).

Be that as it may, the crossover phenomenon has excited as much interest in the United Kingdom as it has in the United States. In 2008 Amanda Craig, children's book critic of *The London Times,* wrote, "Crossover books—novels that appeal to adults as much as they do to children—are the publishing phenomenon of the past decade." Craig (2008) attributes the success of the crossover book to the plodding dullness of contemporary adult literary fiction. "It is the power of story-telling which, however, lies at the heart of the crossover novel's rise."

Perhaps so, though the Canadian academic Jeffrey Canton, credits marketing, not story, and believes the origins of the phenomenon can be traced to the land down under. "This whole notion of cross-marketing is really, in fact, an Australian notion. They've done it very successfully with a number of writers" (MacDonald 2005, 20). Of course, some English observers also credit the Aussies with having introduced YA fiction to England in the first place. "In the UK, fiction for 'young adults' has grown hugely over the past decade," Rachel Cooke (Cooke 2003) wrote in 2003, "we got the idea from Australia"—and from the United States, I would hasten to add!

Be that as it may, Australia does seem to have developed an extraordinary cadre of gifted, home-grown YA authors, whose work is often both cross-marketed and cross-published there. Brilliant writers like Markus Zusak, Margo Lanagan, and Sonya Hartnett belong in this category, though all are published only as YA in the United States, where their work has regularly—and deservedly—received Printz Prize recognition and attracted growing legions of adult readers.

Nevertheless, a certain sense of stigma about being published as YA lingers, at least in the United States. Consider that Sittenfeld's hugely successful first novel *Prep* was reportedly rejected by fourteen American publishers before Random House accepted it; "and at least half of them said no because they thought it was YA," Sittenfeld told fellow author Margo Rabb. Rabb, whose own first novel *Cures for Heartbreak* was written for adults but published by Delacorte as YA, also had firsthand experience of this. When she told another writer at the MacDowell Colony, a prestigious writer's retreat in New Hampshire, that her first novel was being published as young adult, the other's response was a sniffy, "Oh, God. That's such a shame" (Rabb 2008, 23).

The rampant confusion—in England, Australia, Canada, and America—over precisely what constitutes the difference between adult and YA has captured the attention of both the professional and mass media and made the crossover book one of the most buzzed about phenomena in today's publishing world. Consider this sampling of articles that have appeared since 2002:

"Trend in Books: Tales Aimed at All Ages," by Phil Kloer, Cox News Service, October 6, 2002.

"Crossing Over: A Materials Selector Looks at Adult Books for Teen Readers," by Angelina Benedetti, *School Library Journal*, January 2003.

"YA Lit—Not Just for Kids Anymore," by Steve Sherman, *Bookselling This Week*, March 25, 2003.

"What Exactly Is a Children's Book?" by Nicolette Jones, *London Times*, April 30, 2004.

"YA for Everybody," by Steve MacDonald, *Quill and Quire*, February 2005.

"Growing Up," by Judith Rosen, *Publishers Weekly*, February 21, 2005.

"Why YA and Why Not," by Sue Corbett, *Publishers Weekly*, September 5, 2005.

"Crossover Books for Teens and Twentysomethings," by Gillian Engberg, *Booklist*, November 15, 2005.

"The Quest for Crossover Books," by Scott Jaschik, insidehighered.com, May 22, 2006.[3]

"Crossover Books—Time Out," by Amanda Craig, amandacraig.com, 2006.

"Redefining the Young Adult Novel," by Jonathan Hunt, *Horn Book,* March 2007.

"Teen Fiction Not Just for Teens Anymore," by Tina Kapinos, *Chicago Tribune,* June 27, 2007.

"Identity Crisis? Not Really," by Meg Rosoff, *Publishers Weekly,* October 22, 2007.

"The Grand Tradition of Crossover Novels," by Meg Rosoff, *Manchester Guardian,* 2008.

"An Author Looks Beyond Age Limits," by Motoko Rich, *New York Times,* February 20, 2008.

"Patterson Aplenty," by Matthew Thornton, *Publishers Weekly,* May 5, 2008.

"'Madapple': What Is a Crossover Book?" by Christina Meldrum, freshfiction.com, April 7, 2008.

"Young Adult Literature: Not Just for Teens Anymore," by Stephanie A. Squicciarni and Susan Person, *VOYA,* June 2008.

"I'm Y.A. and I'm O.K.," by Margo Rabb, *New York Times Book Review* July 7, 2008.

"Guilty Pleasures," by Misty Harris, *Ottawa Citizen,* October 26, 2008.

"Crossovers," by Michael Cart, *Booklist,* February 15, 2009.

"ALTAFF's 'Books without Boundaries: Crossover Fiction for YAs and Adults," by Barbara Hoffert. *Library Journal,* June 2012.

"Is Young Adult Fiction the New Chick Lit?" by Anna North. *Buzzfeed,* September 11, 2012.

"The Shortlist/YA Crossovers," by Jessica Bruder. *The New York Times Book Review,* September 22, 2013.

The Invasion of Adult Authors

Further confusing the distinction between adult and young adult is the increasing presence of established adult authors among the ranks of those now writing and being published for young adults. Attracted by the increasing profitability of writing for YAs (thanks to Harry Potter) and encouraged by publishers who seek to capitalize on these authors' already-established adult readerships, the list of these grows longer every day. Some of them—writers like Dave Barry, Ridley Pearson, Jodi Picoult, Clive Barker, Isabel Allende, Chitra Banerjee Divakaruni, John Feinstein, Carl Hiaasen, Jacquelyn

Mitchard, Robert B. Parker, Michael Winerip, Terry Pratchett, and James Patterson—are writing commercial or genre fiction. Others, however, attracted by the newly expansive artistic possibilities of the field, are writing literary fiction for YAs. In this category are the likes of Sherman Alexie, Julia Alvarez, Michael Chabon, Francine Prose, Joyce Carol Oates, Joyce Maynard, Cynthia Kadohata, Nick Hornby, Peter Cameron, Alice Hoffman, Ariel Dorfman, and others.

How significant—and sometimes confusing—crossover publishing, marketing, and selling have become is epitomized by the case of James Patterson, the best-selling author in the world from 2001–2014 (Chilton 2014).

His entry into the YA field in 2005 with a new series, Maximum Ride (coauthored by an uncredited Gabrielle Charbonnet), was, accordingly, big news—and an even bigger success. By early 2008 there were reportedly 4.8 million copies of the first three novels in the series in print. Nevertheless, when sales failed to match those of his adult titles, Patterson and his publisher Little, Brown decided to reposition the fourth volume, *The Final Warning*, marketing it as an adult title, redesigning the cover art, and raising the price from $16.99 to $20.00. So as not to lose the still-lucrative YA market, the new book was branded "A James Patterson Pageturner," and billed as being suitable "for readers from ten to a hundred and ten." (The phrase was reportedly coined by Patterson himself, who—before he became an author—was Chairman of the legendary J. Walter Thompson Advertising Agency.) Even more dramatic was Patterson's insistence that all of the Maximum Ride books—and another new YA series, The Dangerous Days of Daniel X—be displayed at the front of bookstores instead of in the children's/YA section and remain there for as long as any of his adult titles would. Subsequently the hardcovers were to be shelved with adult fiction. As a concession to younger fans, the then new titles were released six months after the hardcovers as YA trade paperbacks (Rich 2008).

Civilization will probably survive this, but the Patterson brouhaha is the clearest evidence yet that it is not necessarily readers, but revenue, that continues to drive the crossover phenomenon and that explains why it is not necessarily the editorial staff that determines whether a new book will be published as adult or as YA; instead it is often the sales and marketing staff. Which brings us back to Sittenfeld's *Prep* and Rabb's *Cures for Heartbreak*, both of which—though written as adult titles—could have been published profitably as YA, though only Rabb's was.

What Do You Mean "Young Adult"?

All of this conversation raises another question: what on earth do we now mean by that term *young adult*? Surely it no longer embraces only twelve- to eighteen-year-olds but must now also include nineteen- to twenty-five-year-olds (or even older, as the twelve to thirty-four MTV demographic has become an increasingly desirable market in publishing). Indeed, over the course of the last five or so years, coming of age itself has become a significantly more attenuated process and, as a result, a new category of human development has begun to appear that is being called, variously, "kiddults," "adultescents," "twixters," and "boomerangers."

This category started to show up when, because of economic hard times, more and more twenty-something Americans began returning home to live with their parents,[4] delaying commitments—to professions and partners alike—until their early thirties. And why not, because many of them—given increasing life expectancies and continuing economic hard times—are looking at living into their nineties and working until they're in their seventies. Who can blame them for not rushing to accept adult responsibilities? However, how to market to them and—if you're a librarian—how to serve them remains a continuing conundrum.

Further confusing the issue is new research that confounds our long-held belief that the human brain is fully wired by the age of twelve. Now scientists have demonstrated that the brain continues to grow until the early or mid-twenties and that the last part to mature is the prefrontal cortex, which is responsible for such adult behavior as impulse control, the regulation of emotions and moral reasoning (Raeburn 2004, 26).

"The age at which Americans reach adulthood is increasing," psychologist Robert Epstein told *Psychology Today* in 2007. "30 is the new 20," he continued, "and most Americans now believe a person isn't an adult until age 26" (Marano 2007).

"Most Americans" includes the medical community, too. Between 1994 and 2005 nearly one thousand doctors were certified in a new subspecialty: adolescent medicine. And Massachusetts General Hospital for Children is now (2016) only one of many prestigious institutions to have added a new Division of Adolescent and Young Adult Medicine. As Kantrowitz and Springen (2005, 65) write, "The old view of adolescence was that it ended at 18 or 19. Now, with many young adults in their early 20s still struggling to find their foothold in the world, doctors call the years from 18 to 28 the second decade of adolescence."

These are all complicated issues, but one way to begin addressing them is, as I mentioned earlier, to consider redefining young adult. As it now stands, the term—at least as applied to literature—includes books for readers as young as ten (the category includes middle-school literature for ten- to fourteen-year-olds) and as old as twenty-five. My suggestion would be to leave the middle-school age range as is but to be scrupulously careful to call it "middle school," not YA.

Literature for twelve- to eighteen-year-olds (or thirteen- to nineteen-year-olds) could officially be described as Teen (a descriptor that more and more public libraries are using anyway for what had formerly been called young adult services); and books for eighteen- to twenty-five-year-olds could be categorized as young adult or new adult, the latter of which has increasingly become the popular descriptor of choice and about which we will talk a bit later. Granted, there's a good deal of overlap among these categories but, after all, the folks they contemplate don't fall into rigidly defined demographics— they are all individuals who grow and mature at different rates and, accordingly, have different individual needs, interests, and appetites. And they should be encouraged to range freely among these three divisions, reading up or down as their needs and interests dictate.

I don't offer this suggestion whimsically, fully recognizing that—as I wrote in my January 2005 "Carte Blanche" column—"the biggest impediment to making this change a practical reality is that it contemplates creating a new area" (or areas, I would now say) "in libraries and bookstores; it might also mean reorganizing publishing or, at the very least, encouraging the children's and adult sides of publishing houses to communicate and publish cooperatively" (always the starry-eyed dreamer, I) (838).

According to *Publishers Weekly*, a few independent bookstores had already, in the mid-aughts, started cautiously experimenting with adding new sections for titles with appeal to older adolescents (or younger "adultescents!") (Rosen 2008). And the YALSA Board, at its 2009 annual meeting, approved the Serving New Adults Interest Group and charged it with "discuss[ing] issues relating to serving young adults in their late teens and early twenties. We seek to develop and exchange ideas," the conveners continued, "on how libraries can continue to best serve these 'new adults' as they navigate life after the high school years."[5]

Meanwhile, so many books are now appearing, willy-nilly, with reader appeal that crosses over from eighteen to twenty-five that, since 2004, I've been reviewing them for *Booklist* as a separate category of adult books (Cart 2009) Significantly, *Prep* was one of the first I reviewed.

These books typically have several features in common: many of them are first novels by writers who, themselves, are often in their twenties; their novels typically feature protagonists in their late teens or early twenties, characters who are—like Holden Caulfield before them—coming of age with various degrees of grace and success. Perhaps most significantly, though published as adult, almost all of these titles could easily have been published as YA had someone not determined they would be more advantageously (read profitably) published as adult.

The Alex Awards

Speaking of adult books for young adults brings us to YALSA's Alex Awards, a selection of the ten best adult books for young adults that has been assembled annually since 1998. In light of our lengthy discussion of the ongoing blurring of the boundary between adult and young adult books, this category-driven list might seem, at first blush, a bit regressive. But what Betty Carter noted in 2008 remains true today: "Alex winners put more books on the table for librarians to read and use for readers' advisory. And that's what Margaret Edwards" [the legendary YA librarian for whom the awards are named] "was about: wide reading and solid recommending in order to create lifetime readers of thousands of young adults" (Carter 2008, 22).

Spearheaded by Deborah D. Taylor, the former YALSA president, and funded by the Margaret Alexander Edwards Trust, the Alex Awards began in 1997 as a five-year YALSA project designed to investigate the use of adult books with young adult readers. It was the ad hoc committee appointed to administer this project that then recommended the creation of both an annual list of best books and also the presentation of a program at each annual ALA conference that would focus on some aspect of adult books for YAs. Thus it was that the first program, held in 1998, featured a lecture titled "Back to the Future with Adult Books for the Teenage Reader." Presented by Richard F. Abrahamson, professor of literature for children and young adults at the University of Houston, it offered a retrospective view of the historic importance to young adults and their reading of adult books; it also examined the continuing importance of nonfiction in stimulating teens' interest in reading adult books (Abrahamson is the coauthor with Betty Carter of the important book *Nonfiction for Young Adults from Delight to Wisdom* [1990]) and called for more future research on the relationship of adult books and teen readers while stressing the importance of providing teens with enhanced opportunities for free reading—of both YA and adult books.

The Alex Awards ultimately became a permanent YALSA fixture in 2002 when the five-year project concluded and the Board voted to perpetuate the list under the cosponsorship of *Booklist* magazine, which for a number of years has been adding four categories of repeat notes to adult titles to identify those with special interest to general teen readers, mature teens, teens with special interest in specific subjects, and those books with particular curriculum value. (See issues of *Booklist* for examples.)

As a result, 180 adult books have, to 2016, been named Alex winners. Viewed retrospectively, they are remarkable for the diversity of reading interests they represent, ranging from commercial and genre fiction to serious investigations of race, ethnicity, and civil rights, from sports to memoirs to science. But they also have some important elements in common: one is the large number of nonfiction titles included, particularly in the categories of biography, science, and narrative accounts of adventure; a second is the large number of first novels; and a third is the increasingly large number of what we would now call crossover books; (e.g., *The Curious Incident of the Dog in the Nighttime, Black Swan Green, Anansi Boys, The Kite Runner, Golden Boy, The Lovers' Dictionary, The Magicians, The Bride's Farewell*, and more).

And so it would seem that the Alex Awards themselves, while continuing to acknowledge the historic propensity of teens for reading adult books, have also inevitably reflected the changing nature of those adult books. One imagines that the redoubtable Margaret A. Edwards, who always had one eye firmly fixed on the future of teens and of reading, would be pleased.

And in the larger context of the many changes that continue to visit young adult literature, one thing that Abrahamson said in his above-mentioned Edwards Lecture remains singularly apposite: "If we truly cared about creating lifetime readers," he noted, "we wouldn't be talking about either young adult books or adult books, we'd be discussing the need to use both" (Abrahamson 1998, 383).

New Adult: Steamy or Serious?

A new name for nineteen- to twenty-five-year-olds, New Adult, was coined in 2009 by the publisher St. Martin's Press when it issued a call for "fiction similar to YA that can be published and marketed as adult—a sort of older YA or New Adult."

Has this resulted in the creation in New Adult of a new crossover genre? I decided to find out and reported the results in an August 10, 2014, *Booklist* article.

I queried a clutch of people in publishing to get their take on the situation. I started, appropriately, with St. Martin's itself. Here is what Editor Rose Hilliard had to say:

> My take on it is that New Adult is an offshoot of romance and is not connected to YA, because it's so sexy. New Adult characters are usually in their early twenties, which allows for a lot of emotional intensity, angst and high drama, elements that work very well in E (books), where readers have less patience for subtlety, detail, and nuance. But age of the protagonists aside, the New Adult on our list (and so much of what's working in the self-pubbed world) is aimed at adult romance readers. (Cart 2014a)

The references to self- and E-publishing remind us that New Adult began, and continues to be a vital presence, in the E (online) world. A paradigmatic figure here is surely indie (self-published) author Abbi Glines, whose two novels *The Vincent Boys* and *The Vincent Brothers* were originally published online as YA and—the dream of every indie author—were subsequently picked up by a major publisher, Simon and Schuster's YA imprint Simon Pulse. "We've focused a lot of our list attention on her," Pulse Publisher Mara Anastas acknowledges. "Her books are selling really, really well and she has a huge audience." Simon Pulse is currently publishing Glines's Sea Breeze series, while a Simon and Schuster adult imprint, Atria, is publishing a second series, Rosemary Beach.

Glines clearly has a crossover readership but, Anastas says, Pulse will soon be doing something by Glines that is "completely YA" adding that Pulse is "absolutely open" to publishing other New Adult novels when "the story is really compelling."

Another publisher with a crossover readership is Harlequin. Senior Editor Margo Lipschultz says, "We view the New Adult readership as primarily adult romance fans who enjoy the nostalgia of remembering their college (or college-age) years, though I do think there are older teens and college students who read and love these books as well."

Lipschultz continues: "We tend to look at New Adult as a romance subgenre revolving around college-age and early twenties protagonists and characterized by a younger, often first-person narrative voice. While New Adult rose to popularity as a subgenre that bridged the gap between contemporary YA and contemporary romance, it's gradually expanding to include paranormal romance and romantic suspense stories as well."

Nevertheless, "the vast majority of our New Adult titles are published under our adult romance and fiction imprints Harlequin HQN and Harlequin MIRA and in our flagship Digital Imprint Carina Press."

The importance of a digital readership is once again underscored by the fact that Random House has four adult digital-only imprints: HYDRA for science fiction/fantasy, ALIBI for mystery/suspense, LOVESWEPT for romance and women's fiction and the newest and most relevant, FLIRT, which targets "the rapidly growing college-age New Adult audience."

As for YA, Beverly Horowitz, VP and Publisher of Random House's Delacorte Press imprint, says she is not acquiring New Adult, "which is happening mostly online." Instead she cites "the wonderful YA crossover books" available now. "YA authors may explore older characters, that is, those in their later teens, but they remain rooted in the YA experience."

Like Horowitz, Elise Howard, Editor Publisher of Algonquin Books for Young Readers, reports:

> Right now I'm not planning to publish New Adult per se. My brief is to publish YA and I'm committed to making sure that the titles on my list are books that will appeal to a core YA audience. If these books attract an older readership, that's great. Signaling a readership that a book is published with them in mind doesn't exclude other readers from picking a title up and enjoying it. And my colleagues publishing primarily for an adult audience and I spend a lot of time talking about how we might cross[over] the boundaries of our core markets to reach additional readers. I do sometimes wonder if spending too much time focusing on the explosive growth in the adult readership of YA books will cause

YA publishers to drift more and more into NA at the expense of younger YA readers and I've heard some librarians and book-sellers lament a recent dearth of YA with innocent stories and younger—12–16-year-old—protagonists.

Although we tend to think of New Adult as a new phenomenon, one author, Francesca Lia Block, foreshadowed the genre by several decades with her Weetzie Bat books. "I feel I've been writing New Adult for twenty-five years," she says, "before there was even a term for it. I'm very interested in the years between adolescence and full adulthood as this time marks an important threshold in human development. For me it was a painful period of growth and exploration. I don't know how this category will affect YA. Some people consider it just a marketing ploy to sell more books (Is selling books so bad, anyway?), but for me it's more a case of naming a category that already exists in my oeuvre and my heart."

Stephen Roxburgh, publisher of namelos, cites another concern: "I'm per-plexed by the 'New Adult' category," he says. "Basically I think it's a publish-ing gambit to cross adult books down and YA up, which is as legitimate as any marketing gambit but practically it presents a problem: do we send the books to the adult reviewer or to the children's/YA reviewer? They don't like it when you send it to both. It's a sadness that these kinds of considerations are important. I should be able to send the book to everyone."

The late literary agent George Nicholson echoed that concern; he also felt that "much of this new publishing is for the moment and the season not backlist, which accounts for the continued long life of most serious YA pub-lishing."

This raises the question: Is the entire genre ephemeral? Simon Pulse editor Anastas speaks to that point when she says, "New Adult fiction is essentially escapist (although) I think there will always be contemporary sexy, steamy books but what we choose to call that category may change."

Sexy and steamy or serious? It's interesting that few of those interviewed acknowledged that there are a variety of books being published by YA imprints that are actually New Adult. Little, Brown's Director of School and Library Marketing Victoria Stapleton cites Sara Zarr and Tara Altebrando's *Roomies* (2013) for one. But I would add Libba Bray's *Beauty Queens* (2011) from Scholastic, Rainbow Rowell's *Fangirl* (2013) from St. Martin's Griffin, Paul Rudnick's *Gorgeous* (2013) from Scholastic, Aidan Chambers's *This Is All* (2006) from Abrams, Sharon Biggs Waller's *A Mad Wicked Folly* (2014) from

Viking, Leslye Walton's *The Strange and Beautiful Sorrows of Ava Lavender* (2014) from Candlewick, and many others.

But what's in a name? It's unlikely that readers will be hung up on what this new genre is called. What they're interested in is content regardless of whether it's YA or NA. And after all, it's the readers who will always have the final word (Cart 2014a).

Another Seismic Shift

In a September 13, 2012, press release the R. R. Bowker Company revealed the following stunning information: "More than half the consumers of books classified for young adults aren't all that young. Fully 55 percent of buyers of works that publishers designate for kids aged 12 to 17—nicknamed YA books—are 18 or older, with the largest segment aged 30 to 44. Accounting for 28 percent of sales, these adults aren't just purchasing for others—when asked about the intended recipient, they report that 78 percent of the time they are purchasing books for their own reading."

What could account for this? It was less than a decade ago that teens were regarded as the überconsumers of young adult books and now it's adults? Yes, and the reason is contained in the following three words: Collins, Rowling, Meyer. Thirty percent of those queried in the Bowker survey said they were reading Suzanne Collins. "The remaining 70 percent reported a vast variety of titles (over 220), only two of which commanded more than five percent of overall sales—*Harry Potter and the Deathly Hallows* and *Breaking Dawn*. Although best sellers lead, there's a long tail of rich reading that has interesting implications for the publishers of YA books in terms of discovery and consumer relationships," said Bowker project editor Kristen McLean.

As understatement this is tantamount to saying Godzilla is just a large lizard! The numbers are overwhelming. Reporting in the February 24, 2014 issue of *Publishers Weekly*, Jim Milliot wrote: "The popularity of the young adult category is driven largely by adult book buyers. Readers 18 and older accounted for 79 percent of young adult unit purchases in the December 2012 through November 2013 period, according to Nielsen. The single largest demographic group buying young adult titles in the period was the 18- to 29-year-old age bracket" (Milliot 2014).

The news continues: "When 'PW' recently compiled its list of the top-selling titles of the first half of 2014 using Nielsen BookScan figures, the top six were YA novels: the three books in the Divergent Trilogy, along with three editions of John Green's 'The Fault in Our Stars'" (Rosen 2014).

Meanwhile *The Los Angeles Times* reported

> A spokesperson for Scholastic estimated that half of the 50 mil-lion+ buyers of Suzanne Collins' bestselling young adult series, the "Hunger Games," are adults. A spokesperson for HarperCollins, publisher of Veronica Roth's bestselling "Divergent" series, also said that 50% of the series' readers were older than twenty-five, based on information on the book-referral website Good Reads.com. (Carpenter 2012)

This market shift has obvious implications for book sales. A Flavorwire.com headline, "Are You an Adult Who Reads YA Novels? Congratulations, You Saved Publishing in 2014," may be overdramatic, but it is inarguably true that figures through the first eight months of the year showed that while adult fiction and nonfiction sales were down 3.3 percent, the sales of children's and young adult were up 22.4 percent (Sturgeon 2014).

The message here may well be "don't mess with success," which could mean a continuing emphasis on the publication of serial fiction à la Collins, Rowling, and Meyer, but the stand-alone novel is inarguably getting a boost from John Green, whose *The Fault in Our Stars* has sold more than 10 million copies and grossed more than $300 million worldwide (Wholf 2014) resulting, as Scholastic editor Aimee Friedman told PBS Newshour, in "the pendulum (swinging) toward John Green lit as people call it. Contemporary realistic stories about teens facing everyday things in their lives" (2014). Nevertheless, whether it is serial or stand-alone, the focus clearly remains on event publishing and the relentless search for the next blockbuster. In the meantime, the essential fact remains that adults are buying—and reading—YA books in record numbers.

Not everyone is happy with that fact. In June 2014, the writer Ruth Graham 2014) caused a great stir when, at Slate.com, she published a scathing indictment of adults reading YA.

"Adults," she huffed, "should feel embarrassed about reading literature being written for children. Life is short," she continued, "and the list of truly great books for adults is so long." To make her point she spent most of her screed—er, article—denigrating young adult literature. Her opinions elicited a flurry of articles *contra* Graham; my favorite is headlined "Read Whatever the Hell You Want" (Minkel,2014). In my *Booklist* column "Carte Blanche," I wrote my own piece taking issue with Graham's arguments. Because it encapsulates my thinking on the subject, I'm including it here:

"So, adults, are you ashamed of reading young adult literature? Journalist Ruth Graham thinks you should be. Writing in an article titled "Against YA," which appeared in the online magazine *Slate,* she averred, "Read whatever you want. But you should be embarrassed when what you're reading was written for children." Really? Young adults are children? Since when? Well, apparently since Graham herself was a YA, for, she writes, "Books like *The Westing Game* and *Tuck Everlasting* provided some of the most intense reading experiences of my life." Doesn't she know those are children's books? I wonder if, when she was a YA, she was embarrassed to be reading *them?* Apparently not but she betrays the same kind of confusion when she goes on to write, of John Green's *The Fault in Our Stars,* "Hmm, that's a nicely written book for 13-year-olds." Say what? *13-year-olds?* Either this woman is entirely clueless or she's trying to denigrate *The Fault in Our Stars.* Actually replace the word "or" in the previous sentence with "and" and you may be on to something—the fact that she's trying to denigrate the entire body of young adult literature when apparently she knows only two YA novels: *The Fault in Our Stars* and *Eleanor and Park,* the only two she cites (well, she does mention *Divergent* and *Twilight,* for the opportunity of dismissing them, saying "no one defends [them] as serious literature." But who said they did?).

If her article is, thus, an exercise in extrapolation, how can she reliably generalize by going on to say, "even the myriad defenders of YA fiction admit that the enjoyment of reading this stuff" (YA literature) "has to do with escapism, instant gratification, and nostalgia." Reader, is your blood boiling? Mine is. After all, are adults in pursuit of escapism, instant gratification, and nostalgia when they read Aidan Chambers's *This Is All,* a closely observed, psychologically acute story of a teenage girl that ends (spoiler alert!) with her death? Or how about Markus Zusak's thematically rich, award-winning *The Book Thief,* or Paolo Bacigalupi's darkly dystopian *Ship Breaker?* Are these exercises in escapism or instant gratification or nostalgia? I think not. But wait, Graham has more to say: "But if they" (adult readers) "are substituting maudlin teen dramas for the complexity of great adult literature, then they are missing something."

Sure, there are maudlin teen dramas but not all are maudlin by a long shot and as for complexity, how about the work of David Almond, Philip Pullman, Margo Lanagan, or M. T. Anderson?

And then there are those endings: "YA endings are uniformly *satisfying,*" (her italics, not mine) "whether that satisfaction comes through weeping or cheering." Is the ending of Andrew Smith's most recent, *Grasshopper Jungle,* which concludes with the world's being taken over by giant carnivorous praying mantises, satisfactory? To paraphrase T. S. Eliot, "This is the way the world ends, not with a bang but with your head being bitten off by a big bug!" This is more shudder-inducing than satisfying, I say. Or how about a YA classic, *The Chocolate War?* Is its dark ending "satisfying"? Yes, it is but not in the way Graham uses the word. Nevertheless, she relentlessly continues: "But wanting endings like this" (ones that are "wrapped up neatly") "is no more ambitious than only wanting to read books with 'likable' protagonists." For an unlikable protagonist look no farther than Amanda Maciel's *Tease* and its protagonist, who is a teen who has bullied another teen to death. Or for a book whose ending is *not* wrapped up neatly look no farther than Leslye Walton's *The Strange and Beautiful Sorrows of Ava Lavender.*

Most damning of Graham's allegations is arguably her claim that "These are the books that could plausibly be said to be replacing literary fiction in the lives of their adult readers. And that's a shame." The real shame is that Graham apparently feels there are no literary young adult novels. On the contrary, I can offer as examples all the winners of the Michael L. Printz Award and the many Printz honor titles as well, all of which represent the best YA novels of the year based solely on literary merit.

After all, these books are judged on such considerations as characterization, story, voice, style, setting, theme, etc.—all considerations that define adult literary fiction. In fact, YA literature satisfies all of T. S. Eliot's three permanent reasons for reading: (1) the acquisition of wisdom; (2) the enjoyment of art; and (3) the pleasure of entertainment.

So is it really true that, as Graham claims, "Fellow grown-ups, at the risk of sounding snobbish and joyless and old, we are better than this"? Replace "snobbish" with "pretentious," I say, and you have a nice encapsulation of Graham's entire article. After all, this is a woman who claims that *her* extracurricular reading in high school was John Updike and Alice Munro, and that she's gotten "purer plot-based highs recently from books by Charles Dickens and Edith Wharton."

The bottom line is that readers of any age can empathize with the fully realized characters who inhabit the best of YA. And they can enjoy the pleasures of art, wisdom, and entertainment, too. For all of which I declare—

despite Graham—I'm proud to read young adult literature. And I'll bet you are, too (Cart 2014b).

• • •

Distinguished adult author Meg Wolitzer agrees, writing, in *The New York Times*, "I don't feel obliged to cast off my teenage reading habits as if they were the Earth Shoes I wore at 13. Books not only sometimes stay with you; they can become you. And as for the YA war? When you're deep in a good book, you won't even hear the drumbeats" (Wolitzer 2014).

Let these be the last words on the subject as we move, now, to the real world and its challenges.

Notes

1. I had the pleasure of writing it.

2. This is close to $500,000 today (i.e., 2016).

3. This interesting article demonstrates the ubiquity of the crossover phenomenon, which has now invaded academic publishing where the term describes the attempt to find books with crossover appeal to the mainstream market.

4. In 2012, 36 percent of those aged eighteen to thirty-one were living in their parents' home (Fry 2013).

5. Unfortunately, this group is moribund as of February 2016.

Meanwhile, Back in the Real World

Diversity, Mixed Race, Risk-Taking, and Other Realities of Teen Life

"America reached an important milestone in 2011. That occurred when, for the first time in the history of the country, more minority babies than white babies were born in a year."

—*William. H. Frey, "Diversity Explosion," 2015*

HERE, FOR STARTERS, ARE SOME STATISTICS: ACCORDING TO THE 2010 CEN-sus, the United States population totals 308,745,538. Of that number, 20,677,194 are aged ten to fourteen (an increase of 0.9 percent over the 2000 census), while 22,040,343 are aged fifteen to nineteen (an increase of 9 percent over 2000). Together these numbers represent 13.8 percent of the total population (US Census Bureau 2010). But by themselves they don't reflect the increasing diversity of America. For that, note the following: from 2000 to 2010 the Asian population increased more than four times faster than the total US population, growing from 10.2 million to 14.7 million (The Asian Population 2010; 2010 Census Briefs. March 2012).

During the same period the African American population grew, too, though more slowly from 34.7 million to 38.9 million (The Black Population 2010; 2010 Census Briefs, September 2011).

The Hispanic population reflected the greatest numerical growth, increasing from 35.3 million to 50.5 million (The Hispanic Population 2010; 2010 Census Briefs, May 2011).

By 2012, updated census figures showed that young people aged ten to eighteen represented 13.6 percent of the US population. More than 16 percent of them were African-American, 12.2 percent were Asian-American, and 17.7 percent were Hispanic (Strickland 2014). Together, the minorities totaled 45.9 percent of the youth population, while whites totaled 54.1 percent, but at the present rate of change, it is projected that by 2018, children and teens of color will have become the majority youth population. Furthermore, by 2060, the percentage of Hispanic children is expected to reach 34 percent, while the percentage of white, non-Hispanic children will drop to 36 percent. Add African-American and Asian youth to the mix and together children who belong to ethnic or racial minority groups will comprise 64 percent of the total youth population.

As for all ages, by 2060 Hispanics will comprise 29 to 31 percent (estimates vary) of the total population; African Americans, 13 percent, and Asians, 9 percent, making the overall white population—at 47 percent—a minority (Passel and Cohn 2008).

These are enormous changes but there is at least one more to consider: for the first time in history the 2000 census allowed respondents to self-identify as being of more than one race. This option remained available on the 2010 Census. As a result, "across the country, 9 million people—or 2.9 percent of the population—chose more than one race on the last (2010) census, an increase of about 32 percent over 2000. (Those who reported a single race grew by only 9 percent)" (Deal 2012). It should be mentioned that a 2015 Pew Research study updates these figures, reporting that mixed race persons now constitute 6.9 percent of the population and that population is expected to triple by 2060 (Kunkle 2015).

The Pew Study also finds that the number of interracial marriages has increased dramatically from 1.6 percent in 1980 to 6.3 percent in 2013 (2015). One in seven new marriages is now between spouses of different races or ethnicities (Saulny 2011), 18 percent of unmarried couples (1.2 million), and 21 percent of same sex couples are now interracial (Jayson 2012).

More significantly for our purposes, "since 2000, among American children, the multiracial population has increased almost 50 percent to 4.2 million, making it the fastest growing youth group in the country" (Saulny 2011). Indeed, the percentage of children born to mixed-race parents has grown from 1 percent in 1970 to 10 percent in 2013 (Kunkle 2015).

The cultural implications of this are compelling: as early as 2004 *The New York Times* was reporting that "(ethnic) ambiguity is chic" and "using faces that are ethnically ambiguous is the latest youth marketing trend" (LaFeria 2004, E1). "There's not only less stigma to being in these groups, there's even positive cachet," according to Jeffrey S. Passel, a senior demographer at the Pew Hispanic Center (Saulny 2011).

Accelerating this trend to acceptance is the increasing number of public figures offering mixed-race role models—Tiger Woods, Keanu Reeves, Norah Jones, Halle Berry, Mariah Carey, Bruno Mars, Dwayne Johnson, Alicia Keys, and—not least—President Barack Obama!

A Literature of Diversity?

Given these extraordinary statistics and the sweeping social changes they represent, one wonders if we are any closer to offering young readers a viable literature of similar diversity and complexity? It is very difficult to marshal reliable numbers to answer that question, but the Cooperative Children's Book Center at the University of Wisconsin—Madison, has been making a heroic effort to provide them since 1985. That was the year it began tracking the number of books being published by and about African Americans, but it soon expanded that purview. As the staff explained, "Because of the great interest in these statistics and with the increasing concern for accurate and authentic portrayals of people of color in literature for children, in 1994 we began keeping statistics for the numbers of books by and about American Indians, Asian/Pacific Americans, and Latinos, as well (as African Americans)" (www.education.wisc.edu/ccbc).

Jason Low, publisher of Lee and Low, one of the country's few minority-owned publishing companies says, "Diversity is the missing piece of the puzzle in children's books and the CCBC has had its fingers on the pulse of this issue from the very beginning" (Gilmore 2015a).

In terms of actual numbers, the CCBC estimates that it received 3,500 books from publishers in 2014. Of this number a mere 180 were about African Americans; 38 were about American Indians; 112 were about Asian Americans and only 66 were about Latinos.

The situation is even worse if you limit the number of books to those created by authors and artists working from within the culture. In that case, the totals for African American books shrink from 180 to 84; for Native Americans, from 38 to 20; for Latinos, from 66 to 59 but—more positively—for Asian Americans the number actually increases to 129 (largely due to cases of multiple authorship).

Why such miniscule numbers? There are many reasons, some of which we've already articulated in our discussion of the origins of Latino literature in part one. first and foremost, there still aren't enough editors of color; a 2014 *Publishers Weekly* industry-wide survey revealed the dispiriting reality that the profession is overwhelmingly white—90 percent of the survey's respondents identified as white, 3 percent identified as Asian, 3 percent as Latino, and only 1 percent as African American (Patrick and Reid 2014)

A second reason for the disappointingly small number of multicultural books is the perceived lack of demand for them; a third reason is: "there aren't enough authors and illustrators out there producing books for diverse audiences" (Kirch 2014, 30).

David Gale of Simon and Schuster confirms this, saying, "We're limited by what people are writing and what's being offered to us." He then offers a fourth—and dismaying—reason: "We choose the best of what's offered but the gatekeepers aren't buying it." (David Gale, personal communication, May 28, 2015). One of the survey respondents seconds this: "We publish a ton of diverse (children's) books, but the gatekeepers (booksellers and librarians) need to stock them" (Kirch 2014, 32).

In other words, both publishing and bookselling are businesses, and there simply aren't enough dollars being generated by the sale of multicultural books to warrant a significant expansion of offerings. If sales are a function of popularity (the more popular the book, the higher the sales), consider that over the course of its twelve years of existence, YALSA's annual Teens' Top Ten Lists—books nominated and chosen by teens themselves—have included no more than three multicultural titles. This neglect may be due in part to a lack of worthy titles, but it also says something important about the equation of lack of popularity and miniscule sales, something that has not escaped the attention of publishers despite the fact that another YALSA list, that of Best Fiction for Young Adults, also has teen input but has significantly more diverse content. As a result, publishers are at pains to package multicultural books in any way that might enhance their sales appeal. Sometimes this strategy is effective; sometimes it is not. Consider the case of Justine Larbalestier's *Liar* (2009). Its publisher, Bloomsbury, inadvertently sparked a firestorm of controversy when word reached the blogosphere that this novel about an African American girl with "nappy" hair was being packaged with a dust jacket featuring the photo of a white girl with long, straight hair. The author herself was among those complaining, telling *Publishers Weekly* "The problem is long-standing and industry-wide. Whitewashing of covers, ghettoizing of books by people of color, and low expectations (reflected in the lack of marketing push behind the majority of these books) are not new things."

Happily, Bloomsbury quickly decided to redesign the jacket, saying—in a rather convoluted press release: "We regret that our original creative direction for *Liar*—which was intended to symbolically reflect the narrator's complex psychological makeup—has been interpreted by some as a calculated decision to mask the character's ethnicity" (Springen 2009).

This whole situation is complicated by the fact that since the mid-nineties or thereabouts, the traditional market for multicultural books—libraries and schools—has taken a backseat to the retail market (Barnes and Noble, amazon.com, and, increasingly, the big box stores like Wal-Mart and Target), which is less friendly to books about people of color.

Larbalestier herself seemed to acknowledge this when she told *Publisher Weekly*, "However, we consumers have to play our part, too. If you've never bought a book with someone who isn't white on the cover, go do so now. Start buying and reading books by people of color" (2009).

Otherwise, one suspects, these markets will continue to homogenize output and, in pursuit of sales, continue to turn children's book publishing (and that includes YA) into what I earlier called event publishing.

As a result, it becomes ever more difficult for new writers—of any color—to break into print, especially if their work is perceived as being mid-list. If this is the bad news, the good news is the growing importance of small independent publishers like Lee and Low, Cinco Puntos Press, Arte Publico, and others that remain committed to publishing multicultural literature. "Diversity is happening in the publishing industry, but you are finding it at the small press level," John Byrd, managing editor of Cinco Puntos, confirms (Kirch, 2014).[1] Author Sherman Alexie concurs: "We see it time and time again: Innovation comes from the small press world" (Strickland 2014).

K. T. Horning, director of the CCBC, wonders "Can anything be done to diversify children's books?" (Horning 2014, 20). And why, she wonders, was there so much positive activity in this regard back in the 1960s and 1970s? "What did they have then that we don't have now?" (Horning 2014, 20). Answering her own question, she says, "They had the Council on Interracial Books for Children for one thing." This gadfly organization relentlessly focused on the need for a more diverse literature for children and sponsored an annual contest for unpublished writers of color, launching the careers of such celebrated authors as Walter Dean Myers, Sharon Bell Mathis, Kristin Hunter, and Mildred Taylor. Similarly, the CIB Council on Interracial Books for Children's (CIBC) "Art Directors Take Note" column brought attention to such visual talents as Donald Crews, Leo and Diane Dillon, and Pat Cummings.

Of course, we have no CIBC today but we do have another organization, namely We Need Diverse Books, which sprang from a protest campaign inspired by the lack of diversity among speakers at the 2014 BookCon. WNDB began as a social media campaign fueled by Twitter and Facebook, but gradually gathered steam and incorporated as a volunteer-run nonprofit on July 14, 2014. Subsequently in April 2015, it gained 501(c)(3) nonprofit status (Kirch 2015), WNDB consists of an eight-member executive team headed by its cofounder, the author Ellen Oh, plus an advisory board of eight authors known for incorporating multicultural characters and themes in their works.

WNDB's Mission Statement, "We Need Diverse Books is a grassroots organization of children's book lovers that advocates essential changes in the publishing industry to produce and promote literature that reflects and honors the lives of all young people" (WNDB Official Campaign Site) http://weneeddiversebooks.org, is now being realized by an increasingly ambitious program of activities, including—for established authors—the Walter Award (named in honor of the late Walter Dean Myers) and—for emerging writers—the Walter Dean Myers Grants; it also boasts a publishing intern program, the WNDB in the classroom initiative in collaboration with the National Education Association's Read Across America Program, and the children's literature diversity festival scheduled to be held in Washington, DC, in August 2016 (Kirch 2015).

Cofounder and President Oh sums up the situation neatly when she says, "There was this hopelessness, but now there's such energy. We want to work as hard as we can so that a lack of diversity is no longer an issue" (*Library Journal* 2015).

Though I'm sometimes concerned about the proliferation of awards and prizes—like adding too much water to the soup, it tends to dilute the broth—there's no gainsaying their importance to the evolution of multicultural literature. I've already mentioned the Coretta Scott King Awards, of course, but let me also note—in the context of my earlier jeremiad about the difficulty of breaking into print—that the King awards have done a great service by adding a category for new talent, which encourages publishers to give new voices a chance to be heard. And let's acknowledge, too, the Young Adult Library Services Association's William C. Morris YA Debut Award, which will further encourage publishers to take a chance on new and previously untested creative voices.

Meanwhile, such other prizes as the Pura Belpre, Americas, and Tomas Rivera awards remain hugely important to focusing attention on Latino writers and books, while the American Indian Library Association presents its American Indian Youth Literature Award, and the APALA awards recognize the best in Asian Pacific Literature. Notably the Margaret A. Edwards Award has to date gone to three African American writers—Walter Dean Myers, Jacqueline Woodson, and Sharon Draper—though it has yet to go to either a Latino or Asian writer.

In 2014, the National Book Award was presented to Jacqueline Woodson for her luminous memoir in verse: *Brown Girl Dreaming*, making her the fifth person of color to win this prestigious award.

As someone who was involved with the creation of the Michael L. Printz Award, I'm delighted to note that this youngest of the major prizes seems to have one of the best records of diversity: after all, its first recipient, in 2000, was Walter Dean Myers for his memorable novel *Monster*. In 2002, An NA was the recipient for her first novel *A Step from Heaven*. In 2004 it was Angela Johnson's turn for her novel *The First Part Last*. Marilyn Nelson was a Printz honor recipient in 2006 for her book *A Wreath for Emmet Till*, as were Benjamin Alire Saenz in 2013 for his *Aristotle and Dante Discover the Secrets of the Universe* and Ashley Hope Perez in 2016 for her *Out of Darkness*.

The name of the 2007 recipient offers a natural segue to another newly emergent literature that is literally giving faces to the formerly invisible. I'm talking about Gene Luen Yang, who—in 2007—became the first person to receive the Printz for a graphic novel, *American-Born Chinese*, published by First Second Books (this was also the first graphic novel to be shortlisted for the National Book Award in the young readers category).

Other graphic novel imprints are also expanding our understanding of the world. Pantheon, for example, is the publisher of the Iranian artist Marjane Satrapi's hugely successful (but often challenged) two-volume memoir of her rebellious childhood in Iran, *Persepolis* and *Persepolis 2*, and Knopf has given readers Mark Alan Stamaty's *Alia's Mission: Saving the Books of Iraq*.

As continuing tensions in the Middle East have captured American readers' attention, a handful of traditional print books—virtually all of them published as adult titles with strong crossover appeal—have appeared to address conditions of being there. Several of the most popular—Azadeh Moaveni's *Lipstick Jihad* and Azar Nafisi's *Reading Lolita in Tehran*—deal with Iran, while Khaled Hosseini's *The Kite Runner* (an Alex Award winner) is a coming-of-age novel set in Afghanistan in the 1970s. A crossover nonfiction book about that same country is Said Hyder Akbar's *Come Back to Afghanistan: A California Teenager's Story.*

A small handful of YA novels dealing with people of Middle Eastern heritage have belatedly begun to appear, among them the unfortunately titled *Bestest Ramadan Ever* by Medeia Sharif (2011), Amelie Sarn's *I Love, I Hate, I Miss My Sister,* which is set in France (2014), *Guantanamo Boy* by Anna Perera (2011), *If You Could Be Mine* by Sara Farizan (2013) and also her *Tell Me How a Crush Should Feel* (2014). Virtually the only other author writing about the Middle East for children and young adults is the Palestinian-American poet and novelist Naomi Shihab Nye.

Another people of color who have been almost equally overlooked—at least in terms of authentic representations of their culture—are Native Americans. Only a scattering of authors are currently writing from within that experience, among them Sherman Alexie, Joseph Bruchac, Debby Dahl Edwardson, Louise Erdrich, Eric Gansworth, Linda Hogan, Leslie Marmon Silko, and Cynthia Leitich Smith.

Like YALSA, the International Reading Association sponsors an annual booklist selected by teens. Called "Young Adults' Choices," it has been around since 1986 and involves the participation of seventh- through twelfth-grade students in selected school districts around the country. Perhaps because a book, to be eligible, must have received two positive reviews in professional journals, the resulting Choices lists do offer a slightly better representation of multicultural books than YALSA's. Of the 327 titles selected to date (2016) 10 percent (35) could be called "multicultural." In terms of races, cultures, and ethnicities represented, the titles group as follows: nineteen are about African Americans; seven about Asians; seven about Hispanics; one about Native Americans; and one about an African American/Hispanic mixed-race couple. The authors represented are, for the most part, well-established names like Walter Dean Myers, Sharon M. Draper, Sharon G. Flake, Angela Johnson, Janet McDonald, Lensey Namioka, Gary Soto, and Pam Munoz Ryan.

Before we leave this subject, some small attention to international books is in order. I'm talking here of books first published abroad and also of books written in this country but set in other countries. Neither is a terribly robust body of literature, but are certainly deserving of attention. A reliable guide to the former is ALA's annual Mildred Batchelder Award, given to the most outstanding children's book originally published in a language other than English in a country other than the United States and subsequently translated into English for publication in the United States. Though many of the Batchelder books skew younger than YA, enough are targeted at older readers to justify attention. Of course, as YA has become increasingly international in scope, a plethora of titles are coming to the United States from other Anglophone countries, books by such English writers as Aidan Chambers, Louise Rennison, Marcus Sedgwick, Nick Lake, David Almond, Geraldine McCaughrean, Meg Rosoff, and others, while Australia is represented by such talents as Markus Zusak, Sonya Hartnett, Melina Marchetta, and Margo Lanagan, to name but a few. As for American books set in other countries, consider such reliable authors as Patricia McCormack, Tara Sullivan, and Eliot Schrefer.

Ultimately one wonders how many authors and how many books might be sufficient to represent the variety and richness of America's new racial, cultural, and ethnic populations? There is no answer to this question, of course, but it certainly invites discussion and the observation that, finally, it is not only quantity but also quality of content that should drive such conversations.

Let me conclude this discussion by reiterating my belief that fiction remains essential to understanding our human condition in all its complexities. The heart has its reasons the mind cannot know, which means we come to understanding not only through our head but also through our heart, and it is fiction—the best fiction—that offers us essential opportunities for cultivating empathy, for feeling sympathy and for experiencing emotional engagement with others. This leads me to another essential point: multicultural literature is indispensable not only because it enables us to see ourselves in the pages of good books, but also because it enables us to see others—and not only to see those others but also to eavesdrop on their hearts, to come to understanding, and to what I can only call commonality.

The world is changing apace—for good or for ill; you decide which. But change has always visited our lives whether we're ready for it or not. And it remains literature that can help us cope with this sometimes vexing and often perplexing fact of life.

No one has manifested this more resolutely and powerfully than the late Walter Dean Myers. In a widely discussed *New York Times* opinion piece "Where Are the People of Color in Children's Books?" (Myers 2014) he wrote, "As I discovered who I was, a black teenager in a white-dominated world, I saw that these characters, these lives, were not mine. What I needed, really, was to become an integral and valued part of the mosaic that I saw around me." Myers's work has made it possible for countless young readers of color to become part of that mosaic.

Over the course of his long career (his first book for young readers, *Fast Sam, Cool Clyde and Stuff,* was published in 1975), Myers has built a reputation as one of a handful of the very most important young adult writers in the history of the genre. He did this by trusting his growing legions of readers with the difficult truth about the real world in which they must live their lives. Poverty, violence, drugs, guns—none are strangers to his young adult fiction.

In his Margaret A. Edwards acceptance speech, Myers said, "There are always children that need to be rescued from some obscure hell, to be brought into the light of recognition so that we can no longer avoid looking at their suffering."

"What I can do," he continued, "is help make all our children and all our young adults visible again. I can help begin the process of peeling away labels they have been burdened with, that diminish their humanity" (Frolund 2008, 99).

This is what he does to such good effect in his novel *Monster,* but a similar commitment to humanity, to the humane, is central to all of Myers's work, whether it is written for children or for young adults. A prolific writer (he's published nearly one hundred books), Myers has worked for all ages and in a variety of different forms ranging from picture books to chapter books to nonfiction, and from poetry to memoir to hard-edged young adult fiction. In the process he became one of our most honored writers for youth; he is, for example, the only author to have received both the Margaret A. Edwards Award and the Michael L. Printz Prize; he is a five-time recipient of the Coretta Scott King Award and a four-time recipient of a King honor; he has twice received a Newbery honor and has twice been a National Book Award finalist. And in 2012 he became America's National Ambassador for Young People's Literature.

It's worth noting, too, that he was one of the first to give faces to young soldiers fighting in three American Wars, those in Vietnam (*Fallen Angels*), Iraq (*Sunrise in Falljuah*), and World War II (*Invasion*). In that process he invited his readers to examine not only their own personal values but also those of the nation in which they live.

"If we do not write about all our children," Myers said, "write about them with hard truths and a harder compassion, then we have, in a very significant way, failed our own futures" (Frolund 2008, 101).

Reflecting on his career as a writer, on the future, and on his legacy, Myers once wrote, "I would like to be remembered as giving something back to the world" (Gallo 1990, 149).

There is absolutely no question that he will be.

Note

1. You can download a five-page list of small publishers at the CCBC website, www.education.wisc.edu.ccbc.

Reality Redux

Risky Behaviors

"Adolescence is practically synonymous in our culture with risk taking"[1]
—*Richard A. Friedman*

RANGING FROM PHYSICAL AND EMOTIONAL VIOLENCE TO DRUG AND ALCO-
hol abuse, from risky sexual behavior to driving recklessly and carrying
weapons to school, risky behaviors remain very real factors in the daily
lives of twenty-first century teens. Indeed, the top three killers of teenagers
are accidents, homicides, and suicide (Friedman 2014).

But why should this be? Is it sheer perversity on the part of teens? In a
word, no. The answer now seems to be that their brains are wired for risk.

Frances Jensen, author of *The Teenage Brain,* likens teen brains to defec-
tive spark plugs, writing, "Teens are not quite firing on all cylinders when it
comes to the frontal lobes. Thus, we shouldn't be surprised by the daily stories we hear and read about tragic mistakes" (Kolbert 2015).

"The problem is that the incentive/reward system matures earlier than
the cognitive control system" says Dr. Lisa Freund, a developmental psychologist and neuroscientist at the National Institutes of Health (NIH) (Freund,
2011). That "cognitive control system" is the brain's prefrontal cortex, which
governs reasoning, impulse control, and emotion regulation, and that doesn't
fully develop until the age of twenty-five, making it one of the brain's last
regions to mature. "In other words," Freund continues, "the brain's 'that's so
cool, I want it now' part develops well before the 'stop and think twice' part."

Elizabeth Kolbert puts it simply: "Adolescents are designed to sniff out
treats at a hundred paces!" (Kolbert 2015).

Freund amplifies: "The reward centers of their [teens'] brains respond in heightened fashion to the neurotransmitter dopamine, which may explain why they are particularly vulnerable to addiction" (Schaffer 2015).

The problem is exacerbated when a teen is with peers. "We have also shown that the reason teenagers take more chances when their peers are around is partly because of the impact of peers on the adolescent brain's sensitivity to rewards. When teens were with people their own age, their brains' reward centers became hyperactivated," according to Dr. Laurence Steinberg (2014). It appears the stereotypical parental concern about their child's "dangerous" friends may, in fact, be well founded in physiology!

Not all of this is necessarily bad. Author Arthur Allen writes, "The brain development that can make teens and young adults take scary risks also motivates them to go out on their own, seek new experiences, and sometimes create new things" (Allen 2014).

Adds Maria Szalavitz, "Their greater tolerance for uncertainty and the unknown—and an increased desire for and focus on rewards—probably helps them leave the nest" (Szalavitz 2012).

Violence and Its Consequences

The riskiest of teen behaviors involve violence and related injury, which remain the leading causes of death among all youth aged five to nineteen—67 percent from injury, 16 percent from homicide,[2] and 14 percent from suicide (www.cdc.gov/yrbss).

These are startling—even shattering—statistics. But, wait, there are more: In 2012 there were about 749,200 nonfatal violent victimizations at school among students twelve to eighteen years of age (Kemp, Rathbun, and Morgan 2014).

In a 2013 sample of students in grades nine through twelve, 8.1 percent reported being in a physical fight on school property; 7.1 percent reported they did not go to school on one or more days in the thirty days before the survey because they felt unsafe; 5.2 percent reported carrying a weapon (knife, gun, or club) on school property; and 6.9 percent reported being threatened or injured with a weapon one or more times in the twelve months before the survey (Centers for Disease Control and Prevention 2013).

Why such violent behavior? According to the Centers for Disease Control and Prevention (CDC), "a number of factors can increase the risk of a youth engaging in violence. Among them: a prior history of violence; drug, alcohol, or tobacco use; poor family functioning; poor grades in school; poverty in the community; and association with delinquent peers" (CDC nd).

Speaking of delinquent peers, the Federal Bureau of Investigation reports that there are currently 33,000 violent street gangs, motorcycle gangs, and prison gangs with about 1.4 million members. Gangs are responsible for an average of 48 percent of violent crime in most jurisdictions and up to 90 percent in others (Federal Bureau of Investigation, nd).

Nearly three in four gang members are between the ages of fifteen and twenty-four, though one in six is fourteen or younger (Healthychildren.org 2015). Nor is membership any longer confined to males. Girls are now believed to make up as much as one-quarter to one-third of all urban gangs.

Happily, gang activity has declined in the mid-2010s, but the reasons young people join them have remained essentially the same: (1) to belong; (2) to make money; (3) for protection; (4) to have a place to hang and something to do; (5) for the thrill; and (6) peer pressure.

Gangs, of course, have been a feature of young adult literature since its inception in the pages of S. E. Hinton's *The Outsiders*, and remain popular to this day. In fact, a recent (February 2016) search of *Booklist* magazine's online data base turned up sixty-eight gang-related novels.

As for other causes of violent behavior: it is hard not to think that growing up in a violence-ridden world—the real thing as in the spate of post-Columbine school shootings, 9/11, the Iraq War, the war in Afghanistan, international terrorism—and imagined but powerfully visualized (and sometimes glamorized) violence in movies, on TV, on the Internet, and in video games (*Grand Theft Auto* anyone?) has some impact on teens' lives and psyches.

But the often asked question—exactly what impact do television and video violence actually have on teens' behavior—remains a vexing one.

"We just finished a major review of studies, looking at 381 effects of violent video games on over 130,000 people," says Brad Bushman, a professor of communication and psychology at Ohio State University. "We found that violent video games unmistakably raised levels of aggression and heart rate and decreased feelings of compassion toward others. No one is immune to the effects of violent video games, any more than anyone is immune to the effects of smoking cigarettes" (Savacool 2014).

This is disquieting to say the least, because 97 percent of American children between the ages of twelve and sixteen spend some thirteen hours per week playing electronic games (Savacool 2014), and unlike watching television where they are passive viewers, playing video games makes them active participants.

"Video games could be expected to have a larger effect than media violence. The player is participating. They're being reinforced. The important thing is repetition," says Rowell Huesmann, a psychologist at the University of Michigan (Keim 2013).

And yet, "I don't think we have enough science to suggest that playing video games causes violence in children any more than watching violence on TV," says Ryan Hall, a psychiatrist at the University of Central Florida, referencing a vast body of scientific literature that has failed to find any strong connection between violent television and corresponding bad behavior (Keim 2013).

So the research continues—for good or for ill. "This is a pool of research that, so far, has not been very well done," says Christopher J. Ferguson, associate professor of psychology and criminal justice at Texas A&M International University. "I look at it and I can't say what it means" (Carey 2013).

Fascinatingly, although video game sales have more than doubled since 1996, the number of violent youth offenders has actually fallen by more than half from 1994 to 2010 (Carey 2013). Is there a relationship? Based on a working paper by Dr. Michael R. Ward and two colleagues, there might be. The three researchers have found that higher rates of violent video game sales related to a decrease in crimes and especially violent crimes! *The New York Times* reporter Benedict Carey writes, "No one knows for sure what these findings mean. It may be that playing video games for hours every day keeps people off the streets who would otherwise be getting into trouble. It could be that the games provide 'an outlet' that satisfies violent urges in players. Or the two trends may be entirely unrelated."

If the causes are complex—and sometimes downright confusing—there is nevertheless no gainsaying the presence of violence in the lives of too many teens.

A Literature of Risk

Does it seem counterintuitive, then, to argue that we need more—not less—YA literature that addresses these same issues honestly and realistically?

Not at all. For the great gift literature can give its readers that new—and old—media cannot is the experience of empathy and sympathy. Books can take their readers into the interior lives of characters in ways that television and video can't. They can show not only what is happening to characters, but can also powerfully convey how what is happening feels. Interactive games and media can, doubtless, improve hand-eye coordination. But books can improve heart-eye coordination and even, I would argue, create it when—as increasingly seems to be the case—it is altogether absent in the reader.

One author whose work is particularly relevant to this discussion is Adam Rapp. A successful playwright like Paul Zindel before him, Rapp began writing for young adults in the 1990s; his first novel, *Missing the Piano* was published in 1994 and helped usher in the new golden age of YA literature. In the half dozen novels that have appeared since, Rapp has written some of the most harrowing—and haunting—young adult novels in the history of the field. The protagonists of his unsparingly realistic novels—Blacky Brown (*Little Chicago*), Steve Nugent (*Under the Wolf, Under the Dog*), Custis (*33 Snowfish*), Jamie (*Punkzilla*), and others—live lives *in extremis.* Victimized, incarcerated, bullied, sexually abused, mentally ill, they all struggle to survive the worst a seemingly sociopathic—or perhaps sadistic—world can throw at them. If these sound like the worst of the problem novels of the 1970s, know that they are not. Though the circumstances they reveal are often ugly, so ugly the reader may want to look away, the books themselves are beautiful in their compassion and caring and—thanks to his gifts as a dramatist—lyrical in the unconventional, unforgettable voices Rapp creates for his characters.

> So my name is Steve Nugent. I'm just seventeen. It was my birthday last month, in November. Now it's the middle of December, and the trees around here are caked in ice and sort of silvery in that creepy, wintry way, so right now seventeen seems like a hundred years off. (*Under the Wolf, Under the Dog*)

• • •

> At night the sky glows purple like the light from a TV when a VCR movie is done playing. And the stars get so big they look like

knives coming at you. Some of them stars look like spaceships, too. Especially them blue ones.

It would be cool if one of them blue stars came and a spaceman lit up his insides and showed us his moon bones . . . Them spacemen probably got stronger hearts than humans, too, cuz they don't got no pit bull worries or no money suit worries or no Bob Motley worries. All them worries make your heart small, and the smaller your heart the less it glows . . . (Custis in *33 Snowfish*)

• • •

There's a new subdivision going up and the rain makes the houses look like they were dropped out of the sky.

Nobody lives here yet. It's all piles of bricks and skeleton wood.

From the cab of the bulldozer I can see into the half-made house. It's all skinny wood and chicken wire. I think that houses have bones too.

I wonder when they put the walls in cause the walls are skin.

I wonder how electricity works cause electricity's like veins. Trying to figure this out makes me sleepy. (Blacky in *Little Chicago*)

In a wonderful way, Adam Rapp resembles Maurice Sendak in his outrage at a world that often fails, abuses, and exploits its young. In his recent appreciation of Sendak, "Making Mischief," Gregory Maguire identifies the artist's "steady and unflagging creed: The weak and lowly are not to be abused" (Maguire 2009, 68).

Like Sendak, Rapp is an inveterate risk-taker and fearless truth-teller in dramatizing this creed, and so his work is controversial and no stranger to the censor. But anyone who cares about kids—whether they're named Jack or Guy or Blacky or Steve—needs to be a champion for this work, just as Rapp (and Sendak) are champions for their characters.

Attention must be paid; truth must be told. And that is Rapp's creed:

Ma always says, "No matter how hard it is you gotta tell the truth, Blacky. No matter how hard."

• • •

"I don't mean to be weird P but in your letter you said how you wanted the truth about stuff even if it's ugly and trust me it's going to get a little ugly."

• • •

The truth can be ugly, but the unflagging love that Rapp shows again and again for his characters, inviting his readers to love them, too, even if the world sometimes doesn't is beautiful.

In *Punkzilla,* Rapp's eponymous protagonist receives a letter from a girl named Jenny. In it she writes of her boyfriend Branson, "He cries sometimes when nobody's looking, like when he's in the bathroom or hiding behind a car, and that's why I know his soul has gold in it. And your's does too, Zilla. Your's has gold and silver."

And so, I venture to say, has Rapp's.

Bullying

"The scariest aspect of bullying is the utter lack of empathy."[3]

I have emphasized the importance of literature in fostering empathy because, frankly, there is a shocking absence of it in today's adolescent lives, and that is nowhere more powerfully evidenced than in the epidemic of bullying that is plaguing America's schools, playgrounds, parks, and neighborhoods. Bullying is no respecter of age or gender. Note that, in 2013, according to the National Center for Education Statistics, 22 percent of all students twelve to eighteen reported having been bullied. (Happily, this is down from 28 percent two years earlier) (Hefling 2015).

If any good thing came out of the shootings at Columbine, it was the elevation of attention given to this epidemic problem and the very rapid emergence of a subgenre of young adult literature that continues to explore the many aspects of this issue with insight and, yes, empathy. This is a good thing, because bullying has escalated to the point that it has become something of a *cause cèlébre;* there has even been a White House Conference on bullying prevention (2011), and October is now National Bullying Awareness Month.

Arguably the first book to emerge in this category was Todd Strasser's chilling documentary novel *Give a Boy a Gun* (2000). In it Strasser charts the growing disaffection of two teenage boys, Gary and Brenden, who first dream of taking revenge on the people who have bullied them (principally members of the school's football team) and then transform that dream into reality. In my starred *Booklist* (October 1, 2000) review of this important title, I compared it to the work of the late John dos Passos, for Strasser, like dos Passos before him, enlivens his narrative with a contrapuntal collection of quotations, facts, and statistics about real-life school and gun violence. He concludes his book with appended lists of shootings and other incidents of school violence that occurred while *Give a Boy a Gun* was being written (Cart 2000c).

A number of other novels dealing with school violence due to bullying have appeared in the years since Strasser's. One of the best—and most recent—is Amanda Maciel's *Tease* (2014). Here's its story: Sara Wharton is a bully. But not, she insists, a murderer. However, Emma Putnam is dead, a suicide who was literally bullied to death. And Sara has been criminally charged. But she blames Emma who, she acidly thinks, got off easy. Self-pitying and not a bit sorry, Sara is a classic anti-heroine—or is she? As the story moves back and forth in time, before and after the suicide, a fuller portrait emerges as Sara tells the story in her own first person voice. And perhaps she might, in the end, come to terms with her actions and even find redemption. First novelist Maciel has done an exemplary job of giving readers a multidimensional portrait of a bully, one that is psychologically acute and emotionally resonant. Readers may not like Sara but they will come to empathize with her as she discovers the meaning of remorse.

Other relevant recent titles include: *All the Rage* by Courtney Summers (2015), *The Fearless* by Emma Pass (2015), *Still Waters* by Ash Parsons (2015), *Knockout Games* by G. Neri, (2014), *The Things You Kiss Goodbye* by Leslie Connor (2014), *Graduation Day* by Joelle Charbonneau (2014), and *Yaqui Delgado Wants to Kick Your Ass* by Meg Medina (2013). A slightly older but still interesting nonfiction title is *Dear Bully* (2011), in which seventy authors tell their own stories of bullying and being bullied.

As the Maciel novel suggests, a gravely misguided strategy for coping with bullying is suicide, the third leading cause of death among youth aged fifteen to twenty-four. Approximately one out of every fifteen high-school students reports attempting suicide each year. For each suicide death among young people, there might be, it is hypothesized, as many as 100 to 200 attempts (Youth.gov. nd). Overall, the suicide rate among teens climbed during the years 2009–2011, from 6.3 percent in 2009 to 7.8 percent in 2011 (Neal 2012).

Despite suicide's alarming frequency, this topic was taboo in YA literature for many years (for fear of creating a copycat effect among young readers). This has begun to change since the enormous success of Jay Asher's 2007 novel *Thirteen Reasons Why*, a book in which a teenage girl named Hannah kills herself, leaving a package of cassette tapes articulating her reasons. Laurie Halse Anderson also addresses this issue in *Twisted* (2007), her novel in which a teen boy contemplates killing himself in response to intolerable bullying. Here are another half-dozen recent similar titles: *The Last Leaves Falling* by Sarah Benwell (2015), *Backlash* by Sarah Darer Littman (2015), *The Last Time We Say Goodbye* by Cynthia Hand (2015), *When Reason Breaks* by Cindy L. Rodriguez (2015), *All the Bright Places* by Jennifer Niven (2015), *I Was Here* by Gayle Forman (2015), and *Forgive Me, Leonard Peacock* by Matthew Quick (2013).

Fortunately, not all bullying results in apocalyptic violence. Arguably the best-known book on how the targets of bullying can find a creative way to respond remains James Howe's *The Misfits* (2001), the story of four middle-school students who are, yes, misfits and, accordingly, the targets of painful bullying. Instead of getting even, the four resolve to change their school's climate of abuse by running for class office on a no name-calling platform. Clearly Howe's novel touched a nerve; its huge popularity has inspired a national No Name-Calling Week that is observed by middle and elementary schools all across the country.

Cyberbullying

The newest kind of bullying, however, remains well-nigh pervasive, thanks to the ubiquity of the Internet. I'm referring here to cyberbullying, the posting of innuendo, put-downs, gossip, lies, and—perhaps worst of all—compromising photos online.

"Cyberbullying is the fastest-growing form of bullying happening around the world," according to C. J. Bott, a retired English teacher and author of two books about the subject: *The Bully in the Book and in the Classroom* and *More Bullies in More Books* (2004 and 2009, respectively).

Girls are more likely to have been victims than boys—25.8 percent versus 16 percent. But about 50 percent of all teens and young adults from ages fourteen to twenty-four report having experienced some form of abusive digital behavior (Teen Violence Statistics, Cyberbullying Statistics nd).

One of the attractions of this technique for bullies is that it allows them both anonymity and the ability to inflict pain without being forced to see its effects, which "also seems to incite a deeper level of meanness" (Harmon 2004, A1). Perhaps worst of all, there is no escaping this type of bullying; it spreads virally and follows the victim everywhere. Cyberbullies can be both boys and girls, but the latter tend to predominate. A few recent books about this invidious phenomenon are Sarah Darer Littman's *Backlash* (2015), Laura Ruby's *Bad Apple* (2009), Shana Norris's *Something to Blog About* (2008), and Laurie Halse Anderson's *Twisted* (2007).

Another significant form of bullying that can't go unmentioned is what Bott calls "institutional." In her article "When Institutions Are Libel for Bullying," she notes, "Sometimes the situation is even more complicated. When harassment is not dealt with because the reputation of an organization—perhaps the senior class, the football team, or the whole school—would be tarnished, the environment promotes institutional bullying. More simply, when the individuals in charge support the harassment by being silent, the institution is libel" (Bott, Gregory, and Cohen 2014).

In an e-mail to me (C. J. Bott, personal communication, June 2, 2015), Bott adds, "I find it interesting that this has been going on for years and people always accepted it. Kids killing themselves because they somehow felt they caused their disgrace and there was nowhere to turn."

More about Empathy

Whether in-person or online, bullying seems to betray a lack of empathy in its too often solipsistic perpetrators. Recently, several studies have suggested that teens' brains are simply not yet wired for empathy. This seems to be an oversimplification but it is true, as I have observed elsewhere, that the prefrontal cortex, which governs impulse control and judgment, and is where cognitive empathy originates, is among the last regions of the brain to develop (Shellenbarger 2013).

Recognizing this, the Supreme Court has prohibited the death penalty and even sentences of life without parole for many offenses committed by juveniles. "Given time and guidance, bullies can outgrow their bad patterns of behavior but their lives can be ruined if their awful teenage behavior puts them in the headlines or in jail" (Schwartz 2013).

Interestingly, there are those who say that bullies actually can empathize, but to bad—not good—effect. "Bullies are notorious for their ability to recognize weaknesses or shame in others. They do have a capacity to empathize. However, they destructively use their empathy to manipulate, control, exploit or cause pain. And they are able to withhold their compassion for the distress they cause others to feel" (Lamia 2010).

Cameron, Inzlicht, and Cunningham (2015) agree, saying "Psychopaths and narcissists are able to feel empathy; it's just that they typically don't want to." In this context they go on to state, importantly, "We believe that empathy is a *choice* that we make whether to extend ourselves to others."

That empathy might be a choice is, it seems to me, one of the most important lessons a young person can learn. And how better to learn this than to read good books that inspire the reader to feel empathy? And this is surely one of the most compelling arguments one can offer for *writing* fiction about even the most unpleasant realities of teens' lives, the kinds of realities we have been confronting in this chapter. For life, even at its darkest, can hold the promise of hope and positive change—especially when we read about it with open minds and hearts, with intellectual attention and emotional empathy.

One author whose luminous work epitomizes these points is Jacqueline Woodson. "When I was in fifth grade," she has recalled, "I used to stand in front of the bathroom mirror, holding a hairbrush as a microphone and practice giving my speech for the Pulitzer Prize" (Woodson 2006, 65) She has yet to win the Pulitzer, but this author so essential to young adult literature has won virtually every other award. Most recently The Poetry Foundation's Young People's Laureate, she is the author of more than thirty books for children and young adults. Their uniform excellence is evidenced by the spate of awards and honors she has received, including the Margaret A. Edwards Award, the National Book Award, multiple Newbery Honor Medals, multiple Coretta Scott King awards, the Caldecott Medal, *The Los Angeles Times* Book Award, numerous state awards, and many others. Most recently she has been selected by the American Library Association to deliver the prestigious May Hill Arbuthnot Lecture in 2017.

She began her storied career in 1990 with the publication of her first book *Last Summer with Maizon*. Since then her works have been distinguished by—among other things—their thematic richness, strong female characters, lyrical voice, demonstration that friendship can transcend the barriers society has erected between races and economic conditions, and compassionate treatment of those considered outsiders, including lesbians and gays. "Every character I write about," she has said, "is in some ways outside of the mainstream—black, working class poor white, a pregnant teen, gay" (Cart 1999, 913). She adds, "This sense of being on the outside of things, of feeling misunderstood and invisible is the experience I bring to the story" (Hayn 2000, 380). She also brings a powerful sense of family and history, personal and otherwise, as evidenced in her deeply felt, National Book Award–winning memoir in verse, *Brown Girl Dreaming*.

The result of all of this is a powerful invitation to empathy, further evidenced by her expression of gratitude, in her Margaret A. Edwards Award acceptance speech, to "every young reader who has crossed lines of race and class and gender to imagine their feet in another person's shoes" (Woodson 2006, 70).

This theme continues when she then speaks of the late Margaret A. Edwards's belief in literature and in teenagers and the power of their voices, "the importance of introducing them to people they might not otherwise have met and places they would never have seen" (Woodson 2006, 68). Woodson might have been speaking here of her own writing which the Edwards committee described as "powerful, groundbreaking and very personal explorations of the many ways in which identity and friendship transcend the limits of stereotype."

The originality, integrity, and courage with which she writes so eloquently of youth at risk is a major contribution to the world of young adult literature and richly deserves a Pulitzer Prize; may one be forthcoming.

Notes

1. Richard A. Friedman. 2014. "Why Teenagers Act Crazy." *New York Times*, June 29, SR1.

2. In 2006 nearly 6,000 young people aged 10 through 24 were murdered, an average of sixteen each day.

3. Bazelon, Emily. 2014. *Sticks and Stones*. New York: Random House, 55.

Sex and Other Shibboleths

YA Comes of Age—And Not a Moment Too Soon

IT'S POSSIBLE TO VIEW THE HISTORY OF YOUNG ADULT LITERATURE AS A series of inspired exercises in iconoclasm—of envelope pushing, taboo busting, and shibboleth shattering—Hinton's acknowledgment of teen class warfare, Childress's of heroin abuse, Cormier's of evil's ascendancy, and so on.

The one area of life that has most stubbornly resisted such taboo busting is human sexuality. This is hardly press-stopping news. Puritans invented America, after all, and they viewed sexual expression as something to be denied and suppressed. This attitude has been a hardy perennial ever since. Former *New York Times* television critic John J. O'Connor (1994, B5) put it a bit more acerbically: "It's hardly news," he wrote, "that America is inhabited by large numbers of Puritanical hysterics."

Whether hysterical or more reasoned, such Puritanism has long flowered in the garden of young adult literature. Margaret A. Edwards (1969, 72) herself acknowledged this, writing, "Many adults seem to think that if sex is not mentioned to adolescents, it will go away. On the contrary it is here to stay and teenagers are avidly interested in it. There are excellent factual books on the market, but the best novels on the subject go beyond the facts to the emotional implications of love." Having made that point, Edwards proceeded to discuss what she regarded as eight "exemplary" novels involving sexuality.[1]

That all eight were adult titles says something, I think, about the near total lack of YA titles on the subject even as late as 1969; that the preceding decade had been one of sexual liberation and revolution in real world America seems to have escaped the attention of young adult authors and publishers! At any rate, of the exemplary eight Edwards (1969, 72) writes, "All of these have something to say about love that cannot be learned from informational books. Too many adults wish to protect teen-agers when they should be stimulating them to read of life as it is lived."

Such reticence assumed life-and-death proportions in the 1980s with the appearance of AIDS and its nearly incomprehensible lesson that love can kill. Before we talk about AIDS—and other sexually transmitted diseases—we need, however, to look at the cautious and halting evolution of young adult literature's attitude toward and treatment of sex.

The first important novel to deal with teenage sexuality was Henry Gregor Felsen's *Two and the Town* (1952). Though simplistic and cautious by today's standards, it was, nevertheless, fifteen years ahead of its time in its treatment of premarital sex, pregnancy, and forced marriage.

In it the high-school football star Buff Cody gets dark-haired loner Elaine Truro pregnant, and they are forced by Elaine's father to marry. When a baby, little Buff, is born, big Buff enlists in the Marine Corps to escape this new burden. Happily, in the Corps he learns how to be a real man and take responsibility for his family. He returns home—after a high-school football injury conveniently provides a deus ex machina reason for early separation from the service—determined to be happy with his wife and little Buff. Although the possibility of a happy ending is, thus, held out to the reader, it comes only after a censorious community has thoroughly punished the two teens for their indiscretion. And the implication remains that Buff will probably never get to be the coach he always dreamed of becoming. Such punishment for sexual activity was, of course, a *de rigueur* staple of popular culture at the time.

Despite its carefully cautionary element, Felsen's book was quite controversial. Edwards recalls that

> the book came off the press in the fifties, a few weeks before the American Library Association met in New York City. There was to be a preconference on young adult work in the public library, and I was to sit on a panel where I expected the book to be questioned. Sure enough [the book] came up for discussion and the panel seemed to agree it "was not up to Felsen" [a reference, I pre-

sume, to his usual standards], which simply meant they thought it too hot to handle. I came to the book's defense saying we had no other book that dealt honestly with this problem . . . and asked what they would give to a young person who wanted a book on the subject. One of the true-blue ladies drew herself up and announced, "I would give him 'The Scarlet Letter.'" (Edwards 1969, 82)

Shades of the Puritans.

Those Puritans had little to fret about for the next fifteen years until 1967 brought a second important milestone on the road to YA literature's sexual liberation: Ann Head's *Mr. and Mrs. Bo Jo Jones.* At that, there was no cause for immediate alarm, because the book was published in hardcover as an adult novel. However, within a year it "was offered to high-school students through paperback teenage book clubs" (Cart 1996, 192) and quickly became a harbinger, along with *The Outsiders* and *The Contender,* of more realistic fiction to come. Its lingering influence and enormous popularity are evidenced by the fact that it has appeared on two of YALSA's four retrospective best-of-the-best lists.

Bo Jo is not dissimilar to *Two and the Town* in its bare plot outline. Once again two teenagers, July and Bo Jo (Bo Jo is the boy), are swept away by passion; July becomes pregnant and the two elope. This time, however, the couple's families attempt to break up the marriage. July's father runs the local bank, while Bo's works as a construction foreman. Parental interference is the least of July and Bo Jo's problems, however. They quarrel over money and friends and their baby dies; they break up but in the end they are reunited and go off to college together. In the context of what has preceded it, the happy ending may be more author-imposed than inevitable; nevertheless, as a work of fiction, the book is a more fully realized effort than *Two and the Town,* and its popularity spurred a number of imitators. Witness the fact that only three years later in 1970 "four of the five top books sold through the Xerox Educational Publications' teenage book clubs were about sex and pregnancy" (Kraus 1975, 19).

The same year *Bo Jo* was published for adults, Zoa Sherburne's *Too Bad about the Haines Girl* was published for young adults. This time the teenage girl who becomes pregnant does not marry the father but actually turns, instead, to her parents for help with her problem, one of the rare instances of this happening in early YA.

A year before that, in 1966, Jeanette Eyerly's *A Girl Like Me* (Lippincott) appeared. In this one it's not the protagonist but a friend, Cass Carter, who brings shame on her family and is sent off to a Dickensian home for unwed mothers. At the twelfth hour the baby's father, the wealthy Brewster Bailey Winfield III (you can't make this stuff up) appears and volunteers to make Cass an honest woman but she nobly refuses, having decided to give the baby up for adoption "by somebody who'll love him, even if it turns out to be a girl—a girl like me" (Kraus 1975, 21).

Abortion as an option in resolving an unwanted teenage pregnancy was not offered until Paul Zindel's 1969 novel *My Darling, My Hamburger*. The indefatigable Jeanette Eyerly wasn't far behind, though. Her take on the topic, *Bonnie Jo, Go Home* appeared in 1972 and presented, author Norma Klein (1991, 24) noted, "such a negative, dark view of abortion that it would scare the wits out of almost anyone."

For good or for ill all of these books had one thing in common: All were primarily concerned not with the sexual act but with the (usually dire) consequences. Not so Judy Blume's revolutionary *Forever*, which was published in 1975 as a celebration of the sexual act itself. Not only do Blume's protagonists, high-school seniors Katherine and Michael, have sex, they (shudder) enjoy it, and the reader gets to watch the explicit action!

"This time Michael made it last much, much longer, and I got so carried away I grabbed his backside with both hands, trying to push him deeper and deeper into me—and I spread my legs as far apart as I could—and I raised my hips off the bed—and I moved with him, again and again and again—and at last I came." Whew!

The late Norma Klein (1991, 23), whose own novels offered a similar *cinema véritée* take on teenage sexuality, notes that "'Forever' was the first—I hope not the last—book to show teenagers it was all right to have sexual feelings, to be unashamed of this very natural physical and emotional reality. It showed them that love," [Blume's title is ironic, of course] "even when it doesn't last forever, is still an important part of growing up."

The only trouble with this is that it's *not* love that Blume writes about; it's sex as a rite of passage that Katherine can't wait to experience and have done with. As a result, it too often seems that Blume has not written a novel but a scarcely dramatized sex manual, including a chapter-long account of Katherine's visit to a Planned Parenthood Clinic (after she has read "a whole bunch of pamphlets" her grandmother has sent her from the organization). However courageous and wonderfully well-intentioned it was, *Forever* remains more tract than novel (though a tract probably wouldn't name a boy's penis Ralph as Michael dubs his, providing an occasion for nervous giggling by readers in the years since).

I'm reluctant to offer such negative-sounding criticism of *Forever*, because it earned Blume a Margaret Edwards A. Award in 1996 (it was the only one of her titles the selection committee cited), and also because I wholeheartedly agree with Norma Klein's assertion that "I would like more, not less, explicit sex in books for teenagers" (1991, 25).

Not to include sex in books for contemporary high-school students is to agree to a de facto conspiracy of silence, to imply to young readers that sex is so awful, so traumatic, so dirty that we can't even write about it. That's why I applaud Blume's candor, since it shattered the prevailing conspiracy of silence and made it possible for the writers who came after her to deal more maturely with one of the most important aspects of life. Well, if not *of* life then certainly *to* life, since it wouldn't exist without the sexual act, though until Blume spoke out, most teenage readers might have been forgiven for believing that it was not sex but the stork that brought babies.

Needless to say, times have changed. Nationwide, 46.8 percent of students have now had sexual intercourse; 5.6 percent before the age of thirteen! (CDC 2013). We can't blame—or credit—Blume for that, of course, but it is thanks to her that other writers have had the liberty of beginning the important work of investigating other, less savory aspects of sex—notably its perversion by the interjection of violence in the form of rape and sexual abuse. Thus, in 1976, a year after *Forever* was published, another important pioneering novel, this one by Richard Peck, appeared. *Are You in the House Alone?* was arguably the first YA title to deal with rape, not sensationally or exploitatively, but with Peck's signature sense, sensitivity, and insight. Not surprisingly, it was named an ALA Best Book for Young Adults.

Perhaps the last taboo to fall in the literary sexual arena was not rape, though, but another form of sexual abuse, incest, which—according to the National Center for Victims of Crime—"has been cited as the most common form of child abuse" (www.ncvc.org/). It was, the author Mia Fontaine points out, "the first form of institutional abuse and it remains by far the most widespread" (2013). Sadly, the institution to which she refers is the family.

This sensitive subject was first addressed in the pseudonymous Hadley Irwin's 1985 novel *Abby, My Love*, a title that was also chosen as a Best Book for Young Adults. (As mentioned earlier, Scott Bunn's 1982 novel *Just Hold On* had also addressed the subject—but only peripherally.) Seven and eight years later, respectively, Ruth White dealt with the subject in *Weeping Willow* (1992), and in 1993 it was Cynthia D. Grant's turn in *Uncle Vampire* (1993). In 1994, three of the best books about this issue, in terms of literary quality, were published: Francesca Lia Block's *The Hanged Man*, Cynthia Voigt's *When She Hollers*, and Jacqueline Woodson's *I Hadn't Meant to Tell You This*. Though these books are quite different from one another in their treatment of sexual abuse, all have in common the art their gifted authors employ in transforming what could have been a simple journalistic reporting of the facts of this excruciatingly painful problem into powerfully artful literature, instead—literature that is riveting in its passion and in its righteous anger at the horrors the world sometimes visits on young women.

Incest is defined by the National Center for Victims of Crime as "sexual contact between persons who are so closely related that their marriage is illegal (i.e., parents and children, uncles/aunts and nieces/nephews). This usually takes the form of an older family member sexually abusing a child or adolescent" (www.ncvc.org).

In many cases the perpetrator is portrayed in YA books as a stepfather or a mother's live-in boyfriend (as in the Voigt novel); but more often it is the biological father (Irwin, Block, Woodson, etc.), a reflection of real world circumstance. One expert, with the National Center for Victims of Crime, for example, has estimated that 1 million Americans are victims of father-daughter incest and the number reportedly grows by some 16,000 each year (www.ncvc.org).

The perpetrator need not be a father, however; he may also be an uncle (*Uncle Vampire*) or an older brother, as in Carolyn Coman's *Bee and Jackie* (V. C. Andrews's lurid and histrionic *Flowers in the Attic*, which features a similar "forbidden relationship," was published as an adult book though it has attracted generations of young adult readers).

Not all of these cases are so clear-cut, however. Meg Rosoff's Printz Award–winning novel *How I Live Now* (2004) features a physical relationship between cousins, not a relationship that is forced on the girl protagonist but one she enters willingly, having fallen in love with her male cousin. Though Rosoff delicately and sensitively handles the situation, some adult readers were outraged, though others—who weren't—pointed out such relationships are perfectly legal in many states.

Most YA novels that have featured incest portray a girl as the victim, a reflection of real-world circumstance. However, boys are not immune from such victimization. One in five to seven boys is sexually abused before he turns eighteen, "an overwhelming incidence of which happens *within* the family" (2013).

Stephen Chbosky dramatizes this in his extraordinary novel *The Perks of Being a Wallflower* (1999). His emotionally disturbed, fifteen-year-old protagonist, Charlie, is revealed to have been victimized by a favorite aunt, whom he movingly forgives near the book's end.

Regardless of the relative involved, sexual violence of all sorts—assault, rape, incest—typically strikes close to home. According to the Rape, Abuse and Incest National Network, "approximately four of five victims were attacked by a non-stranger (generally an acquaintance or family member)" (www.rainn.org/statistics).

Some 44 percent of victims are under eighteen and 80 percent are under 30. The highest risk years are 12–34, and girls 16–19 are four times more likely than the general population to be victims. Seven percent of girls in grades five through eight and 12 percent of girls in grades nine through twelve report being sexually abused, while 3 percent of boys in grades five through eight and 5 percent of boys in grades nine through twelve report being victims (www.rainn.org/statistics). The results are devastating. Ninety-five percent of teen prostitutes and at least one-third of female prisoners were abused as kids. Sexually abused youth are twice as likely to be arrested for a violent offense as adults, are at twice the risk for lifelong mental health issues, and are twice as likely to attempt or commit teen suicide (2013).

Prostitutes are hardly a fixture in young adult literature but a moving novel about one, a girl who is tacitly abused by her pimp, is Martine Leavitt's *My Book of Life by Angel* (2012). Consider: Prostitution may be called the oldest profession but too often it's performed by the young—like sixteen-year-old Angel, whose life on the street begins when Call, the man she thinks is her boyfriend, gets her hooked on his "candy" and before she knows it, she's selling herself to support him—and her habit. But when Call brings home an eleven-year-old girl named Melli and demands Angel train her for the street, Angel realizes things must change. But that may require a miracle. As it happens, *My Book of Life by Angel* is something of a miracle itself a compassionate—and passionate—account of a heartbreakingly horrible life. But perhaps there are angels looking after Angel, for her efforts to save Melli and herself are heroic and, ultimately, inspired. Leavitt has created a first person voice for Angel that is a perfect mix of innocence and experience and has underscored that by seamlessly introducing passages from Milton's *Paradise Lost* into her narrative. Death, too, is present in Angel's life, when women she knows begin vanishing from the street, victims, perhaps, of a serial murderer. This last is inspired by an epidemic of murders that began in Vancouver in 1983 and continued through 2002. But Angel's story is uniquely her own and Leavitt has done a brilliant job of imagining and recording it.

A second exemplary novel on this subject is E. R. Frank's highly recommended *Dime* (2015). Fourteen-year-old Dime is a child prostitute whose "Daddy" routinely abuses her. Will she be able to break out of the relationship? *Booklist* magazine called this "gritty, graphic, and shatteringly painful to read" (Booth 2015). But read it one must to learn about the circumstances of a life in the gravest jeopardy.

As in the case with incest, few books deal with the sexual abuse of boys, and those that do are often not altogether successful. One of the first to do so was Catherine Atkins's 1999 novel *When Jeff Comes Home,* the story of a fifteen-year-old boy who is kidnapped by a stranger. Held captive for two and a half years, the boy is routinely forced to have sex with his kidnapper, a man named Ray, who also photographs the boy naked. When Ray rather improbably returns Jeff to his home and the circumstances of the boy's captivity become public, most people believe the boy is gay (he isn't), and subject him to horrible verbal and emotional abuse, which only heightens Jeff's already virulent feelings of self-hatred. The book too often strays into the melodramatic and never clarifies Ray's sexual identity, leaving the reader with the impression that he is gay and that, as one character puts it, "These faggots that prey on our kids, they should be strung up, electrocuted, tortured."

A second early book is Kathleen Jeffrie Johnson's *Target* (2003), in which a sixteen-year-old boy is violently (and graphically) raped by two men, an experience that leaves him so badly traumatized he is virtually catatonic. The motives of his attackers are never clearly delineated, though the author does make the point that most such acts are not sexually motivated but, instead, are exercises in power and domination. Nevertheless, the boy, Grady—like Jeff—is left self-hating and agonizingly questioning his own sexual identity (he wonders why didn't he fight back, a question that plagues Jeff, too). Further muddying the waters are Grady's flashback memories of being abused as a child by the man next door.

A third, Robert Lipsyte's searing *Raider's Night* (2006), recounts the sexual assault of a young football player by one of his teammates, and then focuses on the moral dilemma confronting the team's cocaptain, who has witnessed the violation and must then decide whether or not to report the incident.

A fourth and more recent title is Alex Sanchez's *Bait* (2009). Its teen protagonist Diego is put on probation for assaulting a fellow student. As he begins to know and comes to trust his probation officer, he finally admits the truth about the source of his anger: for years he was molested and raped by his stepfather. Things become complicated, however, when Diego—who fears the assaults will make him gay—learns that his probation officer himself is gay. Will his trust be shattered?

A fifth and still more recent title—is Carl Deuker's *Swagger* (2013), the story of teen basketball star Jonas who, with his parents, moves to a new town and a new basketball team. There he meets and befriends Levi, who, he then discovers, has been sexually abused by their charismatic coach. Will Jonas, who needs a basketball scholarship to attend college, report the crime and compromise his chances? Deuker's excellent novel is far more nuanced than either *When Jeff Comes Home* or *Target* but has in common with them a boy as a target of sexual predators.

Given the incendiary nature of the offenses committed in these five books, it does seem that ambiguities need to be very carefully handled, lest they perpetuate stereotypical thinking (e.g., all gays are predators), and the authors need to be equally careful to ground their material in clinically sound research and avoid any temptations to melodramatic or even gothic treatment of situation and characterization.

There is, however, no ambiguity at all about the fact that although it involves forced sex, rape is not about sex or passion and it certainly has nothing to do with love. Rape is an act of aggression and violence. Nevertheless, one understands why teens may be confused about this subject, because rape and other sexual violence too often take place in the context of a presumed romantic relationship. Indeed, according to the CDC, "Among female rape victims 51.1 percent of perpetrators were reported to be intimate partners. Among male rape victims, 52.4 percent of perpetrators were reported to be acquaintances" (CDC 2012), while "1 in 5 high school girls has been physically or sexually abused by a dating partner." And eighty percent of rape cases are date rape (Teen Violence Statistics, Date Rape, nd).

The CDC explains, "Dating violence is a type of intimate partner violence. It occurs between two people in a close relationship. There are three common types of dating violence: physical (when a partner is pinched, hit, shoved, or kicked), emotional (name calling, teasing, threats, bullying, etc.), and sexual (forcing a partner to engage in a sex act when he or she does not or cannot consent)" (CDC 2014).

As noted above, not all assaults are physical; some are emotional, as in the case of teen dating and harassment in the digital world where "abusers use technology to stalk their partners, send them degrading messages, embarrass them publicly, and pressure them for sex or sexually explicit photos" (Zweig and Dank 2013).

A recent study by the Urban Institute shows that the most frequent form of online harassment or abuse is tampering with a partner's social networking account without permission. Nearly one in ten teens in relationships reports having experienced this. Unfortunately, the cyber-abused are also abused in other ways. A total of 84 percent of them are psychologically abused; half are physically abused, and one-third experience sexual coercion (Zweig and Dank 2013).

Unfortunately, some abused teens choose not to report a sexual assault. Why?

Well, sadly it's because the consequences of going to authorities can sometimes be dire, a reality that has never been better dramatized than in Laurie Halse Anderson's Printz Honor Award novel *Speak*. When Anderson's protagonist, incoming high-school freshman Melinda, calls 911 to report she has been raped at an end-of-summer party, she winds up a virtual outcast, because her assailant was one of the most popular boys in school. Melinda is finally vindicated when the boy attempts to assault her again and this time is discovered in the act.

In the meantime, Melinda has chosen not to tell her parents what has happened. As noted above, this is not uncommon. Many teens choose not to tell their parents they have been assaulted. "Preteens and teenagers often confide only in friends about deeply personal issues—and, unfortunately, something as serious as rape is no exception. And laws in some states don't require that parents be notified if a teenager under eighteen has called a rape crisis center or visited a clinic for evaluation" (KidsHealth.org nd).

Melinda's parents, remain clueless, because they simply don't recognize the symptoms of abuse. Caitlin's parents in Sarah Dessen's *Dreamland* (2000)—another superb novel about this subject—are too distracted to know what's going on: Caitlin's "perfect" older sister has run away with her boyfriend. In the wake of this trauma, Caitlin's life begins to unravel as she experiments with drugs and begins dating wealthy Rogerson Briscoe, forming a relationship that quickly turns violently abusive.

Sometimes the fault lies in the parent himself, as in the case of Alex Flinn's first novel *Breathing Underwater* (2001). In this one, protagonist Nick's father's pattern of abusive behavior has influenced the boy's own understanding of how to behave in a relationship. Accordingly, he soon becomes an abuser, himself, of his girlfriend Caitlin. Fortunately, a court-mandated anger management class will help disabuse him of his unhealthy ideas and habits.

These are all deeply disquieting stories but, as I have attempted to show with my lengthy survey of statistical evidence, they do represent the actual life circumstances of an alarming number of adolescents. And perhaps making their stories available may foster understanding and promote positive change.

More such stories are contained in the following recent novels: Colleen Clayton, *What Happens Next* (2012); Jenny Downham, *You Against Me* (2011); Kimberly Marcus. *Exposed* (2011); Courtney Summers, *All the Rage* (2015); K. M. Walton, *Empty* (2013); and Daisy Whitney, *The Mockingbirds* (2010).

At the risk of redundancy, I will say that statistics alone are informative, essential, and—in the cases we've been discussing—perhaps even lifesaving. Most kids, however, find them boring; worse, they may suspect they're overstated to scare them if not straight, then celibate. Accordingly, we really do need more unapologetically candid and well-crafted fiction about these issues. And it is a very positive thing, I think, that since the turn of the twenty-first century young adult literature has truly come of age in its willingness to address some of the darker aspects of the human experience with honesty and candor.

But let us not close this chapter on a down note but, instead, acknowledge that sex has been treated positively, too, in recent YA literature; my own anthology *Love and Sex: Ten Stories of Truth*, for example, explored the intersection of love and sex, while the redoubtable John Green has put a positive spin on sexual activity in two of his novels, *Looking for Alaska* and *The Fault in Our Stars*. Yes, such books are controversial and often challenged but they do readers a service by acknowledging the fact that teenagers are sexual beings who deserve to see their stories in the pages of good, nonjudgmental young adult books.

Note

1. *Of Human Bondage, Wuthering Heights, The Cruel Sea, Love Is Eternal, Winter Wheat, Gone with the Wind, Bridge to the Sun,* and *Three Came Home.*

Lesbian, Gay, Bisexual, and Transgender Literature

Coming Out and Coming of Age

THOUGH JOHN DONOVAN'S *I'LL GET THERE. IT BETTER BE WORTH THE TRIP*, the first YA novel to treat the subject of homosexuality, may have appeared in 1969, only two years after *The Outsiders* and *The Contender*, no more than eight others about this subject followed over the next eleven years. Worse than their paucity, however, was the fact that, though well-intentioned like *I'll Get There*, they were equally riddled with stereotypes, a subject that I and my coauthor Christine A. Jenkins address at some length in *The Heart Has Its Reasons*, a critical history of young adult literature with gay, lesbian, and queer content (2006). Suffice it to say that these early efforts perpetuated the stereotypical view of homosexual lives as being unrelievedly bleak, lonely, danger-filled, and—as often as not—doomed to a tragically early end, usually in a car wreck, because these books were crowded with the worst drivers this side of my grandmother.

It should also be mentioned that virtually every one of the central characters in these books was white and middle-class. Yes, the first black character, Rosa Guy's eponymous Ruby, had appeared as early as 1976, but no other African Americans would appear until the 1991 publication of Jacqueline Woodson's *The Dear One,* and no Latinos until 1995.

Though the world of LGBT teens remained an all-white one, an otherwise more realistic—and positive—picture of homosexuality did begin emerging in the eighties, starting with Nancy Garden's classic *Annie on My Mind* (1982), the first YA novel to acknowledge that homosexuality was about more than sex(uality): it was also about love, a love that should dare to speak its name.[1]

A year after the publication of *Annie*, another first expanded and enriched the field: the first literary novel with gay content, Aidan Chambers's *Dance on My Grave* (1983); this was also only the second of many gay-themed novels from Great Britain that would be published in the United States (the first was David Rees's *In the Tent*).

Other notable firsts from the eighties include: Norma Klein's *Breaking Up* (1980), the first to include a gay parent; then Gary W. Bargar's *What Happened to Mr. Forster* (1981) became the first to include a working gay teacher (I say "working" because Isabel Holland's, in *Man without a Face* [1972], Justin McLeod was also a teacher though retired one. Unfortunately, the eponymous Mr. Forster established a new stereotype, the self-sacrificing gay teacher who quietly gives up his job rather than cause distress to his students. An exceptionally important first appeared in 1986, M. E. Kerr's *Night Kites*, the first YA novel about AIDS. Even though the pandemic, which in its early years principally affected gay men, had been around since 1981, nervous publishers had been notably reluctant to address the subject in books for teens. Indeed, Kerr, in her Margaret A. Edwards Award acceptance speech, acknowledged that she felt she might have committed a form of professional suicide in writing the book, especially because her AIDS sufferer is a young gay man. She explained: "It seemed to me that *not* to have a homosexual be the AIDS sufferer would be a way of recognizing the illness but not those who have it . . . a sort of don't ask/don't tell proposition, where the reader can know the nature of the plague, without having to deal with those personalities who threaten the status quo" (Cart and Jenkins 2006, 63).

Unfortunately, in the years since, there have been only a handful of other YA novels dealing with this issue, even though at the end of 2012 more than 62,400 youth were living with HIV in the United States. In 2013 an estimated 2,704 were diagnosed with full-blown AIDS, representing 10 percent of the 26,688 people diagnosed with the disease that year (CDC nd, HIV among Youth).

Sadly, 60 percent of these young people didn't know they were infected (Mann 2013). "Only 13 percent of high school students have been tested," according to Dr. Jonathan Mermin, director of the CDC's Division of HIV/AIDS Prevention. "So they're not getting all the information they need at an age when they're starting to be sexually active" (Mann 2013).

Clearly there is a desperate need for good, realistic fiction about this issue and yet, other than *Night Kites,* only two other novels addressed the issue in the eighties; thirteen were added to that number in the nineties; but since the millennium, there have been only four or five more, although one that addressed the pandemic in Africa—Alan Stratton's *Chanda's Secrets* (2004)— was selected as a Printz honor title in 2005. And a second excellent novel, *Sky-scraping* by Cordelia Jensen, was published in 2015. This semiautobiographical novel written in free verse tells the story of Mira, who discovers her father is gay and that his HIV status is deteriorating into full-blown AIDS.

In addition to being a decade of firsts, the 1980s also saw a significant increase in the number of LGBT novels: forty titles compared to a mere eight in the seventies. Of the eighties' total, however, only half-a-dozen would prove to be of enduring literary value. In addition to *Annie on My Mind, Dance on My Grave,* and *Night Kites,* three others offered notable contributions to the gradually emerging field: Ron Koertge's *Arizona Kid* (1988), A. M. Homes's *Jack* (1989) and Francesca Lia Block's *Weetzie Bat* (1989).

Koertge's story of the memorable summer a teenage boy spends with his gay Uncle Wes in Arizona is significant not only because it includes the issue of AIDS, but also—and even more significantly—because it is the first gay-themed novel since M. E. Kerr's *I'll Love You When You're More Like Me* (1977) to include humor, a refreshing change in a field more given to the tragic than the comic. Homes's novel about a boy who discovers his father is gay is notable not only for its wryly humorous voice but also for its realistic depiction of a teen's journey from anger to acceptance. Block's novel is notable, like Koertge's, for its inclusion of AIDS, but also—and more significantly—for its lyrical celebration and open-hearted embrace of love as both an aspect of homosexuality and also an ingredient essential to the human experience.

The field of LGBT literature for Yas continued to expand in the nineties, the number of titles being published—seventy-five—nearly doubling the forty that appeared in the eighties. Unfortunately, once again, advances were more statistical than aesthetic. Too many of the novels in the new decade (fifty-one of seventy-five) continued to focus narrowly on the coming-out experience and too few dealt with the realities of living as an out teen. Also, the literature's gender imbalance, a problem since its beginnings, continued apace. Thus, in the eighties 73 percent of the books featured gay males and only 27 percent lesbians. The numbers in the nineties were, if anything, even more skewed, 69 percent dealing with gays and only 26 percent with lesbians. The remaining 5 percent actually included both gay and lesbian characters, a notable advance for a literature that had previously been rigidly divided between genders. Another interesting—but dubious—trend of the nineties was the movement of the gay or lesbian character from the central role of protagonist to that of secondary character. In the eighties, 40 percent of gay characters had been protagonists and 60 percent secondary characters. But in the nineties, only 27 percent remained protagonists and 73 percent had become secondary characters. This may have made the books more accessible to non-gay readers (like the earlier practice of making the narrator straight even when the central character was gay), but demoting these characters to often one-dimensional supporting roles tended to rob them of their individuality, make them token gay characters, and invite the danger of lazy stereotyping.

Nevertheless, there were a number of 1990s books—at least twenty of the seventy-five—that remain significant either for their literary quality or for the advances they introduced into the field. Sometimes they offered both as in the case of Jacqueline Woodson's novels *The Dear One, From the Notebooks of Melanin Sun,* and *The House You Pass on the Way,* which variously featured characters of color, a mixed-race relationship, fully realized adult lesbian characters, and more. Less successful literarily but equally important in terms of innovation were the two Pride Pack novels of R. J. Hamilton (*Who Framed Lorenzo Garcia* and *The Case of the Missing Mother* [1995], a miniseries that introduced gay Latino characters to the field (a non-series novel that did the same was Gloria Velasquez's *Tommy Stands Alone* [1995]).

Francesca Lia Block added three novels to her Weetzie Bat cycle in the 1990s: *Witch Baby* (1991), *Missing Angel Juan* (1993), and—most notably—*Baby Bebop* (1995), which gave readers the back story of Weetzie's gay best friend Dirk.

The nineties also saw the publication in the United States of important novels from Australia (*Peter* by Kate Walker [1993] and New Zealand (Paula Boock's *Dare Truth or Promise* [1999] and William Taylor's *The Blue Lawn* [1999]) confirming, for American readers, the universality of the homosexual experience.

One of the best written and most emotionally satisfying of the novels about AIDS, Theresa Nelson's *Earthshine* was published in 1994, while Robert Paul Walker's *The Method* (1990) made history by being the first YA novel to include a gay restaurant and a Gay Pride parade, acknowledging in the process that gay and lesbian teens did not have to live in hermetically sealed isolation but could be part of a larger—and even companionable—culture.

As for M. E. Kerr, she continued her long-standing habit of innovation by giving readers the first novel to deal with bisexuality: *Hello, I Lied* (1997), while a second novel by her, *Deliver Us from Evie* (1994), offered an unusual take on stereotyping by presenting perhaps the most fully realized lesbian character to date, the titular Evie, who resembles Elvis Presley and enjoys fixing farm machinery, telling her mother, "Some of us look it, Mom! I know you so-called normal people would like it better if we looked as much like all of you as possible, but some of us don't, can't, and never will!"

Important short stories with gay or lesbian content also appeared in the nineties: Marion Dane Bauer's *Am I Blue?* (1994) was a landmark collection entirely devoted to gay or lesbian characters and themes. And two of the most memorable stories in Chris Crutcher's *Athletic Shorts* (1991) addressed gay themes: *In the Time I Get* featured a character with AIDS, while the unforgettable *A Brief Moment in the Life of Angus Bethune* gave us a teenage boy with not one but two sets of homosexual parents!

Both the growing literary importance of fiction with homosexual content and its increasingly widespread acceptance were evidenced by the 1999 publication of Ellen Wittlinger's *Hard Love*, a book that became one of the first Printz Honor Award recipients, setting the stage for significant progress in this field in the decade to follow.

Sure enough, 2004 would be a singularly important year in the ongoing evolution of LGBT literature. This was the year Aidan Chambers received the Michael L. Printz Award for his extraordinary gay-themed novel *Postcards from No Man's Land*, which subtly and thought-provokingly addressed the complications that visit the nature of sexual identity. That same year, Garret Freymann-Weyr received a Printz honor for her novel *My Heartbeat*, which examines two teenage boys' attempts to define their own sexual identities. Also in 2004, the Margaret A. Edwards Award was presented to Nancy Garden. As in the earlier case of Judy Blume, the selection committee—to underscore its importance—mentioned only one of the recipient's books in the award citation. It was, of course, *Annie on My Mind*.

The volume of titles giving faces to lesbian, gay, and bisexual teens also continued to grow significantly in the new century. From 2000 through 2015, no less than 319 LGBT titles were published,[2] an average of more than 21 per year (compared with 1 per year in the 1970s, 4 in the 1980s, and 7 in the 1990s). The numbers published each year increased dramatically during this period ranging from 4 in 2000 to 64 in 2015—that's 24 more than were published throughout the entire decade of the 1980s and only 12 less than in the 1990s.

In a positive development, new output also reflected many of the diverse trends that have defined young adult literature for the twenty-first century. Thus, LGBT content began enriching literary fiction, genre fiction, commercial fiction, crossover novels, short stories, poetry, and a growing body of ethnically, racially, and culturally diverse literature. Even better, it has finally begun giving faces to those who are among the last invisible teens, those who are transgender. The first transsexual[3] character appeared in Francesca Lia Block's 1996 short story "Dragons in Manhattan" (published in her anthology *Girl Goddess #9*). The first appearance of a transgender character was in Emma Donoghue's *The Welcome*, a story in my 2001 anthology *Love and Sex*. And there are three transgender stories—by Francesca Lia Block, Jennifer Finney Boylan, and Jacqueline Woodson—in my 2009 collection *How Beautiful the Ordinary*. Meanwhile in 2004 a transgender character finally became the focus of an entire novel, Julie Anne Peters's groundbreaking and National Book Award-shortlisted *Luna* (2004). A second novel featuring a transgender character, Ellen Wittlinger's *Parrotfish*, followed in 2007. More recent novels include *Gracefully Grayson* by Ami Polonsky (2014), the first middle-school novel to feature a transgender character. *George* (2015) followed the next year, to tell the story of a ten-year-old boy who realizes he is really a girl inside. *Freakboy*, a novel in verse by Kristen Elizabeth Clark (2013), and *Beautiful Music for Ugly Children* by Kirstin Cronn-Mills (2012) are also important examples as is a lovely work of nonfiction: *Beyond Magenta* by Susan Kuklin (2014). In it six transgender teens tell their own stories, which are illustrated by Kuklin's memorable photographs.

Another important first occurred in 2014: the appearance of an intersex character in Bridget Birdsall's *Double Exposure*. Two more followed in 2015: Alyssa Brugman's *Alex as Well* and I. W. Gregorio's *None of the Above*. The same year Jeff Garvin's *Symptoms of Being Human* became the first to feature a gender fluid character and Robin Talley's *What We Left Behind*, a gender queer character.

A significant number of important new writers have emerged in recent years to continue bringing art, innovation, and diversity to LGBT literature. Among them, certainly, are author and editor David Levithan, whose 2003 novel *Boy Meets Boy* employs a breathtakingly good mixture of realism and fantasy in its creation of an idealized world in which sexual differences are not castigated, but celebrated! More recent novels by the talented Mr. Levithan include *Will Grayson, Will Grayson* (with John Green) (2010); *Two Boys*

Kissing (2013), and *Hold Me Closer* (2015). Evidence of his importance to the field of LGBTQI literature—and to YA literature in general—is his selection as winner of the 2016 Margaret A. Edwards Award.

A second talent, Alex Sanchez, has explored multiple aspects of the gay and lesbian life experience in his Rainbow Boys trilogy, while in his 2004 novel *So Hard to Say* he wrote one of the few gay-themed novels for middle-school readers. Significantly, in his later novel *Boyfriends with Girlfriends* (2011) he became one of the first authors to feature bisexual characters since M. E. Kerr's 1997 novel *Hello, I Lied.* Other significant new writers include Christian Burch, Nick Burd, emily m. danforth, Sara Farizan, Brent Hartinger, Steve Kluger, Bill Konigsburg, Brian Malloy, P. E. Ryan, Sara Ryan, Brian Sloane, Martin Wilson, and Benjamin Alire Saenz, whose novel *Aristotle and Dante Discover the Secrets of the Universe* received a Printz Honor Award in 2013.

Jandy Nelson deserves special attention here and praise for her superb novel *I'll Give You the Sun,* which features a gay co-protagonist and is winner of the 2015 Printz Award, thus becoming the second gay-themed novel to cop the prize, the first—as previously noted—being Aidan Chamber's *Postcards from No Man's Land.*

I should mention here another advance in LGBT literature: the increasing presence of gay and lesbian characters in comics and graphic novels. The most celebrated example of these is surely Alison Bechdel's graphic novel *Fun Home* (2006). Bechdel's award-winning coming-of-age memoir focuses not only on her being a lesbian but also on her closeted father being gay. Another more recent graphic novel for a younger audience is Raina Telgemeier's notable *Drama* (2012). The mainstreaming of LGBT characters in comics is further evidenced by Archie Comics' introduction of its first gay character, Kevin Keller, and the increasing presence of homosexual characters in superhero comics: DC, for example, has given readers two: Batwoman, who is a lesbian, and Midnighter, who is gay. Jim Lee, copublisher of DC, comments: "Our main directive is to make these characters as modern and reflective of the real world (as possible)" (Schmidt 2015).

Shannon Watters, an editor at Boom! Studios, publishers of the lesbian-themed *Lumberjanes,* concludes, "It is very encouraging to see the decisions that DC and Marvel have made in giving marginalized creators more of a platform to tell their stories but we still have a long way to go" (Schmidt 2015).

Clearly LGBTQ literature has come a long way since its 1969 genesis. Especially salutary is its evolution in quality. In fact, when my collaborator Christine A. Jenkins and I set out to survey the field in 2014, we found 250 novels of sufficient quality to include them in our 2015 book *Top 250 LGBTQ Books for Teens*. Other indicators of quality are ALA's Stonewall Awards and its annual Rainbow List of the best LGBTQ books for young adults.

Nevertheless, LGBTQ remains a literature in transition. Despite the many gains in the field, further advances still need to be made. For example, too many titles, especially those that remain focused on coming out, continue to treat being homosexual or transgender as a problem or issue, though—in real world context—this is understandable. For the sad fact is that the lives of gay, lesbian, and bisexual youth too often remain fraught; for example, they are two to five times as likely as their straight peers to attempt suicide and young transgender people are also at heightened risk (Adelson and Knight 2015). Too, according to the latest School Climate Survey conducted by GLSEN (Gay, Lesbian, Straight Educators Network), schools remain hostile environments for a distressing number of LGBT students. Consider that 74 percent of them were verbally harassed in 2014 because of their sexual orientation and 55 percent because of their gender expression. As well, 36 percent were physically harassed (e.g., pushed or shoved); 23 percent were similarly abused because of their gender expression; 17 percent were physically assaulted (e.g., punched, kicked injured with a weapon), as were 11 percent for their gender expression. And, finally, 56 percent reported personally experiencing LGBT-related discriminatory policies or practices at school (Gay Lesbian Straight Educators Network 2014).

Though it certainly remains important to have literature that reflects these disturbing realities, it is also important to publish more novels that feature characters whose LGBT identity is simply a given, as it is in stories about heterosexual characters. Such a literature of assimilation is not without its detractors, who feel it would result in the ultimate elimination of gay culture, but I would argue that it reflects the increasing reality of the lives of at least some LGBT teens and therefore deserves attention.

In other areas of change, because of the increasingly early age at which young people are now coming out, we need more novels for middle-school readers that examine this phenomenon. We continue to need more LGBT novels, too, with characters of color and characters who come from other cultures and ethnicities. A welcome addition to the field is, thus, Sara Farizan, whose *If You Could Be Mine* (Algonquin 2013) is a novel about two lesbian lovers who are Persian and living in Iran. Also noteworthy is Michael Barakiva's *One Man Guy* (Hyperion 2014), a novel about an Armenian-American teen who falls in love with a boy he meets in summer school, and Hannah Moskowitz's *Not Otherwise Specified* (Simon Pulse 2015), with its bisexual African American protagonist. What else do we need? Surely we need more novels with same-sex parents and, finally, we need the genre to continue to come of age as literature. And yet, if ours is not quite the wonderful world that a gay character in *Boy Meets Boy* sees when he looks around himself, we are getting there—and (pace, John Donovan) it will definitely be worth the trip!

Notes

1. Lord Alfred Douglas famously called homosexuality "The love that dare not speak its name."

2. For a number of years my colleague Christine Jenkins and I have been maintaining annual lists of all new LGBT novels published; these figures are based on those lists.

3. A transgender person is one who identifies with the opposite sex; a transsexual is a person whose sex has been surgically changed.

Still the Controversies Continue

Book Challenges and Censorship, Oh My

NO MATTER HOW COMPELLING A CASE ONE MIGHT MAKE FOR BRINGING candor to young adult literature, many people continue to take strenuous exception to the notion. The result is not only a great deal of huffing and puffing by the mainstream media, but also a cascade of book challenges in America's schools and libraries. No one can say precisely how many of these occur, because the American Library Association's Office of Intellectual Freedom estimates that 70 to 80 percent of such cases routinely go unreported. If so, that would mean there are significantly more than the 6,855 challenges that were reported between 2000 and 2015. Of those, the most common challenges were due to the following reasons: sexual explicitness, offensive language unsuited to age group, violence, and homosexuality.

Although some of these cases involved books published as adult titles, they were all challenged—in a majority of the cases by parents—because of their use by or with children and young adults. As a result, the largest incidence of challenges has taken place in school libraries, followed closely by classrooms and, finally, by public libraries (www.ala.org/oif).

The single most challenged book in 2014 was Sherman Alexie's semi-autobiographical YA novel *The Absolutely True Diary of a Part-Time Indian*. The clutch of reasons for which it was challenged include: anti-family sentiment; cultural insensitivity; drugs, alcohol, smoking, and gambling; offensive language; sex education; sexually explicitness; unsuited for age group; violence; and depictions of bullying. One wonders if there is anything in the book the censors don't find offensive! Perhaps accordingly, since its publication in 2007, *True Diary* has been a regular target of would-be censors, but so have many other young adult books, among them, the Gossip Girl books, *The Perks of Being a Wallflower*, the Alice series by Phyllis Reynolds Naylor, Chris Crutcher's *Athletic Shorts*, Robert Cormier's *The Chocolate War*, the TTYL series by Lauren Myracle, *The Earth, My Butt and Other Big, Round Things* by Carolyn Mackler, Walter Dean Myers's *Fallen Angels*, and *Go Ask Alice* (by the notorious Anonymous).

Acknowledging the frequent appearance of YA books on its annual lists of the most challenged books, ALA chose to spotlight them during its 2015 Banned Books Week (September 27–October 3, 2015). "Young adult books are challenged more frequently than any other type of books," said Judith Platt, chair of the week's national planning committee, explaining that the often difficult issues presented in YA titles make them a ripe target for censorship (Maughan 2015).

In fact, forty-five of the top one hundred most censored books of the first decade of the twenty-first century are YA titles, most of them novels. There is, of course, a great deal of other information about censorship, ALA's Office of Intellectual Freedom (OIF) being a staple source of much of it. But there are also a few works of fiction that put a human face on the issue, including Nancy Garden's *The Year They Burned the Books*, *Americus* by M. K. Reed, Chris Crutcher's *The Sledding Hill*, and *Places I Never Meant to Be*, a collection of original short stories edited by Judy Blume and written by often challenged authors. Reading Blume's introduction to this book was—for me—a trip down memory lane. Blume recalls that as a junior in high school she went to her local public library in Elizabeth, New Jersey, in search of a copy of novelist John O'Hara's *A Rage to Live*. "But I couldn't find it," she explains. "When I asked, the librarian told me THAT book was RESTRICTED. It was kept in a locked closet, and I couldn't take it out without permission from my parents" (Blume 1999, 2).

Well, Judy Blume and I are roughly the same age, and while she was growing up in Elizabeth, New Jersey, I was growing up in Logansport, Indiana. Our two hometowns probably had little in common except that the public library in each had a collection of restricted books. In Logansport, ours were kept in something called the locked case. Aside from *A Rage to Live*, I don't know what was restricted in Elizabeth and, alas, I've forgotten the identity of most of the contents of the Logansport locked case except for the Kinsey Reports and copies of the novels *Forever Amber* and *Peyton Place*. I am happy to report that when I grew up to become the library's director—as I did—one of my first acts was to unlock the locked case and release its contents (and I finally got to read *Peyton Place!*).

Well, that was then and this is now, and today it's not locked closets and cases we need to worry about; it's locked minds—minds that are impervious to alternative points of view and terrified of telling young people the sometimes thorny truth about the realities of the world. One certainly understands and sympathizes with parents and other concerned adults who wish to protect their own youngsters from what they perceive as being objectionable, because I believe that parents need to be aware of and responsible for their offspring's reading. However, I draw the line at parents who unilaterally and adamantly decree that not only their own children but also those of other parents may not have access to materials.

Perhaps as troubling to me is the continuing barrage of sensationalistic, often misleading articles that appear in the mainstream media, media that are—or so I was taught in journalism school—supposed to be defenders of intellectual freedom and the people's right to know. As was the case in the 1990s, a never-ending stream of over-the-top, so-called exposés of books for youth continues to flow from the Fourth Estate. Here's a sample of twenty-first century headlines:

> "Young Readers, Harsh Reality" (*The New York Times*, June 13, 2002)
>
> "New Book on Children's Sexuality Causes a Furor" (Associated Press wire story, April 3, 2002)
>
> "It Ain't Half Hot, Mum" (*The Manchester Guardian*, February 23, 2003—yes, some of these stories appeared in the British press)
>
> "So It's Goodbye to Janet and John" (*The London Times*, May 2, 2003)
>
> "City's Ed. Boobs" (*The New York Post*, October 13, 2003—the lede for this story is "The three R's in education were almost racy, raunchy, and risqué")
>
> "What (Sex) Boys (Sex) Think (Sex) About" (*The New York Times*, October 7, 2004—this is actually an article about the television series *Life as We Know It*, but the show was adapted from Melvin Burgess's controversial YA novel *Doing It*.)

"Teen Playas" (*Entertainment Weekly*, March 7, 2005)

"Racy Books for Teens Pondered" (*The New York Journal News*, July 10, 2005)

"Battle of the Books: The Problem with 'Problem' Young Adult Fiction" (*Slate*, June 17, 2005)

"Racy Reads" (*The New York Journal News*, July 10, 2005)

"You're Reading . . . What?" (*The Wall Street Journal*, June 24, 2005)

"Young Readers Pulled into a Rich, Amoral Teen Universe" (*The San Francisco Chronicle*, September 24, 2005)

"Tales of Raw Misery for Ages Twelve and Up" (*The New York Times*, July 30, 2007)

"Teen Fiction Plots Are Darker and Starker" (*The Denver Post*, July 5, 2009)

"It Was Like All Dark and Stormy" (*The Wall Street Journal*, June 6, 2009)

"Rape, Abortion, Incest. Is This What CHILDREN Should Read?" (*Daily Mail*, July 9, 2009)

"Darkness Too Visible" (*The Wall Street Journal*, June 4, 2011)

"Is It Time to Rate Young Adult Books for Mature Content?" (*US News and World Report*, May 18, 2012)

"Childhood, Uncensored" (*The New York Times*, December 30, 2012)

"Sex in Young Adult Fiction—A Rising Trend?" (*The Telegraph*, February 14, 2013)

"Young Adult Books and Sex: What We Learned under the Covers" (CNN.com, January 15, 2014)

"YA Books on Death: Is Young Adult Fiction Becoming Too Dark?" (*Manchester Guardian*, May 11, 2014)

As was the case a decade-and-a-half ago, too many of these articles were written by reporters who had not a clue about young adult literature, nor had they seemed to have read the books they decried. Accordingly, their pieces sometimes approached the ludicrous—at least to knowledgeable professionals. Unfortunately it's not only professionals who are reading them, it's also credulous parents or people who are looking for a cause—*célèbre* or otherwise. And who, in turn, also fail to read the books but, nevertheless, storm the barricades or, more probably, the nearest library, to file a challenge.

Among the many anti-YA screeds, one of the most vitriolic is titled: "Darkness Too Visible: Contemporary Fiction for Teens Is Rife with Explicit Abuse, Violence and Depravity" (Gurdon 2011).

Written by one Meghan Cox Gurdon, it is an often patronizing, even more often sneering indictment of what it perceives to be the depravity of young adult literature. Gurdon sets the tone with her question, "How dark is contemporary fiction for teens? Darker than when you were a child, my dear." The rest of her equally condescending screed is an example of exaggeration and specious extrapolation: "Kidnapping and pederasty and incest and brutal beatings," she writes, "are now just part of the run of things in novels directed, broadly speaking, at children from the ages of 12 to 18." She doesn't, of course, identify which books contain those atrocities. And are eighteen-year-olds really children? She goes on to give the back of her mailed fist to such talents as the great Robert Cormier who, she says, "is generally credited with having introduced utter hopelessness to teen narratives" (see chapter 2 of this book for my implicit rebuttal of this charge) and to the more contemporary Lauren Myracle, whose deeply felt novel *Shine* she dismembers with a verbal broadsword. She saves her most vitriolic remarks, however, for champions of intellectual freedom. "Every year," she sneers, "the American Library Association delights in releasing a list of the most frequently challenged books." I'd say this is done more in sorrow than delight. But nevertheless, Gurdon continues, "The book business exists to sell books; parents exist to rear children and oughtn't be daunted by cries of censorship. No family is obliged to acquiesce when publishers use the vehicle of fundamental free-expression principles to try to bulldoze coarseness or misery into their children's lives."

Author Sherman Alexie (2011) would argue that there is already misery in children's lives, and does so in an article he penned for the journal *Rethinking Schools:* "Why the Best Kids Books Are Written in Blood." Responding to Gurdon's rumblings about what she perceives as the pernicious power of realistic YA fiction, he writes, "Does Ms. Gurdon honestly believe that a sexually explicit YA novel might somehow traumatize a teen mother? Does she believe that a YA novel about murder and rape will somehow shock a teenager whose life has been damaged by murder and rape? Does she believe a dystopian novel will frighten a kid who already lives in hell?"

"I write books for teenagers," he concludes, "because I vividly remember what it felt like to be a teen facing everyday and epic dangers. I don't write to protect them. It's far too late for that. I write to give them weapons—in the form of words and ideas—that will help them fight their monsters. I write in blood because I remember what it felt like to bleed."

Lauren Myracle, who—as noted—is also attacked by Gurdon, says, "Give your kid some credit for being smart—just because they read about something doesn't mean they will do it. Fiction is a safe place to explore" (Saint Louis 2012).

Or not? Sarah Coyne, a professor in Brigham Young University's department of family life, who conducted a 2012 study of profanity in YA books, feels they should be rated and labeled. "I think we put books on a pedestal compared to other forms of media," she says; "I thought long and hard about whether to do the study in the first place—I think banning books is a terrible idea but a content warning on the back I think would empower parents" (Koebler 2012).

I agree that banning books is a terrible idea, but so is rating or labeling them! Just for starters, who is going to define the ratings? Who is going to apply the warning? Who is going to enforce their application? And isn't this an implicit form of banning, anyway?

Beth Yoke, executive director of the Young Adult Library Services Association, speaks to this point when she says, "Books can be a safe way for young people to explore edgier, sensitive or complicated topics. Having a big, nebulous organization decide what your kid can or can't read is not really a democratic process" (Koebler 2012).

By now it should be clear that the twenty-first century has brought new artistic freedom to both writers and publishers of young adult books. With that new freedom has come new responsibility—not only for them but also for librarians, teachers, and reviewers. That responsibility includes reading widely, receiving a grounding in the history of the literature, developing critical evaluative and thinking skills, becoming aware of the realities and problems of YA life, and being on the lookout for the truly exploitative and irresponsible, especially because the ongoing process of liberating young adult literature from some of its former restraints continues to redefine not only its audience but also its marketplace.

Who knows what tomorrow might bring? As for today, this surely remains one of the most exciting, dynamic periods in the whole history of young adult literature.

Let the wild rumpus continue.

The Viz Biz

Transforming the Funnies

Beginnings

THE COMICS HAVE LONG BEEN A STAPLE OF AMERICAN POPULAR CULTURE; IN fact, they were one of the seven "lively arts" identified by cultural critic Gilbert Seldes, in his landmark 1924 book of the same title.[1] Nevertheless, they found neither respect nor place in America's school and public libraries, where, for decades, they were considered at best ephemeral and at worst either subliterate or downright subversive. This impoverished attitude began to turn around in the 1980s and 1990s, but it didn't become a certifiable phenomenon until YALSA devoted an entire 2002 preconference to the subject. To widespread surprise, the event was a sellout and was, in fact, the best attended of all the ALA preconferences that year. How the comics came into the library limelight and, almost overnight, turned into must-have staple constituents of library collections, is a fascinating story.

It began in the 1890s with the first newspaper comic strips. One of the earliest and most influential of these was R. F. Outcault's *Hogan's Alley*, which debuted on May 5, 1895, in the *New York World*. Not a strip but, instead, a single-panel cartoon, the feature introduced the Yellow Kid, who quickly became its signature character. As comics historian Richard Marschall (1989, 24–25) writes, "It was 'Hogan's Alley' starring the Yellow Kid that truly turned the newspaper world upside down. Every paper had to have its own color comic section and every publisher longed to have its own counterpart of the Yellow Kid."

Among those early counterparts were Rudolph Dirks's *The Katzenjammer Kids*, Frederick Opper's *Happy Hooligan*, and Winsor McKay's gorgeously drawn *Little Nemo*, which would influence generations of children's picture book artists to come, ranging from Maurice Sendak to William Joyce.

Created, frankly, to sell newspapers, these comics quickly attracted huge audiences of eager readers, among them the many new immigrants who were arriving in America as part of the greatest wave of immigration in this country's history. The strips appealed not only because they featured immigrants themselves—especially the tenement dwellers of *Hogan's Alley* and the German-American Dirks's *Katzenjammer Kids*—but also because people who did not have English as a first language embraced visual stories that could be comprehended at a glance.

Though at first confined to a single panel, the new comics quickly became a more kinetic exercise, assuming the form of multi-panel strips of sequential images. It didn't take long thereafter for the first spin-offs to appear: book-length compilations of previously published daily strips that, as early as 1902, were being called comic books.

The first comic book to contain all new stories and characters, *New Fun 1* debuted in 1935, the same year that Walt Disney's first comic book, *Mickey Mouse Magazine*, also appeared.

In the meantime, another kind of kinetic reading experience that married words and pictures in a seamless symbiotic unity, the children's picture book, had debuted (Wanda Gag's *Millions of Cats* [Coward-McCann 1928] is often cited as being the first of these) and cartoons had begun to move in the form of animated film even earlier; Winsor McKay, for example, produced a hand-colored film of his *Little Nemo* around 1911, while Disney's first sound cartoon, *Steamboat Willie* came along in 1928. In the decades since, all three of these art forms have continued to maintain a creatively symbiotic relationship, though it is the comic book that has contributed most directly to the emergence of today's library-friendly comics form known as the graphic novel.

In 1938, three years after the first original comic book appeared, the comics made another giant leap forward with the publication in 1938 of *Action Comics #1*, which introduced Jerry Siegel and Joe Shuster's soon-to-be-immortal Superman. A year later, another caped crusader, Bob Kane's Batman, appeared and within a decade another 400 superheroes had joined the ranks. America had never been so well protected!

The next two decades saw such an exponential growth in comic book publishing that the period is now generally regarded as the golden age of comic books. According to industry observer Michael R. Lavin, comic book sales were ranging from 500 million to 1.3 billion copies a year by 1953. In the meantime, however, those same comic books had become much edgier in content thanks to the rise of graphically violent horror, crime, and war "comics," especially those published by William Gaines's EC imprint. In 1954 child psychiatrist Frederick Wertham's controversial book *The Seduction of the Innocent* appeared. Linking comic book violence to the rise of juvenile crime, Wertham's book created a backlash that resulted in the Comic Book Hearings of the United States Senate Subcommittee on Juvenile Delinquency and the creation of the starchy Comics Code Authority. The adverse publicity almost destroyed the comic-book industry as sales plummeted and the number of publishers shrank from some three dozen to no more than nine.

Fortunately, the visual has always had an enduring appeal, and by 1956 a new silver age of comics had begun, soon becoming an even more robust revival with the 1960s debut of two new features from Marvel Comics: *Fantastic Four* and, perhaps more notably in terms of young adult literature, *Spiderman*, who was, in reality, troubled teen Peter Parker, arguably the first psychologically complex superhero. While this was happening, the counterculture movement of the sixties had begun spawning adult, underground comics created, most notably, by R. Crumb, whose work has, over the years since, become so respectable that it is now featured in the *New Yorker!*

The increasing sophistication of characterization and subject matter came together in 1978 in the pages of veteran cartoonist Will Eisner's ambitious book *A Contract with God and Other Tenement Stories*. To describe this novel-length collection of four linked literary stories, Eisner used the term *graphic novel*, which has since become identified with him, though it had actually been used two years before in George Metzger's 1976 book *Time and Again*.

The Comics Come of Age

Nearly another decade would pass, however, before three other important, genre-changing works appeared in the same landmark year of 1986. Together they launched a new age of grown-up comics known as "graphic novels." The three were Art Spiegelman's *Maus*, Frank Miller's *Dark Knight Returns*, and Alan Moore and Dave Gibbons's *Watchmen*. Until this time, comic books had been sold at newsstands or, increasingly, at specialty comic book stores. As the developments we've been charting began to broaden the comic book audience, however, some publishers like Fantagraphics, Drawn and Quarterly, Viz, and Dark Horse started selling their output through general bookstores. This, in turn, began attracting the attention of librarians. Thus, as early as 1984, the Hawaii State Public Library System had started acquiring this form of visual and verbal communication. California's Berkeley Public Library followed suit in 1989. Enough other libraries had hopped onto the comic book bandwagon by 1994 that *VOYA* magazine launched a regular column, "Graphically Speaking," in which librarian Kat Kan became one of the first to review graphic novels for a library-based readership. In the meantime, Spiegelman's *Maus* and its sequel *Maus II*, released in a single volume in 1992 by Harper, received the Pulitzer Prize, and signaled that the venerable comic book had finally come of age as a newly vibrant and vital art form that deserved a place even on respectable library shelves.

In the wake of *Maus*, established comics publishers like DC, Fantagraphics, Top Shelf, and Drawn and Quarterly began experimenting with similarly serious graphic novels or alternative comics as they were also called. DC actually started two imprints—Vertigo and Paradox Press—to differentiate its new darker, more sophisticated efforts from its traditional superhero series. The former imprint, launched in 1993, published such early classics as Alan Moore and David Lloyd's *V for Vendetta* and Neil Gaiman's *Sandman* (an original Sandman graphic novel, *The Sandman: Endless Nights*, published in 2003, became the first graphic novel to make *The New York Times* Best Seller List). The latter imprint, formed the same year, published both Howard Cruse's novel of the civil rights era *Stuck Rubber Baby* and Max Allan Collins and Richard Rayner's *Road to Perdition*, which, some years later, would become a movie starring Tom Hanks and Paul Newman.

The trend to the alternative continued in 1995, when Canadian publisher Drawn and Quarterly began issuing Adrian Tomine's serially published *Optic Nerve*, while in 1998 Fantagraphics published Daniel Clowes's *Ghost World*, and in 2000 Joe Sacco's innovative exercise in graphic journalism *Safe Area Gorazde*.

At the same time, a handful of major trade book publishers began experimenting with what—to them—was still a new form. One of the first was Avon; its imprint Neon Lit debuted in 1994 with a graphic version of Paul Auster's noir novel *City of Glass*. Three years later, Bob Mecoy, who had become vice president and senior editor at Simon and Schuster after launching the Avon imprint, told *Publishers Weekly:* "Basically what we were doing was making paper movies." He continued, "Book publishing now competes with the rest of the entertainment industry and that means finding other viable ways to tell a story, especially at a time when the public seems so interested in multimedia entertainment" (Morales 1997, 49).

Not only was the public interested but so, increasingly, were other traditional book publishers. In 1996, Little, Brown, the longtime American publisher of Belgian cartoonist Herge's internationally celebrated *Tintin*, published Ben Katchor's critically hailed *Julius Knipl: Real Estate Photographer* and Pantheon, which has since become the most important trade publisher of literary graphic novels, followed in 1998 with Katchor's next novel, *The Jew of New York.* Pantheon subsequently published Clowes's *David Boring* (2000) and Chris Ware's extraordinary *Jimmy Corrigan: The Smartest Kid on Earth* (2000), which is regarded by some as being the field's first masterpiece.

Though avidly read by teens, all of these books were technically published for adults. One of the first titles to be published expressly for young adults was Karen D. Hirsch's original anthology *Mind Riot: Coming of Age in Comix* (1997), and in 2000 the Joanna Cotler imprint at HarperCollins launched the Little Lit series, coedited by Art Spiegelman and his wife Francoise Mouly, the Art Editor of the *New Yorker.* Clearly, as Spiegelman quipped, "Comics aren't just for grownups any more" (Reid and Macdonald 2000, 44–45). And they certainly weren't just for collectors, aging fan boys, or other habitués of specialty comic bookstores, either. By the time the silver anniversary of the graphic novel arrived in 2003, *Time* magazine had claimed, "Graphic novels have finally reached a point of critical mass in both popular consciousness and sales. Micha Hershman of the chain bookstore Borders confirms the trend, saying, 'Over the last four years graphic novels have shown the largest percentage of growth in sales over any other book category'" (Arnold 2003).

As noted earlier, libraries had begun purchasing this vital new art form as early as the mid-eighties; indeed, as Judith Rosen (2003, 52) pointed out, "Initially libraries led the way in embracing comics as a way to get young people to read. And wholesalers that service libraries developed catalogues, e-mailings and Web sites to help with building graphic novel collections."

This hope—that the popularity of comics and graphic novels might lure kids to the library and induce them to read—was a fundamental reason for librarians' initial interest in developing these collections. Other reasons that have stood the test of time include:

- Comics' proven capacity to increase visual literacy, an essential skill in a digital age
- Their high visual content, which recommends their use with reluctant readers and English language-learners
- Their established viability as a new—and continuously evolving—art form
- Their indispensable place in popular culture
- And—more pragmatically—their demonstrated capacity for increasing circulation and enhanced use of other library collections

Libraries Enter the Picture

Nevertheless, as previously noted, it wasn't until 2002 that a true turning point arrived; not only did YALSA hold its first graphic novel preconference, its Popular Paperbacks Committee issued a recommended list of graphic novels for teens, and "Get Graphic @ Your Library" was selected as the theme for national Teen Read Week. Just three years later, YALSA launched its annual Great Graphic Novels for Teens list, an act that invited serious consideration of how to review and evaluate this evolving art form. The policies and procedures for the Great Graphic Novels Committee list the following criteria:

- Reflect an integration of images and words
- Exhibit a clarity of visual flow on the page
- Ability of images to convey necessary meaning
- Outstanding quality of the artwork's reproduction
- Narrative enhanced by the artwork
- Narrative dominated by sequential art component

Curious about this same issue of evaluation, I interviewed six-time Eisner Award–winning[2] graphic novelist Eric Shanower, creator of *The Age of Bronze*, an epic retelling of the Trojan War in comic book form. To my question, "How should librarians go about assessing work like yours?" he replied, "They should ask: Is the artwork engaging? Does it draw a reader into the story? Is the movement of the story from one panel to the next clear? The visual storytelling doesn't necessarily need to be 'easy' or even linear but it does need to be comprehensible. Also, does the artwork serve the story? The evaluation of its technical aspects should be specific to the medium of the comics, but the evaluation of the emotional and intellectual content and impact—the aesthetic experience as a whole—will generally have much more in common with the ways other media are evaluated" (Cart, 2002b).[3]

One area of evaluation that shouldn't be ignored is the different impact of the written and visual experiences. In many cases the visual can offer the more visceral, inviting the attention of would-be censors.

Brigid Alverson (2014a, 43) cites one example, that of the Chicago Public Schools' 2013 removal of Marjane Satrapi's *Persepolis* from all classrooms because of "powerful images of torture" on a single page of the award-winning book. Another similar reason for challenges is what the researcher Steven Cary calls "the naked buns test" (Alverson 2014a). "It's the rare student or parent who objects to the words 'naked buns,' he writes, but an image of naked buns can set off fireworks."

Speaking of fireworks, Charles Brownstein, executive director of the Comic Book Legal Defense Fund, notes, "The number and profile of challenges that CBLDF participates in has risen dramatically in recent years" (Alverson 2014a, 43). Acknowledging this, ALA chose comic books and graphic novels as the focus of its 2014 Banned Books Week.

"Prose books and comics are challenged for the same reasons," Brownstein explains. "Content addressing the facts of life about growing up like sexuality, sexual orientations, race issues, challenging authority, and drug and alcohol use are causes for challenges. Profanity is as often a factor as is violence."

As is the case with books, a comprehensive selection policy is essential to fending off and responding to challenges of graphic novels and comics. It is also highly recommended that selectors examine comics before purchase. Happily, the presence of specialty comic book shops in most cities makes this possible. And if worse comes to worst, both the Comic Book Legal Defense Fund and ALA's Office of Intellectual Freedom are available to help.

The continuing—and even expanding—library interest in graphic novels spurred a number of trade publishers (among them Abrams Amulet, Random House, Puffin, and Hyperion) to start publishing graphic novels specifically targeted at young readers. In 2005, Scholastic became the first children's book publisher to inaugurate its own graphic novel imprint, which it called, appropriately, Graphix. Though initially focused on books for younger readers—including an ambitious, multivolume colorized release of Jeff Smith's classic Bone series—Graphix published its first YA title, *Breaking Up* by Aimee Friedman and Christine Norrie in 2007.

That same year, Simon and Schuster children's publishing announced an ambitious division-wide effort to encourage the publication of comics and graphic novels by all of its imprints, and Ginee Seo/Athenaeum quickly responded with *Chiggers*, an original graphic novel by award-winning cartoonist Hope Larsen.

By far the most promising and ambitious new imprint, however, was Roaring Brook/Macmillan's First Second. Led by Editorial Director Mark Siegel, himself a comics artist and book designer, the line launched in the spring of 2006; within a year one of its books had garnered remarkable recognition: *American Born Chinese* by Gene Luen Yang became the first graphic novel to receive the Michael L. Printz Award; it was also the first graphic novel to be shortlisted for the National Book Award in the young readers category.

Siegel, who grew up in France, brings a cosmopolitan sensibility to his imprint, which publishes not only American comic artists, but also editions of distinguished comic art from all over the world in a high-end, soft-cover format with French flaps and a uniform six-by-eight-and-a-half-inch trim size.

In light of the growing sophistication and aesthetic ambition of the highly visual form, one must ask what, exactly, a graphic novel is these days—is it, as some have asserted, just "a long comic book" (Estrada 2006, C4), or "a comic book that needs a bookmark?" (McGrath 2004a, 26).

Yes and no. The form certainly has its roots in the humble comic book. And in the comic book industry itself, graphic novels are still often called "trade comics" and many graphic novelists continue to call themselves cartoonists. That said, graphic novels are, in fact, distinguished from comic books, first, by their greater length and, second, by their sturdier format; traditional comic books remain a cross between a pamphlet and a magazine; they're single-issue publications that usually appear monthly, are stapled rather than bound, and are seldom longer than thirty-six pages. Graphic novels, on the other hand, are square bound, original, never-before-published, book-length stories or collections of (previously unpublished) short stories.

They are a medium, not a genre; a form that combines words, pictures, and iconic language presented in sequential panels to create a whole work that is larger than the sum of its parts. They require an investment of creative energy and imagination by the reader to supply actions and events implied by breaks between the panels. And before we get too lost in their analysis, graphic novels are technically different not only from comic books but also from trade paperbacks, which are book-length compilations of previously published material, usually consecutive issues of an ongoing series. To further confuse the issue, trade paperbacks can be published in either soft or hardcover formats, and graphic novels can also be nonfiction.

Though the field of comics and graphic novels has clearly been in flux since the mid-1980s, one thing about them has remained fixed for far too long: the medium's tendency to attract significantly more male readers than females (as evidence, consider that a hallmark of comics has always been their unfortunate tendency to objectify women). In 1990 Chris Oliveros, founder of the Canadian publisher Drawn and Quarterly, called the world of comics "a private boys' club" (Jennings 2015). Which is not to say that there have been no girl-friendly comics. Consider the popularity of two very different classics: *Little Lulu* and *Wonder Woman.*

Little Lulu was the creation of cartoonist Marjorie Henderson Buell, who signed her work "Marge,"[4] but *Wonder Woman* was the creation of a man, William Moulton Marston, a psychologist who is famous for having been involved in the invention of the polygraph.[5] His superheroine debuted in *All Star Comics* No. 8 for December 1941, was immediately popular, and has been published, more or less continuously, since. The character's popularity received a boost, of course, with the debut of the television series starring Lynda Carter in 1975 (it remained on the air until 1979). But the comic's popularity gradually waned in the 1980s and it was actually discontinued for a year in 1986 before being reintroduced in 1987. It was not until 2006, however, that the adventures of the superheroine were, for the first time, written and drawn by a woman, the cartoonist Gail Simone.

Though few women actually worked in the field, *Little Lulu* and *Wonder Woman* weren't the only comics targeted at girl readers. A whole subgenre of romance comics came into existence in the late 1940s (at the same time that romance fiction for teens was the reigning genre in book publishing) and stuck around until the 1970s. With titles like *Young Romance, Falling in Love,* and *Heart Throbs,* they were as full of clichés, stereotypes, and dialogue as overripe as that of a B movie. And, of course, they were all written by men. As the romance comics gradually faded into oblivion in the 1970s, Paul Levitz, the president and publisher of DC Comics told *Publishers Weekly,* "Publishers essentially abandoned the [female] demographic. Nobody put a lot of effort into trying to reach them for the next couple of decades" (Deahl 2007).

Manga

This situation began to change dramatically with the mid-1990s explosion of manga—Japanese comics. Like *graphic novel*, the term *manga* describes a format, not a genre, because manga can be about any subject and addressed to an audience of virtually any age, though the earliest manga to reach the United States were typically for children, such as Pokemon. Despite the diversity of their content—which includes media tie-ins, superheroes, fantasy, science fiction, romance, sports, action/adventure, humor, and more—manga tend to conform to a readily recognizable artistic style: their characters all have enormous eyes and tiny noses; most of the books are done in black and white; and—most challenging to older American readers—they are read from right to left and back to front. Most manga are also part of seemingly endless series (Jason Thompson identifies more than 900 of them in his 2007 book *Manga: A Complete Guide*), each of which may fill thirty or more paperback volumes and—like TV soap operas—may run for years (Oh, My Goddess, arguably the first manga to become popular in the United States, is also the longest-running series to date, having lasted twenty-one years! Another epic is Masashi Kishimoto's Naruto. A total of seventy-two volumes of the adventures of this young ninja-in-training were published before the series was discontinued in October 2015. With more than 200 million copies in print, it is the third best-selling series of this genre in history.)

There are a prodigious number of manga subcategories, but two of the most prominent are called *shojo* and *shonen*, the former—targeted at girl readers—tend to be character-driven, while the latter—aimed at boys—are typically plot-driven.

Manga have been a fixture of Japanese popular culture for more than sixty-five years.[6] It wasn't until women began writing and drawing manga for the first time in the late 1960s, however, that shojo became an indispensable part of the Japanese comic mix. And even then they didn't begin to attract an audience of American readers until the late 1980s and early 1990s when Viz, Dark Horse, and Tokoyopop (which shut down in 2011 but plans to begin publishing again in 2016) were founded (Aoki 2015).

Manga quickly became one of the fastest-growing segments of the publishing industry, and girls were among its fastest-growing groups of readers; indeed, manga were the first comics that many modern girls ever read. Why them and not American comics? Well, in part because of the diversity of shojo's content. If American comics focused on superheroes, shojo explored a much wider, girl-friendly world ranging from fantasy to fashion and from high-school stories to romantic comedy.

Not surprisingly, many of the most popular shojo titles are not only written and drawn by women, they also feature female characters and, perhaps accordingly, are sometimes called the chick lit of the graphic novel world (especially *josei*, manga aimed at adult women readers).[7]

Sailor Moon is probably the classic example of shojo. Created by Naoko Takeuchi, it's the story of a fourteen-year-old schoolgirl who is granted magical powers after she meets a talking cat named Luna. (The shojo tradition of female characters having magic powers may derive, the critic Paul Gravett argues, from the Shinto tradition of female deities and priestesses.).

Arguably even more popular than Sailor Moon is Fruits Basket, by a female artist who works under the pseudonym Natsuki Takaya. *Fruits Basket* is the story of an orphan girl named Tohru who lives in a tent in the woods. There she is befriended by a mysterious family named Sohma, the members of whom, when hugged by a person of the opposite sex, turn into one of the animals of the Chinese zodiac.

Speaking of the opposite sex: Ranma ½—though drawn and written by the female artist Rumiko Takahashi—is the story of a male teenage martial artist. Well, he's a male some of the time, anyway. It turns out that Ranma is enchanted and turns into a woman whenever he is splashed by cold water. To turn back into a male, he must be splashed by—you guessed it—hot water.

As Ranma demonstrates, some shojo do feature male characters. Another notable example of this is Clamp's xxxHolic, the story of a teenage boy who goes to work for a witch (the series concluded in 2011). Clamp is not a single artist but, rather, a four-woman studio that, over the past twenty-two years, has produced at least twenty-two popular manga series, including, in addition to xxxHolic, Chobits, Cardcaptor, Sekura, Tsubasa, X, and more recently xxxHolic:Rei. Finally, another form of shojo that features male protagonists is *shonen-ai*. Translated as "boy love," these books do, indeed, feature idealized romantic relationships between two boys. Shonen-ai are seldom sexually explicit, though a form called *yaoi*, aimed at older readers, often is.

The appeal and influence of manga of all sorts on the US market have been significant. By 2005 the form had even spawned a still-popular American version called "OEL" (original English-language) manga, that is, comics created for the American market by non-Japanese artists.

But it is manga's role in establishing a female audience for graphic novels that may be its most enduring contribution. As a result, not only are more women now entering the field, but mainstream American graphic novel publishers are also beginning to aggressively court girl readers.[8] The publisher NBM, founded in 2005, initially targeted the tween market for young girls by issuing graphic adaptations of the classic Nancy Drew mysteries. In 2006 DC introduced an entire new imprint called Minx, a line of original graphic novels aimed at young female readers. In reaching out to this new audience, DC took an unusual step for a comics publisher: it joined forces with Alloy Marketing and Media, the packager responsible for such successful book series as Gossip Girl and Sisterhood of the Traveling Pants. The Minx line debuted in May 2007 with a graphic novel titled *The Plain Janes.* Written by established YA novelist Cecil Castellucci, the novel had art by Jim Rugg and recounted the doings of a nonconformist girl gang. Unfortunately, despite significant media attention and the publication of nearly a dozen critically praised graphic novels, DC retired the new imprint barely two years after its 2007 launch.

There is no question, however, that graphic novels by women author-artists have become an important part not only of manga but also of the entire graphic novel scene. A well-attended panel at the 2008 New York Comic Con was devoted to the growing number of comics aimed at girls, and four of the most critically hailed graphic novels of the last ten years are by women: Marjane Satrapi's *Persepolis* and *Persepolis II,* a two-volume graphic memoir of her life during and after the Iranian Revolution, and Alison Bechdel's memoir *Fun Home* (2006) (Rosen 2009b) and its companion *Are You My Mother?* (2012). Most recently, a third woman, Raina Telgemeier, has sprung to prominence. Her first graphic novel, the semiautobiographical *Smile,* was published in 2010, and has been followed by two other autobiographical works *Drama* (2012) and *Sisters* (2014). Hugely successful both critically and commercially (*Smile* has more than 1.5 million copies in print), Telgemeier, as Milton Griepp put it, "is blowing the doors off! She by herself is a real force that affects the whole category" (Maloney 2014).

This is a welcome phenomenon. As Peggy Burns, current editor of Drawn and Quarterly, says, "When the medium has more women creating comics, more women reading comics, more women studying comics, more women working in comics, both the industry and comics literary canon become more reflective of the real world" (Jennings 2015, 20).

"When" seems increasingly to be now. The headline of a *New York Times* article covering the 2015 Comic-con was "At Comic-Con, It Feels Like the Year of the Woman" (Scott 2015). The article cites, as one of the best attended con panels, "Nobody's Damsel: Writing for Tomorrow's Women." One of the panelists, Sam Maggs, author of *The Fangirls's Guide to the Galaxy*, pointed out that women and girls now make up roughly half of all comic-book buyers, video game players, and Comic-Con badge holders (Scott 2015). In an interview accompanying the *Times* article, Maggs noted that social media has been influential in expanding the female presence in the comics world. "We're able through places like Twitter and Tumblr to form communities of women and other diverse people in which we feel empowered to say, 'These are the things that we like' and 'These are the things we're missing.' Not only can we say them with a large and loud voice, we can say them directly to the content creators. So we can go directly to Marvel and directly to DC and say: 'We have all this money, all this buying power. Why aren't you catering to us?' and they kind of have to listen" (Scott 2015).

Comic Art—Oxymoron or Appraisal?

Speaking of comic art—Satrapi, Bechdel, and Telgemeier are distinguished writers as well as artists and evidence another trend that has been building in the field since about 2005. Television journalist Rachel J. Allen explains: "Graphic novels have gotten bigger because they're, well, better. The past five years have often been trumpeted by the comic book industry as 'The Golden Age of Writers'" (Allen 2006).

First Second's Mark Siegel agrees: "With the advent of an author-driven market—as opposed to series-driven or merchandising-driven—creators have a platform and potential to reach a great audience by developing their own personal vision, their own unique voice" (Brill 2006).

As a result, a number of celebrated authors continue to be drawn to the graphic novel as a new form of self-expression. Such luminaries as Michael Chabon, Jonathan Lethem, Jodi Picouolt, Greg Rucka, Brad Meltzer, Joss Whedon, and—most recently—Margaret Atwood have all tried their hands at writing graphic novels.

The new popularity of the form with writers has also manifested itself in the appearance of young adult books with protagonists who want to be cartoonists. Some of these books, like Daniel Ehrenhaft's 2006 novel *Drawing a Blank*, Barry Lyga's *The Astonishing Adventures of Fan Boy and Goth Girl* (2006), Sherman Alexie's 2007 National Book Award-winning *The Absolutely True Diary of a Part-Time Indian*, Stephen Emond's *Happyface* (2010),

Cherie Priest's *I Am Princess X* (2015), Shaun David Hutchinson's *The Five Stages of Andrew Brawley* (2015), Andrew Smith's *Winger* (2013) and *Stand Off* (2015), and Laurent Linn's *Draw the Line* (2016) include their characters' artwork; others—like Cheryl Rainfield's *Stained* (2013), about a girl who longs to emulate the comic book hero she has created; Suzanne Kamata's *Gadget Girl* (2013), which is about a girl with cerebral palsy who creates a manga alter-ego; Susan Juby's *The Truth Commission* (2015), which features a protagonist whose older sister is a celebrated graphic novelist; Adam Silvera's *More Happy Than Not* (2015), about a Bronx teen who is struggling to forget elements of his life; and Cori McCarthy's *You Were Here* (2016) about a girl on a quest to memorialize her dead brother, do not.

The Market

The market for alternative comics and graphic novels has grown steadily since the late nineties, which has meant a continuing shift from the traditional comics specialty bookstore as the prime sales outlet to general bookstores, especially the chains (though this was compromised when the giant Borders chain went out of business in 2011). The market shift was accompanied by other dramatic changes. For example, the sales of graphic novels in 2006 actually exceeded those of comics for the first time ($330 million compared to $310 million) (Reid 2007).

Some 2,800 graphic novels were published that year, according to Milton Griepp (2009) of ICv2, a pop culture website that tracks the market. A total of 144 of these were targeted at teens and tweens, up from only 64 in 2005. And, fully 1,200 of the 2,800 were manga, a growing number of them coming not from Japan but from Korea, where they're called *manhwa*. Statistics for 2007 were even more positive: sales rose 12 percent to $375 million, and the total number of graphic novels grew to 3,391, of which 1,513 were manga (MacDonald 2008a).

An incipient recession in 2008 caused the market, especially for manga, to slow though not decline. Sales totaled $395 million, "but," Milton Griepp said, a bit archly, "if flat is the new up, graphic novels are doing just great" (Griepp 2009).

Though the growth in the number of teen and tween titles for the period 2005–2006 slowed to only 1 percent and that of "literary" graphic novels to 2 percent, the library portion of the market remained significant, as demonstrated by an entire day of the 2006 New York Comic Con being devoted to a conference within a conference. Stackfest, cosponsored by *Library Journal* and the distributors Diamond and BroDart, was targeted specifically at librarians and those who were interested in reaching them. The next year, the 2007 Book Expo America (BEA)—the book trade's leading exposition and trade show—featured a large panel with the topic "The Science, Art, and Magic of Graphic Novel Selection for Libraries," and the 2009 BEA boasted three such panels (www.publishersweekly.com/pw/by-topic/new -titles/adult-announcements/article/9365-bookexpo-america-2009-despite -no-shows-many-comics-graphic-novels-at-bea.html). A seminal article, "How Graphic Novels Became the Hottest Section in the Library," by Heidi Mac-Donald, appeared in the May 3, 2013, issue of *Publishers Weekly*.

Earlier evidence of the importance of the library market had come in 2005 when, for the first time, a librarian was added to the panel of judges that select the winners of the annual Eisner Awards, the Oscars of the comic book industry. Kat Kan was the first librarian judge; she has been followed in the years since by such experts as Robin Brenner, Eva Volin, Mike Pawuk, Francisca Goldsmith, Jesse Karp, Richard Graham, and Karen Green.

Clearly there is no question about the growing popularity of the graphic novel form with librarians and teachers. The books are now regularly reviewed by all the professional journals (*Booklist* even publishes an annual "spotlight on graphic novels" issue) and virtually every publisher of series nonfiction—Rosen, Capstone, Stone Arch, World Almanac, Lerner, ABDO, and others—has been releasing titles in this format.

The popularity of comics extends even to college and university libraries. According to Karen Green, graphic novel selector at Columbia University, "Graphic novels are the most frequently requested material in our Ivy League request system" (MacDonald 2013).

Anxious to expand their market, juvenile trade publishers have been busily mining their backlists for print books—both fiction and nonfiction—that can be adapted as graphic novels. HarperCollins, for example, has published graphic versions of Neil Gaiman's *Coraline* and his Newbery Medal–winning *The Graveyard Book,* and Simon and Schuster early on launched continuing adaptations of its Pendragon and Childhood of Famous Americans series, Scholastic did a graphic version of Ann Martin's popular Babysitter's Club series, and Yen Press (the graphic novel division of Hachette Book Group) launched adaptations of James Patterson's Maximum Ride series and produced a graphic novel version of Stephanie Meyer's wildly popular Twilight series. Meanwhile, Marvel published graphic novel versions of Margaret A. Edwards Award–winner Orson Scott Card's *Ender's Game* and *Ender's Shadow*, as well as a multivolume adaptation of Stephen King's *The Stand*. More recently still, Del Rey has done an adaptation of Scott Westerfeld's *Uglies* ("Shay's Story"); IDW has done Peter Beagle's classic *The Last Unicorn*, and Yen Press has produced both Ransom Riggs's *Miss Peregrine's Home for Peculiar Children* and Kami Garcia and Margaret Stohl's *Beautiful Creatures*.

Despite all this activity, the comics market is not sacrosanct. Sales declined in both 2009 and 2010. Milton Griepp explains why: "Part of that was the economy and people pulling back on buying but I also think a lot of the business is driven creatively and I think there was a little creative drought in that period" (Alverson 2014b).

Nevertheless, sales remained a strong enough part of the overall book market that, in the spring of 2009 *The New York Times* launched its first graphic books Best Seller List. And then, over the course of the next three years—thanks to an improving economy, an infusion of creative energy, new convention venues, and retail channels—the market rebounded and across-the-board sales shot up 35 percent, reaching a bullish $870 million by the end of 2013. Graphic novels commanded the greatest share of that ($415 million), followed by comics ($365 million), and digital ($90 million). The $870 million figure is the highest dollar value since 1993 (Reid 2014). And the upward trend continues: sales in 2014 hit a twenty-year high at $935 million, a 7 percent increase over 2013 (Griepp 2015).

Aside from sales, one trend that has hugely impacted the comic market, just as it has that of regular publishing, is its burgeoning symbiotic relationship with motion pictures and television. The graphic novelist and cartoonist Eric Shanower (*Age of Bronze*) comments: "Marvel Comics/Disney has, of course, been seeing success with adaptations of its properties into movies and TV shows. DC Comics, less so, though DC seems to be chasing the success that Marvel has found. So one might be seeing a trend among publishers with a lot of corporate-owned comics properties to try to tailor those properties to movie and TV adaptations. I don't think these adaptations have had much impact on the rest of the field, though" (Eric Shanower, private communication, May 29, 2015).

By mid-2015, all prospects were pleasing. According to Shanower: "cartooning is strong and healthy. The trends of more diverse visions and strong material that have been developing over the past couple decades show no sign of abating" (personal correspondence, 2015).

Milton Griepp is even more optimistic: "From my perspective of 40 years in the comics business, the variety and quality of what is being published today is the greatest it's been in my lifetime" (Alverson 2014b).

First Second Founder and Editorial Director Mark Siegel concurs, calling this "an amazing time, a golden age, bigger than any of the others before it."

To get Siegel's take on other current aspects of the field, I interviewed him on May 21, 2015. Here is some of what he had to say: he began by confirming that this is not only a golden age for the form but for the creators of it as well, citing the "creative explosion of these people working in the field." From what he shared, it seems an especially good time for writers. He cites, for example, the "blossoming of true authors aiming for depth and great writing," noting that many are transcending the constraints of both the superhero and manga forms. Further, he says that in the past, prose authors have had devoted followings, but now graphic novelists do as well. He offers, as an example, the wildly popular Raina Telgemeier.

In this same connection, he points to both the growing number of influential women creators like Telgemeier ("Some of the most outstanding books of the past three years have come from women") and also the growing population of female readers, who, he says, now constitute 60 percent of the graphic novel and comics audience. In 2015 young women 17 to 30 became the fastest-growing demographic among comics readers (Dockterman 2015). "Young women have been really responding to the comics where the female characters are designed to appeal to girls, not boys," says Juliette Capra, events director at Fantastic comics in Berkeley, California (Dockterman 2015).

Like me, Siegel acknowledges the positive influence of manga on the development of female readers. Though calling it inherently "disposable entertainment," Siegel concedes that there are nevertheless some "amazing and wonderful manga being written and drawn," and accordingly, the field has "evolved upward." There was a time, though, he wryly suggests, when the market for manga was saturated ("You could shovel it out by the pound") but now "more and more of it is rising to the top." Indeed, as Deb Aoki points out in a July 15, 2015, *Publishers Weekly* article, "The North American Manga market is back and stronger than ever" (Aoki 2015).

As for nonfiction, we are seeing more and more of it, Siegel points out, noting the field still has lots of room to grow. "What's great is that it's a ticket to a whole other reader," that is, those who are attracted by the subject rather than the form. Shanower is somewhat less sanguine, though: "Maybe there are a few more nonfiction comics being published," he says, "although it's hard for me to tell. There always seem to be nonfiction comics coming out, often from smaller publishers. What I have seen recently are some really bad nonfiction comics brought out by creators who don't seem to have any idea how to handle the comics form. These bad comics seem to me to be aimed primarily at the education market, which I think is a shameful situation" (Mark Siegel, personal correspondence, May 21, 2015).

One positive trend that seems to have arrived is the enhanced critical attention graphic novels are receiving, including major award consideration. The perfect example is First Second's *This One Summer,* which—written by Mariko Tamaki and illustrated by Jillian Tamaki—was selected as both a 2015 Caldecott honor and a Printz honor title, arguably the first time one book has received such dual recognition.

Siegel reserves special praise for libraries and librarians. "There is no way we could have had this sea change without librarians," he says. "Librarians are champions of the medium," he continues, noting that "When we started, librarians—mainly teen librarians–were the lone voice in support." Clearly their faith has been vindicated by the evolution of the field. One thing librarians are now talking about that particularly excites Siegel is what he calls "the new mainstream." Essentially author-driven, it manifests itself in how collections are organized in libraries. More and more libraries, Siegel explains, are offering three sections of content: superheroes, manga, and the new mainstream, or the author comics. In this third section, he continues, there are some series, but there are also many one-offs (i.e., stand-alone titles). "It's the authors, not the series or brands that are attracting readers to this third section, which contains the kinds of books that First Second was formed for."

Meanwhile "the market is growing and growing and growing." Siegel notes that 2013 was a breakthrough year for First Second (and for the field itself). As for 2014, graphic novel sales were up 7 percent industry-wide, the only area of publishing aside from young adult that showed an increase. In this connection Siegel hails the salutary influence of YALSA's Great Graphic Novels for Teens list. "Having that call out from ALA is like a way of underscoring that graphic novels are hitting the mark."

As for the future of the form, Siegel says First Second has felt little impact from the newly digital ("It's kind of negligible"). Shanower agrees: "If there's a large audience rushing to read the digital editions, I have yet to hear of it. I know from the sales of my own comics published digitally that they are downloaded but not in huge numbers."

As Siegel speaks, it's obvious that he highly values the book as a physical object, as an artifact. "These are books you're going to save for the next generation to read and savor. There is now a graphic novel for every kind of reader," he concludes.

Good news for them and for the industry, as well.

But what about other visual forms? For that we turn to the next chapter.

Notes

1. *The Seven Lively Arts* (New York: Harper and Brothers, 2014). For the record the other six were movies, musical comedy, vaudeville, radio, popular music, and dance.

2. The Eisner Awards are the Oscars of the comic book industry.

3. The fundamental introduction to the comics medium remains Scott McCloud's *Understanding Comics* (Kitchen Sink Press, 1993), while a good introduction to library use of the medium is Francisca Goldsmith's *Graphic Novels Now* (ALA 2005).

4. In 2015 Buell was inducted into the prestigious Will Eisner Comic Awards Hall of Fame.

5. Though Buell did the single panel Lulu cartoons that appeared in the *Saturday Evening Post*, the Lulu comic books were, in large part, also the work of a man, John Stanley, who—along with Carl Barks who drew Uncle Scrooge for Disney—is regarded as one of the two great creative talents in the history of comic books.

6. A comprehensive and beautifully designed history of manga is Paul Gravett's *Manga: Sixty Years of Japanese Comics* (Harper Design International).

7. Shonen manga for adult men is called *seinen*.

8. The Friends of Lulu, a nonprofit organization was founded in 1994 to promote female readership and participation in the comics field.

16

The New Nonfiction

The Eyes Have It

Today's children are the first generation to grow up more accustomed to digital screens than the printed page; as wireless devices proliferate, kids increasingly understand and appreciate data that is transmitted to them in visual forms. —*James Bickers, "The Young and the Graphic Novel," Publisher's Weekly, 2007*

THE IDEA THAT PICTURES CAN CONVEY INFORMATION AND UNDERSTANDING as well as or better than text is hardly a new one. Bishop Comenius, the Czech educational reformer whose 1658 visual encyclopedia *Orbis Pictus* is often regarded as the first children's picture book, once observed, "Pictures are the most intelligible books that children can look upon" (Avery 1995, 7).

Nevertheless, for many years American nonfiction remained earnestly unadorned. And no wonder—from its beginnings work of Samuel Griswold Goodrich (Peter Parley) in the 1820s, its purpose was utilitarian and its presentation dryly didactic.

The purpose-driven, curriculum-related nature of nonfiction continued to dominate the field for more than a century and, as a result, most (though not all) nonfiction came in the form of series from institutional publishers. Its appearance was often forbidding, distinguished by pages of dense, pedestrian text unbroken by pictures; when images did appear, they were often small, poorly reproduced, black-and-white, and, as often as not, culled from the files of the Bettman Archives.

This finally began to change in the 1950s when children's publishing entered a period of expansion, and Random House launched Landmark Books, its influential and wildly popular series of history and biography titles. In 1958, a Congress worried that America was losing the space race to Russia passed the National Defense Education Act, which generously funded libraries' purchase of books in the sciences; this, in turn, led to the appearance of still more nonfiction series—such as Crowell's Let's Read and Find Out—as well as the debut of such soon-to-be-celebrated writers of nonfiction as Isaac Asimov, Franklyn Branley, Millicent E. Selsam, Herbert S. Zim, and others. The boom years continued through the sixties, thanks in large part to another infusion of federal money, this from the Elementary and Secondary Education Act, which was part of President Lyndon Johnson's Great Society legislation. Anxious to spend their windfalls quickly, libraries issued a de facto demand to publishers for more new books.

And, the publisher and author James Cross Giblin (1988, 29) recalls, "Publishers scurried to meet [the demand] by launching new series of information books for every age group in every conceivable subject area."

Unfortunately, the well of federal funding abruptly ran dry in 1969 when, as a result of its focus on the Vietnam War, the Nixon administration turned its attention from books to bullets, and juvenile nonfiction was one of the first victims.

Publishing being a famously cyclical business, however, the depressed—and depressing—situation of nonfiction began gradually to improve in the mid-seventies, thanks, this time, not to an infusion of funds but of exciting visual content. These visuals were crisply produced photographs offered in the form of what soon came to be called the "photo essay." Though pioneered by *Life* magazine photographers Alfred Eisenstaedt, Margaret Bourke-White, Thomas McAvoy, and Peter Stackpole, it is editor Norma Jean Sawicki, then at Crown, whom Giblin credits with establishing "the photoessay as a genre unto itself. Led by the interest in photoessays," Giblin continues, "the juvenile nonfiction area made a quiet but steady comeback in the early 1980s" (1988, 30).

The texts of these books improved appreciably, too, thanks to the entrance into the field of a new generation of accomplished writers like Brent Ashabranner, Betsy Maestro, Gail Gibbons, Dorothy Hinshaw Patent, Milton Meltzer, Jean Fritz, and Russell Freedman. And when engaging text and captivating, impeccably researched visual content came together in an artistically seamless whole in Freedman's *Lincoln: A Photobiography* (Clarion 1987), a nonfiction book won the Newbery Medal for the first time in thirty-two years and a new kind of informational book was born.

Also contributing to that birth was British publisher Dorling Kindersley (DK), which—in the late 1980s—had launched its revolutionary series of Eyewitness Books, which were published in the United States by Knopf. Employing what it called a "lexigraphic approach," DK devised a new way of publishing nonfiction. Publisher Peter Kindersley explained, "One of the problems with words is that they're incredibly slow, while pictures are incredibly fast. When you put them together, they work in completely different ways" (*Children's Software Review* 1997).

As I wrote in *Booklist* in 2002, "What DK did—with almost revolutionary panache—was essentially reinvent nonfiction books by breaking up the solid pages of gray type that had previously been their hallmark, reducing the text to bite-size, nonlinear nuggets and surrounding them with lavish white space and pictures that did more than adorn—they also conveyed information. Usually full-color, they were so brilliantly reproduced they seemed almost to leap off the page. Carter and Abrahamson, in their essential book *Nonfiction for Young Adults,* call the images 'stunning visuals . . . all artfully arranged on the pages for visual appeal.'" (Cart 2002a, 399). Kindersley may have best explained the new approach when he wrote, "Through the picture I see reality and through the word I understand it" (Cart 2002a, 399).

In the Know: Libraries and the New Nonfiction

The word (i.e., the text) was the focus of yet another important YALSA preconference, important because it underscored the growing prominence of nonfiction in libraries. Held in 1990 and called "Just Say Know," this one devoted two days to an exhaustive examination of the newfound importance and allure of nonfiction and information materials for young people. As Linda Waddle (1991, 361) wrote in the *Journal of Youth Services in Libraries,* "The sessions were designed to help participants become better evaluators and users of the increasing quantity and variety of nonfiction materials." Presentations ranged from "Booktalking Nonfiction" to "Apartheid in South Africa," and from "Evaluation and Review of Current Self-Help Books" to "Magazine Publishing: The *Sassy* Approach."

The keynote speakers were Betty Carter and Richard Abrahamson, whose book *From Delight to Wisdom: Nonfiction for Young Adults* was published by Oryx Press that same year. The coauthors addressed "The Role of Nonfiction in Developing Lifetime Readers." Staunch advocates of the form, they asserted that "young adults who want to know about this world, or this planet, or this society don't care to continually extrapolate their ideas from fiction; they want to examine more reliable sources. Only nonfiction responds to this need" (Waddle, 1991, 366–67). And what about those who want to know about themselves, instead? "Young adults read for identification. Neither fiction nor nonfiction dictates a reader's stance; the reader always does. Frequently, the reader interacts on a personal level with nonfiction" (366). In other words, nonfiction provides the facts; it is the reader who provides the same kind of emotional response he or she would while reading fiction.

Surprisingly, only one presentation addressed the visual aspect of nonfiction. James Cross Giblin and Norma Jean Sawicki offered their answer to the often-heard complaint "But All They Do Is Look at the Pictures: Illustrations in Nonfiction Books." And clearly they did look, for the impact of those pictures continued to inform the evolution of the informational book, as established writers like Freedman, Jim Murphy, Rhoda Blumberg, Kathryn Lasky, and Patricia Lauber were joined by Albert Marrin, Janet Bode, Laurence Pringle, Susan Kuklin, Elizabeth Partridge, and James Cross Giblin himself (who had retired from publishing to devote full-time to his own career as a writer of award-winning information books). All of these authors were extraordinarily good writers, but they also understood the importance of incorporating significant, carefully researched visual material into their texts.

At the same time, another editor and publisher, Marc Aronson, was continuing to develop nonfiction for older young adults at Holt and later at Carus Publishing, where he had his own imprint, Marcato Books. However, he, too, retired from publishing and has since become not only one of America's most eloquent advocates for nonfiction, but also the author of some of its most intellectually challenging and stimulating books, like *Sir Walter Ralegh and the Quest for El Dorado* (2000), *The Real Revolution* (2005), *Trapped: How the World Rescued 33 Miners from 2000 Feet below the Chilean Desert* (2011), and *Master of Deceit: J. Edgar Hoover and America in the Age of Lies* (2012).[1]

There is no fictionalizing to be found in any of these fine writers' books—no imagined conversations, no messing with history or chronology to make a better story, but—speaking of story—all do demonstrate the importance of creating a narrative and, to that end, they borrow techniques from novelists without violating the accuracy or the integrity of their books' content. Freedman (1994, 138–39) has addressed this aspect of his work, saying, "I think of myself first of all as a storyteller, and I do my best to give dramatic shape to my subject whatever it may be . . . By storytelling, I do not mean making things up, of course. I don't mean invented scenes, or manufactured dialogue, or imaginary characters."

Freedman goes on to discuss the importance of developing character by including telling details (the contents of Lincoln's pockets the night he was assassinated), using anecdotes, creating vivid scenes (including William Herndon's description of the chaos wrought in his law office by Lincoln's two sons), and—to give readers a sense of what historical personages actually sounded like—quoting from letters, diaries, journals, speeches, and other written matter. When handled expertly, the result is a compelling narrative that offers the power of story without sacrificing any of the authenticity of fact.

Writing about the art of narrative nonfiction, Lee Gutkind (2012), founder and editor of *Creative Nonfiction* magazine, asks, "In our fervor to be cinematic and provide readers with compelling characters, how do we avoid crossing the murky line between fact and fiction?"

"Nonfiction," he explains, "means that our stories are as true and accurate as possible." To ensure that, Gutkind then offers three R's of narrative nonfiction: first is *research* ("in fact, narrative requires more research than traditional reportage"), then comes *real world exploration* (conducting interviews, visiting sites, etc.), "and finally and perhaps most important, *a fact checking review* of all that has been written."

Though I have been referring to narrative nonfiction, it is obvious from the title of Gutkind's magazine that there are others who prefer the term *creative nonfiction*. The celebrated author John McPhee (2015) is one of them. Writing in the *New Yorker*, he asks, "What is creative about nonfiction? The creativity lies in what you choose to write about, how you go about doing it, the arrangement through which you present things, the skill and the touch with which you describe people and succeed in developing them as characters, the rhythms of your prose, the integrity of the composition, the anatomy of the piece (does it get up and walk around on its own?), the extent to which you see and tell the story that exists in your material, and so forth. Creative nonfiction is not making something up but making the most of what you have."

As for Marc Aronson, he, too, underscores the continuing importance of the narrative, noting the surprising fact that once heavily illustrated work is now often appearing—like novels—without ancillary visual content (Aronson, personal communication, May 4, 2015). With or without pictures, nonfiction has been and is increasingly becoming an art, and it is no wonder that since the mid-1970s, award attention has begun to be paid to this formerly overlooked form. The Boston Globe-Horn Book Awards, for example, added a category for nonfiction as early as 1976. The Society of Children's Book writers followed in 1977, and the Book Guild of Washington initiated a body of work award for nonfiction that same year. In 1983, a total of three Newbery Honors was presented for nonfiction (to Kathryn Lasky, Rhoda Blumberg, and Patricia Lauber); in 1988, Freedman, as already noted, received the Newbery itself for *Lincoln: A Photobiography.* Two years later the National Council of Teachers of English (NCTE) initiated its nonfiction Orbis Pictus Award (the first winner was Jean Fritz for her *Great Little Madison*); and in 2000 the Association of Library Service for Children, which presents the Newbery and Caldecott Medals, created the Robert F. Sibert Medal to be awarded annually to the author(s) and illustrator(s) of the most distinguished informational book for children published in English during the preceding year. The first award, presented in 2001, went to Marc Aronson for his *Sir Walter Ralegh and the Quest for El Dorado,* which many considered a young adult book. Interestingly, one of the four Honor Books that year—Judd Winick's *Pedro and Me*—was also regarded as young adult and was a graphic novel to boot. In the years since, award and honor recipients have included both children's and YA titles—among the latter being the 2003 winner James Cross Giblin's *The Life and Death of Adolf Hitler* and—that same year—an honor to Jack Gantos for his edgy memoir *A Hole in My Life,* which was also the recipient of a Printz honor award. Other more recent crossover Sibert recipients include *The Family Romanov* by Candace Fleming (2014); *Bomb* by Steve Sheinkin (2012); and *The Boys Who Challenged Hitler* (2015), *Moonbird* (2012), and *Claudette Colvin* (2009) by Phillip Hoose. Aronson, however, now sees an emerging trend to younger Sibert title winners, even picture books (e.g., Brian Floca's *Locomotive* [2013]). Why? Well, perhaps because of the Printz Award–like presence of the still new YALSA Award for Excellence in Nonfiction.

Why YALSA did not immediately follow the Sibert example and create a similar prize excited a great deal of discussion. Some pointed to the fact that nonfiction is eligible for the Printz (witness the Gantos book), but others have pointed out that no informational book has actually won this most prestigious YA award, and only four such books over the past fifteen years have even received honors—Gantos's *A Hole in My Life* (2002), Elizabeth Partridge's *John Lennon* (2005), Stephanie Hemphill's *Your Own Sylvia* (2007), and Deborah Heiligman's *Charles and Emma* (2009).

Too, nonfiction had always received recognition on YALSA's annual Best Books for Young Adults lists, but even there the news has not always been salutary. As Betty Carter noted in the first edition of her *Best Books for Young Adults,* "Not only has BBYA changed from an almost exclusively adult list to a strongly juvenile one but it has also reversed from including mostly nonfiction books to containing a predominance of fiction titles . . . In 1993 seventy-five percent of the books were fiction" (Carter 1994, 39–40). In the second edition of her book, Carter again wrote, "Nonfiction fails to appear in representative numbers on BBYA lists. Part of that failure may be because of the reading tastes of the committee, but part is also because of publishing output" (2000, 12).

In the third edition of the book, published in 2007, the new editor Holly Koelling reported that only 20 percent of the titles on the 2001–2007 lists were nonfiction (80 percent, thus, were fiction). The number of nonfiction titles on the accompanying Top Ten lists was equally puny. During the period described by Koelling, only five of the seventy titles selected between 2001 and 2007 were nonfiction. And when one looks at the thirteen Teens Top Ten lists that YALSA teens have generated since 2003, the results are even more discouraging: the teens themselves have chosen not a single nonfiction title.

Much of this became moot in 2010 when the YASLA Board restructured the Best Books for Young Adults Committee, eliminating nonfiction from its purview and transforming it into the Best Fiction for Young Adults Committee. If that is (for nonfiction lovers) the bad news (it certainly is for Aronson, who considers it disastrous), the good news is that the same year, YALSA finally created its Excellence in Nonfiction Book Award, its first winner being *Charles and Emma* (a joint biography of Charles Darwin and his wife) by Deborah Heiligman.

The purpose of the new award is fivefold: "To recognize the best in the field of nonfiction books, promote the growing number of nonfiction books published for young adults, inspire a wider readership in the genre, give recognition to the importance of the genre, and position YALSA as an authority in the field of nonfiction for young adults."

Thus far, six years after the award's founding, these purposes seem to have been fulfilled. In the meantime, the field has continued to evolve, the most significant factor to impact it in these years of the 2010s being the establishment of the Common Core Standards. Now a Rutgers professor, Aronson, in a May 4, 2015, interview with me, noted that the Common Core is represented in forty states, and pointed out that it has exponentially increased classroom interest in nonfiction (at the expense of fiction, some worry). Lionel Bender, cofounder of the UK book packager Bender Richardson White, agrees: "The icing on the cake is the Common Core standards, which are making nonfiction important and making nonfiction writers finally feel like fiction's equals" (Goddu 2013).

This newfound classroom interest has, in turn, caused a nonfiction market shift to schools and away from libraries and the retail market, which was never much of a factor, at least in nonfiction sales, having been, Aronson points out, the most neglected area in the many Barnes and Noble bookstores. Beverly Horowitz, vice president and publisher of Delacorte Press, agrees, saying, "You used to go to the nonfiction children's section in a bookstore and often they just had dinosaur and potty books." Of course, nonfiction has always been represented in the classroom in the form of textbooks and, to a lesser extent, institutional series nonfiction, but trade nonfiction is now claiming an ever greater market share.

"We are seeing a huge lift in nonfiction sales," Shanta Newlin, executive director of publicity at Penguin Young Readers Group, confirms (Rosen 2015). According to her, sales of the division's top 200 nonfiction titles were up 38 percent in 2014.

Another significant new trend is the appearance of young people's editions of adult nonfiction titles. "These slimmed-down, simplified and sometimes sanitized editions of popular nonfiction titles are fast becoming a vibrant, growing and lucrative niche," writes Alexandra Alter in *The New York Times* (Alter 2014). It's understandable why this should be, as publishers are clearly hoping to capitalize on and imitate the flourishing crossover market in fiction. "They are following the money," Alter confirms. To further expand the market, publishers are hoping adult readers will discover these adaptations for themselves. "Adults are now so used to reading young adult books that there may be some nice crossover," Horowitz notes.

The viability—or integrity—of these adaptations, however, remains another matter: "If they're cutting out controversy and assuming that teens won't be able to absorb some of these bigger ideas, we go back to the adult version," says Chris Shoemaker, former president of the Young Adult Library Services Association (Alter 2014). An example of this situation is Laura Hillenbrand's *Unbroken* (2014), a biography of erstwhile Olympic athlete and WWII POW survivor Louis Zamperini. In the book's young adult version, Hillenbrand expunged a scene of a prison guard's torturing and killing a duck. "I know that if I were twelve and reading it, that would upset me," she says (Alter 2014). These considerations aside and speaking, now, of the nonfiction field as a whole, Aronson calls it "a tremendously exciting moment," noting that, like YA in general, the field is exploding; "like June," he adds a bit poetically, "it is busting out all over!" (Aronson, personal communication, May 4, 2015).

He goes on to point to a number of new forms enriching the field, citing poetry, graphic novel nonfiction, memoirs, and more. As for the future, he is particularly intrigued by the emerging shift from "just the facts" nonfiction to passionately argued, point-of-view nonfiction à la Paul Fleischman's *Eyes Wide Open* (2014), a clarion call to environmental action.

Aronson believes one area remains deficient, however: that of diversity. He feels publishers could do a better job of importing relevant titles from abroad to give readers a more global perspective. As for the Internet, Aronson feels a positive impact of its presence is that one can assume most readers now have relatively easy access to it and, accordingly, authors are free to include in their texts references to Internet-accessible materials. "Think of it as weaving together the book and the Internet," he says.

Finally, though acknowledging that changes in the field are occasioning "growing pains," Aronson remains sanguine about the evolution of this long-neglected literary form.

Now if only young people are able to read it! To examine that issue, we turn to the next chapter.

Note

1. Aronson writes insightfully about nonfiction and many other aspects of young adult literature and publishing in his two collections of essays and speeches: *Exploding the Myths* and *Beyond the Pale* (Scarecrow, 2001 and 2003, respectively).

Of Books and Bytes

Multiple Literacies, the Death of Print, and Other Imponderables

MY MORE CULTURALLY AWARE READERS MAY ALREADY HAVE NOTED THAT what I've been calling the new golden age of young adult literature coincides almost exactly with what is also being widely regarded as the age of irony.[1] I mention this because I find it so wonderfully ironic that the field's renaissance, which has driven the publication of more YA books than ever before, should have occurred during the same period in which many people are also saying that—thanks to a dazzling array of digital distractions—no one is reading books any longer.

Are Young Adults Reading?

The catalyst for such dire muttering was a 2004 National Endowment for the Arts study titled *Reading at Risk,* which found that "the percentage of Americans reading literature has dropped dramatically over the past 20 years" (2004, ix). Although this sounds suspiciously like hyperbole, the statistics reported were, indeed, startling, showing that the percentage of US adults reading literature had dropped from 56.9 in 1982 to 46.7 in 2002. More to our point, the most precipitous drop (from 59.8 percent in 1982 to 42.8 percent in 2002) took place among eighteen- to twenty-four-year-olds, which led the report writers to note, "The trends among younger adults warrant special concern, suggesting that unless some effective solution is found, literary culture and literacy in general will continue to worsen" (xiii).

Critics of the report—and there were many—pointed out that the NEA's definition of reading was a very narrow one ("confoundingly narrow," charged the journalist and cultural observer Charles McGrath), limited—as it was—to novels, poetry, and plays. Nonfiction was not included, nor were magazines or newspapers or any reading that was done in association with work or study. Even more interestingly, though quick to imply it might be partly responsible for the decline, the report did not consider the Internet at all, even though, as McGrath (2004c, WK3) pointed out, "When people surf the Web, what they are doing, for the most part, is reading."

Perhaps sensitive to these criticisms, the NEA issued a follow-up report in 2007. Titled *To Read or Not to Read,* it expanded its definition of reading to include all kinds, including reading done online. It also broadened its statistical base to include data from some two dozen other studies by the Education and Labor Departments, the Census Bureau, and selected academic, foundation, and business surveys. Despite this expansion, the 2007 findings were no more positive than those of 2004, showing a continuing decline in both reading and reading proficiency, especially among those between the ages of nine and seventeen. "These trends," the new study claimed, "are concurrent with a falloff in daily pleasure reading among young people as they progress from elementary to high school. In 2006, for example, the data found that 15- to 24-year-olds were spending only 7 to 10 minutes a day voluntarily reading anything at all" (B. Thompson 2007).

This is especially unfortunate, because the new study also showed that students who did read for fun nearly every day performed better in reading tests than those who reported reading never or hardly at all.

This study, too, excited considerable debate and criticism, ranging from reservations about its data[2] to its perceived lack of nuance. Timothy Shanahan, past president of the International Reading Association, told *The New York Times,* "I don't disagree with the NEA's notion that reading is important, but I'm not as quick to discount the reading that I think young people are really doing" (a reference, according to the *Times,* to reading on the Internet) (Rich 2007).

Marc Aronson concurred, arguing that the problem was not a crisis in reading "but, rather, a problem on the part of adults who idolize a certain kind of fiction reading and have trouble making sense of the mixture of fiction, digital information, nonfiction and assigned reading that make up the diet of the YA reader" (Cart 2007, 42).

Similarly, the former YALSA President Linda Braun said, "The more willing adults are to recognize the important role that technology-based reading—blogs, wikis, text messages, and the like—has in teen lives, the more likely it is that teens will start to think of themselves as readers" (Cart 2007, 42).

We will address the role of the Internet in young adult reading in a moment, but first we should acknowledge that a third report followed in 2009. Surprisingly, this one, *Reading on the Rise*, found that after twenty years of decline, "literary reading has risen among adult Americans" (National Endowment for the Arts, 2004, 1).

And "best of all," NEA Chairman Dana Gioia wrote, "the most significant growth has been among young adults, the group that had shown the largest declines in earlier surveys. The youngest group (ages 18–24) has undergone a particularly inspiring transformation," he continued, "from a 20% decline in 2002 to a 21% increase in 2008" (National Endowment for the Arts 2009, 1).

What on earth caused such a dramatic and salutary about-face? "There is no statistical answer to this question," Goia wrote—a bit coyly, I fear, because he then went on to credit "the heightened sense of urgency created by alarming studies like 'Reading at Risk' and 'To Read or Not to Read'" ("to cite only NEA's own contributions to the genre," he added).

Certainly some credit is owed to the NEA, but might an increase in online reading also have played a part in this rise? Goia doesn't say, only reiterating earlier equations of reading declines with "an unprecedentedly large variety of electronic entertainment and communication options" (National Endowment for the Arts 2009, 1–2).

And yet, as for children and teens, a separate study—the 2008 Kids and Family Reading Report commissioned by Scholastic and conducted by the Yankelovitch consumer trends research company—found that nearly two in three of nine- to seventeen-year-olds surveyed had extended their reading experience via the Internet (e.g., visited a fan site, visited an author's website, used the Internet to find books by a particular author) and "high frequency Internet users are more likely to read books for fun every day" (Sellers 2008b).

In the years since 2009, the NEA has issued two more reports, one in 2013 (*How a Nation Engages with Art*) and one in 2015 (*A Decade of Arts Engagement*). Unfortunately, the 2013 report found that reading among young adults had once again declined—from 63.8 percent in 2009 to 51.8 percent. At that, this was better than the adult findings, which showed that in 2012 only

46.9 percent of adults had read at least one work of literature, compared with 50.2 percent in 2008 and remaining even with 2002 figures. Unfortunately, the level of literary reading in 2002 was also down, estimated to have fallen from 1992's high of 54 percent (*Publishers Weekly* 2013) As for the subsequent 2015 report, it added no new data, as it was a retrospective survey of reading for the decade 2002–2012.

New—and positive—data is now available, however, from both the Pew Research Center (Zuckhur and Rainie 2014) and the 2014 Nielsen Children's Book Industry Report. According to the former, "The youngest age groups are significantly more likely than older adults to read books, including print books. Reading and research required for schoolwork contributes to this, along with a decline in overall reading rates for adults aged 65 and older. As a group," the report continues, "younger Americans under age 30 are more likely than those 30 and older to report reading a book (in any format) at least weekly (67% vs 58%)" (Zuckhur and Rainie 2014).

As for Nielsen, its report found that children's book sales have risen steadily across all categories, though performing strongest is middle-grade and YA fiction and that 67 percent of kids read for fun "fairly often" (unfortunately, "fairly often" remains undefined) (Gilmore and Burnett 2014).

Though this smorgasbord of reports, findings, and statistics isn't exactly a comparison of apples and oranges, one wishes it might have been a bit more congruent. Nevertheless, it does seem to evidence that teens and younger kids do, indeed, appear to be reading but that begs another, more basic question:

Can Young Adults Actually Read?

The short answer is "yes but not nearly as well as they should." Consider that, according to the Alliance for Excellent Education, "The majority of students are leaving high school without the reading and writing skills needed to succeed in college and a career" (Alliance for Excellent Education 2014).

This is hardly a new situation: "Over the past four decades, the literacy performance of seventeen-year-olds on the National Assessment of Educational Progress has remained flat."

"The stagnation is unacceptable," says David Driscoll, chairman of the NAEP Governing Board, adding "Achievement at this very critical point in a student's life must be improved to ensure success after high school" (Hefling 2014).

According to the NAEP, more than 60 percent of middle- and high-school students scored below the "proficient" level in reading achievement on the 2013 test. "These results reveal that millions of young people cannot understand or evaluate text, provide relevant details, or support inferences about the written documents they read" (Hefling 2014).

Worse is the fact that only 26 percent of American Indian and Alaska Native, 23 percent of Hispanic, and 16 percent of African American twelfth-graders scored at or above "proficient" on the NAEP reading assessment, compared to 47 percent of white and Asian students.

What to do? Bob Wise, President of the Alliance for Excellent Education and a former governor of West Virginia, says that the new national results speak to "a desperate need for the aggressive implementation" of the Common Core standards (Associated Press 2014).[3] It must be noted that these standards are highly controversial but their implementation could be, many feel, at least a step in the right direction. Another such step is the acknowledgment of the importance of adolescent literacy itself, which went unremarked for far too long. As recently as 1999 Carol Santa, then President of the International Reading Association (IRA), was saying, "Adolescents are being shortchanged. Nobody is giving their literacy needs much press; there is little funding for adolescent literacy, and the topic is not a priority among educational policy makers or in the schools" (*Reading Today*, 1999, 1).

To redress this oversight, the IRA issued its first position statement on adolescent literacy that same year, flatly asserting, "The reading, writing, and language development of adolescents is just as important and requires just as much attention as that of beginning readers" (*Reading Today* 1999, 22).

In a field that had always focused on elementary school reading instruction, the idea that literacy might be a developmental process and the acquiring of its skills a continuum was a new one that began exciting considerable professional attention. In 2004, for example, The National Council of Teachers of English issued a position-action statement of its own, "A Call to Action," which stated, "Reading is not a technical skill acquired once and for all in the primary grades, but rather a developmental process. A reader's competence continues to grow through engagement with various types of texts and wide reading for various purposes over a lifetime" (NCTE Guideline: "A Call to Action").

As literacy skills continued to stagnate or decline, both the IRA and NCTE began searching for ways to engage students with books and other means of reading. Marsha Sprague, author of the IRA-published book *Their Voices: Engaging Adolescent Girls with Young Adult Literature*, suggested that teachers "give adolescents books that help teens make sense of their lives, with the idea that if they see reading as meaningful, they will want to read more" (*Reading Today* 2007, 12).

Jonathan Eakle, director of the Reading Program at Johns Hopkins University agreed, saying, "One of the key pieces that must be present in the instruction of adolescent readers is authenticity. Reluctance is often related to relevance. Students don't see how what they're being asked to do is related to their lives, in the present or the future. Making the connection between literacy education and real life means teaching students how to gather, organize and design multimedia texts . . . to navigate the architectures of digital and real space" (Flanagan 2008, 7–8).

The Rise of Multiple Literacies

Whether you call them "multiple literacies," "new literacies," or "twenty-first century literacies" one thing is obvious: they aren't your father's literacies and they require a new definition if we are to understand them. The simplest is that the term *new literacies* refers to the evolving forms of literacy made possible by digital technology developments. However, NCTE has given us a more prolix one. Literacy has always been a collection of cultural and communicative practices shared among members of particular groups. As society and technology change, so does literacy. Because technology has increased the intensity and complexity of literate environments, the twenty-first century demands that a literate person possess a wide range of abilities and competencies, many literacies. These literacies are multiple, dynamic, and malleable. As in the past, they are inextricably linked with particular histories, life possibilities, and social trajectories of individuals and groups (National Council of Teachers of English nd).

The Young Adult Library Services Association also deals in some depth with considerations of multiple literacies and technology in its essential Future Library Services and Teens Project Report, see www.ala.org/yaforum/future-library-services-and-teens-project-report.

Meanwhile the International Reading Association has its own views on the matter, expressed in a position statement titled *New Literacies and 21st Century Technologies*. It reads, in part, "The Internet and other forms of information and communication technologies (ICTs) are redefining the nature of reading, writing and communication. These ICTs will continue to change in the years ahead, requiring continuously new literacies to successfully exploit their potentials. Although many new ICTs will emerge in the future, those that are (already) common in the lives of our students include search engines, webpages, e-mail, instant messaging, blogs, podcasts, e-books, wikis, nings, YouTube, video and many more." (To which one might add Twitter, Instagram, Edmodo, Facebook, Google Docs, Socrative, Notability, and more.)

No wonder YALSA chose "How We Read Now" as the theme of its first-ever YA Literature Symposium, held in Nashville in 2008. Or that Howard Gardner—with an eye to the future—predicted that "literacy—or an ensemble of literacies—will continue to thrive but in forms and formats we can't yet envision" (Gardner 2008, B01).

Some might think our present forms and formats are difficult enough to envision, never mind those of the future. Collectively they flourish in an online environment that continues to challenge older observers, though it's familiar territory to teens. Consider that, according to the Pew Internet and American Life Project, 92 percent of teens go online on a daily basis and 24 percent go online "almost constantly." Add to this the fact that a total of 88 percent of American teens ages thirteen to seventeen have or have access to a mobile phone of some kind. More than half of teens have access to a tablet, while 87 percent have a desktop or laptop computer (Lenhart 2015).

Whether teens ever use these devices to read during the approximately 15.5 hours per day they spend on them (as well as watching TV and listening to the radio) (Chang 2013) is moot but the idea invites a question:

Is Reading Online Actually Reading?

The answer is "yes," but apparently it differs significantly from traditional reading done on a printed page. The renowned Web researcher Jakob Nielsen, who tested 232 people to determine how they read pages on screens, found they followed a pattern that looks like a capital letter *F*. Mark Bauerlein, author of *The Dumbest Generation*, explains: "At the top [of the screen] users read all the way across, but as they proceed, their descent quickens and horizontal sight contracts, with a slowdown around the middle of the page. Near the bottom eyes move almost vertically, the lower-right corner of the page largely ignored" (Bauerlein 2008). Speed is the hallmark of such reading and—no surprise—another Nielsen test has found that teenagers skip through the Web even faster than adults do, but with a lower success rate for completing tasks online (55 percent compared to 65 percent).

A study from University College London (2008) reported similar findings: "It is clear that users are not reading online in the traditional sense; indeed, there are signs that new forms of 'reading' are emerging as users 'power browse' horizontally through titles, contents pages, and abstracts going for quick wins. It almost seems they go online to avoid reading in the traditional sense."

"The result [of such reading]," Nicholas Carr (July/August 2008) wrote in an influential *Atlantic Monthly* article, "Is Google Making Us Stupid?" "is to scatter our attention and diffuse our concentration. In Google's world, the world we enter when we go online, there's little place for the fuzziness of contemplation. Ambiguity is not an opening for insight but a bug to be fixed."

If true, this finding will be particularly discouraging to fans of the newly literary young adult fiction that has finally made a place in its pages for just such ambiguity, a staple of artful fiction, but one that—apparently—commands no place in fiction or other literary forms that one might encounter online.

Indeed, it seems the Internet is no friend to any kind of complex or long-form reading. Naomi Wolf, author of *Proust and the Squid: The Story and Science of the Reading Brain,* worries that "the style of reading promoted by the Net, a style that puts 'efficiency' and 'immediacy' above all else may be weakening our capacity for the kind of deep reading that emerged when an earlier technology, the printing press, made long and complex works of prose commonplace" (Carr 2008).

"If the rise of nonstop cable TV news gave the world a culture of sound bites," Wolf more recently argues, "the Internet is bringing about an 'eye bite' culture." "This is nonlinear reading," Michael S. Rosenwald (2014) adds, "and it has been documented in academic studies."

Naomi S. Baron (2014), a professor of linguistics at American University, offers a similar assessment: "What's the problem? Not all reading works well on digital screens. The bottom line is that while digital devices may be fine for reading that we don't intend to muse over or reread, text that requires what's been called 'deep reading' is nearly always better done in print. Digital reading," she concludes, "encourages distraction and invites multitasking."

As researchers Heather and Ruetschlin Schugar and Jordan Schugar found in a 2014 study, there are significant differences between reading online and on paper. In their research they discovered that when they asked middle-school students to read either traditional books or e-books, the students' reading comprehension was noticeably higher when they read conventional books (Paul 2014).

What the Internet favors, it seems, is the presentation of information and the most successful information is that which is immediately available and in bite-size form. The long-range consequence of this may actually be a change in cognition. "What the Net seems to be doing," Carr lamented (almost confessionally), "is chipping away my capacity for concentration and contemplation. My mind now takes in information the way the Net distributes it: in a swiftly moving stream of particles. Once I was a scuba diver in the sea of words. Now I zip along the surface like a guy on a jet ski."

Indeed, neuroscientists argue that humans "seem to be developing digital brains with new circuits for skimming through the torrent of information online." Wolf worries we will develop what she calls "Twitter brains." Others see the development of a "biliterate" brain that accommodates both reading online and in print (Rosenwald 2014).

As for print, teens—despite the rush to an online and e-book environment—continue to prefer words on paper! A survey eagerly discussed at the December 2014 Nielsen Children's Book Summit revealed that 67 percent of teens showed "a significant preference for print over digital books" (Gilmore and Burnett 2014).

Why the preference? The journalist Sue Corbett offers a hypothesis: "Publishers speculate that because teens already spend so much of their day reading and writing on screens, reading for pleasure may mean deliberately getting away from electronics" (Corbett 2014).

In fact, only 20 percent of teens buy e-books, and express a strong preference for print (Stampler 2014). Another Nielsen survey suggests several more reasons for print preference: one is the parental habit of buying traditional print format for their teens; another is teens' penchant for borrowing and sharing books rather than buying them. And "over half of teens are still looking for books on library or bookstore shelves" (Nielsen Media 2014).

Don't Rush to Judgment

In the interest of fairness, it should be noted that there have been those—though not recently—who welcomed reading on the Internet. Writing in the

New Yorker, for example, Caleb Crain said, "The Internet, happily, does not so far seem to be antagonistic to literacy." In support of his claim he cited a study of Michigan children and teenagers that found "grades and reading scores rose with the amount of time spent online. Even visits to pornography websites improved academic performance!" (Crain 2007).

Even more optimistic than Crain was Steven Johnson, author of the book *Everything Bad Is Good for You: How Today's Popular Culture Is Actually Making Us Smarter,* a paean to video gaming, film, television, and the Internet. But even Johnson (2005, 185)—although claiming that "thanks to e-mail and the Web, we're reading text as much as ever, and we're writing more"— admitted, "it is true that a specific, historically crucial kind of reading has grown less common in this society: sitting down with a 300-page book and following its argument or narrative without a great deal of distraction. We deal with text now in shorter bursts, following links across the Web, or sifting through a dozen e-mail messages."

Speaking of "shorter bursts," some online magazines like *Slate* and *Medium* are now actually including small captions with stories telling how long it will take to read them. "This is the new currency of the realm when reading online. It may not be content anymore but rather time. How much time am I going to need to spend on this?" This from communications professor Arthur D. Santana (North 2014). "Maybe this is our cultural lot," he concludes. "We live in an age of skimming."

And listening, perhaps?

Audio Books

The sixteenth-century Spanish writer Francisco de Quevedo once said of reading that "it enables us to listen to the dead with our eyes." *Plus* ça *change*—today's movement away from print is not only toward the electronic but also towards the aural, as more and more people read with their ears. Recorded books are hardly a new phenomenon, however. They date to the 1930s and the establishment of the Library of Congress's program of recording for the blind, whereas Caedmon Records—the first to offer literature in the form of the spoken word—was founded in 1952. Nevertheless, most major publishers did not establish audio divisions until the mid-1980s; the Audio Publishers Association was founded in 1986, but it wasn't until the early nineties that recorded books became a significant industry that has, since then, grown apace. Indeed, in recent years the field has exploded. For example, nearly 36,000 audiobook titles were produced in 2013, up from 13,255 in 2012 and only 6,200 in 2010 (Cobb 2015).

As a result, audio books have ballooned into a $1.2 billion industry, up from a paltry(!) $480 million in 1997 (Alter 2013). And a total of 6 million more audiobooks were sold in 2012 than in 2011 (Eldridge 2014).

According to *Forbes* magazine, as of 2011 "37 percent of people say they've listened to an audio book, and the medium continues to become an important substitute for old-fashioned reading. Thanks in part to the ubiquity of iPods . . . audio books remain popular" (Khazan 2011).

If anything they are even more popular in 2015. *The New York Times Book Review* now regularly includes a section on audiobooks and maintains an audiobook best-seller list. And, of course, all the professional media regularly review them. "Audiobooks have gone mass market," Alexandra Alter (2013) writes. "Shifts in digital technology have broadened the pool of potential listeners to include anyone with a smartphone."

As the industry has matured, it has become more like producers of other entertainment, especially in its current habit of creating original content specifically for the audio format. According to Michele Cobb, Executive Director of the Audio Publishers Association, "major authors now write stand-alone pieces that are released in audio only" (Cobb 2015). The novelist Orson Scott Card is one of those. He was recently hired by Audible, amazon.com's audiobook arm, to write a six-hour dramatization of his novel *Ender's Game*. "It is not a simple adaptation," Card claims, "it is a new telling of the same story" (Alter 2013).

But, people inevitably ask, is listening to a text actually reading? *The New York Times* published an amusing article in 2007 about the hot debate over this issue that was then occurring in the growing ranks of America's book discussion groups. Though the jury is still out these nine years later, what one expert witness, Daniel T. Willingham, a University of Virginia cognitive neuroscientist, had to say remains apposite: "If the goal is to appreciate the aesthetic of the writing and understand the story, then there won't be much difference between listening and reading. The basic architecture of how we understand language is much more similar between reading and listening than it is different" (Newman 2007).

"In some cases," Olga Khazan (2011) writes, "listening offers major advantages over reading, even with material as tough to parse as Shakespeare."

Not everyone is so sure, however. Nicholas Carr, author of *The Shallows. What the Internet Is Doing to Our Brains*, says, "If we come to think reading is this secondary activity we do while doing other stuff, then we lose the deepest and most important kind of reading. The broader danger is that technology will give us the illusion that everything can be done while multitasking, including reading" (Alter 2013).

Pam Spencer Holley, a former president of YALSA and reviewer of audiobooks, isn't so sure. "The more I listen," she says, "the more ready I am to accept that listening can be interchanged with reading" (Holley, personal communications, December 6, 2009, and June 6, 2015). When I asked her why audiobooks have become so popular with teens, she pointed to "the increase in the number of titles, which affords teens a wide range of selections. For pleasure or school assignments, listening is a natural for this teen population." To enhance their listening skills, she notes that for the last several summers there has been a joint program from AudioFile and OverDrive called SYNC, which encourages teens to download two free audiobooks a week from early May through August. One of these is a classic; the other, a similarly themed current young adult novel. "With teens sporting earbuds or headphones and carrying some sort of MP3 player this program is a natural for them," Holley concludes.

That word "sync" is becoming an increasingly important aspect of the maturing field. According to Alter, "Digital innovation isn't just changing the way audio books are created, packaged and sold. It's starting to reshape the way readers consume literature, creating a new breed of literary omnivores who see narrated books and text as interchangeable. Last year, the audio book producer and retailer Audible unveiled a long-awaited syncing feature that allows book lovers to switch seamlessly between an e-book and a digital audio book, picking up the story at precisely the same sentence" (Alter 2013).

As the technology—and content—continue to develop and expand, more and more librarians are becoming—along with teachers—staunch advocates of the viability of listening as a literary experience. As early as 2006, the Young Adult Library Services Association and the Association of Library Service to Children jointly created a new annual prize for excellence in audiobook production. Named the Odyssey Award and sponsored by *Booklist*, it was first presented in 2008. Holley, one of the creators of the award, explains it "gives recognition to the entire audiobook from ensuring there are no distortions of sound, mispronunciations, or variations in sound quality to acknowledging the seamless partnership created by the best readers with their texts" (Holley, personal communications, December 6, 2009, and June 6, 2015).

With this demonstration of increasing library interest, the producers of audio for children and teens have dramatically increased their output and, aided by technology, have also increased the number and variety of formats in which audiobooks are available.

With ever-better and ever more dramatic production values, audiobooks' entertainment value has become a given. But what about their educational value?

According to *Becoming a Nation of Readers,* a study by the Commission on Reading, "The single most important activity for building the knowledge required for eventual success in reading is reading aloud to children."

Audio book mavens and librarians Mary Burkey, Sharon Grover, and Liz Hannegan offer some other educational benefits of audiobooks:

> They build and enhance vital literacy skills such as fluency, vocabulary, language acquisition, pronunciation, phonemic awareness, and comprehension.
> They develop critical thinking and active listening skills.
> They increase literacy skills and the reading ability of readers with learning disabilities and English language learners.
> They augment the quantity of spoken, sophisticated vocabulary that research shows increases academic achievement (Audio Publishers Association, 2014).

The creators of the Odyssey Award agree "It's important," they write, "that we, as a group of professionals committed to lifelong literacy, recognize the role of audiobooks in the development of literacy" (www.ala.org/alsc/awards grants/bookmedia/odysseyaward/odysseyabout).

"Listening," the Odyssey Award founders conclude, "is an important skill to be both taught and learned." Their conclusion seems to prove that all old is new again! As long ago as 1985, the poet Donald Hall (who went on to serve as America's Poet Laureate in 2006) wrote the essay "Bring Back the Out-Loud Culture" in *Newsweek.* In it, he noted that "before the late 1920s and 1930s American culture was *out loud.* We continually turned print into sound. Mother read or recited to infant (memorization allowed entertainment even while both hands made bread). Grandfather read from Prophet and Gospel; his grandson performed chapters from Scott and Dickens . . . When we stopped memorizing and reciting literature, our ability to read started its famous decline. As children speak poems and stories aloud," he continued, "by the pitch and muscle of their voices they will discover drama, humor, passion and intelligence in print. In order to become a nation of readers, we need again to become a nation of reciters" (Hall 1985, 12).

Let ALA's Odyssey Award founders have the final word here: "Children of this century live in a world where media is a dominant form of communication, and imagination's greatest champion in this technological realm is the spoken word. Through the years our cultures have been nurtured and our customs passed on by storytellers—audiobooks carry on that tradition."

To which one can only add a hearty, "Hear hear!"

Here and Now

Surely it's obvious by now that story, in whatever form or format it may be presented, will survive. But so, I predict, will paper. Ease of access offered by technology is one thing; the aesthetic pleasure of the book as a physical object, as an artifact is quite another, however. Nothing in my experience can beat the tactile and visual pleasure of holding, examining, and reading a beautifully designed, bound, and printed book. By comparison the act of reading a book on a screen is a cold, sterile, and eye strain–inducing exercise. And I suspect that enough other people share my sympathies to ensure that the book, as a physical object, is going to be around for a while—quite a while. What is interesting, even exciting, in this context is the perhaps unintended impact that the omnipresence of the digital in the lives of today's young netizens is having on the design of books. More and more publishers, it seems, are finding the future in the past, as books begin to replicate the visual appeal of illustrated books from the nineteenth century.[4]

One of the best cases in point of the new-old aesthetic importance of books for young readers remains Scott Westerfeld's novel *Leviathan* (2009), a book that—though aimed at YAs—was lavishly illustrated and featured beautifully intricate, full-color endpaper maps. It also was printed on seventy-pound paper, the whole point of the obviously expensive exercise being Westerfeld's desire to re-create the look of Victorian books, as his novel itself was a work of steampunk science fiction (though set during an alternate World War I instead of the more customary Victorian Era). Happily, Westerfeld had the best-selling clout with his publisher to make such an expensive publishing event happen (even if he did, as one reads, have to pay for a large part of it himself). (Volumes two and three in this trilogy—*Behemoth* [2010] and *Goliath* [2011] were equally attractive.)

A more recent case in point is Ben Tripp's *The Accidental Highwayman* (2014), an antic mashup of historical fiction and fantasy that is lavishly illustrated with black-and-white drawings by the author. Other recent examples of this type of book are Adele Griffin's *The Unfinished Life of Addison Stone* (2014), which is illustrated with photographs commissioned for the volume; Kiersten White and illustrator Jim DiBartolo's *In the Shadows* (2014), a novel told in text and portfolios of pictures; and Emil Sher's *Young Man with a Camera* (2015), illustrated—as the title suggests—with photographs. Yet another is Ransom Riggs's eccentric *Miss Peregrine's Home for Peculiar Children* (2011), which is illustrated with eerie vintage photographs; and Stephen Emond's *Bright Lights, Dark Nights* (2015), with its black- and-white pictures.

Text and image, which can be enjoyed both visually and tactilely, offer an agreeable combination. But the most agreeable combination imaginable is that of young adults and young adult literature. When I wrote the first edition of this book in the 1990s, there was widespread doubt that one half of this equation—young adult literature—would survive but, as I hope I have demonstrated in the preceding pages, not only has the genre survived; it has thrived! Despite some occasional problems with the economy—both here and abroad[5]—the future of YA seems secure. Publishers continue to add new YA imprints and means of distribution, for example, the big box stores, and as "the walls between marketing channels are beginning to crumble," the new mass merchandise market is also proving especially beneficial to teen book sales (Rosen 2009a).

As for teen demographics, the National Center for Education Statistics (2009) forecasts record levels of total elementary and secondary enrollment through at least 2017; indeed, new records are anticipated every year until then. Overall, public school enrollment is expected to increase 9 percent between 2008 and 2017 and secondary enrollment will grow by 5 percent.

At this rate, the golden age of young adult literature promises to become a permanent fixture of publishing, libraries, bookstores, and teen lives. It will be fascinating to watch the field continue to grow, to continue to invite creative and technological innovations, to continue to welcome traditional and nontraditional means of sharing stories and information in ways that will delight our imaginations, expand our minds, teach us new means of cultivating empathy and understanding, and—perhaps above all else—securing a civilization of enlightenment, comity, and compassion for future generations of teens and young adults yet to come.

Notes

1. See "The Age of Irony Isn't Over After All," Michiko Kakutani. *New York Times*, 10/9/01, and "The Age of Irony Is Alive and Well" by Brian Unger, *The Unger Report*, NPR, 9/11/06. www.npr.org.

2. A particularly withering analysis, "Reading Responsibly," was offered by Nancy Kaplan, Executive Director of the School of Information Arts and Technologies at the University of Baltimore. See www.futureofthebook .org/blog/archives/2007/11/reading_responsibly_nancy_kaplan.

3. The Common Core Standards Initiative is the largest-ever attempt to set unified expectations for what students in grades K-12 should know and be able to do in preparation for college and the workforce.

4. One of the best books on this subject is Percy Muir's "Victorian Illustrated Books" (New York: Praeger 1971).

5. A September 16, 2009 article by Caroline Horn in Britain's "The Bookseller" was headlined "Children's Publishers Cutting Acquisitions and Advances."

References

21st Century Schools. nd. "Multiple Literacies." www.21stcenturyschools.com/Multiple_Literacies.htm.

Abrahamson, Richard. 1998. "Back to the Future with Adult Books for the Teenage Reader." *Journal of Youth Services in Libraries* 11 (Summer): 383.

Abramson, Jane. 1976. "Playing It Safe: Restricted Realism in Teen Novels." *School Library Journal* 22 (May): 38.

Adelson, Stewart and Kyle Knight. 2015. "The Right Therapy for LGBT Youth." *The Washington Post*, May 1. www.washingtonpost.com/opinions/the-right -therapy-for-LGBT-youth/2015/05/01/b43965e6-eeb43965e6-eeb4–11ed4–8666 -a1d756d0218e_story.html.

Alderdice, Kit. 1996. "How Random Created a YA Crossover." *Publishers Weekly* 243 (April 1): 28.

———. 2004. "Chick Lit for Teens and Tweens." *Publishers Weekly* 251 (November 15): 26.

Alexie, Sherman. 2011. "Why the Best Kids Books Are Written in Blood." *Wall Street Journal*, June 9. http://blogs.wsj.com/speakeasy/2011/06/09/why-the-best-kids -books-are-written-in-blood.

Allen, Arthur. 2014. "Risk Behavior by Teens Can Be Explained in Part by How Their Brains Change." *The Washington Post*, September 1. www.washington post.com/national/health-science/risky-behavior-by-teens-can-be-explained -in-part-by-how-their-brains-change/2014/08/29/28405df0–27d2–11e4–8953 -da634b334390_story.html.

Allen, Rachel. 2006. "From Comic Book to Graphic Novel: Why Are Graphic Novels So Popular?" CBSNews.com, July 31. www.cbsnews.com/stories/2006/07/27/ entertainment/main1843318.shtml?tag=mncol;1st;1.

Alliance for Excellent Education. 2014. "Adolescent Literacy, Fact Sheet." June. http://all4ed.org/issues/adolescent-literacy.

Alm, Richard S. 1955. "The Glitter and the Gold." *English Journal* 44 (September): 315.

Alter, Alexandra. 2013. "The New Explosion in Audio Books." *Wall Street Journal*, August 1. www.wsj.com/articles/SB10001424127887323854904578663785004909 8298.

———. 2014. "To Lure Young Readers, Nonfiction Writers Sanitize and Simplify." *The New York Times*, October 7: A1.

Alverson, Brigid. 2014a. "The Graphic Advantage." *School Library Journal*, September 14, 43.

———. 2014b. "ICv2 White Paper: Rise of the New Comics Customer." *Comic Book Resources*, October 10. www.comicbookresources.com/?page=article&id=56168.

American Library Association Washington Office Newsline. 1977. News release, August 21.

Anderson, Richard C. 1985. *Becoming a Nation of Readers*. Champaign, IL: National Academy of Education. Commission on Reading. Centre for the Study of Reading.

Anonymous. 1988. *Go Ask Alice*. New York: Aladdin.

Aoki, Deb. 2015. "Manga Resurgent at Comic-Con 2015 and Anime Expo." *Publishers Weekly*, July 15. www.publishersweekly.com/pw/by-topic/industry-news/comics/article/67505-manga-resurgent-at-comic-con-2015-and-anime-expo .html.

Aratani, Lori. 2006. "Upper Grades, Lower Reading Skills." *The Washington Post*, July 13, B1.

Arnold, Andrew D. 2003. "The Graphic Novel Silver Anniversary." *Time*, November 14. http://content.time.com/time/arts/article/0,8599,542579,00.html.

Aronson, Marc. 1995. "The YA Novel Is Dead, and Other Fairly Stupid Tales." *School Library Journal* 41 (January): 36.

Associated Press. 2014. "Report: Nation's High School Seniors Lack Critical Math and Reading Skills." Syracuse.com, May 7. www.syracuse.com/news/index .ssf/2014/05/nations_report_card_results_math_science_high_school.html.

Audio Publishers Association. Nd. "FAQ." www.audiopub.org/faq.asp.

———. 2014. "Sound Learning Overview." www.soundlearningapa.org.

Avery, Gillian. 1995. "The Beginnings of Children's Reading to c. 1700." In *Children's Literature: An Illustrated History*, edited by Peter Hunt. New York: Oxford University Press.

Bacon, Perry. 2002. "Libraries, Stores Face a Teenage Mystery." *The Washington Post*, July 13.

Badavi, Mary Ann. 2014. "No, *The Fault in Our Stars* Is Not Young Adult Fiction's Savior." *Atlantic.com*, June 10. www.theatlantic.com/entertainment/archive/2014/06/no-em-the-fault-in-our-stars-em-is-not-young-adult-fiction -s-savior/372441.

Baldwin, Neal. 1984. "Writing for Young Adults." *Publishers Weekly*, October 19, 15.

Bantam Doubleday Dell. 1994. *Fall Catalog.*

Barnes, Brook. 2012. "Hunger Games' Ticket Sales Set Record." *The New York Times*, March 25. www.nytimes.com/2012/03/26/movies/hunger-games-breaks-box -office-records.html.

Baron, Naomi S. 2014. "How E-Reading Threatens Learning in the Humanities." *The Chronicle of Higher Education*, July 14. http://chronicle.com/article/ How-E-Reading-Threatens/147661/.

Barr, Donald. 1986. "Should Holden Caulfield Read These Books?" *The New York Times Book Review*, May 4.

Barson, Michael, and Steven Heller. 1998. *Teenage Confidential: An Illustrated History of the American Teen.* San Francisco: Chronicle Books.

Bass, Dina. 1997. "Poll Finds Sharp Rise in Drug Use among Youngsters." *The Los Angeles Times*, August 14, A4.

Bauerlein, Mark. 2008. "Online Literacy Is a Lesser Kind." *Chronicle of Higher Education.* September 19. http://chronicle.com/article/Online-Literacy-Is -a-Lesser/28307.

Bellafante, Gina. 2003. "Poor Little Rich Girls Throbbing to Shop." *The New York Times*, August 17. www.nytimes.com/2003/08/17/fashion/17GIRL.html.

Berger, Laura Standley, ed. 1994. *Twentieth Century Young Adult Writers.* Detroit: St. James.

Bernstein, Elizabeth. 1996. "Don't Throw the Small Ones Back." *Publishers Weekly*, November 18, 25. www.publishersweekly.com/article/CA6417183.html.

Billman, Carol. 1986. *The Secret of the Stratemeyer Syndicate.* New York: Ungar.

Blume, Judy, ed. 1999. *Places I Never Meant to Be.* New York: Simon and Schuster.

Bolle, Sonja. 2008. "Why 'Twilight' Isn't for Everybody." *The Los Angeles Times*, December 14, www.latimes.com/features/books/la-caw-wordplay14–2008 dec14,0,5100531.

Booth, Heather. 2015. Review of *Dime*, *Booklist*. April 15.

Borelli, Christopher. 2013. "Veronica Roth the Next Literary Superstar?" *Chicago Tribune*, October 21. http://articles.chicagotribune.com/2013–10–21/ entertainment/chi-veronica-roth-profile-20131021_1_veronica-roth-allegiant -anderson.

Bott, C. J. 2008. "Bullybooks." *VOYA*, 31 (June): 118.

Bott, C. J., David Gregory, and Josh C. Cohen. 2014. "When Institutions Are Libel for Bullying." *The ALAN Review* (Winter).

Boylston, Helen. 1936. *Sue Barton Student Nurse.* Boston: Little, Brown.

Brill, Ian. 2006. "A New Era in Comics Publishing." *Publishers Weekly*, June 27. www.publishersweekly.com/article/CA6347385.html.

Burton, Dwight L. 1951. "The Novel for the Adolescent." *English Journal* 40 (September): 362.

Calvino, Italo. 1988. *Six Memos for the Next Millennium.* Cambridge, MA: Harvard University Press.

Cameron, Daryl, Michael Inzlicht, and William Cunningham. 2015. "Empathy Is Actually a Choice." *The New York Times,* July 12, SR12.

Campbell, Patty. 1993. "The Sand in the Oyster." *Horn Book* 69 (September/October): 568.

———. 1997. "Rescuing Young Adult Literature." *Horn Book* 73 (May/June): 365.

Carey, Benedict. 2013. "Shooting in the Dark." *The New York Times,* February 11. www.nytimes.com/2013/02/12/science-studying-the-effects-of-playing-violent-video-games.html.

Carlsen, G. Robert. 1980. *Books and the Teen-Age Reader,* 2nd ed. New York: Harper.

———. 1984. "Teaching Literature for the Adolescent: A Historical Perspective." *English Journal* 73 (November): 29.

Carpenter, Dave. 2000. "When Teens Spend, Business Listens." *Sacramento Bee,* November 20.

Carpenter, Susan. 2012. "Most Young Adult Book Buyers Are Not Young Adults." *The Los Angeles Times,* September 13. http://articles.latimes.com/2012/sep/13/books/la-bk-young-adult-book-buyers-20120913.

Carr, Nicholas. 2008. "Is Google Making Us Stupid?" *Atlantic Monthly,* July/August. www.theatlantic.com/magazine/archive/2008/07/is-google-making-us-stupid/306868.

Cart, Michael. 1995a. "Of Risk and Revelation: The Current State of Young Adult Literature." *Journal of Youth Services in Libraries* 9 (Winter): 151.

———. 1995b. "The Stinky Cheese Man Goes to College." *Booklist,* December 15, 695.

———. 1996. *From Romance to Realism: 50 Years of Growth and Change in Young Adult Literature.* New York: HarperCollins.

———. 1997a. "Let's Do a Month." *Booklist,* May 15, 1570.

———. 1997b. "Not Just for Children Anymore." *Booklist,* November 15, 553.

———. 1999. "Jacqueline Woodson." *St. James Guide to Young Adult Writers.* Detroit: St. James Press.

———. 2000a. "The Dream Becomes a Reality." *Booklist,* March 15, 1370.

———. 2000b. "Robert Cormier Remembered. Eulogy Delivered at St. Peter's Church." New York City, December 6.

———. 2000c. Review of *Give a Boy a Gun. Booklist,* October 1, 337.

———. 2001. "Poetry Changes the World." *Booklist,* March 15, 1390.

———. 2002a. "Eyewitness Books." *Booklist,* October 15, 399.

———. 2002b. "Got Graphic?" *Booklist,* December 15.

———. 2007. "Teens and the Future of Reading." *American Libraries* 38 (October): 42.

———. 2009. "Core Collection: Crossovers." *Booklist,* February 15, 74.

———. 2012a. Review of *The Fault in Our Stars. Booklist,* January, 98.

———. 2012b. "Review of *My Book of Life by Angel.*" *Booklist,* October, 53.

———. 2014a. "YA or NA?" *Booklist.* August. 10.

———. 2014b. "Against Graham." *Booklist.* August.

Cart, Michael, and Christine A. Jenkins. 2006. *The Heart Has Its Reasons.* Lanham, MD: Scarecrow Press.

Carter, Betty. 1988." Let's Take Taitte to Task." *School Library Journal* 35 (November): 60.

———. 1994. *Best Books for Young Adults: The Selections, the History, the Romance.* Chicago: American Library Association.

_____. 2000. *Best Books for Young Adults,* 2nd ed. Chicago: American Library Association.

———. 2008. "The Alex Award." In *The Official YALSA Awards Guidebook,* edited by Tina Frolund. New York: Neal-Schuman.

Carter, Kim. 2009. "It's a Web 2.0 World." *VOYA* 32 (June): 114.

Carvajal, Doreen. 1997. "Book Chains' New Role: Soothsayers for Publishers." *The New York Times,* August 12.

Cavanna, Betty. 1946. *Going on Sixteen.* Philadelphia: Westminster.

Centers for Disease Control and Prevention. nd. "HIV among Youth." www.cdc .gov/hiv/risk/age/youth/index.html.

———. nd. "Injury Prevention and Control." www.cdc.gov/ViolencePrevention/ youthviolence/riskprotectivefactors.html.

———. 2009. "Youth Violence Facts at a Glance." www.cdc.gov/ViolenceProtection/ pdf/yv-datasheet-a.pdf.

———. 2012. "Sexual Violence. Facts at a Glance." www.cdc.gov/ViolencePrevention/ pdf/sv-datasheet-a.pdf.

———. 2013. "Trends in the Prevalence of Sexual Behaviors." National Youth Risk Behavior Survey: 1991–2013. www.cdc.gov/healthyyouth/yrbs/pdf/trends/ us_sexual_trend_yrbs.pdf.

———. 2014. "Understanding Teen Dating Violence. Fact Sheet." www.cdc.gov/ violenceprevention/pdf/teen-dating-violence-2014-a.pdf.

———. MMWR. 2013. "Youth Risk Behavior Surveillance—United States." June 13. www.cdc.gov/mmwr/pdf/ss/ss6304.pdf.

Chang, Andrea. 2013. "Digital-Media Use to Average 15.5 Hours a Day by 2015, Study Predicts." *Los Angeles Time,* October 30. http://articles.latimes.com/2013/ oct/30/business/la-fi-tn-media-consumption-20131030.

Charles, Ron. 2015. "Juan Felipe Herrera Becomes the First Mexican American US Poet Laureate." *The Washington Post,* June 10. www.washingtonpost.com/ entertainment/books/juan-felipe-herrera-becomes-first-hispanic-american -us-poet-laureate/2015/06/09/12de5168–0e60–11e5-adec-e82f8395c032_story .html.

Children's Software Review. 1997. "A Conversation with Dorling Kindersley's Peter Kindersley." November/December. www.childressoftwarre.com /Kindersley .html.

Chilton, Martin. 2014. "James Patterson Tops the Best-Selling Authors Since 2001." *The Telegraph,* March 20. www.telegraph.co.uk/culture/books/booknews/ 10710399/James-Patterson-tops-the-list-of-best-selling-authors-since -2001.html.

Cobb, Michele. 2015. "Audiobooks: Where They've Been and Where They're Headed." *Dear Author.* http://dearauthor.com/tag/audiobooks.

Comerford, Lynda Brill. 2009. "Q and A with Virginia Euwer Wolff." *Publishers Weekly,* February 5. www.publishersweekly.com/pw/by-topic/new-titles/ adult-announcements/article/3348-q-amp-a-with-virginia-euwer-wolff.html.

Commission on Reading. 1985. *Becoming a Nation of Readers.*

Cooke, Rachel. 2003. "It Ain't Half Hot, Mum." *Guardian,* February 23. www .theguardian.com/books/2003/feb/23/booksforchildrenandteenagers-features.

Corbett, Sue. 2014. "All Teen, All the Time." *Publishers Weekly,* September 29, 23.

Corliss, Richard. 1995. "To Live and Buy in L.A." *Time,* July 31. www.time.com/ magazine/article/0,9171,983251,00.html.

Cormier, Robert. 1974. *The Chocolate War.* New York: Pantheon.

———. 1988. "Probing the Cellars of a Young Adult Writer's Heart." Frances Clarke Sayers Lecture. University of California, Los Angeles, May 17.

Cornish, Sarah, and Patrick Jones. 2002. "Retro Mick Printz." *VOYA* 25 (December): 353.

Craig, Amanda. 2008. "Crossover Books—Time Out." www.amandacraig.com/ pages/childrens-book-reviews-reviews/crossover-books.htm.

Crain, Caleb. 2007. "Twilight of the Books." *New Yorker,* December 24. www.new yorker.com/arts/critics/atlarge/2007/12/24/071224crat_atlarge_crain.

Daly, Maureen. 1942. *Seventeenth Summer.* New York: Dodd, Mead.

———, ed. 1951. *Profile of Youth.* Philadelphia: J. B. Lippincott.

Deahl, Rachel. 2007. "DC Goes Where the Girls Are." *Publishers Weekly,* April 20. www.publishersweekly.com/pw/by-topic/1-legacy/24-comic-book-reviews/ article/12082-where-the-girls-are-html.

Deal, Melanie. 2012. "2010 Census Shows Multiple-Race Population Grew Faster Than Single-Race Population." *United States Census Bureau News,* September 27. www.prnewswire.com/news-releases/2010-census-shows-multiple -race-population-grew-faster-than-single-race-population-171528431.html.

DiMassa, Cara Mia. 2001. "New Chapter for Young Adult Books." *The Los Angeles Times,* January 29.

Dockterman, Eliana. 2015. "Everyone's a Superhero." *Time,* September 7, 80.

Donston-Miller, Debra. 2014. "Why Young Adults Hunger for The Hunger Games and Other Post-Apocalyptic Dystopian Fiction." *Forbes,* November 20. www

.forbes.com/sites/sungardas/2014/11/20/why-young-adults-hunger-for-the
-hunger-games-and-other-post-apocalyptic-dystopian-fiction.

Du Jardin, Rosamund. 1949. *Practically Seventeen*. Philadelphia: Lippincott.

Dunleavy, M. P. 1993. "The Crest of the Wave." *Publishers Weekly*, July 19, 31.

Eaglen, Audrey. 1990. "Don't Argue with Success." *School Library Journal* 36 (May): 54.

Edwards, Margaret A. 1954. "The Rise of Teen-Age Reading." *Saturday Review*, November 13, 88.

———. 1969. *The Fair Garden and the Swarm of Beasts*. New York: Hawthorn.

Egoff, Sheila. 1980. "Beyond the Garden Wall." In *The Arbuthnot Lectures 1970–1979*, compiled by Zena Sutherland, 190–96. Chicago: American Library Association.

Eldridge, Dan. 2014. "Have You Heard? Audiobooks Are Booming: Here's What You Need to Know." *Book Business*, April.

Elleman, Barbara. 1998. "To Market, to Market." *School Library Journal* 44 (April): 44.

Engberg, Gillian. 2004. "Choosing Adult Romances for Teens." *Booklist* 101 (September 15): 237.

Epstein, Connie. 1990. "A Publisher's Perspective." *Horn Book* 66 (March/April): 237.

Erikson, Erik. 1950. *Childhood and Society*. New York: W. W. Norton.

Estrada, Jackie. 2006. "The Rise of the Graphic Novel." *ForeWord*, January/February C4.

Fantozzi, Joanna. 2012. "Harry Potter, The Hunger Games Books Top NPR's Poll of Best Young Adult Literature Ever." *New York Daily News*, August 8. www.ny dailynews.com/entertainment/music-arts/harry-potter-hunger-games-books -top-npr-poll-best-young-adult-literature-article-1.1132007.

Farish, Terry. 2013. "Why Verse?" *School Library Journal* 59 (November): 11.

Federal Bureau of Investigation. nd. "Gangs." https://www.fbi.gov/about-us/ investigate/vc_majorthefts/gangs.

Flanagan, Anna. 2008. "The Role of Research in Improving Adolescent Literacy." *The Council Chronicle* 17 (March): 6.

Fontaine, Mia. 2013. "America Has an Incest Problem." *Atlantic.com*, January. www.theatlantic.com/national/archive/2013/01/america-has-an-incest -problem/272459/.

Forman, Jack. 1994. "Paul Zindel." In *Twentieth-Century Young Adult Writers*, edited by Laura Standley Berger, 931–33. Detroit: St. James.

Freedman, Russell. 1994. "Bring 'Em Back Alive." *School Library Journal* 40 (March): 138.

Freund, Lisa. 2011. "Risky Business: Dealing with Your Teen's Behavior." *NIH News in Health*, September. http://newsinhealth.nih.gov/issue/Sep2011/Feature1.

Frey, William H. 2015. *Diversity Explosion*. Washington, DC: Brookings Institution Press.

Friedman, Richard A. 2014. "Why Teenagers Act Crazy." *New York Times*, June 29.

Frolund, Tina, ed. 2008. *The Official YALSA Awards Guidebook*. New York: Neal–Schuman Publishers.

Frost, Helen. 2006. *The Braid*. New York: Farrar, Strauss and Giroux.

Fry, Richard. 2013. "A Rising Share of Young Adults Live in Their Parents' Home. A Record 21.6 Million in 2012." Pew Research Center, August 1. www.pewsocial trends.org/2013/08/01/a-rising-share-of-young-adults-live-in-their-parents -home.

Gallo, Don, ed. 1990. *Speaking for Ourselves*. Urbana, IL: NCTE.

Gardner, Howard. 2008. "The End of Literacy? Don't Stop Reading." *The Washington Post*, February 15, B01.

Gaudios, John. 2012. "Hunger Games Trilogy Beats Harry Potter Series to Become All-Time Bestselling Series." *Forbes*, August 1. http://onforb.es/NtPRnI.

Gay, Lesbian, Straight Educators Network. 2014. "GLSEN Releases New National School Climate Survey on America's Middle and High Schools," October 22. www.glsen.org/article/glsen-releases-new-national-school-climate-survey.

Getlin, Josh. 1997. "Future of Books Isn't Written in Stone." *The Los Angeles Times*, October 1.

Giblin, James Cross. 1988. "The Rise and Fall and Rise of Juvenile Nonfiction, 1961–1988." *School Library Journal* 35 (October): 27.

Gilmore, Natasha. 2015a. "CCBC Stats Show Children's Books Shifting toward Diversity." *Publishers Weekly*, February 18. www.publishersweekly.com/pw/ by-topic/childrens-industry-news/article/65628-ccbc-stats-show-children -s-books-shifting-toward-diversity.htm.

———. 2015b."New York Times' Changes Children's Bestseller Lists." *Publishers Weekly*. August 19.

Gilmore, Natasha, and Matia Burnett. 2014. "Kids Are Thriving, Reading, and Hungry for More: Crunching Numbers at the Nielsen Children's Book Summit." *Publishers Weekly*, December 16. www.publishersweekly.com/pw/by-topic/ childrens/childrens-industry-news/article/65068-kids-are-thriving-reading -and-hungry-for-more-crunching-numbers-at-the-nielsen-children-s-book -summit.html.

Goddu, Krystyna. 2013. 21st "Century Children's Nonfiction: A Conference Recap." *Publishers Weekly*, June 20. www.publishersweekly.com/pw/by-topic/ childrens/childrens-industry-news/article/57894–21st-century-children-s -nonfiction-a-conference-recap/html.

Graham, Ruth. 2014. "Against YA." *Slate.com*. June 5. www.slate.com/articles/arts/ books/2014/06/against_ya_adults_should_be_embarrassed_to_read_children _s_books.html.

Gray, Paul. 1993. "Carnage: An Open Book." *Time* 142 (August 2): 54.

———. 1999. "Wild about Harry." *Time* 154 (September 20): 67.

Green, John. 2004. "Review of *ttyl* by Lauren Myracle." *Booklist* 100 (May 15): 1615.

Griepp, Milton. 2009. "NYCC: The Graphic Novel Conference. ICv2." February 9. www.comicbookresources.com/page=article&id=19938.

———. 2015. "Comics and Graphic Novel Market Sales Hit New 20 Year High." *ICv2*. http://icv2.com/articles/markets/view/31916/comics-graphic-novels-sales-hit -new-20-year-high.

Gurdon, Meghan Cox. 2011. "Darkness Too Visible: Contemporary Fiction for Teens Is Rife with Explicit Abuse, Violence and Depravity." *Wall Street Journal*, June 4. www.wsj.com/articles/SB10001424005270230365740457635762259269703B.

Gutkind, Lee. 2012. "Three R's of Narrative Nonfiction." *The New York Times*, December 17. http://opinionator.blogs.nytimes.com/2012/12/17/three-rs-of -narrative-nonfiction/.

Hall, Donald E. 1985. "Bring Back the Out-Loud Culture." *Newsweek*, April 15, 12.

Hall, G. Stanley. 1904. *Adolescence: Its Psychology and Its Relations to Anthropology, Sociology, Sex, Crime, Religion and Education.* 2 vols. New York: D. Appleton.

Harmon, Amy. 2004. "Internet Gives Teenage Bullies Weapons to Wound from Afar." *The New York Times*, August 26.

Havighurst, Robert James. 1950. *Developmental Tasks and Education.* New York: David McKay.

———. 1988. *Developmental Tasks and Education* Quoted in David A. Russell. "The Common Experience of Adolescence." *Journal of Youth Services in Libraries*, 2 (Fall): 61.

Hayn, Judith. 2000. "Jacqueline Woodson." In *Writers for Young Adults Supplement.* New York: Charles Scribner's Sons.

Healthychildren.org. 2015. "Teenagers and Gangs." May 5. https://www.healthy children.org/English/ages-stages/teen/Pages/Teenagers-and-Gangs.aspx.

Hefling, Kimberly. 2014. "Nation's Report Card: 12th-Graders Show No Growth." *Associated Press*, May 7.

———. 2015. "Survey: School Bullying at Lowest Level in a Decade." *The Republic*, A9.

Hentoff, Nat. 1967. "Tell It as It Is." *The New York Times Book Review*, May 7.

Hertz, Sarah H., and Donald R. Gallo. 1996. *From Hinton to Hamlet. Building Bridges between Young Adult Literature and the Classics.* Westport, CT: Greenwood Press.

Hesse, Monica. 2009. "When Romance Writers Gather." *The Washington Post*, July 18.

Hine, Thomas. 1999. *The Rise and Fall of the American Teenager.* New York: Avon Books.

Hinton, S.E. 1967a. *The Outsiders.* New York: Viking.

———. 1967b. "Teen-Agers Are for Real." *The New York Times Book Review*, August 27.

Hochschild, Adam. 1994. "War and Peace, Part II." *The Los Angeles Times Book Review,* August 7.

Horning, Kathleen T. 2014. "Still an All-White World?" *School Library Journal* 60 (May): 20.

Huntwork, Mary M. 1990. "Why Girls Flock to Sweet Valley High." *School Library Journal* 36 (March): 137.

Hutchinson, Margaret. 1973. "Fifty Years of Young Adult Reading: 1921–1971." *Top of the News* 30 (November) 24–53.

International Reading Association. nd. "New Literacies and 21st Century Technologies." www.reading.org/general/About/IRA/PositionStatements/21stCenturyLiteracies.aspx.

Ivins, Molly. 1997. "America Turns on Its Kids." *San Francisco Chronicle,* July 2.

Jackson, Richard. 1998. "The Beast Within." *Booklist* 94 (August): 1985.

Jacobs, Thomas A. 1997. *What Are My Rights? 95 Questions and Answers about Teens and the Law.* Minneapolis, MN: Free Spirit.

Jayson, Sharon. 2012. "Census Shows Big Jump in Interracial Couples." *USA Today,* April 26. www.usatoday30.usatoday.com/news/nation/story/2012–04–24/census-interracial-couples/54531706/1.

Jefferson, Margo. 1982. "Sweet Dreams for Prom Queens." *The Nation* 234 (May 22): 613.

Jenkins, Christine. 1999. "Two Hundred Years of Young Adult Library Services History." *VOYA,* March. www.voya.com/2010/03/30/chronology.

Jennings, Dana. 2015. "Drawn & Quarterly's Cartoonist Mystique." *The New York Times,* June 14. AR 1, 20–21.

Jennings, Frank G. 1956. "Literature for Adolescents—Pap or Protein?" *English Journal* 45 (December): 226.

Jensen, Kelly. 2013. "Killer Books." *School Library Journal* 59 (September): 41.

Johnson, Steven. 2005. *Everything Bad Is Good for You: How Today's Popular Culture Is Actually Making Us Smarter.* New York: Riverhead.

Kantrowitz, Barbara, and Karen Springen. 2005. "A Teen Health Gap." *Newsweek,* December 12, 65.

Kaufman, Leslie. 2013. "A Novelist and His Brother Sell Out Carnegie Hall." *The New York Times,* January 16. www.nytimes.com/2013/01/17/books/john-and-hank-green-bring-their-show-to-carnegie-hall.html.

Keim, Brandon. 2013. "What Science Knows about Video Games and Violence." *NOVA next,* February 28. www.pbs.org/wgbh/nova/next/body/what-science-knows-about-video-games-and-violence/.

Kellogg, Mary Alice. 1983. "The Romance Book Boom." *Seventeen,* 42 (May): 158.

Kemp, Robert S, J. Rathbun, and R. E. Morgan. 2014. "Indicators of School Crime and Safety." 2013. National Center for Education Statistics. United States

Department of Education. http://nces.ed.gov/pubsearch/pubsinfo
.asp?pubid=2014042.

Kett, Joseph E. 1977. *Rites of Passage. Adolescence in America 1790 to the Present.*
New York: Basic Books.

Khazan, Olga. 2011. "Is Listening to Audio Books Really the Same as Reading?"
Forbes, September 12. www.com/forbes.com/sites/olgakhazan/2011/9/12/is
-listening-to-audio-books-really-the-same-as-reading/.

KidsHealth. nd. "If Your Child Is Raped." http://kidshealth.org/parent/positive/
talk/rape.html.

Kirch, Claire. 2014. "Looking to Move Beyond the 11%." *Publishers Weekly,* October
13, 30.

———. 2015. "We Need Diverse Books Becomes 501-c-3 Nonprofit." *Publishers
Weekly,* April 7. www.publishersweekly.com/pw/by-topic/childrens/childrens
-book-news/article/66127-we-need-diverse-books-becomes-501-c-3-nonprofit
.html.

Klein, Norma. 1991. "Thoughts on the Adolescent Novel." In *Writers on Writing for
Young Adults,* edited by Patricia E. Feehan and Pamela Petrick Barron. Detroit:
Omnigraphics.

Koebler, Jason. 2012. "Is It Time to Rate Young Adult Books for Mature Content?"
US News and World Report, May 18. www.usnews.com/news/articles/2015/
05/18/is-it-time-to-rate-young-adult-books-for-mature-content.

Koelling, Holly. 2007, ed. *Best Books for Young Adults,* 3rd ed. Chicago: American
Library Association.

Kohlberg, Lawrence, and Carol Gilligan. 1971. *The Adolescent as Philosopher.*
New York: Daedalus.

Kolbert, Elizabeth. 2015. "The Terrible Teens." *New Yorker.* August 31. 84.

Kraus, Daniel. 2012. "Review of *Midwinterblood.*" *Booklist,* December 1, 52.

Kraus, W. Keith. 1975. "Cinderella in Trouble Still Dreaming and Losing." *School
Library Journal* 21 (January): 18.

Kunkle, Fredrick. 2015. "Pew: Multiracial Population Changing the Face of the U.S."
Washington Post, June 11.

Kushman, Rick. 1999. "Youth Market." *Sacramento Bee,* May 28.

LaFeria, Ruth. 2004. "Generation Mixed." *San Diego Union-Tribune,* January 4.

Lamia, Mary C. 2010. "Do Bullies Actually Lack Empathy?" *Psychology Today,* October 30. https://www.psychologytoday.com/blog/intense-emotions-and-strong
-feelings/2010010/do-bullies-actually-lack-empathy.

Lane, Rose Wilder. 1933. *Let the Hurricane Roar.* New York: Longmans, Green.

Larrick, Nancy. 1965. "The All White World of Children's Books." *Saturday Review,*
September 11, 63–65.

Latrobe, Kathy Howard. 1994. "Report on the Young Adult Library Services Association's Membership Survey." *Journal of Youth Services in Libraries* 7 (Spring): 238.

Lawrence-Pietroni, Anna. 1996. "The Tricksters, The Changeover, and the Fluidity of Adolescent Literature." *Children's Literature Association Quarterly* 21 (Spring): 34.

Lenhart, Amanda. 2015. "Teens, Social Media and Technology Overview." *Pew Research Center Internet, Science and Tech*, April 9. www.pewinternet.org/2015/04/09/teens-social-media-technology-2015/.

Library Journal. 2015. "We Need Diverse Books™ | Movers and Shakers 2015—Change Agents." *Library Journal*, March. http://lj.libraryjournal.com/2015/03/people/movers-shakers-2015/we-need-diverse-books-movers-shakers-2015-change-agents/.

Lipsyte, Robert. 1967. *The Contender*. New York: Harper.

Lodge, Sally. 1992. "The Making of a Crossover." *Publishers Weekly* 239 (November 23): 38.

———. 1998. "Breaking Out of Format Formulas." *Publishers Weekly* 245 (November 9): 31.

———. 2008. "Gossip Girl Dishes On." www.publishersweekly.com/article/CA6547202.html?

Logan, William. 2014. "Poetry: Who Needs It?" *The New York Times*, June 15. www.nytimes.com/2014/06/15/sunday-review/poetry-who-needs-it.html.

Lynch, Chris. 1994. "Today's YA Writers: Pulling No Punches." *School Library Journal* 40 (January): 37.

Macaulay, David. 1991. "Caldecott Medal Acceptance Speech." *Horn Book* 67 (July-August): 419.

MacDonald, Heidi. 2008a. "Big NYCC Crowds Enjoy Good Mood, Weather, Comics." *Publishers Weekly*, April 22. www.publishersweekly.com/article/CA6553777.html.

———. 2008b. "Graphic Novels Hit $375 Million." *ICv2*. http://icv2.com/articles/comics/view/12416/graphic-novels-hit-375-million.

———. 2008c. "ICv2 Confab Reports 2007 Graphic Novel Sales Rise 12%." *Publishers Weekly* www.publishersweekly.com/pw/by-topic/new-titles/adult-announcements/article/37-nycc-icv2-briefs.html.

———. 2013. "How Graphic Novels Became the Hottest Section in the Library." *Publishers Weekly*, May 13. www.publishersweekly.com/pw/by-topic/industry-news/libraries/article/57093-how-graphic-novels-became-the-hottest-section-in-the-library.html.

MacDonald, Scott. 2005. "YA for Everybody." *Quill and Quire*, February.

Maguire, Gregory. 2009. *Making Mischief*. New York: Morrow.

Maloney, Jennifer. 2014. "The New Wave of Graphic Novels." *Wall Street Journal*, December 31. www.wsj.com/articles/the-new-wave-of-graphic-novels -1420048910.

Mann, Leslie. 2013. "HIV Infection Risk Especially High for Teens." *Chicago Tribune*, January 2. http://articles.chicagotribune.com/2013–01–02/news/ ct-x-0102-teens-hiv-20130102_1_hiv-infection-risk-young-gay-men-hiv-rates.

Marano, Hara Estroff. 2007. "Trashing Teens." *Psychology Today*, March 1, www.psychologytoday.com/node/23774.

Marcus, Leonard. 2008. *Minders of Make-Believe*. Boston: Houghton Mifflin.

Marschall, Richard. 1989. *America's Great Comic Strip Artists*. New York: Abbeville Press.

Matthews, Virginia, et. al. 1990. "Kids Need Libraries." *Journal of Youth Services in Libraries* 3 (Spring): 197–207.

Mattson, Dirk. 1997. "Should We Be Aware of Donors Bearing Book Prizes? Questioning the Walden Award." *School Library Journal* 43 (9): 115–17.

Maughan, Shannon. 1999. "The Harry Potter Halo." *Publishers Weekly* 246 (July 19): 92.

———. 2000. "Teenage Growing Pains." *Publishers Weekly*, 247 (October 23): 28.

———. 2007. "Way Cool: Marketing and the Internet." *Publishers Weekly*, February 16. www.publishersweekly.com/pw/by-topic/new-titles/adult -announcements/article/6423-way-cool-marketing-and-the-internet.html.

———. 2015. "Banned Books Week to Showcase YA." *Publishers Weekly*. April 23. www.publishersweekly.com/pw/by-topic/childrens/childrens-industry-news/ article/66377-banned-books-week-to-showcase-ya.html.

Maughan, Shannon, and Jim Milliot. 2001. "Time-Life Trade, Teen People Book Club to Close." *Publishers Weekly*, April 2, 12.

McElderry, Margaret K. 1994. "Across the Years, Across the Seas." *Journal of Youth Services in Libraries* 7 (Summer): 369–80.

McGrath, Charles. 2004a. "Not Funnies." *The New York Times Magazine*, July 11.

———. 2004b. "The Short Story Shakes Itself out of Academe." *The New York Times*, August 25.

———. 2004c. "What Johnny Won't Read." *The New York Times*, July 11.

McPhee, John. 2015. "Omission." *New Yorker*, September 14, 46–47.

Mead, Rebecca. 2009. "The Gossip Mill." *New Yorker*, October 19. www.newyorker .com/magazine/2009/10/19/the-gossip-mill.

Miller, Laura. 2004. "Lad Lit." *New York Times*, May 23.

———. 2005/2006. "Far from Narnia." *New Yorker*, December 2005–January 2006, 52.

———. 2010. "Fresh Hell." *New Yorker*. June 14. www.newyorker.com/magazine/ 2010/06/14/fresh-hell-2.

Milliot, Jim. 2014. "Children's Books: A Shifting Market." *Publishers Weekly*, February 24. www.publishersweekly.com/pw/by-topic/children's/childrens-industry-news/article/61167-children-s-books-a-shifting-market.html.

Minkel, Elizabeth. 2014. "Read Whatever the Hell You Want: Why We Need a New Way of Talking about Young Adult Literature." *New Statesman*, October 14.

Mondale, Sarah, and Sarah B. Patton, eds. 2001. *School. The Story of American Public Education*. Boston: Beacon Press.

Moore, John Noell. 1997. *Interpreting Young Adult Literature. Literary Theory in the Secondary Classroom*. Portsmouth, NH: Boynton/Cook Heinemann.

Morales, Robert. 1997. "That's Entertainment." *Publishers Weekly*, June 30, 49.

Mydans, Seth. 1993. "A New Tide of Immigration Brings Hostility to the Surface, Poll Finds." *The New York Times*, June 27.

Myers, Walter Dean. 2008. "Margaret A. Edwards Award Acceptance Speech." In *The Official YALSA Awards Guidebook*, edited by Tina Frolund, 98–101. New York: Neal-Schuman.

———. 2014. "Where Are the People of Color in Children's Books?" *The New York Times*, March 16, SR1.

National Center for Education Statistics. 2009. Digest of Education Statistics: 2008. March, http://nces.ed.gov/programs/digest/d08/.

National Council of Teachers of English. nd. Position Statement. The Definition of 21st Century Literacies. www.ncte.org/positions/statements/21stcent definition.

National Endowment for the Arts. 2004. *Reading at Risk*. Washington, DC: National Endowment for the Arts.

———. 2007. *To Read or Not to Read*. Washington, DC: National Endowment for the Arts.

———. 2009. *Reading on the Rise*. Washington, DC: National Endowment for the Arts.

———. 20013. *How a Nation Engages with Art*. Washington, DC: National Endowment for the Arts.

———. 2015. *A Decade of Arts Engagement*. Washington, DC: National Endowment for the Arts.

Neal, Meghan. 2012. "1 in 12 Teens Have Attempted Suicide: Report." *New York Daily News*, June 9. www.nydailynews.com/life-style/health/1-12-teens-attempted-suicide-report-article-1.1092622.

Newman, Andrew Adam. 2007. "Your Cheatin' Listenin' Ways." *The New York Times*, August 2.

Nielsen Media. 2014. "Don't Judge a Book by Its Cover: Tech-Savvy Teens Remain Fans of Print Books." December 9. www.nielsen.com/us/en/insights/news/2014/don't-judge-a-book-by-its-cover-tech-savvy-teens-remain-fans-of-print-books.html.

Nilsen, Alleen Pace. 1994. "That Was Then, This Is Now." *School Library Journal*, 40 (April): 30.

Nilsen, Alleen Pace, and Kenneth L. Donelson. 1988. "The New Realism Comes of Age." *Journal of Youth Services in Libraries* I (Spring): 275.

———. 1993. Literature for Today's Young Adults. 4th ed. New York: HarperCollins.

———. 2009. *Literature for Today's Young Adults*, 8th ed. Boston: Pearson.

North, Anna. 2012. "Is Young Adult Fiction the New Chic Lit?" *Buzzfeed*, November 9. www.buzzfeed.com/annanorth/is-young-adult-fiction-the-new-chick-lit# .jsEbmYKVa.

———. 2014. "Do You Have Time to Read This Story?" *The New York Times*, October 2. http://op-talk.blogs.nytimes.com/2014/10/02/do-you-have-time-to-read -this-story.

Nussbaum, Emily. 2005. "Psst, Selena Is a Slut, Pass It On." *New York*, December 8. http://nymag.com/nymetro/arts/books/12058/.

O'Connor, John J. 1994. "Is the BBC Too Adult for American Viewers?" *The New York Times*, December 29.

Ohanian, Susan. 1991. "Learning 'Whole Language.'" *Publishers Weekly*, February 22, 127.

Olsen, Ray. 2002. "The Booklist Interview: Neil Gaiman." *Booklist*, 98 (August): 1949.

Palladino, Grace. 1996. *Teenagers. An American History*. New York: Basic Books.

Pareles, Jon. 1995. "They're Rebels without a Cause and Couldn't Care Less." *The New York Times*, July 16.

Passel, Jeffrey S., and D'Vera Cohn. 2008. Pew Research Center. Hispanic Trends. US Population Projections: 2005–2050.February 11. www.pewhispanic.org/ 2008/02/11/us-population-projections-2005–2050.

Paterson, Katherine. 1999. "Historical Fiction: Some Whys and Hows." *Booklist* 95 (April 1): 430.

Patrick, Diane, and Calvin Reid. 2014. "Got Diversity?" *Publishers Weekly*, December 15, 23.

Paul, Annie Murphy. 2014. "Students Reading E-Books Are Losing Out, Study Suggests." *The New York Times*, April 10. http://parenting.blogs-nytimes.com/ 2014/04/10/students-reading-e-books-are-losing-out-study-suggests.

Peck, Richard. 1993. "The Silver Anniversary of Young Adult Books." *Journal of Youth Services in Libraries* 6 (Fall): 19–23.

———. 1994. *Love and Death at the Mall*. New York: Delacorte.

Penny, Laurie. 2014. "Laurie Penny on Fiction." *New Statesman*, April 3. www .newstatesman.com/2014/03/no-wonder-teens-love-stories-about-dystopian -futures-they-feel-they-re-heading-one.

Pierce, Tamora. 1993. "Why Kids Read It, Why Kids Need It." *School Library Journal* 39 (October): 50.

Pogrebin, Robin. 1996. "Magazines Learning to Take Not-So-Clueless (and Monied) Teen-Agers More Seriously." *The New York Times*, November 4.

Pollack, Pamela D. 1981. "The Business of Popularity: The Surge of Teenage Paperbacks." *School Library Journal* 28 (November): 25.

Poniewozik, James. 1999. "Their Major Is Alienation." *Time*, September 20, 77–78.

Publishers Weekly. 2008. "NYCC: ICV2 Briefs."

———. 2013. "NEA Study Finds Reading Levels Steady, though 'Literature' Reading Dips." *Publishers Weekly*, September 26. www.publishersweekly.com/pw/by-topic/industrynews/publisher-news/article/59260-nea-study-finds-reading-levels-steady-though-literature-reading-dips.html.

Rabb, Margo. 2008. "I'm Y.A. and I'm O.K." *The New York Times Book Review*, July 20.

Raeburn, Paul W. 2004. "Too Immature for the Death Penalty?" *New York Times Magazine*, October 17.

Rafferty, Terrence. 1994. "Superhero." *New Yorker*, May 23, 93.

Ramsdell, Kirsten. 1983. "Young Adult Publishing: A Blossoming Market." *Top of the News* 39 (Winter): 177.

———. 1987. *Happily Ever After*. Littleton, CO: Libraries Unlimited.

Rapp, Adam. 2002. *Little Chicago*. Honesdale, PA. Front Street.

———. 2003. *33 Snowfish*. Somerville, MA: Candlewick.

———. 2004. *Under the Wolf, Under the Dog*. Somerville, MA: Candlewick.

———. 2009. *Punkzilla*. Somerville, MA: Candlewick.

Reading Today. 1999. "Adolescent Literacy Comes of Age." *Reading Today* 17 (August/September): 1.

———. 2007. "Adolescent Literacy: The Hottest Topic." *Reading Today* 25 (February/March): 12.

Reed, J. D. 1982. "Packaging the Facts of Life." *Time* 120 (August 23): 65.

Reid, Calvin. 2007. "Graphic Novel Hits $330 Million." *Publishers Weekly*. February 22. www.publishersweekly.com/pw/by-topic/industry-news/comics/article/24/graphic-novel-market-hits-330-million.html.

———. 2014. "Comics, Graphic Novels Market Hits $870 Million in 2013." *Publishers Weekly*, July 16. www.publishersweekly.com/pw/by-topic/industry-news/comics/article/63319-comics-graphic-novels-market-hits-870-million-in-2013.html.

Reid, Calvin, and Heidi MacDonald. 2000. "The Literature of Comics." *Publishers Weekly* 247 (October 16) 44–45.

———. 2009. "BookExpo America 2009. Despite No-Shows, Many Comics, Graphic Novels at BEA." *Publishers Weekly*, May 26. www.publishersweekly.com/pw/by-topic/new-titles/adult-announcements/article/9365-bookexpo-america-2009-despite-no-shows-many-comics-graphic-novels-at-bea-html.

Rich, Motoko. 2007. "Study Links Drop in Test Scores to a Decline in Time Spent Reading." *New York Times*, November 19. www.nytimes.com/2007/11/19/arts/19nea.html.

———. 2008. "An Author Looks Beyond Age Limits." *New York Times*, February 20. www.nytimes.com/2008/2/20/books/20patt.html.

Riley, Jenelle. 2014. "The 'Giver' Author Lois Lowry Thinks 'Dystopian Fiction' Is Passé." *Variety*. August 13. http://variety.com/lois-lowry/.

Rinaldi, Ann. 2009. "In Defense of Historical Fiction." *Publishers Weekly*, April 2. www.publishersweekly.com/pw/by-topic/neew-titles/adult-announcements/article/1813-in-defense-of-historical-fiction.html.

Roan, Shari. 1994. "Next! When Abnormal Becomes Normal." *The Los Angeles Times*, September 6.

Robehmed, Natalie. 2015. "Why Are There So Many Young Adult Writers on the Top-Earning Authors List?" *Forbes*, July 22. www.forbes.com/sites/natalierobehmed/2015/07/22/why-are-there-so-many-young-adult-writers-on-the-top-earning-authors-list/.

Rochman, Hazel. 1993. *Against Borders: Promoting Books for a Multicultural World*. Chicago: American Library Association.

———. 1998. "The Art of the Anthology." *Booklist* 94 (March 15): 1234.

Rodriguez, Roberto, and Patrisia Gonzalez. 1994. "Censorship by Omission." *The Los Angeles Times*, December 30.

Roiphe, Katie. 2009. "A Lovely Way to Burn." *The New York Times Book Review*, April 12.

Rollin, Lucy. 1999. *Twentieth-Century Teen Culture by the Decades. A Reference Guide*. Westport, CT: Greenwood Press.

Romance Writers of America. nd. www.rwa.org/p/cm/1d/fid=578.

Rosen, Judith. 1997. "Breaking the Age Barrier." *Publishers Weekly*, September 8, 28.

———. 2003. "Selling Graphic Novels to Retailers." *Publishers Weekly*, October 20, S2.

———. 2005. "Growing Up." *Publishers Weekly*, February 21, 79.

———. 2009a. "Children's Books: Channel Surfing." *Publishers Weekly*, July 20, www.publishersweekly.com/pw/by-topic/1-legacy/23-children-s-book-reviews/article/2314-children-s-books-channel-surfing-.html.

———. 2009b. "McNally Jackson Books: Turn, Turn, Turn." *Publishers Weekly*, May 12. www.publishersweekly.com/pw/by-topic/-new-titles/adult-announcements/article/10914-mcnally-jackson-books-turn-turn-turn-html.

———. 2014. "Middle Grade and YA: Where to Draw the Line?" *Publishers Weekly*, July 18. www.publishersweekly.com/pw/by-topic/childrens/childrens-industry-news/article/63358-middle-grade-and-ya-where-to-draw-the-line.html.

———. 2015. "Is Children's Nonfiction Having Its Moment?" *Publishers Weekly*, July 17. www.publishersweekly.com/pw/by-topic/childrens/childrens-industry-news/article/67549-is-nonfiction-having-its-moment.html.

Rosenwald, Michael S. 2014. "Serious Reading Takes a Hit from Online Scanning and Skimming, Researchers Say." *The Washington Post*, April 6. www.washington post.com/local/serious-reading-takes-a-hit-from-online-scanning-and-skimming -researchers-say/2014/04/06/088028d2–11e3-b899–20667de76985_story.html.

Rudman, Masha Kabakow. 2006. "Multiculturalism." In *The Oxford Encyclopedia of Children's Literature*, vol. 3, edited by Jack Zipes. New York: Oxford University Press.

Saint Louis, Catherine. 2012. "Childhood, Uncensored." *The New York Times*, December 30.

Salinger, J. D. 1951. *The Catcher in the Rye*. Boston: Little, Brown.

Saricks, Joyce. 2008. "Revisiting Historical Fiction." *Booklist* 104 (April 15): 33.

Saulny, Susan. 2011. "Black? White? Asian? More Young Americans Choose All of the Above." *The New York Times*, January 29. www.nytimes.com/2011/01/30/ us/30mixeed.html?pagewanted.

Savacool, Julia. 2014. "Think You're Immune to Video-Game Violence? Think Again." *USA Today*. March 30. www.usatoday.com/story/tech/gaming/ 2014/03/30/video-games-violence/6437253/.

Schaffer, Amanda. 2015. "Review of *The Teenage Brain*" by Frances E. Jensen with Amy Ellis Nutt. *The New York Times Book Review*, April 15, 28.

Schiffrin, Andre. 1995. "Between Us." *American Bookseller*, April, 17.

Schmidt, Gregory. 2015. "Pow! Gay Comic Book Characters Zap Stereotypes." *The New York Times*. July 5, B6.

Scholastic News Room. *The Hunger Games*. nd. http://mediaroom.scholastic.com/ hunger games.

Schuker, Lauren A. E. 2009. "Harry Potter and the Rival Teen Franchise." *Wall Street Journal*, July 9. http://online.wsj.com/article/SB10001424052970204261704574276261288253316.html.

Schwartz, John. 2013. "Words That Hurt and Kill: Lessons for Society from Bullying and Its Psychic Toll." *New York Times*, March 10.

Scott, A. O. 2014. "Young Love, Complicated by Cancer." *The New York Times*, June 5. www.nytimes.com/2014/06/06/movies/the-fault-in-our-stars-sets-out-to -make-you-cry.html.

———. 2015. "At Comic-Con, It Feels Like the Year of the Woman," *The New York Times*, July 11, C1.

Seldes, Gilbert. 1924. *The Seven Lively Arts*. New York: Harper and Brothers.

Sellers, John A. 2008a. "Q & A with M. T. Anderson." *Publishers Weekly*. www .publishersweekly.com/pw/by-topic/authors/interviews/article/9085-q-a -with-m-t-anderson.html.

———. 2008b. "Scholastic Report." *Publishers Weekly*. www.publishersweekly.com/ pw/by-topic/childrens/childrens-book-news/article/3251-scholastic-report -kids-still-read-for-fun-teens-less-so.html.

Shaffer, Kenneth R. 1963. "What Makes Sammy Read?" *Top of the News* 19 (March): 9.

Shellenbarger, Sue. 2013. "Teens Are Still Developing Empathy Skills." *Wall Street Journal,* October 15. www.wasj.com/articles/SB100014240527023045610045791375 14122387446.

Silvey, Anita. 2006. "The Unreal Deal." *School Library Journal* 52 (October): 45.

Slater, Janie. 2011. "Why Teens Love and Need Dystopian Literature." *The Examiner,* August 1. www.examiner.com/young-adult-literature-in-atlanta/janie-slater.

Smith, Henrietta. 1995. "African American Children's Literature." In *Children's Books and Their Creators,* edited by Anita Silvey, 4–7. Boston: Houghton Mifflin.

Smith, Karen Patricia. 1993. "The Multicultural Ethic and Connection to Literature for Children and Young Adults." *Library Trends* 41 (Winter): 341.

Smith, Lynn. 1997. "What Americans Say about Their Children." *The Los Angeles Times,* June 26, E3.

Spitz, David. 1999. "Reads Like Teen Spirit." *Time,* July 19.

Springen, Karen. 2009. "Justine Larbalestier's Cover Girl." *Publishers Weekly,* July 29. www.publishersweekly.com/pw.by-topic/childrens/childrens-book-news/article/16014-justine-larbalestier-s-cover-girl.html.

———. 2010. "Apocalypse Now." *Publishers Weekly,* February 15, 21–22.

Stampler, Laura. 2014. "Adult Book Sales Are Down and Young Adult Soars in 2014." *Time.* December 16. http://time.com/3636601/young-adult-book-sales-2014/.

Stavn, Diane Gersoni. 1969. "Watching Fiction for Today's Teens. Notes of a Critical Voyeur." *School Library Journal* 16 (November): 139.

Steinberg, Lawrence. 2014. "Friends Can Be Dangerous." *The New York Times,* April 27, SR 12.

Stevens, Dana. 2014. "Why Teens Love Dystopia." *Slate,* March 21. www.slate.com/articles/arts/movies/2014/03/divergent_starring_shailene_woodley_and_the_hunger_games_why_teens_love.html.

Stevenson, Nanette. 1997. "Hipper, Brighter, and Bolder." *Publishers Weekly,* February 17, 139.

Strickland, Ashley. 2013a. "'Fear Street': R. L. Stein and the Return of Teen Horror." CNN, November 25. www.cnn.com/2013/11/25/living/young-adult-fear-street-books/index.html.

———. 2013b. "Young Adult Books from Page to Screen." CNN, October 22. www.cnn.com/2013/10/22/living/young-adult-book-movie-adaptations/index.html.

———. 2014. "Where Is the Diversity in Young Adult Fiction?" CNN, April 9. www.cnn.com/2014/04/09/living/young-adult-books-diversity-identity/index.html.

Sturgeon, Jonathan. 2014. "Are You an Adult Who Reads YA Novels? Congratulations! You Saved Publishing in 2014." *Flavorwire,* December 16. http://flavorwire.com/494377/are-you-an-adult-who-reads-ya-novels-congratulations-you-saved-publishing-in-2014.

Sutton, Roger. 1982. "The Critical Myth: Realistic YA Novels." *School Library Journal* 29 (November): 33.

Szalavitz, Maria. 2012. "Why the Teen Brain Is Drawn to Risk." *Time*, October 8. http://healthand.time.com/2012/10/02/why-the-teen-brain-is-drawn-to-risk.

Talbot, Margaret. 2014. "The Teen Whisperer." *New Yorker*, June 9–16, 60–68.

Tarkington, Booth. 1916 *Seventeen*. New York: Harper.

Teen Violence Statistics. nd. "Cyberbullying Statistics." www.teenviolencestatistics .com/content/cyberbullying.html.

———. nd. "Date Rape." www.teenviolencestatistics.com/content/date-rape.html.

Thompson, Bob. 2007. "A Troubling Case of Reader's Block." *The Washington Post*, November 19. www.washingtonpost.com/wp dyn/content/article/2007/11/19/ AR20071119415.html.

———. 2009. "Unexpected Twist." *The Washington Post*, January 12. www.washington post.com/wp-dyn/content/article/2009/01/11/AR2009011102337.html.

Thompson, Jason. 2007. *Manga: A Complete Guide*. New York: Del Rey.

Time. 1993. "The Numbers Game—Fall Special Issue," 14.

Toffler, Alvin. 1970. *Future Shock*. New York: Random House.

Townsend, John Rowe. 1980. "Standards of Criticism for Children's Literature." In *The Arbuthnot Lectures, 1970–1979*, compiled by Zena Sutherland. Chicago: American Library Association.

Tucker, Ken. 1993. "Nameless Fear Stalks the Middle-Class Teen-Ager." *The New York Times Book Review*, November 14.

Tunis, John R. 1977. "What Is a Juvenile Book?" In *Crosscurrents of Criticism*, edited by Paul Heins, 22–26. Boston: Horn Book.

Unger, Brian. 2006. "The Age of Irony Is Alive and Well." *Unger Report*, September 11. www.npr/templates/archives.php?thingID=4465030&date=05–10–2010&p=106.

University College London. 2008. "Information Behavior of the Researcher of the Future." January 11, www.bl.uk/news/pdf/googlegen.pdf.

United States Census Bureau. 2010. United States Census. 2010. www.census.gov/ 2010census.

Valby, Karen, 2008. "Stephenie Meyer: Inside the 'Twilight' Saga." *Entertainment Weekly*, July 31. www.ew.com/article/2008/07/31/stephenie-meyers-vampire -empire.

Van Gelder, Robert. 1942. "An Interview with Miss Maureen Daly." *The New York Times*, July 12.

Waddle, Linda. 1991. "Just Say Know." *Journal of Youth Services in Libraries* 4 (Summer): 361.

Waters, Henry F. 1994. "Teenage Suicide: One Act Not to Follow." *Newsweek* 123 (April): 49.

We Need Diverse Books. 2015. "Mission Statement." http://weneeddiversebooks .org.

Wertham, Frederick. 1954. *The Seduction of the Innocent.* New York: Rinehart.

Wholf, Tracy. 2014. "Why Adults Are Buzzing about YA Literature." *PBS Newshour,* October 4. www.pbs.org/newshour/bb/ya-literature-buzzing-just-young -adults.

Winerip, Michael. 2008. "In Novels for Girls, Fashion Trumps Romance." *The New York Times,* July 13.

Wojciechowska, Maia. 1968. "An End to Nostalgia." *School Library Journal* 15 (December): 13.

Wolf, Naomi. 2006. "Young Adult Fiction: Wild Things." *The New York Times,* March 12. www.nytimes.com/2006/03/12/books/review/12wolf.html.

Wolitzer, Meg. 2014. "Look Homeward, Reader." *The New York Times,* October 17. www.nytimes.com/2014/10/19/fashion/a-not-so-young-audience-for-young -adult-books_html?_r=0.

Woods, George. 1966. "Screening Books for Review." *Wilson Library Bulletin* 41 (October): 169.

Woodson, Jacqueline. 2006. Margaret A. Edwards Award Acceptance Speech. In *The Official YALSA Awards Guidebook,* edited by Tina Frolund. New York: Neal-Schuman.

Wren, Christopher. 1997. "Drugs Common in Schools, Survey Shows." *The New York Times,* September 19, A12.

Yao, Lauren. 2008. "Bitten and Smitten: Readers Crave Stephenie Meyer's 'Twilight' Tales of Vampire Love." *The Washington Post,* August 1. www.washingtonpost .com/wp-dyn/content/article/2008/08/01/AR2008080100064.html.

Yardley, Jonathan. 1994. "The Moral of the Story." *The Washington Post Book World,* April 17, 3.

Yep, Laurence, ed. 1993. *American Dragons.* New York: Harper.

Yolen, Jane. 1994. "An Empress of Thieves." *Horn Book* 70 (December): 705.

Young, Moira. 2011. "Why Is Dystopia So Appealing to Teens?" *The Guardian,* October 22. www.theguardian.com/books/2011/oct23/dystopian-fiction.

Youth.gov. nd. "Youth Suicide Prevention." http://youth.gov/youth-topics/ youth-suicide-prevention.

Zindel, Paul. 1968. *The Pigman.* New York: Harper.

Zuckhur, Kathryn, and Lee Rainie. 2014. "Younger Americans' Reading Habits and Technology Use." Pew Research, September 10. www.pewinternet.org/ 2014/09/10/younger-americans-reading-habits-and-technology-use.

Zweig, Jamie, and Meredith Dank. 2013. "Teen Dating Abuse and Harassment in the Digital World." *Urban Institute.* www.urban.org/research/publication/ teen-dating-abuse-and-harassment-digital-world.

Appendix

IN 2007 I WAS ASKED BY YALSA TO WRITE A WHITE PAPER ON THE VALUE OF young adult literature. The following document was subsequently adopted by the YALSA Board of Directors in January 2008.

YALSA WHITE PAPER

The Value of Young Adult Literature

Abstract: This White Paper will discuss the nature and evolution of young adult literature with particular emphasis on its current condition and its value to its intended readership. In discussing its increased viability as a body of critically lauded literature, it will also discuss its importance in meeting the life needs of young adults and its increasing value in enhancing adolescent literacy. It will conclude by affirming the Young Adult Library Services Association's commitment to evaluating, promoting, and supporting the most widespread availability possible of this literature to American youth.

Background: The term *young adult literature* is inherently amorphous, for its constituent terms "young adult" and "literature" are dynamic, changing as culture and society—which provide their context—change. When the term first found common usage in the late 1960s, it referred to realistic fiction that was set in the real (as opposed to imagined), contemporary world and addressed problems, issues, and life circumstances of interest to young readers aged approximately 12–18. Such titles were issued by the children's book divisions of American publishers and were marketed to institutions—libraries and schools—that served such populations.

While some of this remains true today, much else has changed. In recent years, for example, the size of this population group has changed dramatically. Between 1990 and 2000 the number of persons between 12 and 19 soared to 32 million, a growth rate of 17 percent that significantly outpaced the growth of the rest of the population. The size of this population segment has also increased as the conventional definition of "young adult" has expanded to include those as young as ten and, since the late 1990s, as old as twenty-five.

"Literature," which traditionally meant fiction, has also expanded to include new forms of literary—or narrative—nonfiction and new forms of poetry, including novels and book-length works of nonfiction in verse. The increasing importance of visual communication has begun to expand this definition to include the pictorial, as well, especially when offered in combination with text as in the case of picture books, comics, and graphic novels and nonfiction.

As a result of these newly expansive terms, the numbers of books being published for this audience have similarly increased, perhaps by as much as 25 percent, based on the number of titles being reviewed by a leading journal. Similarly, industry analyst Albert Greco states that the sales of young adult books increased by 23 percent from 1999 to 2005.

Though once dismissed as a genre consisting of little more than problem novels and romances, young adult literature has, since the mid-1990s, come of age as literature—literature that welcomes artistic innovation, experimentation, and risk-taking.

Evidence of this is the establishment of the Michael L. Printz Award, which YALSA presents annually to the author of the best young adult book of the year, "best" being defined solely in terms of literary merit. Further evidence is the extraordinary number of critically acclaimed adult authors who have begun writing for young adults—authors like Michael Chabon, Isabel Allende, Dale Peck, Julia Alvarez, T. C. Boyle, Joyce Carol Oates, Francine Prose, and a host of others. As a result of these and other innovations young adult literature has become one of the most dynamic, creatively exciting areas of publishing.

Position: YALSA is acknowledging this growing diversity by expanding the number of book-related awards and lists it presents and publishes. Audio books and graphic novels are only two of the new areas that YALSA is targeting. Meanwhile it continues to promote excellence in the field through such established prizes as the Printz, ALEX, and Margaret A. Edwards Awards and such recommended lists as Best Books for Young Adults and Quick Picks for Reluctant Young Adult Readers.

YALSA also acknowledges that whether one defines young adult literature narrowly or broadly, much of its value cannot be quantified but is to be found in how it addresses the needs of its readers. Often described as "developmental," these needs recognize that young adults are beings in evolution, in search of self and identity; beings who are constantly growing and changing, morphing from the condition of childhood to that of adulthood. That period of passage called "young adulthood" is a unique part of life, distinguished by unique needs that are—at minimum—physical, intellectual, emotional, and societal in nature.

By addressing these needs, young adult literature is made valuable not only by its artistry but also by its relevance to the lives of its readers. And by addressing not only their needs but also their interests, the literature becomes a powerful inducement for them to read, another compelling reason to value it, especially at a time when adolescent literacy has become a critically important issue. The Alliance for Excellent Education has declared a "literacy crisis among middle and high school students" in the wake of research from the National Assessment of Educational Progress that finds 65 percent of graduating high school seniors and 71 percent of America's eighth graders are reading below grade level.

As literacy has become another developmental need of young adults, organizations like the International Reading Association and the National Council of Teachers of English have begun to recognize the imperative need for "a wide variety of reading material that they (young adults) can and want to read" (IRA), books that "should be self-selected and of high interest to the reader" (NCTE), young adult books, in short.

As a literature of relevance that meets developmental needs—including literacy skills—young adult literature also becomes a developmental *asset,* which YALSA's *New Directions for Library Service to Young Adults* defines as "a factor promoting positive teenage development." The independent, non-profit Search Institute offers a framework of forty such developmental assets.

YALSA finds another of the chief values of young adult literature in its capacity to offer readers an opportunity to see themselves reflected in its pages. Young adulthood is, intrinsically, a period of tension. On the one hand young adults have an all-consuming need to belong. But on the other, they are also inherently solipsistic, regarding themselves as being unique, which—for them—is not cause for celebration but, rather, for despair. For to be unique is to be unlike one's peers, to be "other," in fact. And to be "other" is to not belong but, instead, to be outcast. Thus, to see oneself in the pages of a young adult book is to receive the reassurance that one is not alone after all, not other, not alien but, instead, a viable part of a larger community of beings who share a common humanity.

Another value of young adult literature is its capacity for fostering understanding, empathy, and compassion by offering vividly realized portraits of the lives—exterior and interior—of individuals who are *unlike* the reader. In this way young adult literature invites its readership to embrace the humanity it shares with those who—if not for the encounter in reading—might forever remain strangers or—worse—irredeemably "other."

Still another value of young adult literature is its capacity for telling its readers the truth, however disagreeable that may sometimes be, for in this way it equips readers for dealing with the realities of impending adulthood and for assuming the rights and responsibilities of citizenship.

By giving readers such a frame of reference, it also helps them to find role models, to make sense of the world they inhabit, to develop a personal philosophy of being, to determine what is right and, equally, what is wrong, to cultivate a personal sensibility. To, in other words, become civilized.

Conclusion: For all of these reasons the Young Adult Library Services Association values young adult literature, believes it is an indispensable part of public and school library collections, and regards it as essential to healthy youth development and the corollary development of healthy communities in which both youth and libraries can thrive.

References

Alliance for Excellent Education. Press Center. www.all4ed.org/press/pr_062907 .html and www.all4ed.org/press/pr_022207.html. Both accessed 9/28/07.

Cart, Michael. "Teens and the Future of Reading." *American Libraries*. October 2007.

———. "Young Adult Literature: The State of a Restless Art." In *Passions and Pleasures* by Michael Cart. Lanham, MD: The Scarecrow Press. 2007.

International Reading Association. "Adolescent Literacy." www.reading.org/resources/issues/positions_adolescent.html. Accessed 9/28/07.

Magazine Publishers of America. *Teen Market Profile.* www.magazine.org/content/files/teenprofile04.pdf. Accessed 9/28/07.

NCTE. "A Call to Action." www.ncte.org. Accessed 9/28/07.

New Directions for Library Service to Young Adults. YALSA with Patrick Jones. Edited by Linda Waddle. Chicago: ALA. 2002.

Search Institute. www.search-institute.org.

Michael Cart is a nationally known expert in young adult literature, which he taught at UCLA before his relocation to the Midwest. A columnist and reviewer for ALA's *Booklist* magazine, he is also the author or editor of twenty-three books and countless articles that have appeared in *The New York Times, The Los Angeles Times, The San Francisco Chronicle, Parents Magazine, American Libraries, School Library Journal*, and elsewhere. The former president of both YALSA and ALAN, he is the recipient of the 2000 Grolier Award and the first recipient—in 2008—of the YALSA/Greenwood Publishing Group Service to Young Adults Award. He appointed and chaired the Task Force that created the Michael L. Printz Award and subsequently chaired the 2006 Printz Committee. He lives, surrounded by books, in Columbus, Indiana.

Index

A

A List series (Von Ziegesar), 113, 114
Abby, My Love (Irwin), 179
abortion, 36, 178
Abrahams, Peter, 106
Abrahamson, Richard F.
    "Back to the Future with Adult Books
        for the Teenage Reader," 141–142
    Nonfiction for Young Adults, 225
    as speaker at nonfiction preconference,
        225–226
Abramson, Jane, 36–37
*The Absolutely True Diary of a Part-Time
    Indian* (Alexie), 197–198
Academy of American Poets, 92
The Accidental Highwayman (Tripp), 247
Action Comics #1 (Siegel & Shuster), 204
Adelson, Stewart, 194
adolescence
    poetry and, 92
    stages of, 7, 25–26
    Stanley G. Hall's theories on, 4–5
    young adult, meaning of, 139–141
*Adolescence: Its Psychology and Its
    Relations to Physiology, Anthropology,
    Sociology, Sex, Crime, Religion and
    Education* (Hall), 4
adolescents
    See teenagers
Adult Books for Young People (ALA), 9
adults
    adult authors writing for YAs, 137–138

Alex Awards, 141–142
    as buyers of YA books, ix–x, 146–150
African Americans
    diversity in YA literature and,
        153–154
    emergence of authors/artists, 48–49
    population growth in U.S., 151, 152
    reading abilities of YAs, 237
"Against YA" (Graham), 147–148
age, 139–141
The Age of Bronze (Shanower), 208
AIDS, 188–189, 190
Akbar, Said Hyder, 157
ALA
    See American Library Association
ALAN (Assembly on Literature for
    Adolescents), 64, 75
Alcott, Louisa May, 8
Alderdice, Kit, 114–115, 134
Aldrich, Henry, 6
Alex as Well (Brugman), 192
Alex Awards, 141–142
Alexander, William, 126
Alexie, Sherman
    *The Absolutely True Diary of a Part-
        Time Indian*, 197–198
    on small presses, 155
    "Why the Best Kids Books Are Written in
        Blood," 201
Alger, Horatio, Jr., 8
Algonquin Books for Young Readers,
    144–145

Alia's Mission: Saving the Books of Iraq (Stamaty), 157
Alice in Wonderland (Carroll), 98
Alice series (Naylor), 198
All the Bright Places (Niven), 171
All the Broken Pieces (Burg), 94
All the Rage (Summers), 170, 185
Allen, Arthur, 164
Allen, Rachel J., 215
Alliance for Excellent Education, 236
Alloy Entertainment, 114
Alloy Marketing and Media, 214
"The All-White World of Children's Books" (Larrick), 48
Alm, Richard S., 24, 26
Almond, David, 82, 99
Altebrando, Tara, 145
Alter, Alexandra
  on audiobooks, 243
  on reading, 244
  on YA editions of adult nonfiction titles, 230
Alverson, Brigid
  on censorship of graphic novel, 209
  on graphic novels, golden age of, 219
  on sales of graphic novels, 218
Am I Blue? (Bauer), 191
The Amber Spyglass (Pullman), 99–100
ambiguity, 82, 240
The Amboy Dukes (Shulman), 19
Amelia Elizabeth Walden Award, 75
American Bookseller magazine, 67
American Born Chinese (Yang)
  Michael L. Printz Award for, 85, 157
  recognition of, 210
American Dragons (Yep), 49
American Graffiti (movie), 42
American Indian Library Association, 157
American Indian Youth Literature Award, 157
American Library Association (ALA)
  Best Books for Young Adults for 1986, 131
  challenged books and, 197, 198
  Coretta Scott King Awards, establishment of, 49
  "On the Edge: Personal Perspectives on Writing for Today's Young Adults" discussion, 72
  Meghan Cox Gurdon on, 201
  Michael L. Printz Award, first, 81
  Mildred Batchelder Award, 158–159
  Washington Office Newsline, on school enrollment, 69

YALSA program at conference of, 65–67
Young Adult Services Division, formation of, 7
Young People's Reading Roundtable, 9
American Sports Poems (Knudson & Swenson), 91
Americas award
  creation of, 50
  importance of, 156
Americus (Reed), 198
An Abundance of Katherines (Green), 126
An Na, 157
Anastas, Mara, 143, 145
Anaya, Rudolfo, 52
Anderson, Laurie Halse
  Speak, 82, 184
  Twisted, 171, 172
Anderson, M. T.
  The Astonishing Life of Octavian Nothing, 102
  Octavian Nothing: Traitor to the Nation, 86
  Thirsty, 104
Andrews, V. C., 180
Anelli, Melissa, 117
Angus, Thongs and Full-Frontal Snogging (Rennison), 107
Annie on My Mind (Garden), 188, 191
Another Jekyll, Another Hyde (Nayeri), 106
Aoki, Deb, 212, 219
APALA award, 157
Appelt, Kathi, 90
Apt, Vicki, 56
Archie Comics, 193
Are You in the House Alone? (Peck), 60, 179
Are You My Mother? (Bechdel), 214
Are You There God? It's Me Margaret (Blume), 34
Aristotle and Dante Discover the Secrets of the Universe (Saenz), 193
The Arizona Kid (Koertge), 94, 189
The Ark (Benary-Isbet), 20
Arnold, Andrew D., 207
Aronson, Marc
  on crossover titles, 65
  Michael L. Printz Award, creation of, 76
  on narrative in nonfiction, 227
  on NEA reading study, 234–235
  nonfiction of, 226
  on nonfiction today, 230–231
  One Death, Nine Stories, 90
  Robert F. Sibert Medal for, 228

"The Young Adult Novel Is Dead and Other Fairly Stupid Tales," 64
on young adult publishing, 59
Arte Publico (publisher), 155
Asher, Jay, 171
Asian Americans
    diversity in YA literature and, 153–154
    population growth in U.S., 151, 152
    use of term, 49
Assembly on Literature for Adolescents (ALAN), 64, 75
Associated Press, 237
Association of American Publishers, 110
Association of Library Service for Children
    on audiobooks, 246
    Odyssey Award, 244, 245
    Robert F. Sibert Medal, 228
The Astonishing Life of Octavian Nothing (Anderson), 102
"At Comic-Con, It Feels Like the Year of the Woman" (Scott), 214–215
Athletic Shorts (Crutcher)
    book challenges, 198
    gay themes in, 191
    publication of, 89
Atkins, Catherine, 182
Atlantic Monthly magazine, 240
Atwater, Montgomery, 10
Atwater-Rhodes, Amelia, 104
Audible, 244
Audio Publishers Association
    on audiobooks, 243
    on educational benefits of audiobooks, 245
    founding of, 242
audiobooks
    educational benefits of, 245–246
    history of, 242–243
    listening as literary experience, 243–245
AudioFile, 244
Auster, Paul, 206
Australia, crossover books in, 135–136
Avery, Gillian, 223
Avon, Neon Lit, 206–207
awards
    Alex Awards, 141–142
    Eisner Awards, 217
    for graphic novels, 220
    for Jacqueline Woodson, 173
    for LGBT literature, 191
    Michael L. Printz Award, 75–77
    Michael L. Printz Award winners, 2000, 81–83
    for multicultural literature, 156–157
    Newbery Medal, 74, 228
    for nonfiction, 228
    Odyssey Award, 244, 245
    for YA literature, new awards, 74–75

B

Baby Bebop (Block), 190
Babysitter's Club series (Martin), 217
Bacigalupi, Paolo, 98
"Back to the Future with Adult Books for the Teenage Reader" (Abrahamson), 141–142
Backlash (Littman), 171, 172
Bacon, Perry, 109
Bad Apple (Ruby), 172
Badavi, Mary Ann, 128
Bait (Sanchez), 183
Baldwin, Neal, 44, 45–46
Banks, Lynn Reid, 53
Banned Books Week, 198
Bantam (publisher), 43
Bantam Doubleday Dell (publisher), 56
Barakiva, Michael, 194
Bargar, Gary W., 188
Barker, Clive, 104
Barnes, Brook, 122
Barnes and Noble
    middle-school literature and, 58
    number of stores, 68
    paranormal romance section, 121
    in publishing/marketing to teens, 108–109
    YA areas in, 65–66
Baron, Naomi S., 240
Barr, Donald, 50
Barson, Michael, 19, 42
Baseball in April (Soto), 89
Bass, Dina, 73
Bauer, Joan, 68
Bauer, Marion Dane, 191
Bauerlein, Mark, 239
Baum, L. Frank, 106
Bazelon, Emily, 169
BEA (Book Expo America), 217
Beagle, Peter, 218
Beautiful Creatures (Garcia & Stohl), 218
Beautiful Music for Ugly Children (Cronn-Mills), 192
Beauty Queens (Bray), 145
Bechdel, Alison
    as distinguished writer/artist, 215
    Fun Home, 193

Bechdel, Alison (cont'd)
    graphic novels of, 214
Becoming a Nation of Readers (Commission on Reading), 245
Bee and Jackie (Coman), 180
Behemoth (Westerfeld), 247
Bellafante, Gina, 112, 113
Benary-Isbert, Margot, 20
Bender, Lionel, 229–230
Benson and Benson (research company), 13
Benton, Lori, 63
Benwell, Sarah, 171
Berck, Judith, 61
Berger, Ellie, 129
Berger, Laura Standley, 11–12, 129
Berkeley Public Library, California, 206
Bernstein, Elizabeth, 68, 71
The Best American Nonrequired Reading YA series (Houghton Mifflin), 108–109
Best Books for Young Adults (Carter), 229
Best Books for Young Adults List (BBYA) (YALSA)
    books selected to be on, 74
    fantasy titles on, 98
    inclusion of YA titles, 34
    nonfiction on, 228–229
    Printz winners and, 87
Best Fiction for Young Adults (BFYA) (YALSA), 87, 154
Best of the Best Books lists (YALSA), 91
Bestest Ramadan Ever (Sharif), 158
Beverly Hills 90210 (television show), 69
"Beware of Donors Bearing Book Prizes?" (Mattson), 75
Beyond Magenta (Kuklin), 192
Beyond the Chocolate War (Cormier), 45
Bickers, James, 223
Bill Haley and His Comets, 19
Billman, Carol, 8
Black and White (Macaulay), 132–133
Black Juice (Lanagan), 87, 90
Blackboard Jungle (movie), 19
Blake, William, 82
bleak books, 71–74
Bless Me, Ultima (Anaya), 52
Blind Date (Stine), 45
Block, Francesca Lia
    debut of, 45
    The Hanged Man, 180
    marketing of Weetzie Bat books, 133
    transgender character in "Dragons in Manhattan," 192
    Weetzie Bat, 81, 189, 190

    Weetzie Bat books as New Adult, 145
    "X-Over" name of, 66
Blood and Chocolate (Klause), 74, 121
Bloomsbury (publisher)
    Harry Potter series, phenomenon of, 117
    Harry Potter series (Rowling), 116
    Liar (Larbalestier), 154–155
The Blue Lawn (Taylor), 190
Blume, Judy
    Are You There God? It's Me Margaret, 34
    Forever, 178–179
    Places I Never Meant to Be, 198
Bobby Rex's Greatest Hit (Gingher), 131, 134
The Body of Christopher Creed (Plum-Ucci), 105
Bolle, Sonya, 120
Bomb (Sheinkin), 228
Bonham, Frank, 28
Bonnie Jo, Go Home (Eyerly), 36, 178
Boock, Paula, 190
book challenges/censorship
    The Absolutely True Diary of a Part-Time Indian (Alexie), 197–198
    censorship in libraries, 198–199
    content warning for books, 202
    graphic novels, 209
    media articles attacking YA literature, 199–201
    number of challenges, 197
    YA literature on, 198
Book Expo America (BEA), 217
Book Guild of Washington, 228
book packagers, 114
The Book Thief (Zusak), 86, 102
Booklist magazine
    Alex Awards, 142
    article on New Adult in, 143
    bleak books and, 72
    "Carte Blanche" column, 64
    graphic novels issue of, 217
    Michael L. Printz Award and, 76
    Odyssey Award, 244
    review of novels in verse, 93
books
    audiobooks, 242–246
    e-books, 143, 144
    print books, 239–242, 246–248
    See also crossover books
Books and the Teen-Age Reader (Carlsen), 25
Boone, Josh, 127
Booth, Heather, 182
Boston Globe-Horn Book Awards, 228

Bott, C. J., 171, 172
Bowen, Brenda, 110
Boy Meets Boy (Levithan), 192
The Boy Who Couldn't Die (Sleator), 104–105
Boyfriends with Girlfriends (Sanchez), 193
Boyle, Danny, 71
Boylston, Helen, 9–10
The Boys Who Challenged Hitler (Hoose), 228
Bradburn, Frances, 76
The Braid (Frost), 94
brain
    of adolescents, 163–164
    empathy and, 172–173
    reading online and, 241
Brando, Marlon, 19
Brashares, Anne, 115
Braun, Linda, 235
Brave New World (Huxley), 123
Bray, Libba
    Beauty Queens, 145
    The Diviners/Lair of Dreams, 102
    Gemma Doyle trilogy, 115
Breaking Dawn (Meyer), 119–120, 146
Breaking Up (Friedman & Norrie), 210
Breaking Up (Klein), 188
Breathing Underwater (Flinn), 185
Brian, Kate, 115
Bridgers, Sue Ellen, 45
A Brief Moment in the Life of Angus Bethune (Crutcher), 191
Bright Lights, Dark Nights (Emond), 247
Brill, Ian, 215
The Brimstone Journals (Koertge), 94
"Bring Back the Out-Loud Culture" (Hall), 245–246
Brody, Jessica, 115
Bronx Masquerade (Grimes), 94
Brooks, Bruce, 45, 90
Brooks, Kevin, 105
Brown Girl Dreaming (Woodson)
    National Book Award for, 157
    sense of family in, 174
    versatility of verse novels, 95
Brownstein, Charles, 209
Brugman, Alyssa, 192
Bryan, Ashley, 48
Buell, Marjorie Henderson, 211
The Buffalo Tree (Rapp), 71
Bullard, Sarah, 47
The Bully in the Book and in the Classroom (Bott), 171

bullying
    cyberbullying, 171–172
    empathy and, 172–173
    YA literature on, 169–171
The Bumblebee Flies Anyway (Cormier), 45
Bunn, Scott
    Just Hold On, as problem novel, 37
    Just Hold On, on incest, 179
    Just Hold On, synopsis of, 38
Burg, Ann, 94
Burkey, Mary, 245
Burnett, Matia, 236, 241
Burns, Peggy, 214
Burton, Dwight L., 24
Bushman, Brad, 165
Bushnell, Candace, 115
Butler, Samuel, 123
Byrd, John, 155

C
Cabot, Meg, 115
Caedmon Records, 242
"A Call to Action" (NCTE), 237
Calling All Girls magazine, 14
Calvino, Italo, 62
Cameron, Daryl, 173
Campbell, Patty
    on age of YA, 65
    on bookstores in 1990s, 68
    "The Sand in the Oyster," 64
Canton, Jeffrey, 135
Card, Orson Scott
    audiobook of *Ender's Game*, 243
    graphic novel versions of books by, 218
    science fiction of, 97–98
Carey, Benedict, 166
Carlsen, G. Robert
    on developmental tasks, 26
    on reading development stages, 25
    on stories of foreign culture, 20
Carlson, Lori, 91, 92
The Carlyles series (Von Ziegesar), 113
Carpenter, Dave, 109
Carr, Nicholas
    on online reading, 240, 241
    on reading as secondary activity, 243–244
Cart, Michael
    on Adult Books for Young People list, 9
    on adults reading YA, 148–150
    awards, creation of, 74–75
    censorship experience of, 198–199
    on chain bookstores, 58
    on Eyewitness Books, 225

Cart, Michael (cont'd)
  on Goosebumps series, 45
  Harry Potter series and, 117–118
  The Heart Has Its Reasons, 187
  "How Adult Is Young Adult?" program,
    65–67
  on Jacqueline Woodson, 174
  Love and Sex: Ten Stories of Truth, 185
  Michael L. Printz Award, creation of,
    75–77
  on Michael L. Printz Award winners, 83
  on NEA reading study, 234–235
  on New Adult, 143
  on packagers, 57
  quote of M. E. Kerr, 188
  quote of Robert Cormier, 34
  review of *The Fault in Our Stars*, 126–127
  "Of Risk and Revelation," 61–62
  on *Sue Barton*, 10
  on theme in poetry, 91
  work with Houghton Mifflin, 108–109
  on YA publishing, 60
"Carte Blanche" column (Cart)
  on adults reading YA, 148–150
  debut of, 64
  on Michael L. Printz Award winners, 83
  on YA category, 140
Carter, Betty
  on age of young adults, 8
  on Alex winners, 141
  on *Bobby Rex's Greatest Hit*, 134
  on crossover book, 131
  Nonfiction for Young Adults, 225
  on nonfiction on BBYA, 229
  as speaker at nonfiction preconference,
    225–226
Carter, Lynda, 211
Carvajal, Doreen, 108
Cary, Steven, 209
The Case of the Missing Mother (Hamilton),
  190
Castellucci, Cecil, 214
The Castle of Otranto (Walpole), 103
The Catcher in the Rye (Salinger), 30
Cavanna, Betty, 14–15, 42
CCBC
  See Cooperative Children's Book Center
CDC
  See Centers for Disease Control and
    Prevention
The Celebutantes series (Pagliarulo), 113
censorship
  of comic books, 205

of graphic novels, 209
  See also book challenges/censorship
Centers for Disease Control and Prevention
  (CDC)
  on dating violence, 183–184
  on rape, 183
  on sexual activity of teenagers, 179
  on youth violence, 164–165
chain bookstores
  evolution of, 44–45
  in late 1990s, 68
  middle-school literature and, 58–59
Chambers, Aidan
  Dance on My Grave, 188
  Postcards from No Man's Land, 85–86,
    102, 191
  This Is All, 145, 148
Chanda's Secrets (Stratton), 189
Chaney, Lon, Jr., 103–104
Chang, Andrea, 239
Chaos Walking trilogy (Ness), 123
character, 85
Charbonneau, Joelle, 170
Charbonnet, Gabrielle, 138
Charles, Ron, 95
Charles and Emma (Heiligman), 228, 229
Chbosky, Stephen, 111, 181
Cherry Ames, Student Nurse (Wells), 10
chick lit
  emergence of, 107–108
  mean girl books, 112–115
  popularity of contemporary romance,
    115
Chiggers (Larsen), 210
Childhood and Society (Erikson), 7
children's literature
  children's picture book, debut of, 204
  Harry Potter series, phenomenon of,
    115–119
  marketing/chain bookstores, 108
  picture book crossovers, 132–133
  reading/sales trends, 236
  YA crossover titles, 65–66
Children's Literature Association, 64
Children's Literature Association Quarterly,
  66
Childress, Alice
  emergence of, 48
  A Hero Ain't Nothin' But a Sandwich, 32,
    34, 60
Chinese Americans, 49
The Chocolate War (Cormier)
  book challenges, 198

description of, 33–34
determinism in, 37
CIB Council on Interracial Books for Children (CIBC), 155
Cimarron (Ferber), 9
Cinco Puntos Press, 155
City of Glass (Auster), 206
Clamp, 213
Clare, Cassandra, 125–126
Clark, Anne Nolan, 20
Clark, Kristin Elizabeth, 94, 192
Clark, Larry, 71
Claudette Colvin (Hoose), 228
Clayton, Colleen, 185
Clique series (Harrison), 114
Clowes, Daniel
    David Boring, 207
    Ghost World, 206
Clueless (movie), 69
Cobb, Michele, 243
Coben, Harlan, 106
Cohen, Josh C., 172
Cohn, D'Vera, 152
Cold New World (Finnegan), 70
Cole, Brock
    debut of, 45
    The Facts Speak for Themselves, 71, 74
    speaker at 1998 ALA conference, 72
Collins, Max Allan, 206
Collins, Suzanne
    adult purchases of YA books, 146, 147
    book sales of, x
    The Hunger Games trilogy, 121–122
    Panem, 123
    science fiction comeback, 98
Columbia University, 217
Coman, Carolyn, 180
Come Back to Afghanistan: A California Teenager's Story (Akbar), 157
Comenius, Bishop, 223
Comerford, Lynda Brill, 93
Comic Book Hearings of the United States Senate Subcommittee on Juvenile Delinquency, 205
Comic Book Legal Defense Fund, 209
comics
    early history of, 203–205
    gay/lesbian characters in, 193
    graphic novels, 205–208
    graphic novels, golden age of, 215–216
    graphic novels vs., 210–211
    libraries and, 208–211
    manga, 212–215
    market for, 216–221
Comics Code Authority, 205
Commission on Reading, 245
Common Core standards
    nonfiction and, 229–230
    reading abilities of YAs and, 237
complexity, 86
Connections (Gallo), 89
Connor, Leslie, 170
consumers, 44
The Contender (Lipsyte), 31–32
A Contract with God and Other Tenement Stories (Eisner), 205
controversy, 85–86
    See also book challenges/censorship
Cooke, Rachel, 135
Cool Salsa: Bilingual Poems on Growing Up Latino in the United States (Carlson), 91
Cooner, Donna, 115
Cooper, Ilene, 72
Cooperative Children's Book Center (CCBC)
    on multicultural literature, x–xi
    tracking of diversity in books, 153
Coraline (Gaiman), 104, 217
Corbett, Sue
    on *Eleanor and Park*, 128
    on preference for print books, 241
    on teen focus group, 112
    on YA imprints, 110
Coretta Scott King Awards
    category for new talent, 156
    establishment of, 49
    for Walter Dean Myers, 160
Corliss, Richard, 69
Cormier, Robert
    The Chocolate War, 198
    determinism, 37
    Fade, 67, 133–134
    Meghan Cox Gurdon on, 201
    Tenderness, 71, 74
    works of, 33–34, 45
Cornish, Sarah, 86
Cosmo Girl magazine, 69
Cotler, Joanna, 133–137
Council on Interracial Books for Children, 43, 155
Coward-McCann (publisher), 204
Coyne, Sarah, 202
Craig, Amanda, 135
Crain, Caleb, 242
Craven, Wes, 56
creative nonfiction, 227
Creative Nonfiction magazine, 227

"Critical Theory and Young Adult Literature" (Children's Literature Association), 64
Cronn-Mills, Kirstin, 192
crossover books
    adult authors, invasion of, 137–138
    adults purchasing YA books, 146–150
    Alex Awards, 141–142
    books made into movies, 129
    marketing/maturing of, 133–137
    multicultural literature, 157–158
    New Adult category, 143–146
    picture books, 132–133
    reluctance to capitalize on, 131
    young adult term, meaning of, 139–141
crossover readership
    bleak books targeted, 71
    of Harry Potter series, 118–119
    of mean girl books, 114–115
    of mystery/suspense, 106
    YA imprints aimed at, 111
    of YA literature, x, 65–66
Crumb, R., 205
Cruse, Howard, 206
Crutcher, Chris
    Athletic Shorts, 89, 191, 198
    debut of, 45
    The Sledding Hill, 198
culture
    multicultural literature in 1980s, 45–50
    renaissance of youth culture in 1990s, 68–71
    youth culture, emergence of, 5–8
Cunningham, Sean, 56
Cunningham, William, 173
Cures for Heartbreak (Rabb), 90, 136
The Curious Incident of the Dog in the Nighttime (Haddon), 134–135
cyberbullying, 171–172

D

Daly, Maureen
    praise for, 24
    Profile of Youth, 16–18, 19–20, 23–24, 27
    Seventeenth Summer, 11–13, 26
Dance on My Grave (Chambers), 188
Dancing on the Edge (Nolan), 71, 74
Dangerous Angels (Block), 133
Daniel Weiss Associates, 57
Dank, Meredith, 184
Dare Truth or Promise (Boock), 190
Dark Horse (publisher), 206
Dark Knight Returns (Miller), 205

"Darkness Too Visible: Contemporary Fiction for Teens Is Rife with Explicit Abuse, Violence and Depravity" (Gurdon), 200–201
dating violence, 183–184
David Boring (Clowes), 207
Davis, Gwendolyn, 76
A Day No Pigs Would Die (Peck), 34, 61
DC Comics
    graphic novel adaptations, 218
    graphic novel imprints, 206
    Minx imprint, 214
De La Cruz, Melissa, 115
Deahl, Rachel, 211
Deal, Melanie, 152
Dean, James, 19
Dean, Zoey, 115
Dear America series (Scholastic), 101
Dear Bully (Hall & Jones), 170
The Dear One (Woodson), 187, 190
The Death and Life of Zebulon (Kraus), 104
deaths
    teen suicide rate, 171
    of teenagers from violence/related injury, 164
A Decade of Arts Engagement (National Endowment for the Arts), 235, 236
Del Rey (publisher), 134, 218
Delacorte (publisher), 109
Deliver Us from Evil (Kerr), 191
Dell (publisher), 43
Dessen, Sarah, 115, 184–185
Deuker, Carl, 183
developmental tasks, 25–26
Developmental Tasks and Education (Havighurst), 7
diary form, 101
The Diary of Bridget Jones (Fielding), 107
DiBartolo, Jim, 247
digital technology
    audiobooks and, 243–244
    multiple literacies, rise of, 238–239
DiMassa, Cara Mia, 109
Dime (Frank), 182
Dinky Hocker Shoots Smack (Kerr), 34
Dirks, Rudolph, 204
discrimination, 194
Divergent trilogy (Roth), 122–123, 147
diversity
    books on Middle East, 157–158
    international books, 158–159
    of Michael L. Printz Award winners, 85

multicultural literature, awards for, 156–157
multicultural literature, lack of, 153–155
multicultural literature, trends in, x–xi
in nonfiction, 231
in U.S. population, 151–152
Walter Dean Myers and, 159–161
We Need Diverse Books, 156
The Diviners (Bray), 102
Dockterman, Eliana, 219
Doctorow, Cory, 98
Donelson, Kenneth L.
    on early YA literature, 8
    quote of George W. Norvell, 23
    on realism in YA literature, 32
    on YA literature, 25
Donnelley, Jennifer, 86
Donoghue, Emma, 192
Donovan, John, 30, 33, 187
Donston-Miller, Debra, 124
Don't Look and It Won't Hurt (Peck), 34
Dorling Kindersley (publisher), 224–225
Dorothy Must Die (Paige), 106
Dos Passos, John, 170
Downham, Jenny, 185
Dr. Frankenstein's Daughters (Weyn), 106
Dracula (Bram Stoker), 103
"Dragons in Manhattan" (Block), 192
Dragonwings (Yep), 49
Drama (Telgemeier), 193, 214
Drawn and Quarterly (publisher), 206
Dreamland (Dessen), 184–185
Dresang, Eliza, 132
Driscoll, David, 236
Drop Out (Eyerly), 36
Du Jardin, Rosamund, 15, 42
Duncan, Lois, 34, 60
Dunning, Stephen, 91
Durango Street (Bonham), 28
Dylan, Bob, 27
dystopian fiction, 123–125

E
Eagen, Cynthia, 113, 114–115
Eaglen, Audrey
    on decline of YA titles, 59
    on middle-school literature, 58
    on publishing, 57
Eakle, Jonathan, 238
The Earth, My Butt and Other Big, Round Things (Mackler), 198
Earthshine (Nelson), 190
e-books, 143, 144
Eclipse (Meyer), 119
Ed, Carl, 6
The Edge of Nowhere series (George), 106
education
    audiobooks, benefits of, 245–246
    poetry associated with classroom, 91
    reading abilities of YAs, 236–238
    school enrollment, forecasts for, 247
    school enrollment numbers in 1990s, 69
    teenagers in school, increase in, 4–5
    YA literature in classroom, 63–65
Edwards, Kirsten, 76
Edwards, Margaret Alexander
    Alex Awards and, 141
    on first young adult novel, 11
    on sexuality in literature, 175–177
    Sue Barton Student Nurse and, 9
Egoff, Sheila, 35
Eisner, Will, 205
Eisner Awards, 217
Eleanor and Park (Rowell), 128–129
Elementary and Secondary Education Act, 224
Eliot, T. S., 149
Elle Girl magazine, 69
Elleman, Barbara, 108
Ellison, Harlan, 98
Emery, Anne, 42
Emond, Stephen, 247
empathy
    bullying and, 172–173
    lack of with bullying, 169
    literature of risk and, 167
    literature on, 173–174
Empty (Walton), 185
Enchanted Air (Engle), 94–95
Ender's Game (Card), 218, 243
Ender's Shadow (Card), 218
Endore, Guy, 103–104
Engberg, Gillian, 120
Engle, Margarita, 94–95
Entertainment Weekly, 120
Entrekin, Morgan, 68
Epstein, Connie C., 55
Epstein, Robert, 139
Erehwon (Butler), 123
Erikson, Erik, 7
Escape from Nowhere (Eyerly), 36
Estrada, Jackie, 210
Etiquette for Young Moderns (Hauser), 6
event publishing
    introduction of, 119
    for Twilight series, 120

Everything Bad Is Good for You: How Today's Popular Culture Is Actually Making Us Smarter (Johnson), 242
Excellence in Nonfiction Book Award, 229
Exposed (Marcus), 185
Eyerly, Jeanette
    A Girl Like Me, 178
    problem novels of, 35–36
Eyewitness Books (Dorling Kindersley), 224–225

F
"Facts of Life" (Cooper), 72
The Facts Speak for Themselves (Cole), 71, 74
Fade (Cormier)
    as crossover book, 133–134
    cross-promotion of, 67
    publication of, 45
Fallen Angels (Myers)
    adult paperback edition of, 67
    book challenges, 198
    as crossover book, 134
    personal face of soldiers, 160
A Family Affair (movie), 6
The Family Romanov (Fleming), 228
Fangirl (Rowell), 145
Fantagraphics (publisher), 206
Fantastic Four (Marvel Comics), 205
fantasy
    David Almond/Philip Pullman, 99–100
    Harry Potter series, phenomenon of, 115–119
    Laurence Yep, 49
    speculative fiction, 97–98
    success of, 98
Fantesky, Beth, 106
Fantozzi, Joanna, 122
Farish, Terry, 93, 95
Farizan, Sara, 158, 194
Fast Sam, Cool Clyde and Stuff (Myers), 34
Father Figure (Peck), 61
The Fault in Our Stars (Green)
    adult purchases of, 147, 148
    sexual activity in, 185
    success of, 126–129
The Fault in Our Stars (movie), 127, 129
Fear Street novels (Stein), 104
The Fearless (Pass), 170
Federal Bureau of Investigation, 165
Feelings, Tom, 48
Feinstein, John, 106

Feiwel, Jean, 101
Felsen, Henry Gregor
    car gang fiction of, 19
    Two and the Town, 176–177
    vocational stories of, 10
Ferber, Edna, 9
Ferguson, Christopher J., 166
fiction
    multicultural literature as indispensable, 159
    for wisdom, 61–62
    See also genre fiction
Fielding, Helen, 107
films
    See movies
The Final Warning (Patterson), 138
Finnegan, William, 70
The Fire Eaters (Almond), 99
First Love (Hauser), 6
First Second imprint
    on graphic novel trends, 220
    launch of, 210
Flanagan, Anna, 238
Flavorwire.com, 147
Fleming, Candace, 228
Flinn, Alex, 185
Flowers in the Attic (Andrews), 180
Fontaine, Mia, 179
Forbes magazine
    on audiobooks, 243
    on high-school students in 1980s, 44
Forester, C. S., 24
Forever (Blume), 178–179
Forgive Me, Leonard Peacock (Quick), 171
Forman, Gayle, 171
Forman, Jack, 31
Francis, Lee, 92
Franco, Betsy, 92
Frank, E. R., 182
Frankenstein: Or the Modern Prometheus (Shelley), 103
Frankie Lyman and the Teenagers, 6
Franks, E. R., 90
Freakboy (Clark), 94, 192
Freaks and Geeks (television show), 70
free verse, 93–94
Freedman, Russell
    Lincoln: A Photobiography, 224–225, 228
    on storytelling, 226–227
Freewill (Lynch), 86
Freund, Lisa, 163–164
Frey, William H., 151

Freymann-Weyr, Garret, 191
Friday the Thirteenth (movie), 56
Friedman, Aimee, 147, 210
Friedman, Richard A., 163
The Friends (Guy), 34
Fritz, Jean, 228
Frolund, Tina, 160
From Delight to Wisdom: Nonfiction for Young Adults (Carter & Abrahamson), 225
From Hinton to Hamlet: Building Bridges between Young Adult Literature and the Classics (Hertz & Gallo), 64–65
From the Notebooks of Melanin Sun (Woodson), 190
Frost, Helen, 87, 94
Fruits Basket series (Takaya), 213
Fun Home (Bechdel), 193, 214
Future Library Services and Teens Project Report (YALSA), 238
future shock, 53

G
Gadget Girl (Kamata), 216
Gag, Wanda, 204
Gaiman, Neil
    Coraline, 217
    horror fiction of, 104
    Sandman, 206
Gaines, William, 205
Gale, David
    on books made into movies, 129
    on diversity in literature, 154
    Michael L. Printz Award, creation of, 76
    on return of realism, 126
    on YA literature industry, 109
    on young adult publishing, 59, 60
Gallo, Donald
    From Hinton to Hamlet: Building Bridges between Young Adult Literature and the Classics, 64–65
    quote of Walter Dean Myers, 160
    short story collections by, 89
gangs
    in *The Outsiders*, 27–28, 29–30
    youth involvement in, 165
Gantos, Jack, 228
Garcia, Kami, 218
Garden, Nancy
    Annie on My Mind, 188
    Margaret A. Edwards Award for, 191
    The Year They Burned the Books, 198

Gardner, Howard, 239
Gardner, John, 62
Garvin, Jeff, 192
Gates, Katherine, 71
Gaudios, John, 122
Gay, Lesbian, Straight Educators Network (GLSEN), 194
Gemma Doyle trilogy (Bray), 115
Generation Dead (Waters), 105
genre fiction
    blurred lines between, 115
    collections of genre stories, 90
    historical fiction, 100–103
    horror, 103–105
    mystery/suspense, 105–106
    romance, 103
    speculative fiction, 97–100
George (Gino), 192
George, Elizabeth, 106
Getlin, Josh, 68
Ghost World (Clowes), 206
The Ghosts of Heaven (Sedgwick), 85, 90
Gibbons, Dave, 205
Giblin, James Cross
    The Life and Death of Adolf Hitler, 228
    on publishing of information books, 224
    on visual aspects of nonfiction, 226
Gibson, H. W., 6
Gilbert, Eugene, 13, 44
Gilmore, Natasha
    on diversity, 153
    on *The New York Times* Best Seller List, 116
    on preference for print books, 241
    on reading rates, 236
Gingher, Marianne, 131, 134
Ginsburg, Ruth Bader, 106
Gioia, Dana, 235
The Girl Inside (Eyerly), 36
A Girl Like Me (Eyerly), 36, 178
Give a Boy a Gun (Strasser), 170
The Giver (Lowry), 123
Glenn, Mel, 91, 93
Glines, Abbi, 143
Glovach, Linda, 37–38
GLSEN (Gay, Lesbian, Straight Educators Network), 194
Go Ask Alice (Anonymous)
    book challenges, 198
    description of, 37–38
    on YALSA's 1994 best books list, 60
Goblin Secrets (Alexander), 126

Godbersen, Anna, 115
Goddu, Krystyna, 229–230
Godwin, Laura, 124
Going on Sixteen (Cavanna), 14–15
Golden Compass (Pullman), 134
Golding, Julia, 105
Goliath (Westerfeld), 247
Gonzalez, Patrisia, 50, 52
GoodReads.com, 147
Goodrich, Samuel Griswold, 223
Goodwillie, Susan, 61
Goosebumps series (Stine), 45
Gordon, Ruth, 91–92
Gorgeous (Rudnick), 145
Gossip Girls series (Von Ziegesar)
    book challenges, 198
    overview of, 112–115
Gracefully Grayson (Polonsky), 192
Graduation Day (Charbonneau), 170
Graham, Ruth
    on adults reading YA, 147–148
    responses to article by, 148–150
Grant, Cynthia D., 180
Grant, Gavin J., 126
graphic novels
    American Born Chinese (Yang), 85, 157
    author-driven market, 215–216
    emergence of, 205–208
    first use of term, 205
    gay/lesbian characters in, 193
    libraries and, 208–211
    manga, 212–215
    market for, 216–221
"Graphically Speaking" column (Kan), 206
Graphix (publisher), 209–210
Grasshopper Jungle (Smith), 149
Gravett, Paul, 213
The Graveyard Book (Gaiman), 104, 217
Gray, Paul, 55, 116
Great Depression, 5
Great Graphic Novels for Teens list
    (YALSA), 208
Green, John
    book sales of, x
    The Fault in Our Stars, adult purchases
        of, 147, 148
    realistic fiction by, xi
    return of realism with, 126–129
    sexual activity in books of, 185
Green, Karen, 217
Greenberg, Jan, 87, 92
Greene, Graham, 34
Gregorio, I. W., 192

Gregory, David, 172
Griepp, Milton
    on graphic novels, golden age of, 219
    on Raina Telgemeier, 214
    on sales of graphic novels, 216, 218
Griffin, Adele, 247
Grimes, Nikki, 94
Grove, Karen, 124
Grover, Sharon, 245
Growing Up Digital (Tapscott), 70
*The Growth of Logical Thinking from
    Childhood to Adolescence* (Piaget),
    7
Guantanamo Boy (Perera), 158
Gulliver's Travels (Swift), 123
Gurdon, Meghan Cox, 200–201
Gutkind, Lee, 227
Guy, Rosa, 34, 48

H
Haddon, Mark, 134–135
Half-Blood Prince (Rowling), 118
Hall, Donald, 245–246
Hall, G. Stanley
    on adolescence, 4
    focus on male adolescents, 6
    on gender differences in literature,
        8
Hamilton, R. J., 190
Hamilton, Virginia, 48
Hand, Cynthia, 171
The Hanged Man (Block), 180
Hannegan, Liz, 245
Happy Days (television show), 42
Happy Hooligan (Opper), 204
Harcourt, Brace (publisher), 59
Hard Love (Wittlinger), 82–83, 191
hardcover books
    dwindling market for, 58–59
    focus on, post-Millennium, 110
Harlequin (publisher), 144
Harmon, Amy, 172
Harold Teen (Ed), 6
HarperCollins
    graphic novels of, 216–221
    Little Lit series, 207
Harry: A History (Anelli), 117
Harry Potter and the Deathly Hallows
    (Rowling), 116, 118, 146
Harry Potter and the Order of the Phoenix
    (Rowling), 117, 118
"Harry Potter and the Rival Teen Franchise"
    (*Wall Street Journal*), 120

Harry Potter and the Sorcerer's Stone (Rowling), 118
Harry Potter series (Rowling)
    comparison with Twilight series, 120, 121
    phenomenon of, 115–119
Hartnett, Sonya, 86, 135–136
Hauser, Margaret L. (Gay Head), 6
Havighurst, Robert James, 7, 25–26
Hawaii State Public Library System, 206
Hayes, Regina, 132
Hayn, Judith, 174
Head, Ann, 177
Healthychildren.org, 165
Hearst, Patty, 38
The Heart Has Its Reasons (Cart & Jenkins), 187
Heart to Heart: New Poems Inspired by Twentieth Century Art (Greenberg), 87, 92
Heaven Eyes (Almond), 99
Heckerling, Amy, 69
Hefling, Kimberly, 169, 236
Heiligman, Deborah, 228, 229
Heinlein, Robert A., 20
Heller, Steven, 19, 42
Hello, I Lied (Kerr), 191
Hemphill, Stephanie, 87, 94, 228
Hentoff, Nat, 28, 33
Her Dark Curiosity (Shepherd), 106
"Here We Go Again . . . 25 Years of Best Books" (YALSA), 60–61
A Hero Ain't Nothin' But a Sandwich (Childress), 32, 34, 60
Herrera, Juan Felipe, 95
Hersch, Patricia, 70
Hershman, Micha, 207
Hertz, Sarah K., 64–65
Hesse, Monica, 120
Hi There, High School! (Hauser), 6
Hiaasen, Carl, 106
high school, 4–5
    See also school
High School Poems (Glenn), 91
Highwater, Jamake, 52–53
Higson, Charlie, 106
Hillenbrand, Laura, 230
Hilliard, Rose, 143
Hine, Thomas, 6
Hinton, S. E.
    The Outsiders, 27–28, 29–30, 165
    on reading by teenagers, 23
    Tex/Taming the Star Runner, 45
    That Was Then This Is Now, 32

"Hipper, Brighter, and Bolder" (Stevenson), 71
Hirsch, Karen D., 207
His Dark Materials trilogy (Pullman), 99–100
His Fair Assassins trilogy (LaFevers), 102
Hispanics
    population growth in U.S., 151, 152
    reading abilities of YAs, 237
    See also Latinos/Latinas
historical fiction
    beliefs about, 100–101
    rise of, 101–103
Hochschild, Adam, 56
Hogan's Alley (Outcault), 203–204
Hold Me Closer (Levithan), 193
A Hole in My Life (Gantos), 228
Holland, Isabel, 188
Holley, Pam Spencer, 244
Holman, Felice, 60
Holt, Victoria, 42
Homes, A. M., 67, 134, 189
homosexuality, 187–195
Hoobler, Dorothy and Thomas, 105
Hoose, Phillip, 228
Horn Book magazine, 64
Horning, K. T., xi, 155
Horowitz, Alex, 105
Horowitz, Beverly
    on nonfiction, 230
    on Pacer Books, 44
    on publishing, 129
    on publishing fiction/nonfiction, 57
    on YA crossover books, 144
horror fiction
    in early 1990s, 55–56
    overview of, 103–105
    success of, 45
Hosseini, Khaled, 157
Hot Rod magazine, 20
Houghton Mifflin (publisher), 108–109
The House You Pass on the Way (Woodson), 190
Houston, Jeanne Wakatsuki, 49
How a Nation Engages with Art (National Endowment for the Arts), 235–236
How Beautiful the Ordinary (Cart), 192
"How Graphic Novels Became the Hottest Section in the Library" (MacDonald), 217
How I Discovered Poetry (Nelson), 95
How I Live Now (Rosoff), 85–86, 135, 180

Howard, Elise
   on Alloy Entertainment, 114
   on Daniel Weiss Associates, 57
   on hardcovers, 110
   on YA crossover books, 144–145
Howe, James, 171
Hubert, Jen, 100–101, 102
Huesmann, Rowell, 166
Hughes, John, 69
The Hunger Games (movie), 122
The Hunger Games trilogy (Collins), 121–122, 147
Huntwork, Mary M., 43
Hutchinson, Margaret, 11
Huxley, Aldous, 123
Hyde (Levine), 106

I
I Hadn't Meant to Tell You This (Woodson), 180
I Know What You Did Last Summer (Duncan), 34, 60
I Love, I Hate, I Miss My Sister (Sarn), 158
I Was Here (Forman), 171
ICTs (information and communication technologies), 238–239
IDW (publisher), 218
If You Could Be Mine (Farizan), 158, 194
I'll Get There. It Better Be Worth the Trip (Donovan), 30, 33, 187
I'll Give You the Sun (Nelson), 193
I'll Love You When You're More Like Me (Kerr), 189
illustrations, 246–247
I'm Really Dragged but Nothing Gets Me Down (Hentoff), 33
images
   See pictures
IMDB (International Movie Data Base), 129
immigration
   future shock and, 53
   multicultural literature and, 46–47
"In Novels for Girls, Fashion Trumps Romance" (Winerip), 113–114
In the Shadows (White & DiBartolo), 247
In the Time I Get (Crutcher), 191
incest, 179–181
information and communication technologies (ICTs), 238–239
institutional bullying, 172
international books, 158–159
International Movie Data Base (IMDB), 129
International Reading Association (IRA)
   on adolescent literacy, 237
   on multiple literacies, 238–239
   "Young Adults' Choices" booklist, 158
Internet
   cyberbullying, 171–172
   multiple literacies, rise of, 238–239
   poetry opportunities with, 92
   reading online, 234, 239–242
   reading trends and, 235
Interpreting Young Adult Literature: Literary Theory in the Secondary Classroom (Moore), 65
interracial marriage, 152
intersex characters, 192
Invasion (Myers), 160
Inzlicht, Michael, 173
IRA
   See International Reading Association
The Iron Duke (Tunis), 11, 12
Irwin, Hadley, 179
"Is Google Making Us Stupid?" (Carr), 240
The It Girls series (Von Ziegesar), 113
Ivins, Molly, 73

J
J. B. Lippincott (publisher), 16
Jack (Homes), 67, 134, 189
Jackaby (Ritter), 106
Jackson, Richard
   on age of YA, 58
   speaker at 1998 ALA conference, 72
   on young adult publishing, 59
Jacobs, Helen Hull, 10
Jacobs, Thomas A., 73
James, Will, 9
Janeczko, Paul B., 91
Japanese Americans, 49
Jayson, Sharon, 152
Jazz Country (Hentoff), 28
Jefferson, Margo, 41
Jekyll Loves Hyde (Fantesky), 106
Jellicoe Road (Marchetta), 86
Jenkins, Christine A.
   The Heart Has Its Reasons, 187
   quote of M. E. Kerr, 188
   Top 250 LGBTQ Books for Teens, 193–194
   "young adult" term, use of, 7
Jennings, Dana, 211, 214
Jennings, Frank G., 24–25
Jensen, Cordelia, 95, 189
Jensen, Frances, 163
Jensen, Kelly, 104
The Jew of New York (Katchor), 207

Jimmy Corrigan: The Smartest Kid on Earth (Ware), 207
John Lennon (Partridge), 228
Johnson, Angela, 157
Johnson, Kathleen Jeffrie, 182
Johnson, Lyndon, 224
Johnson, Maureen, 115
Johnson, Steven, 242
Jones, Patrick, 86
Juby, Susan, 216
Julius Knipl: Real Estate Photographer (Katchor), 207
Just Hold On (Bunn), 37, 38, 179
"Just Say Know" preconference, 225
juvenile delinquency, 18–19

K
Kamata, Suzanne, 216
Kan, Kat, 206, 217
Kane, Bob, 204
Kantrowitz, Barbara, 139
Karl, Jean, 46
Katchor, Ben, 207
Katims, Jason, 70
The Katzenjammer Kids (Dirks), 204
Kaufman, Leslie, 128
Keesha's House (Frost), 87, 94
Keim, Brandon, 166
Kemp, Robert S., 164
Kerr, M. E.
    bisexual/lesbian characters in novels of, 191
    Dinky Hocker Shoots Smack, 34
    I'll Love You When You're More Like Me, 189
    Night Kites, 188
    works in 1980s, 45
Kett, Joseph E.
    on "boyology," 6
    on gangs, 29
    on Hall's theories of adolescence, 4, 5
    on juvenile delinquency, 18
    on readers of YA fiction, 17
Khazan, Olga, 243
Kids (movie), 71
Kids and Family Reading Report (Scholastic), 235
"Kids Need Libraries" (Matthews et al.), 46–47
Killing Mr. Griffin (Duncan), 60
Kindersley, Peter, 225
King, Stephen, 218
Kirch, Claire, 154, 156

Kishimoto, Masashi, 212
Kissing Tennessee (Appelt), 90
The Kite Runner (Hosseini), 157
Kit's Wilderness (Almond), 86, 99
Klause, Annette Curtis, 72, 121
Klein, Norma
    Breaking Up, 188
    on *Forever*, 178
    Mom, the Wolfman and Me, 33
Knight, Kyle, 194
Knockout Games (Neri), 170
Knopf (publisher), 134
Knudson, R. R., 91
Koebler, Jason, 202
Koelling, Holly
    on fantasy, 98, 118
    on nonfiction on BBYA, 229
    on poetry, 91
Koertge, Ron
    Arizona Kid, 189
    debut of, 45
    poetry of, 94
Kohlberg, Lawrence, 7
Kolbert, Elizabeth, 163
Korine, Harmony, 71
Kraus, Daniel, 104
Kraus, Nicola, 115
Kraus, W. Keith, 177, 178
Kriney, Marilyn, 37
Kuklin, Susan
    Beyond Magenta, 192
    Speaking Out: Teenagers Take on Race, Sex, and Identity, 61
Kunkle, Frederick, 152
Kushman, Rick, 70

L
ladders, reading, 25–26
LaFeria, Ruth, 152
LaFevers, Robin, 102
Lair of Dreams (Bray), 102
Lambert, Janet, 42
Lamia, Mary C., 173
Lanagan, Margo
    Black Juice, 87, 90
    as crossover author, 135–136
    Tender Morsels, 86
The Land (Taylor), 102
Lane, Andrew, 106
Lane, Rose Wilder, 9
Lanes, Selma, 68
Larbalestier, Justine, 154–155
Larrick, Nancy, 48

Larsen, Hope, 210
The Last Leaves Falling (Benwell), 171
Last Summer with Maizon (Woodson), 173
The Last Time We Say Goodbye (Hand), 171
The Last Unicorn (Beagle), 218
Latinos/Latinas
    awards for Latino writers, 156–157
    Bless Me, Ultima, 52
    diversity in YA literature and, 153–154
    use of term, 49
    YA literature by, 50
    See also Hispanics
Latrobe, Kathy Howard, 61
Laughing Out Loud, I Fly (Herrera), 95
Lavin, Michael R., 205
Lawrence-Pietroni, Anna, 66
Leaky Cauldron website, 117
Leavitt, Martine, 94, 181–182
Lee, Jim, 193
Lee and Low (publisher), 155
LeGuin, Ursula K., 97–98
Lenhart, Amanda, 239
Lennertz, Carl, 134
Lesbian, Gay, Bisexual, Transgender, Queer/
    Questioning, Intersex (LGBTQI)
    early YA literature, 187–188
    increase in number of books, xi
    literature about AIDS, 188–189
    literature in 1980s, 189
    literature in 1990s, 189–191
    literature in 2000s, 191–195
Lester, Julius, 48
Let the Hurricane Roar (Lane), 9
Leviathan (Westerfeld), 126, 246–247
Levine, Arthur, 72
Levine, Daniel, 106
Levithan, David
    on John Green, 128
    LGBT literature, 192–193
    The Realm of Possibilities, 94
Levitz, Paul, 211
Lewis, Elizabeth Foreman, 20
LGBTQI
    See Lesbian, Gay, Bisexual, Transgender,
        Queer/Questioning, Intersex
Liar (Larbalestier), 154–155
librarians
    audiobooks and, 244–245
    decline in young adult librarians in
        1990s, 61
    graphic novels, attention on, 206
    graphic novels, impact of librarians on,
        220

graphic novels, purchase of, 207–208
    as judges for Eisner Awards, 217
library
    graphic novels, interest in, 208–211
    market for comics/graphic novels,
        216–217
    new nonfiction and, 225–231
Library of Congress, 242
The Life and Death of Adolf Hitler (Giblin),
    228
Life Is Funny (Franks), 90
Life of Pi (Martel), 134, 135
Lincoln: A Photobiography (Freedman),
    224–225, 228
Link, Kelly, 126
Lipschultz, Margo, 144
Lipstick Jihad (Moaveni), 157
Lipsyte, Robert
    The Contender, 31–32
    Raider's Night, 182–183
    Summer Rules/The Summer Boy, 45
listening skills, 244, 245–246
literacy
    multiple literacies, rise of, 238–239
    reading abilities of YAs, 236–238
    reading online, 239–241
literary merit
    popularity vs., 87
    Printz Award Task Force on, 83–87
literature, definition of, 3
Little, Brown (publisher)
    Gossip Girls series, 113, 114–115
    graphic novels published by, 207
    publication of *Sue Barton Student
        Nurse*, 9–10
Little Chicago (Rapp), 167, 168
Little Lit series (Joanna Cotler imprint), 207
Little Little (Kerr), 45
Little Lulu (Buell), 211
Little Nemo (McKay), 204
Little Women (Alcott), 8
Littman, Sarah Darer, 171, 172
Lloyd, David, 206
Lodge, Sally
    on The Carlyles series, 113
    on crossover books, 132, 134
    on historical fiction diary series, 101
Logan, William, 91, 93
Lone Cowboy (James), 9
A Long Way from Chicago (Peck), 90
Longmans Green (publisher), 9
Looking for Alaska (Green)
    as controversial book, 85–86

Michael L. Printz Award for, 126
sexual activity in, 185
Los Angeles Times
on adult buyers of YA books, 147
on adult opinions of teenagers, 73
on books made into movies, 129
on Twilight series, 120
on YA literature industry, 109
"Young Adult Novel" award, 68
Love and Sex: Ten Stories of Truth (Cart), 185, 192
Lovecraft, H. P., 105
Low, Jason, 153
Lowry, Lois
on dystopian novels, 125
The Giver, 123
A Summer to Die, 34
Lucas, George, 42
Luna (Peters), 192
Luxe series (Godbersen), 115
Lyga, Barry, 105–106
Lynch, Chris
Freewill, 86
"Today's YA Writers: Pulling No Punches," 64
Whitechurch, 90

M

M. C. Higgins the Great (Hamilton), 48
Maberry, Jonathan, 105
Macaulay, David
picture book crossovers of, 132–133
The Way Things Work, 67
MacDonald, Heidi
on comics, 207
on graphic novels, 217
on market for comics/graphic novels, 216
MacDonald, Scott, 135
Maciel, Amanda, 149, 170
Mackler, Carolyn, 198
Macmillan (publisher)
First Second imprint, 210
ReaLITyReads program, 126
A Mad Wicked Folly (Waller), 145
magazines, teen, 69
Maggs, Sam, 215
Maguire, Gregory, 168
Make Lemonade (Wolff), 93
"Making Mischief" (Maguire), 168
Making up Megaboy (Walter), 72, 74
Mall Rats (movie), 69
Maloney, Jennifer, 214

Man without a Face (Holland), 188
manga
females and, 219
market for, 216–221
overview of, 212–215
Manga: A Complete Guide (Thompson), 212
Mann, Leslie, 188
Marano, Hara Estroff, 139
Marcus, Kimberly, 185
Marcus, Leonard, 118
Margaret A. Edwards Award
for African American writers, 157
for authors in 1970s, 34
for Jacqueline Woodson, 173, 174
for Judy Blume, 179
for Nancy Garden, 191
for Robert Lipsyte, 32
for S. E. Hinton, 29
science fiction titles awarded, 97–98
for Walter Dean Myers, 160
Margaux with an X (Koertge), 94
market, for comics/graphic novels, 216–221
marketing
books made into movies, 129–130
of crossover books, 133–137, 138
Harry Potter series and, 117, 119
mean girl books and, 114–115
of multicultural literature, 154–155
to teenagers, by chain bookstores/publishers, 108–110
to teenagers in 1980s, 44
to teenagers in 1990s, 68–71
See also retail
marriage, interracial, 152
Marschall, Richard, 203–204
Marshall, James, 132
Marston, William Moulton, 211
Martel, Yann, 134, 135
Martin, Ann, 217
Martinez, Victor, 68
Marvel Comics, 205, 218
Massachusetts General Hospital for Children, 139
Matthews, Virginia, 46–47
Mattson, Dirk P., 75
Maughan, Shannon
on censorship, 198
on hardcover books, 110
on Teen People Book Club, 111
Maus (Spiegelman), 205, 206
Maus II (Spiegelman), 206
Maximum Ride series (Patterson & Charbonnet), 138

Maxwell, William, 24
May B (Rose), 95
Mazer, Norma Fox
    speaker at 1998 ALA conference, 72
    When She Was Good, 71, 74
McCafferty, Megan, 115
McCaffrey, Anne, 97–98
McCarthy, Cori, 216
McDaniel, Lurlene, 115
McDermott, Gerald, 53
McElderry, Margaret K.
    on foreign children's literature, 20
    on immigrant literature, 47
    on multicultural literature, 50
McGrath, Charles
    on graphic novels, 210
    on NEA reading study, 234
    on short stories, 88–89
McKay, Winsor, 204
McLaughlin, Emma, 115
McLean, Kristen, 146
McPhee, John, 227
Me, Me, Me, Me, Me: Not a Novel (Kerr), 45
Mead, Rebecca, 114
Meader, Stephen W., 10
mean girl books, 112–115
Mecoy, Bob, 206–207
media, mainstream, 199–201
Medina, Meg, 170
Medium.com, 242
mental illness, 30–31
Merit Books, 112
Mermin, Jonathan, 188
The Method (Walker), 190
Metzger, George, 205
Meyer, Stephanie
    adult purchases of YA books, 146
    book sales of, x
    graphic novel version of Twilight series,
        217–218
    Twilight series, 119–121
MH-18 magazine, 69
Michael L. Printz Award
    for *American Born Chinese* (Yang), 210
    creation of, 68, 75–77
    diversity record of, 157
    honor title for *Angus, Thongs and Full-
        Frontal Snogging* (Rennison), 107
    for *I'll Give You the Sun* (Nelson), 193
    list of winners, 84–85
    literary merit, defining, 83–87
    for *Looking for Alaska* (Green), 126
    for *Monster* (Myers), 81–82

for *Postcards from No Man's Land*
    (Chambers), 191
Printz Honor books, 82–83
    winners, exclusion from other awards/
        lists, 87–88
Mickey Mouse Magazine (Walt Disney),
    204
Middle East, literature on, 157–158
middle-school literature
    birth of, 57–59
    YA as synonymous with, 65
Midwinterblood (Sedgwick), 85, 86, 90
Mildred Batchelder Award, 158–159
Miller, Edwin, 41–42
Miller, Frank, 205
Miller, Laura
    on chick lit, 107
    on dystopian novels, 124
    on Philip Pullman, 100
Millions of Cats (Gag), 204
Milliot, Jim
    on popularity of YA category, 146
    on sales of YA books, 109
    on Teen People Book Club, 111
Mind Riot: Coming of Age in Comix
    (Hirsch), 207
Minx imprint, 214
The Misfits (Howe), 171
Miss Peregrine's Home for Peculiar Children
    (Riggs), 218, 247
Missing the Piano (Rapp), 167
Mistress of Mellyn (Holt), 42
Mitchard, Jacquelyn, 110
mixed-race people, 152
Moaveni, Azadeh, 157
mobile devices, 239
The Mockingbirds (Whitney), 185
Mom, the Wolfman and Me (Klein), 33
Monahan, Brian, 123
Mondale, Sarah, 4
Monster (Myers), 81–82
Monti, Joe, 108–109
Moonbird (Hoose), 228
Moore, Alan, 206
Moore, John Noell, 65
Moore, Ruth, 24
Morales, Robert, 207
More Bullies in Books (Bott), 171
More Happy Than Not (Silvera), 216
Morgan, R. E., 164
Moskowitz, Hannah, 194–195
Mosle, Sara, 72
Mouly, Francoise, 207

movies
    books made into, impact of, 129–130
    dark films in 1990s, 71
    The Fault in Our Stars, 127
    graphic novels and, 218
    The Hunger Games, 122
    teen-oriented movies in 1990s, 69
Mr. and Mrs. Bo Jo Jones (Head), 177
MTV, 69–70
multicultural literature
    after World War II, 20
    awards for, 156–157
    books on Middle East, 157–158
    emergence of in 1980s, 45–50
    international books, 158–159
    lack of, reasons for, 153–155
    political correctness, 51–53
    trends in, x–xi
    Walter Dean Myers and, 159–161
    We Need Diverse Books, work of,
        156
multiculturalism, 47–48
multiple literacies, 238–239
Murdock, Catherine Gilbert, 115
My Book of Life by Angel (Leavitt), 94,
    181–182
My Darling, My Hamburger (Zindel), 32–33,
    178
My Father's Scar (Cart), 119
My Friend's Got This Problem, Mr. Candler
    (Glenn), 93
My Heartbeat (Freymann-Weyr), 191
My Name Is America series (Scholastic),
    101
Mydans, Seth, 46
Myers, Christopher, 82
Myers, Walter Dean
    book challenges, 198
    diversity, work towards, 159–161
    emergence of, 48
    Fallen Angels, 67, 134
    Fast Sam, Cool Clyde and Stuff, 34
    Michael L. Printz Award for, 157
    Monster, 81–82
    145th Street, 90
Myracle, Lauren
    Meghan Cox Gurdon on, 201
    popularity of, 115
    response to criticism, 201
    TTYL series, 198
Mystery Writers of America Edgar Awards,
    105
mystery/suspense, 105–106

N
Nafisi, Azar, 157
Namioka, Lensey, 49
Nancy Drew series (Keene), 106
Naruto series (Kishimoto), 212
Nation, 67
National Assessment of Educational
    Progress, 236–237
National Book Award
    for Jacqueline Woodson, 157
    for young adult literature, 68, 74
National Book Foundation, 68
National Center for Education Statistics
    on age of young adults, 8
    on bullying, 169
    on libraries with young adult specialists,
        61
    on school enrollment, 247
National Center for Victims of Crime, 179,
    180
National Council of Teachers of English
    (NCTE)
    "A Call to Action," 237
    "Exploding the Canon" theme at
        workshop of, 64
    on multiple literacies, 238
    nonfiction Orbis Pictus Award, 228
National Defense Education Act, 224
National Endowment for the Arts
    How a Nation Engages with Art/A
        Decade of Arts Engagement, 235–236
    To Read or Not to Read study, 234–235
    Reading at Risk study, 233–234
    Reading on the Rise study, 235
National Poetry Month, 92
Native Americans
    diversity in YA literature and, 153–154
    lack of literature about, 158
    political correctness in literature, 52–53
    reading abilities of YAs, 237
Nayeri, Daniel and Dina, 106
Naylor, Phyllis Reynolds, 198
NBM (publisher), 214
NCTE
    See National Council of Teachers of
        English
Neal, Meghan, 171
Nelson, Jandy, 193
Nelson, Marilyn
    How I Discovered Poetry, 95
    as Printz honor recipient, 157
    renaissance of short story, 87
    verse novels, 94

Nelson, Theresa, 190
Neon Lit (publisher), 206–207
Nerdfighters, 127–128
Neri, G., 170
Ness, Patrick, 123
New Adult
    audience, x, xi
    overview of, 143–146
    as popular descriptor, 140
New Fun 1 (comic book), 204
New Literacies and 21st Century
    Technologies (International Reading
    Association), 238–239
New Moon (Meyer), 119
The New York Times
    on audiobooks, 243
    criticism of YA literature in, 28
    on ethnic ambiguity, 152
    graphic books Best Seller List, 218
    on mean girl books, 112, 113
    on publishing/chain bookstores, 108
    on reading YA literature, 150
    review of Teen Angel (Gingher), 131
    Robert Lipsyte and, 31
    on Seventeenth Summer, 11
    on short stories, 88–89
    on teen spending, 69
    Teen-Age Bill of Rights, 13–14
    on video games and violence, 166
The New York Times Best Seller List
    Harry Potter and the Sorcerer's Stone
        on, 116
    Hunger Games trilogy on, 122
The New York Times Book Review, 50, 243
The New York Times Sunday Magazine, 72
Newbery Medal, 74, 228
Newlin, Shanta, 230
Newman, Andrew Adam, 243
Nicholson, George
    on chain bookstores, 44–45, 58
    "How Adult Is Young Adult?" program,
        65–67
    on New Adult category, 145
Nielsen, Jakob, 239, 240
Nielsen Children's Book Industry Report,
    236
Nielsen Children's Book Summit, 241
Nielsen Media, 241
Night Kites (Kerr), 188
The Night of the Living Dead (movie), 105
Nightmare on Elm Street (movie), 56
Nilsen, Alleen
    on decline in realistic YA fiction, 56

    on early YA literature, 8
    on health of YA literature, 55
    quote of George W. Norvell, 23
    on realism in YA literature, 32
    on sale of fiction, 60
    on YA literature, 25
1984 (Orwell), 123
Niven, Jennifer, 171
Nixon, Joan Lowery, 115
No Name-Calling Week, 171
No Place to Be. Voices of Homeless Children
    (Berck), 61
Nolan, Han
    Dancing on the Edge, 71, 74
    speaker at 1998 ALA conference, 72
None of the Above (Gregorio), 192
nonfiction
    in early 1990s, 61
    libraries and, 225–231
    pictures in, 223–225
Nonfiction for Young Adults (Carter &
    Abrahamson), 225
Norrie, Christine, 210
Norris, Shana, 172
North, Anna, 115
A Northern Light (Donnelley), 86
Norton, Mary Alice (Andre Norton), 20
Norvell, George W., 23
nostalgia, 41–43
Not Otherwise Specified (Moskowitz),
    194–195
Nothing (Teller), 86
"The Novel for the Adolescent" (Burton), 24
novels, verse, 93–95
"Numbers Game" (Time magazine), 46
Nussbaum, Emily, 112
Nye, Naomi Shihab, 92, 158

O
O'Connor, John J., 175
O'Connor, Sandra Day, 106
Octavian Nothing: Traitor to the Nation
    (Anderson), 86
Odyssey Award, 244, 245
"Of Risk and Revelation: The Current State
    of Young Adult Literature" (Cart),
    61–62, 64
Office of Intellectual Freedom, 197, 198
Oh, Ellen, 156
Ohanian, Susan, 63
O'Hara, John, 198
Okutoro, Lydia Omolola, 92
Oliveros, Chris, 211

Olsen, Ray, 104
One Death, Nine Stories (Aronson & Smith), 90
145th Street (Myers), 90
One Man Guy (Barakiva), 194
One of Those Hideous Books Where the Mother Dies (Sones), 94
Oppel, Kenneth, 106
Opper, Frederick, 204
Optic Nerve (Tomine), 206
Orbis Pictus (Comenius), 223
Orwell, George, 123
O'Shea, Michael V., 5
Outcault, R. F., 203–204
"The Outlook's Bleak" (Mosle), 72
The Outsiders (Hinton), 27–28, 29–30, 165
OverDrive, 244

P

Pacer Books, Putnam, 44
packagers, 57
Pagliarulo, Antonio, 113
Paige, Danielle, 106
Palladino, Grace
   on juvenile delinquency, 18
   on marketing to teenagers, 12
   on *Seventeen* magazine, 13
   Teenagers: An American History, 70
   on topics addressed by Margaret Hauser, 6
   on young people in school, 5
Pamela (Richardson), 103
Panem (Collins), 123
Pantheon (publisher), 207
Paper Towns (Green), 126
paperback series
   in early 1990s, 55–57
   revival of romance fiction in 1980s, 41–45
paperbacks, 60
Paradox Press (publisher), 206
paranormal romance
   popularity of, 121
   Twilight series (Meyer), 119–121
Pareles, Jon, 71
Parker, Carla, 65–66
Parrot in the Oven (Martinez), 68
Parrotfish (Wittlinger), 192
Parsons, Ash, 170
Partridge, Elizabeth, 228
Pascal, Francine, 43
Pass, Emma, 170
Passel, Jeffrey S., 152
Paterson, Katherine, 100

Patrick, Diane, 154
Patterson, James, 106, 138, 217
Patton, Sarah B., 4
Paul, Annie Murphy, 241
Paulsen, Gary, 45
Pease, Howard, 11
Peck, Richard
   Are You in the House Alone? 60, 179
   Don't Look and It Won't Hurt, 34
   Father Figure, 61
   A Long Way from Chicago, 90
   on multiculturalism, 51
   on *The Outsiders* (Hinton), 28
   on reality in books, 32
   Remembering the Good Times/Princess Ashley, 45
   on S. E. Hinton, 29
   Secrets of the Shopping Mall, 44
Peck, Robert Newton, 34, 61
Pedro and Me (Winnick), 228
peers, 164, 165
Peet, Mal, 102
Penny, Laurie, 124
Perera, Anna, 158
Perez, Ashley Hope, 157
Perfect Summer (Pascal), 43
The Perks of Being a Wallflower (Chbosky), 111
The Perks of Being a Wallflower (Chbosky)
   book challenges, 198
   incest in, 181
Permanent Connections (Bridgers), 45
Persepolis/Persepolis 2 (Satrapi)
   censorship of, 209
   graphic novels by women, 214
   Pantheon as publisher of, 157
Peskin, Joy, 128, 129
Peter (Walker), 190
Peters, Julie Anne, 192
Pew Internet and American Life Project, 239
Pew Research Center, 152, 236
photo essay, 224
Piaget, Jean, 7
picture books, 132–133
pictures
   in modern YA books, 246–247
   in new nonfiction, 223–225, 226
Pierce, Tamora, 99
The Pigman (Zindel), 30–31
Pike, Christopher, 45, 55
Pinkney, Jerry, 48
Pinkwater, Daniel M., 38

Pinsky, Robert, 92
The Place My Words Are Looking For: What Poets Say about and through Their Poems (Janeczko), 91
Places I Never Meant to Be (Blume), 198
The Plain Janes (Castellucci & Rugg), 214
Platt, Judith, 198
Plum-Ucci, Carol, 105
Pocket Books' MTV Books, 111
poetry
    renaissance of, 91–95
    revival of, 88
Pogrebin, Robin, 69
political correctness, 51–53
Pollack, Pamela, 42, 43
Polonsky, Ami, 192
Poniewozik, James, 70
"Poor Little Rich Girls Throbbing to Shop!" (Bellafante), 112
Popular Science Monthly, 6
popularity, 87
Postcards from No Man's Land (Chambers)
    as controversial book, 85–86
    gay theme of, 191
    historical/contemporary elements in, 102
Practically Seventeen (Du Jardin), 15
Prep (Sittenfeld), 134, 136
Pride Pack novels (Hamilton), 190
Princess Ashley (Peck), 45
print books
    preference for, 241
    reading online, support for, 241–242
    reading online vs., 239–240
    survival of, 246–248
Printz Award Task Force
    on literary merit, 83–84
    Michael L. Printz Award, creation of, 75–77
prizes
    See awards
problem novel
    demise of, 55
    problem with, 34–38
Profile of Youth (Daly)
    on cars, 19–20
    profiles of young people in, 16–17
    social student in, 27
    student feedback about reading, 23–24
    topical essays in, 17–18
Project for Awesome, 128
prostitutes, 181–182
public libraries, 197

publishers
    bleak books and, 71–74
    books made into movies and, 129
    crossover books, marketing of, 133–137
    decline of YA publishing, 59–62
    future of YA literature, 247
    of graphic novels, 206–207, 209–210
    of manga, 212, 213–214
    market for comics/graphic novels, 216–221
    middle-school literature, 57–59
    multicultural literature and, 45–50, 154, 155
    packagers, 56–57
    poetry collections by, 92
    romance novels in 1980s, 41–45
    YA imprints, 110–112
    youth culture renaissance and, 70–71
    See also retail
Publishers Weekly magazine
    "Hipper, Brighter, and Bolder," 71
    on institutional market, 57
    Justine Larbalestier's interview with, 154, 155
    on reading trends, 236
publishing
    chick lit, 107–108
    comics/graphic novels, market for, 216–221
    Harry Potter series, phenomenon of, 115–119
    international media conglomerates, 67–68
    marketing, chain bookstores and, 108–110
"Publishing on the Edge" (Cooper & Zvirin), 72
Pulitzer Prize, 206
Pullman, Philip
    fantasy works of, 99–100
    Golden Compass as crossover book, 134
Punkzilla (Rapp), 167, 169
Pura Belpre award, 50, 156
Puritanism, 175, 177
Purucker, Mary, 76
Putnam (publisher), 44

Q
quality, 83–87
Quevedo, Francisco de, 242
Quick, Matthew, 171
Quiet Storm: Voices of Young Black Poets (Okutoro), 92

R

R. R. Bowker Company, 146
Rabb, Margo
    Cures for Heartbreak, 90
    Curtis Sittenfeld and, 136
    on YA literature in Britain, 135
race/ethnicity
    books on Middle East, 157–158
    diversity in U.S. population, 151–152
    international books, 158–159
    multicultural literature, 46–50
    multicultural literature, awards for,
      156–157
    multicultural literature, lack of, 153–155
    political correctness, 51–53
    reading abilities of YAs and, 237
    Walter Dean Myers and, 159–161
    We Need Diverse Books, work of, 156
*Radical Change: Books for Youth in a
    Digital Age* (Dresang), 132
Raeburn, Paul W., 139
Rafferty, Terrence, 29
A Rage to Live (O'Hara), 198
Ragged Dick (Alger), 8
Raider's Night (Lipsyte), 182–183
Rainfield, Cheryl, 216
Rainie, Lee, 236
Ramsdell, Kristin
    on adult romances, 42
    on marketing to teenagers, 44
    on romance novels, 43
Random House (publisher)
    adult digital-only imprints, 144
    Golden Compass as crossover book, 134
    Landmark Books series, 223
    Prep (Sittenfeld), 136
Ranma ½ series (Takahashi), 213
rape
    Are You in the House Alone? (Peck), 179
    of boys in YA literature, 182–183
    dating violence, 183–184
    reporting of, 184–185
    sexual abuse/incest, 179–182
Rape, Abuse and Incest National Network,
    181
Rapp, Adam
    The Buffalo Tree, 71
    literature of risk, 167–169
Rathbun, J., 164
Rawlings, Marjorie Kinnan, 24
Rayner, Richard, 206
reading
    abilities of teenagers/YAs, 236–238

audiobooks and, 242–246
ladders, 25–26
multiple literacies, rise of, 238–239
online, 239–241
online, support for, 241–242
by teenagers/YAs, trends in, 233–236
Reading at Risk (National Endowment for
    the Arts), 233–234
Reading Lolita in Tehran (Nafisi), 157
Reading on the Rise (National Endowment
    for the Arts), 235
Reading Today, 237
The Real World (television show), 69–70
realism
    in Adam Rapp's books, 167–169
    bleak books, 71–74
    criticism of teen realistic novels, 36–37
    problem novel, 34–38
    reaction to in 1980s, 41
    return of, 126–130
    rise of, 27, 31–33
    Robert Cormier and, 33–34
ReaLITyReads program, Macmillan, 126
The Realm of Possibilities (Levithan), 94
Rebel without a Cause (movie), 19
Red Planet (Heinlein), 20
Reflections on a Gift of Watermelon Pickle
    (Dunning), 91
Reid, Calvin
    on comics, 207
    on lack of multicultural books, 154
    on market for comics/graphic novels, 216
Remembering the Good Times (Peck), 45
Rennison, Louise, 107
retail
    chick lit, 107–108
    Divergent trilogy (Roth), 122–123
    dystopian fiction, 123–125
    Harry Potter series, phenomenon of,
      115–119
    The Hunger Games trilogy (Collins),
      121–122
    marketing, chain bookstores and,
      108–110
    mean girl books, 112–115
    realism, return of, 126–130
    steampunk, 125–126
    Twilight series (Meyer), 119–121
    YA imprints, 110–112

Reed, J. D., 38
Reed, M. K., 198
Reese, James, 106
Reeve, Philip, 98

Rich, Motoko, 138, 234
Richardson, Samuel, 103
Riggs, Ransom, 218, 247
Riley, Jenelle, 125
Rinaldi, Ann
    on historical fiction, 100, 102–103
    Native Americans in work of, 53
risky behavior
    brain development of teenagers, 163–164
    bullying, 169–171
    cyberbullying, 171–172
    empathy and, 172–174
    literature of risk, 166–169
    violence/consequences of, 164–166
Ritter, William, 106
Road to Perdition (Collins & Raynor), 206
Roan, Shari, 56
Roaring Brook (publisher), 210
Robehmed, Natalie, 129
Robert F. Sibert Medal, 228
Robinson, M. R. "Robbie," 6
Rochman, Hazel
    Michael L. Printz Award, creation of, 76
    on multicultural books, 47
    on multiculturalism, 52
    short story collections assembled by, 89
"Rock Around the Clock" (Bill Haley and
    His Comets), 19
Rocket Ship Galileo (Heinlein), 20
Rodriguez, Cindy L., 171
Rodriguez, Roberto, 50, 52
Roiphe, Katie, 92
Roll of Thunder, Hear My Cry (Taylor), 49
Rollin, Lucy
    on high school enrollment, 5
    on high-school students in 1980s, 44
    on middle school, 58
    on the 1970s, 38
    on nostalgia, 42
romance fiction
    in early 1990s, 56
    early YA literature, 14–16
    genre bending/blending in, 115
    New Adult category and, 143–146
    popularity of, 103
    revival of in 1980s, 41–45
    romance comics, 211
    Twilight series (Meyer), 119–121
Romance Writers of America
    on elements of romances, 103
    on romance readers, 120
Romano, George A., 105
romanticism, 29–30

Roomies (Zarr & Altebrando), 145
Rooney, Mickey, 6
Rose, Caroline Starr, 95
Rosen, Judith
    on bookstore areas for new adults, 140
    on graphic novels, 207
    on marketing of Dangerous Angels, 133
    on popularity of YA category, 147
    on YA literature, 247
Rosen, Julia, 74
Rosenberg, Liz, 92
Rosenwald, Michael S., 240, 241
Rosoff, Meg, 135, 180
Roth, Veronica
    book sales of, x
    Divergent trilogy, 122–123, 147
Rotters (Kraus), 104
Rowell, Rainbow
    Fangirl, 145
    realistic fiction by, xi
Rowling, J. K.
    adult purchases of YA books, 146
    book sales of, x
    comparison with Stephanie Meyer, 120,
        121
    Harry Potter series, phenomenon of,
        115–119
Roxburgh, Stephen, 145
Ruby, Laura, 172
Rudman, Masha Kabakow, 48
Rudnick, Paul, 145
Rugg, Jim, 214
Rules of the Road (Bauer), 68
Run Softly, Go Fast (Wersba), 60–61
Rush Hour (YA literary journal), 109
Rylant, Cynthia, 91

S
Sacco, Joe, 206
Saenz, Benjamin Alire, 157, 193
Safe Area Gorazde (Sacco), 206
Sailor Moon series (Takeuchi), 213
Saint Louis, Catherine, 201
Salinger, J. D., 30
Sanchez, Alex, 183, 193
"The Sand in the Oyster" (Campbell), 64
Sandman (Gaiman), 206
The Sandman: Endless Nights (Gaiman),
    206
Santa, Carol, 237
Santana, Arthur D., 242
Saricks, Joyce, 101–102
Sarn, Amelie, 158

Satrapi, Marjane
    as distinguished writer/artist, 215
    Persepolis, censorship of, 209
    Persepolis/Persepolis 2, 157, 214
Saulny, Susan, 152
Savacool, Julia, 165–166
Saved by the Bell (television show), 69
Sawicki, Norma Jean, 224, 226
Schaffer, Amanda, 164
Schiffrin, Andre, 67
Schmidt, Gregory, 193
Scholastic (publisher)
    Dear America series, 101
    graphic novels of, 217
    Graphix, graphic novels of, 209–210
    Harry Potter series and, 116, 117
    Kids and Family Reading Report, 235
    Wildfire romance series, 43
Scholastic magazine, 6
school
    book challenges in, 197
    bullying in, 169–171
    enrollment, forecasts for, 247
    LGBT students, hostile environment at,
        194
    violence at, 164–166
school libraries, books challenges in, 197
School Library Journal, 64, 108
Schugar, Heather, 240–241
Schugar, Jordan, 240–241
Schugar, Ruetschlin, 240–241
Schuker, Lauren A. E., 121
science fiction
    in 1940s/1950s, 20
    collections of genre stories, 90
    as speculative fiction, 97–98
    steampunk, 125–126, 246–247
Scieszka, Jon, 132
Scoggin, Margaret, 7
Scott, A. O., 127, 214–215
Scott, Walter, 100
Scowler (Kraus), 104
Secret Heart (Almond), 99
Secrets of the Shopping Mall (Peck), 44
Sedgwick, Marcus, 85, 90
The Seduction of the Innocent (Wertham),
    205
See Dave Run (Eyerly), 36
Seldes, Gilbert, 203
Sellers, John A., 86, 235
Sendak, Maurice, 168
series books
    Divergent trilogy (Roth), 122–123

early history of, 8–9
    Harry Potter series (Rowling), 115–119
    historical fiction, 101–102
    horror fiction, 104–105
    The Hunger Games trilogy (Collins),
        121–122
    manga, 212
    popularity of genre series in early 1990s,
        56–57
    Sue Barton Student Nurse (Boylston),
        9–10
    Twilight series (Meyer), 119–121
Serving New Adults Interest Group, 140
Seventeen (Tarkington), 6
Seventeen magazine
    on nostalgia, 41
    popularity of, 69
    publication of, 13
    on return to romance novels, 43
Seventeenth Summer (Daly)
    developmental tasks in, 26
    publication of, popularity of, 11–13
sexual abuse
    dating violence, 183–184
    in YA literature, 179–182
sexuality
    absence of in early YA fiction, 18
    incest/sexual abuse in YA literature,
        179–185
    LGBTQI literature, 187–195
    in Michael L. Printz Award winners, 86
    taboo of, 175–176
    in Twilight series, 120–121
    in YA literature, 176–179
sexually transmitted disease, 188–189
Shaffer, Kenneth R., 7
Shakespeare Bats Cleanup (Koertge), 94
*The Shallows. What the Internet Is Doing to
    Our Brains* (Carr), 243
Shanahan, Timothy, 234
Shanower, Eric
    on evaluation of graphic novels, 208–209
    on graphic novel adaptations, 218
    on graphic novels, digital editions of, 220
Sharif, Medeia, 158
Sheinkin, Steve, 228
Shellenbarger, Sue, 172
Shelley, Mary, 103
Shepherd, Megan, 106
Sher, Emil, 247
Sherburne, Zoa, 177
Shine (Myracle), 201
Shoemaker, Chris, 230

Shoemaker, Joel, 75–77
shojo (manga category), 212–213
shonen (manga category), 212
shonen-ai (manga category), 213
shopping mall, 44
short story, 88–90
Shulman, Irving, 19
Shuster, Joe, 204
Shusterman, Neal, 98
Siegel, Jerry, 204
Siegel, Mark
    on author-driven market, 215
    First Second imprint, 210
    on graphic novels, golden age of, 219–221
Silver Kiss (Klause), 121
Silvera, Adam, 216
Silverberg, Ira, 108
Silvey, Anita, 98
Simon and Schuster (publisher)
    First Love romance series, 43
    graphic novels and, 210, 217
    Spotlight Entertainment, 111
Simon Pulse (publisher)
    on New Adult fiction, 145
    publication of Abbi Glines's books, 143
Simone, Gail, 211
Sir Walter Raleigh and the Quest for El Dorado (Aronson), 228
Sis, Peter, 133
Sisters (Telgemeier), 214
Sittenfeld, Curtis, 134, 136
Six Memos for the Next Millennium (Calvino), 62
Sixteen (Gallo), 89
Skellig (Almond), 82, 99
Skyscraping (Jensen), 95, 189
Slake's Limbo (Holman), 60
Slate.com, 147–148, 242
Slater, Janie, 125
Sleator, William, 104–105
The Sledding Hill (Crutcher), 198
Slumber Party (Pike), 45
Smile (Telgemeier), 214
Smith, Andrew, 110, 149
Smith, Charles R., Jr., 90
Smith, Dora V., 25
Smith, Jeff, 209–210
Smith, Karen Patricia
    on multiculturalism, 47, 48
    on white authors, 51
Smith, Kevin, 69
Smith, Lane, 132
Smith, Lynn, 73

Snowfish (Rapp), 167–168
So Hard to Say (Sanchez), 193
social media
    female presence in comics world and, 215
    We Need Diverse Books, campaign of, 156
Society of Children's Book writers, 228
Somehow Tenderness Survives (Rochman), 89
Something Permanent (Rylant), 91
Something to Blog About (Norris), 172
Sones, Sonya, 93–94
Soto, Gary, 89
Sotomayor, Sonia, 106
Space Cadet (Heinlein), 20
Sparks, Beatrice, 37–38
Speak (Anderson), 82, 184
Speaking Out: Teenagers Take on Race, Sex, and Identity (Kuklin), 61
speculative fiction
    overview of, 97–100
    steampunk, 125–126
Spiderman (Marvel Comics), 205
Spiegelman, Art
    Little Lit series, 207
    Maus, 205, 206
Spitz, David, 74
Spotlight Entertainment, Simon and Schuster, 111
Sprague, Marsha, 237–238
Springen, Karen
    on dystopian novels, 124
    on marketing of *Liar* (Larbalestier), 155
    on young adults, 139
St. Martin's Press (publisher)
    Eleanor and Park (Rowell), 128
    New Adult category coined by, 143
Stackfest conference, 217
Stained (Rainfield), 216
Stamaty, Mark Alan, 157
Stampler, Laura, 109, 241
The Stand (King), 218
Stapleton, Victoria, 145
Star Man's Son, 2250 A.D (Norton), 20
Stavn, Diane Gersoni, 36
Steamboat Willie (cartoon), 204
Steampunk! An Anthology of Fantastically Rich and Strange Stories (Link & Grant), 126
steampunk fiction
    Leviathan (Westerfeld), 246–247
    overview of, 125–126
Stein, R. L., 104

Steinberg, Laurence, 164
A Step from Heaven (An Na), 85
"Stephanie Meyer: A New J. K. Rowling?"
    (*Time*), 120
Steptoe, John, 48
stereotypes
    of adults, 31
    of African Americans, 48
    of immigrants, 17
    in LGBT literature, 187, 188
    in romance fiction, 43
Stevens, Dana, 124–125
Stevenson, Nanette, 71
"Still Playing It Safe: Restricted Realism in
    Teen Novels" (Abramson), 36
Still Waters (Parsons), 170
Stine, R. L., 45, 55
The Stinky Cheese Man (Scieszka & Smith),
    132
Stohl, Margaret, 218
Stoner and Spaz (Koertge), 94
*Stop Pretending: What Happened When My
    Big Sister Went Crazy* (Sones), 93–94
Storm, Gale, 6
*The Strange and Beautiful Sorrows of Ava
    Lavender* (Walton), 146, 149
*The Strange Case of Doctor Jekyll and
    Mademoiselle Odile* (Reese), 106
Strasser, Todd, 170
Stratemeyer, Edward, 8–9
Stratemeyer Syndicate, 8–9
Stratton, Alan, 189
Street, James, 24
Strickland, Ashley
    on population of U.S., 151
    R. L. Stein and, 104
    on small presses, 155
Stuck Rubber Baby (Cruse), 206
Sturgeon, Jonathan, 147
Such Wicked Intent (Oppel), 106
Sue Barton Student Nurse (Boylston), 9–10
suicide
    bullying and, 170–171
    of LGBTQ youth, 194
    as top killer of teenagers, 163
Sullivan, Ed, 76
The Summer Boy (Lipsyte), 45
Summer Rules (Lipsyte), 45
A Summer to Die (Lowry), 34
Summers, Courtney, 170, 185
Sunrise in Fallujah (Myers), 160
Surrender (Hartnett), 86
The Surrender Tree: Poems of Cuba's

Struggle for Freedom (Engle), 95
Sutton, Roger
    on problem novel, 35, 36
    quote of Robert Cormier, 33
Swagger (Deuker), 183
Sweet Valley High series (Pascal), 43, 56
Sweetwater (Yep), 49
Swenson, May, 91
Swift, Jonathan, 123
sympathy, 167
Symptoms of Being Human (Garvin), 192
SYNC program, 244
Szalavitz, Maria, 164

T

Takahashi, Rumiko, 213
Takaya, Natsuki, 213
Takeuchi, Naoko, 213
Talbot, Margaret, 126, 128
Talley, Robin, 192
Tamaki, Jillian, 220
Tamaki, Mariko, 220
Tamar (Peet), 102
Taming the Star Runner (Hinton), 45
Tapscott, Don, 70
Target (Johnson), 182
Tarkington, Booth, 6
The Tattooed Man (Pease), 11
Taylor, Deborah D., 75–77, 141
Taylor, Mildred
    emergence of, 48
    The Land, 102
    Roll of Thunder, Hear My Cry, 49
Taylor, William, 190
Tease (Maciel), 149, 170
technology
    audiobooks and, 243–244
    multiple literacies, rise of, 238–239
Teen Angel (Gingher), 131
Teen magazine, 69
Teen People Book Club, 111–112
Teen People magazine, 69
Teen Research Unlimited, 44
Teen Vogue magazine, 69
Teen-Age Bill of Rights (*New York Times*),
    13–14
The Teenage Brain (Jensen), 163
Teenage Confidential (Barson & Heller), 42
Teenage Prayer record (Storm), 6
teenagers
    bleak books and, 71–74
    book review by, 112
    brain development of, 163–164

teenagers *(cont'd)*
    bullying, 169–171
    cyberbullying, 171–172
    dystopian fiction and, 123–125
    empathy and, 172–174
    first use of term, 6
    LGBTQI literature, 187–195
    marketing to, chain bookstores and, 108–110
    poetry renaissance and, 91, 92
    population of U.S., percent of, 151
    population spike, 63
    reading, interest in, 23–24
    reading, trends in, 233–236
    reading abilities of, 236–238
    reading online, 239–241
    reading online, support for, 241–242
    risk, literature of, 166–169
    romance novels, return to in 1980s, 41–45
    sexuality in YA literature, 175–185
    societal/personal problems in early 1990s, 61
    stages of development/developmental tasks, 25–26
    theories on adolescence, 4–5
    violence/consequences of, 164–166
    YA literature in 1940s/1950s, 11–21
    young adult, meaning of, 139–141
    youth culture, emergence of, 5–8
    youth culture renaissance in 1990s, 68–71
Teenagers: An American History (Palladino), 70
"Teen-Agers Are for Real" (Hinton), 23
Teens' Top Ten Lists (YALSA), 154
television
    confessional reality shows, 56
    focus on teens in 1990s, 69–70
    graphic novels and, 218
    impact on youth violence, 165, 166
Telgemeier, Raina
    as distinguished writer/artist, 215
    Drama, 193
    graphic novels of, 214
Tell Me How a Crush Should Feel (Farizan), 158
Teller, Janne, 86
Tender Morsels (Lanagan), 86
Tenderness (Cormier), 71, 74
Tex (Hinton), 45
That Was Then This Is Now (Hinton), 32
Their Voices: Engaging Adolescent Girls with Young Adult Literature (Sprague), 237

theme, 91
The Things You Kiss Goodbye (Connor), 170
Thirsty (Anderson), 104
Thirteen Reasons Why (Asher), 171
This Dark Endeavour (Oppel), 106
This Is All (Chambers), 145, 148
This One Summer (Tamaki & Tamaki), 220
Thompson, B., 234
Thompson, Jack, 212
Thompson, Page, 69
Thrasher, Frederic, 29
The Three Golden Keys (Sis), 133
Tibet: Inside the Red Box (Sis), 133
The Tight-Rope Walkers (Almond), 99
Time and Again (Metzger), 205
Time magazine
    article on movies in, 69
    on bleak books, 74
    on high school vogue, 70
    on J. K. Rowling, 116
    on *Just Hold On* (Bunn), 38
    "Numbers Game," 46
A Time to Dance (Venkatraman), 94
"The Times, They Are A' Changin" (Dylan), 27
To Read or Not to Read (National Endowment for the Arts), 234–235
"Today's YA Writers: Pulling No Punches" (Lynch), 64
Toffler, Alvin, 53
Tomas Rivera award, 156
Tomine, Adrian, 206
Tommy Stands Alone (Velasquez), 190
Too Bad about the Haines Girl (Sherburne), 177
Top 250 LGBTQ Books for Teens (Cart & Jenkins), 193–194
Top Ten Best Books for Young Adults, 93
Townsend, John Rowe, 3
Trainspotting (movie), 71
transgender literature, 192
The Tree of Life (Sis), 133
A Tribe Apart: A Journey into the Heart of American Adolescence (Hersch), 70
Tripp, Ben, 247
True Believer (Wolff), 87
The True Story of the Three Little Pigs (Scieszka & Smith), 132
The True Tale of the Monster Billy Dean as Telt by Hisself (Almond), 99
The Truth Commission (Juby), 216
Tucker, Ken, 55–56
Tunis, John R., 11, 12

Twilight (movie), 121
Twilight series (Meyer)
    graphic novel version of, 217–218
    overview of, 119–121
Twisted (Anderson), 171, 172
Two and the Town (Felsen), 176–177
Two Boys Kissing (Levithan), 192—193

U

Uchida, Yoshiko, 49
Uglies (Westerfeld), 124, 218
Unbroken (Hillenbrand), 230
Uncle Vampire (Grant), 180
Under the Wolf, Under the Dog (Rapp), 167
Underland Chronicles series (Collins),
    121–122
The Unfinished Life of Addison Stone
    (Griffin), 247
United Kingdom, crossover books in, 135
United States, population of, 151–152
University College London, 240
U.S. Census Bureau, 151, 152
U.S. Department of Education, 69
USA Today, 109

V

V for Vendetta (Moore & Lloyd), 206
Valby, Karen, 120
Van Draanen, Wendelin, 105
Van Gelder, Robert, 11, 12
Velasquez, Gloria, 190
Venkatraman, Padma, 94
verse novels, 93–95
Vertigo (publisher), 206
video games, 165–166
Viking (publisher), 132
The Vincent Boys (Glines), 143
The Vincent Brothers (Glines), 143
violence
    against LGBT youth, 194
    by teenagers, consequences of,
        164–166
    in teenagers' lives, 29
Virtue Rewarded (Richardson), 103
Visions (Gallo), 89
Viz (publisher), 206
Vlogbrothers (YouTube videos), 127–128
*Voices from the Future: Our Children
    Tell Us about Violence in America*
    (Goodwillie), 61
Voigt, Cynthia, 45, 180
Von Ziegesar, Cecily, 112–115
VOYA magazine, 206

W

Waddle, Linda, 75–77, 225–226
Walden, Amelia Elizabeth, 75
Walker, Kate, 190
Walker, Paul, 190
The Wall (Sis), 133
Wall Street Journal
    on John Green, 128
    on Twilight series, 120, 121
Waller, Sharon Biggs, 145
Walpole, Horace, 103
Walter, Virginia, 72, 74
Walter Award, 156
Walter Dean Myers Grants, 156
Walton, K. M., 185
Walton, Leslye, 146, 149
Ward, Michael R., 166
Ware, Chris, 207
Warner Brothers, 116
Warren, Robert
    as Poet Laureate, 92
    at YALSA conference, 59, 60
Washington Post, 109, 120
Watchmen (Gibbons), 205
Waters, Daniel, 105
Waters, Henry F., 61
Watters, Shannon, 193
The Way Things Work (Macaulay), 67
WB television network, 70
We Need Diverse Books (WNDB), xi, 156
websites, for poetry, 92
Weeping Willow (White), 180
Weetzie Bat (Block), 81, 189
Weetzie Bat series (Block)
    gay character in, 190
    as New Adult, 145
The Welcome (Donoghue), 192
Wells, Helen, 10
Welsh, Irvine, 71
The Werewolf of Paris (Endore), 103–104
Werlin, Nancy, 105
Wersba, Barbara, 60–61
Wertham, Frederick, 205
Westerfeld, Scott
    Leviathan, 126, 246–247
    on success of *Uglies*, 124
    Uglies, graphic novel of, 218
Weyn, Suzanne, 106
Whaley, John Corey, 85
*What Are My Rights? 95 Questions and
    Answers about Teens and the Law*
    (Jacobs), 73
What Happened to Mr. Forster (Bargar), 188

What Happens Next (Clayton), 185

What Hearts (Brooks), 90

What My Girlfriend Doesn't Know (Sones), 94

What My Mother Doesn't Know (Sones), 94

What We Left Behind (Talley), 192

What's in a Name? (Wittlinger), 90

"When Institutions Are Libel for Bullying" (Bott), 172

When Jeff Comes Home (Atkins), 182

When Reason Breaks (Rodriguez), 171

When She Hollers (Voigt), 180

When She Was Good (Mazer), 71, 74

When the Rain Sings: Poems by Young Native Americans (Francis), 92

"Where Are the People of Color in Children's Books?" (Myers), 159

Where Things Come Back (Whaley), 85

Whitbread Book of the Year, 99–100

White, Kiersten, 247

White, Ruth, 180

The White Darkness (McCaughrean), 86

White House Conference on Children and Youth, 18

Whitechurch (Lynch), 90

whites, 151–152

Whitney, Daisy, 185

Who Do You Think You Are? Stories of Friends and Enemies (Rochman & McCampbell), 89

Who Framed Lorenzo Garcia (Hamilton), 190

whole-language movement, 63

Wholf, Tracy, 147

"Why the Best Kids Books Are Written in Blood" (Alexie), 201

"Why 'Twilight' Isn't for Everybody" (Bolle), 120

Wickenden, Dan, 24

The Wild One (movie), 19

Wilder, Laura Ingalls, 52

Will Grayson, Will Grayson (Green & Levithan), 126, 192

William C. Morris YA Debut Award, 156

Willingham, Daniel T., 243

Winerip, Michael, 106, 113–114

Winick, Judd, 228

Wise, Bob, 237

Wise Up to Teens: Insights into Marketing and Advertising to Teenagers (Zollo), 70

Wittlinger, Ellen

    Hard Love, 82–83, 191

    Parrotfish, 192

    What's in a Name? 90

WNDB (We Need Diverse Books), xi, 156

Wojciechowska, Maia, 28–29

Wolf, Naomi, 114, 240

The Wolf Man (movie), 103–104

Wolfe, Thomas, 24

Wolff, Virginia Euwer

    debut of, 45

    Make Lemonade, 93

    True Believer, 87

Wolitzer, Meg, 150

women

    comics and, 211

    graphic novels from, 219

    manga and, 212–215

    mean girl books and, 114–115

Wonder Woman (Marston), 211

Woods, George, 28

Woodson, Jacqueline

    Brown Girl Dreaming, 95

    The Dear One, 187

    empathy in works of, 173–174

    I Hadn't Meant to Tell You This, 180

    LGBT characters in books by, 190

    National Book Award to, 157

workforce, adolescents in, 5

The World of Ellen March (Eyerly), 36

A Wreath for Emmet Till (Nelson), 87, 94

Wren, Christopher, 73

X

xxxHolic (Clamp), 213

Y

YALSA

    See Young Adult Library Services Association

Yang, Gene Luen

    American Born Chinese, 85, 210

    Michael L. Printz Award for, 157

Yao, Lauren, 120

Yaqui Delgado Wants to Kick Your Ass (Medina), 170

Yardley, Jonathan, 62

YASD (Young Adult Services Division), 7

A Year Down Yonder (Peck), 90

The Year They Burned the Books (Gordon), 198

Yen Press (publisher), 217

Yep, Laurence, 49

YM magazine, 69

Yoke, Beth, 202

Yolen, Jane, 43, 51–52
You Against Me (Downham), 185
You Hear Me? Poems and Writing by Teenage Boys (Franco), 92
You Were Here (McCarthy), 216
Young, Moira, 124, 125
Young Adult Library Services Association (YALSA)
  Alex Awards, 141–142
  on audiobooks, 246
  awards, creation of, 74–75
  Best Books for Young Adults List, 34, 228–229
  Best of the Best conference, 2005, 87
  comics, preconference on, 203
  conference in 1994, 59–60
  graphic novels and, 208
  Great Graphic Novels for Teens list, 220
  "How Adult Is Young Adult?" program, 65–67
  Margaret A. Edwards Award for Hinton, 29
  Miami Beach conference, 1994, 63
  Michael L. Printz Award, 68, 75–77
  on multiple literacies, 238
  nonfiction preconference, 225–226
  Odyssey Award, 244, 245
  Serving New Adults Interest Group, 140
  Teens' Top Ten Lists, 154
  YA Literature Symposium, 2008, 239
Young Adult Literature: From Romance to Realism (Cart)
  features in new edition, xi–xii
  new trends in this edition, ix–xi
"The Young Adult Novel Is Dead and Other Fairly Stupid Tales" (Aronson), 64
Young Adult Novel (Pinkwater), 38
Young Adult Services Division (YASD), 7
young adult (YA) imprints, 110–112
young adult (YA) literature
  audience age group expansion, 65–68
  bleak books, 71–74
  book challenges/censorship, 197–202
  bullying addressed in, 169–171
  changes in 1960s, 27–33
  chick lit, 107–108
  comics, 203–221
  decline of YA publishing, 59–62
  Divergent trilogy (Roth), 122–123
  dystopian fiction, 123–125
  in early 1990s, 55–62
  early history of, 8–11
  future of, 247–248

genre fiction, 97–106
Harry Potter series, phenomenon of, 115–119
literary merit, 83–87
marketing, chain bookstores and, 108–110
meaning of category, 139–141
meaning of term, 3–4
Michael L. Printz Award, 75–77
Michael L. Printz Award winners, 81–83
middle-school literature, 57–59
multiculturalism, 45–50
new trends in, ix–xii
in 1980s, 41–53
in 1950s, criticism of, 24–25
in 1940s/1950s, 11–21
in 1960s/1970s, 23–38
nonfiction, new, 223–231
poetry renaissance, 91–95
political correctness, 51–53
prizes, 74–75
problem novel, 34–38
realism, return of, 126–130
revival of, 63–65
revival/renaissance in later 1990s, 63–77
on risk, 166–169
Robert Cormier/1970s, 33–34
romance novels in 1980s, 41–45
short story revival, 88–90
stages of development/developmental tasks, 25–26
teenagers' interest in reading, 23–24
Twilight series (Meyer), 119–121
YA imprints, 110–112
Young Adult Services Division, formation of, 7–8
youth culture, emergence of, 5–8
youth culture in 1990s, 68–71
young adults
  reading, trends in, 233–236
  reading abilities of, 236–238
  reading online, 239–241
  See also teenagers
"Young Adults' Choices" booklist (International Reading Association), 158
"The Young and the Graphic Novel" (Bickers), 223
Young Man with a Camera (Sher), 247
Young People's Reading Roundtable (ALA), 9

Your Own Sylvia: A Verse Portrait of Sylvia Plath (Hemphill)
    Printz Honor for, 87, 228
    versatility of verse novels, 94
youth culture
    emergence of, 5–8
    renaissance of in 1990s, 68–71
Youth Marketing Company, 44
Youth Runs Wild (movie), 19

Z
Zamperini, Louis, 230
Zarr, Sara, 145

Zindel, Paul
    My Darling, My Hamburger, 32–33, 178
    The Pigman, 30–31
    realistic writing of, 32
Zollo, Peter, 70
Zolotow, Charlotte, 45–46
Zuckerman, Linda, 59–60
Zuckhur, Kathryn, 236
Zusak, Markus
    The Book Thief, 86, 102
    as crossover author, 135–136
Zvirin, Stephanie, 72
Zweig, Jamie, 184